D1568970

The New Progressive Era

The New Progressive Era

*Toward a Fair and
Deliberative Democracy*

Peter Levine

ROWMAN & LITTLEFIELD PUBLISHERS, INC.
Lanham • Boulder • New York • Oxford

ROWMAN & LITTLEFIELD PUBLISHERS, INC.

Published in the United States of America
by Rowman & Littlefield Publishers, Inc.
4720 Boston Way, Lanham, Maryland 20706
http://www.rowmanlittlefield.com

12 Hid's Copse Road
Cumnor Hill, Oxford OX2 9JJ, England

Copyright © 2000 by Rowman & Littlefield Publishers, Inc.

British Library Cataloguing in Publication Information Available

Library of Congress Cataloging-in-Publication Data

Levine, Peter, 1967–
    The new Progressive Era : toward a fair and deliberative democracy / Peter Levine.
        p. cm.
    Includes bibliographical references.
    ISBN 0-8476-9573-5 (cl. : al. paper)—ISBN 0-8476-9574-3   (alk. paper)
    1. Civil society—United States.   2. Democracy—United States.
3. Progressivism (United States politics)   4. United States—Politics and
government—20th century.   I. Title.
JK1759.L57   2000
320.973'09'041—dc21   99-045647

Printed in the United States of America

♾ ™ The paper used in this publication meets the minimum requirements of American
National Standard for Information Sciences—Permanence of Paper for Printed Library
Materials, ANSI/NISO Z39.48-1992.

Contents

ments

generous grant from the Florence
encouragement of its president,

associate at Common Cause, the
pirit of the original Progressive

deputy director of the National
ded by the Pew Charitable Trusts
lliam Bennett. As a result, I had
ed through the following pages.
ng Foundation, for which I have
d its president, David Mathews,
ice of civil society.
e University of Maryland's Insti-
itomize the democratic virtues of
. None of the people who work in
ament, but they are responsible for
to my family: my wife, daughters,

Introduction

As the nineteenth century came to a close, Americans confronted powerful forces that transformed almost everyone's life and that seemed beyond the capacity of government to shape or control. The frontier was closed; cities had grown to unprecedented size. There were terrible slums and factories that perpetually darkened the sky. Corporations had accumulated astounding wealth but seemed insensible to the needs of workers and consumers. Social classes had become more distinct, self-conscious, and mutually hostile than ever before in American history. An elaborate system of discrimination was being erected to oppress former slaves. Diesel engines, electric dynamos, assembly lines, and skyscrapers promised a golden age, but in the short term they produced wrenching changes. The whole world was now a single marketplace, so that a crisis in one continent was quickly felt in all the others. Finally, at least according to some, deep moral corruption had permitted saloons and brothels to pollute the nation's cities.

American democratic government seemed unable to handle any of these challenges; its incompetence was matched only by its corruption and bias. Nor were civic institutions—from private clubs to newspapers and political parties—capable of addressing the challenges of the era. Troubled by the new social and economic forces and cynical about their public institutions, millions of Americans embraced third-party protest movements, and significant numbers turned to violence. The 1890s were defined by the People's Party and urban bosses, by anarchist bombings and racist lynchings, by a terrible depression and conspicuous consumption.

Parallels to our own period abound. Global competition and automation are to our age what incorporation and industrialization were to the late 1800s. The citizens' militias and urban rioters of our decade are relatively mild echoes of their Victorian counterparts. Those on the Left still favor state action to address economic problems, and the Right still defends the free market, but neither ideology enjoys broad or stable support. Although virtually all adult citizens are legally able to vote, fewer than half chose to participate in the 1996 election—the worst showing in seventy-two years.[1] In 1998, 111.45 million eligible voters stayed home, an all-time record.[2] This mass abstention was no surprise, since large majorities had been saying for several decades that they fundamentally disliked politics and distrusted public institutions. General confidence in the government, for example, fell from nearly 80 percent in the early 1960s to below 30 percent in the 1990s. Today, just one in five Americans thinks that Congress generally does the right thing. Under these circumstances, we might expect voters to admire politicians who promise to trim federal power, but they—like their liberal rivals—are objects of general contempt. Twenty percent of the public now says that the *whole* governing elite is "involved in a conspiracy." This is the grievance of an alienated minority, but most people agree that the government works for "a few big interests looking out for themselves," and not the "benefit of all."[3]

Alexander Hamilton once proposed as a "general rule" that people's "confidence in and obedience to a government will commonly be proportioned to the goodness or badness of its administration."[4] If this rule still applies, then our government must be corrupt or inept, for it certainly inspires scant confidence. No one who seeks a reason can overlook money. Private interests spent $4 billion to finance the 1996 elections, and politicians sometimes adjust their behavior to benefit the wealthiest donors. But even when campaign money is irrelevant, laws and regulations often seem incomprehensible and arbitrary, the result of incessant private bargaining among organized interests. No concept of the "public good," no matter how misconceived, can be detected in large sections of the U.S. Code.

Meanwhile, important civic institutions have weakened dangerously. Union membership has been cut in half since the 1950s. Daily newspaper readership has declined by a third since 1977, so that readers now constitute a minority of the adult population. The press suffered a dramatic drop in public esteem between 1988 and 1993; today just one in ten Americans has full confidence in the news media. This dissatisfaction is largely warranted, for journalists fail to perform their civic functions. To make matters worse, individual citizens have become distinctly less likely to trust one another, so they are often unwilling to cooperate on common problems. Although some aspects of our political culture have improved, the overall picture is troubling.[5]

The crisis that arose a century ago was broadly similar to the current one. But Americans rethought, repaired, and revived their democratic institutions, building structures that were able to handle modern challenges. This was the achievement of the Progressive Era, and its success has recently inspired calls for a revival. President Bill Clinton has said that we "are living through another time of great change, standing on the threshold of a new progressive era." The First Lady, Senators Bill Bradley (D-NJ) and Ted Kennedy (D-MA), Representative Dick Gephardt (D-MO), and Republican presidential candidates Patrick Buchanan and Steve Forbes have made similar predictions. E. J. Dionne, Jr., Jacob Weisberg, and Michael Sandel have published books defending progressive principles. The British Labour leader, Tony Blair, has joined the chorus, advocating a progressive movement for his country.[6] The only dissenters are some conservative intellectuals who believe that recent Republican victories in Congress mark the belated *demise* of progressivism. Referring to the House Democrats' defeat after forty years in the majority, William Kristol writes, "November 8, 1994 could be said to cap and conclude the Progressive Era of American history."[7] But even Kristol and his colleagues measure their achievements against those of the progressives eighty years before. The new conservatism, they argue, is comparable to the old progressivism in its significance and originality; Republicans will reform American institutions by "standing [progressivism] on its head."[8]

Apparently, everyone would like to reflect a little of the progressives' glory. Unfortunately, the more we learn about them, the more diverse they appear, and the more difficult it seems to define them. "An American," Walter Lippmann wrote in 1921, "will endure almost any insult except the charge that he is not progressive."[9] Since the word sounded unequivocally positive during the Progressive Era, practically everyone embraced it. Thus, for example, the founders of the NAACP were self-styled progressives, but so were many of the white supremacists who perfected racial apartheid in the South. The urban reformers who replaced popularly elected officials with technical experts called themselves progressives—but so did the activists who enhanced direct democracy by winning the vote for women, the popular election of senators, and initiative, referendum, and recall provisions. Some progressives wanted to replace voluntary, private associations with government bureaucracies, but others founded independent organizations and defended them against the state.

Since racists and liberals, elitists and populists, technocrats and democrats all called themselves "progressives," the term often meant nothing more specific than an enthusiasm for change. In 1909, Herbert Croly observed: "Each of our leading reformers is more or less a man on horseback, who is seeking to popularize a particular brand of reform, and who is inclined to doubt whether the other brands are available for public consumption without rigid inspection. Consequently, the party of reform is broken up into a number of insurgent personalities."[10] Any movement that attracted Upton Sinclair and J. Edgar Hoover, W. E. B. Du Bois and Robert Taft, Herbert Hoover and the young Franklin D. Roosevelt can hardly be called a movement at all.

Given all this diversity, historians must generalize if they want to use the word "progressivism" to denote a coherent program or coalition. A standard contemporary view holds that the progressives were quasi-authoritarian figures, enamored of efficiency, discipline, order, and centralization to the detriment of grassroots democracy. If we could poll people who thought that they were "progressives" in the early decades of this century, we might find that a majority favored these elitist goals. But an emphasis on their version of progressivism would exclude the Progressive Party's 1924 nominee, Senator Robert ("Fighting Bob") La Follette, Sr., and his prominent supporters: Governors Hiram Johnson of California and Albert Cummins of Iowa; Representative Fiorello La Guardia of New York; the muckraking journalists Lincoln Steffens, Henry Lloyd, and David Graham Phillips; and such public intellectuals as Du Bois, Louis Brandeis, Jane Addams, Frederic Howe, John Dewey, Walter Rauschenbusch, and the young Reinhold Niebuhr. My purpose is to understand and defend the ideals of these people—not because they were the most powerful reformers of their time, but because I believe that they were right. No label fits them better than the one they chose for themselves. So I will reserve the capitalized term "Progressive" for their philosophy, while conceding that many other "progressives" were far less democratic.

What, then, defined La Follette's version of Progressivism? "It can be expressed in a single sentence," he told the Republican National Convention in 1910; and then (characteristically) he offered a whole paragraph:

> The will of the people shall be the law of the land. Constitutions, statutes, and all the complex details of government are but instruments to carry out the will of the people, and when they fail—when constitutions and statutes and all of the agencies employed to execute statutes and constitutions fail—they must be changed to carry out and express the well formulated judgment and the will of the people. For over all and above all, and greater than all, and expressing the supreme sovereignty of all, are the people.[11]

Read out of context and casually, this statement sounds like a trite endorsement of democracy, with which any American politician could agree. But understood in the context of La Follette's other writings and actions, it reveals a trenchant political philosophy. Progressivism, as he defined it, involved no definite social or economic program. In fact, a rejection of economic dogma was essential to La Follette's position. He promised to support almost any course of action that the public embraced—whether that meant adding regulations or trimming them, raising taxes or lowering them. But if public institutions were corrupt or incompetent, then the state would never obey the people's will. Thus social reform was pointless without good government and healthy politics.

Although La Follette proposed no general theory to explain how social evils arose or how they might be remedied, he did have specific ideas about democracy. In a reformed system, he thought, leaders would debate and act openly, overseen by a public composed of citizens who were politically equal. Neither private money, nor restrictions on voting, nor powerful lobbies, nor a biased press, nor political machines, nor an obstructive judiciary would dilute the principle of one-person, one-vote. Nor would popular government be hampered by any economic ideology with which the voters disagreed. For example, to those who said that the unregulated free market was "natural" (and therefore beyond criticism), La Follette replied that only the people, expressing their will democratically, were sovereign—so they could act however they chose.

La Follette championed popular sovereignty, but he did not believe that every position supported by an electoral majority necessarily represented the people's "well formulated judgment." The government had to be open and fair, but citizens had a corresponding responsibility to act cooperatively and wisely: otherwise, they would forfeit their legitimacy. The surest way for voters to form wise judgments, La Follette thought, was for them to *deliberate* together about public affairs. He therefore supported a variety of practical measures to increase the quantity, quality, and inclusiveness of public deliberation.

The core of La Follette's Progressivism, in short, was a belief in fair, deliberative democracy. Political reform came before social action. To reform politics meant to improve both the fairness of political institutions and the quality of public dialogue. From these core convictions, La Follette developed a whole political program that guided him as Wisconsin's governor (1901–1905), U.S. senator (1906–1925), and two-time presidential candidate (1912 and 1924). He achieved some important reforms, especially in Wisconsin, but he left much to be done.

Chapter 1 of this book is a description and defense of La Follette-style Progressivism. It is meant to be both inspirational and cautionary, for the political obstacles that ultimately defeated Progressivism are likely to recur. But even if Fighting Bob had won every battle, some of his ideas would have become obsolete in our age of television advertisements, think tanks, computerized mailing-lists, and political action committees. As our institutions have changed, so have our expectations, habits, and values—both for better and worse. In chapters 2 and 3, I will discuss these new realities and ask how Progressivism must adjust to handle them. The purpose of this discussion will be diagnostic: to give a picture of our chief civic and political problems, their origins and mutual connections.

I will then outline a full Progressive agenda, devoting a chapter to each of the most troubled elements of American democracy: campaigns and elections, the mass media, legislation and regulation, and voluntary associations. In the course of this argument, I will describe reform movements that have already formed under such names as Public Journalism, Civil Investing, social unionism, service-learning, civic environmentalism, study circles, and Deliberative Polling. Seen together, these movements mark the birth of a civic renaissance like the one that took place between 1900 and the First World War. Combined with concrete and enforceable political reforms, they could spur a New Progressive Movement.

NOTES

1. This is the standard view, endorsed by Curtis Gans of the Committee on the Study of the American Electorate and widely reported in the press. But methods of counting eligible citizens are problematical. See Peter Bruce, "How the Experts Got Voter Turnout Wrong Last Year," *The Public Perspective* (October/November 1997): 39–43. According to Bruce, the year 1988 set the record for lowest turnout in a presidential election.

2. Richard L. Berke, "Democrats' Gains Dispel Notion That the G.O.P. Benefits from Low Turnout," *New York Times*, November 6, 1998, p. A28.

3. National Election Studies (NES); James Davison Hunter and Carl Bowman, "The State of Disunion: 1996 Survey of American Political Culture," executive summary; NES.

4. *Federalist,* no. 27, in *The Federalist Papers* ed. Clinton Rossiter (New York, 1961), p. 174.

5. Herbert Alexander, University of Southern California; *New York Times*/CBS poll of adults, reported in the *New York Times*, April 8, 1997, p. A14; General Social Survey.

6. Federal News Service, remarks by President Bill Clinton at the Princeton University Commencement, Nassau Hall, June 4, 1996; Sean Scully, "Expect Progressive Era, Hillary Tells Graduates," *Washington Times*, May 24, 1996, p. C5; speech by Senator Bill Bradley, "Freeing Democracy from the Power of Money," John F. Kennedy School of Government, January 16, 1996: Federal Document Clearing House, Inc., Congressional Press Releases; "Kennedy Proposes New Progressive Era," *Milwaukee Journal Sentinel*, February 9, 1996, p. 10; Thomas Oliphant, "Gephardt Went Too Far in His Oration against White House," *The Boston Globe*, December 9, 1997, p. A31; by Jeffrey Rosen, "Just a Quirk; Pat Buchanan's Speech on Judicial Restraint Was Largely Composed by Author William J. Quirk," *The New Republic,* vol. 214, no. 12 (March 18, 1996): 16; David Yepsen, "Forbes: U.S. Always Faces Its Problems," *The Des Moines Register,* December 16, 1995, p. 6; E. J. Dionne, *They Only Look Dead: Why Progressives Will Dominate the Next Political Era* (New York, 1996); Jacob Weisberg, *In Defense of Government: The Fall and Rise of Public Trust* (New York, 1996); Michael Sandel, *Democracy's Discontent: America in Search of a Public Philosophy* (Cambridge, Mass., 1996); Tony Blair, "Switch on the Bright Ideas," *The Observer*, May 26, 1996, p. 13.

7. William Kristol, "The Politics of Liberty, the Sociology of Virtue," in *The New Promise of American Life* ed. Lamar Alexander and Chester E. Finns, Jr. (Indianapolis, 1995), p. 120.

8. Michael S. Joyce, and William A. Schambra, "A New Citizenship, a New Civic Life," in ibid., p. 162.

9. Walter Lippmann, *Public Opinion* (New York, 1922), p. 71.

10. Herbert Croly, *The Promise of American Life* edited by Arthur M. Schlesinger, Jr. (1909; reprint Cambridge, 1965), p. 144.

11. Address at the Republican Platform Convention, 1910, in *The Political Philosophy of Robert M. La Follette, as Revealed in His Speeches and Writings* ed. Ellen Torelle (Madison, Wis., 1920), p. 182.

PART ONE

BACKGROUND AND DIAGNOSIS

1

Lessons from the First Progressive Movement

POPULAR SOVEREIGNTY

If you have strong ideas about how an economy or a culture ought to work, then you may view democracy with a certain ambivalence. This was true of laissez-faire conservatives around 1900, who maintained that the unregulated market would produce ideal outcomes, thanks to Darwinian competition, the Invisible Hand, or the sheer virtue of American entrepreneurs. Afraid that the public might favor government regulation, they used private money and lawsuits to advance their agenda.

William Jennings Bryan and his Populist supporters had equally definite ideas. The People's Party, which endorsed Bryan in 1896, had begun as a heterogeneous collection of reformers: prohibitionists and anti-monopolists, African-American farmers of the National Colored Alliance, union members and radical journalists, followers of the economist Henry George, and what the *New York Herald* called "a good sprinkling of crazy-brained cranks."[1] They were united only in their belief that more democratic procedures would produce better outcomes. But Bryan committed them to a specific economic agenda, free silver, which he presented as a virtual cure-all.

Meanwhile, the Socialists argued that all industrial economies required nationalization, graduated income taxes, strong unions, and public ownership of natural resources. Because they believed that they possessed sure knowledge about economics, they had somewhat ambivalent feelings about democratic politics. Attacking "the spirit of bourgeois reform," Eugene V. Debs (the perennial Socialist presidential candidate) said: "Voting for socialism is not socialism any more than a menu is a meal."[2] Even a fair vote might not produce worthy results, he thought, because majorities might pick the wrong policies. And if they did choose wisely, the government might prove fatally weak in a contest with private industry. Indeed, Karl Marx had called the idea of fair elections in a capitalist society "democratic nonsense, political windbaggery."[3]

American Socialists were not doctrinaire; they often cared as much about democratic principles as about Marxist ones. In 1924, they endorsed the Progressive Party ticket and its platform of democratic reform, even though the Progressives had called the "dictatorship of the proletariat" an "undemocratic and un-American" idea.[4] However, ten years later, the Socialists adopted a clearly undemocratic, quasi-Leninist platform that called for the "bogus democracy of capitalist parliamentarianism" to be replaced "by a genuine workers democracy." The Socialist Party, they declared, "whether or not it is a majority, will not shrink from the responsibility of organizing and maintaining a government under the workers' rule."[5]

It seems that Bryanite Populists, conservatives, and Socialists—despite their mutual contempt—had something in common. For them, the purpose of political reform was to get good outcomes, to achieve policies consistent with their beliefs. By contrast, Robert La Follette and his allies were social and economic pragmatists (or "empiricists"), who did not claim to possess sure and general knowledge about public policy.[6] As the saying went, the man who wears the shoe knows best where it pinches; and the public could best identify its own problems.

La Follette himself lacked any coherent economic program, believing that a true democracy could learn from experience what was the best approach to any issue. Defending railroad regulation as an alternative to nationalization, he wrote: "I *think* it will work, and I know it *ought to be thoroughly tested*. If it proves the correct solution to the problem, we have no further to go; if it does not, we can take the next full step with confidence that we have behind us that great body of the people who can only be convinced by events."[7] Soon enough, regulation was "thoroughly tested"—thanks to La Follette's legislation in Wisconsin and the U.S. Senate. As a result of this experience, he gradually came to believe that the railroads should be publicly owned after all.

John Dewey elevated such pragmatism to a philosophical principle:

> There is no more an inherent sanctity in a church, trade-union, business corporation, or family institution than there is in the state. Their value is . . . to be measured by their consequences. The consequences vary with concrete conditions; hence at one time and place a large measure of state activity may be indicated and at another time a policy of quiescence and *laissez-faire*. . . . There is no antecedent universal proposition which can be laid down because of which the functions of a state should be limited or should be expanded. Their scope is something to be critically and experimentally determined. . . . The person who holds the doctrine of "individualism" or "collectivism" has his program determined for him in advance. It is not with him a matter of finding out the particular thing which needs to be done and the best way, under the circumstances, of doing it.[8]

Some Progressives agreed with conservatives that it would be foolish to meddle with markets, but they maintained that the people had dominion over the economy if they chose to exercise it. Democracy without the power to regulate capital would be meaningless in an age when corporations governed people's lives. In 1910, William Allen White imagined a dialogue between Demos (the people) and Croesus (capital), in which Demos starts "catechising the capitalist, . . . asking him to define his uses, . . . demanding that he show cause why he should not follow the soldier, the priest, and the baron"—previous rulers who had lost their power to the people. "'This is my business, I have a right to its profits,' declares Croesus. 'I am your partner,' retorts Demos; 'but for me you would have no patronage. Let's see the books.'"[9]

In this debate—which should be perennial—the capitalist has some valid points to make. If business regulation and taxation are too onerous, jobs may be lost, innovation may be frustrated, and wealth may be squandered. However, Demos always has the right to do the catechizing and to make the ultimate decisions, without any improper influence (such as bribes and threats) from Croesus. As White wrote: "With the breaking of these shackles upon democracy—direct bribery, party bribery, machine rule, and unresponsive legislative control of the states—democracy is now setting out on her real mission: to define the rights of the owner and the user of private property according to the dictates of an enlightened public conscience."[10]

Democratic sovereignty over the market would be a mistake if capitalism reflected pure principles of reason or embodied natural and inalienable rights. But Charles Beard lectured Amherst students about the foolishness of such ideas. Even if free exchange was a natural phenomenon, the institutions of modern capitalism (corporations, currencies, patents, securities markets) were deliberate political creations. In the nineteenth century, he said, "The state was regarded as a badge of original sin, not to be mentioned in economic circles. Of course, it was absurd for men to write of the production and distribution of wealth apart from the state which defines, upholds, taxes, and regulates property, the very basis of economic operations; but this absurdity does not stay the hand of the apologist."[11] According to Progressives, the market was the people's creation, hence their servant, and it could not be allowed to turn into a Frankenstein-monster with purposes of its own.

As Theodore Roosevelt said: "I believe in corporations. They are indispensable instruments of modern civilization; but I believe that they should be so supervised and regulated that they shall act for the interest of the community as a whole."[12] For similar reasons, Progressives supported the Sixteenth Amendment (ratified in 1916), which permitted the federal government to levy income taxes if it so chose; and they generally defended the constitutionality of regulatory provisions that seemed to enjoy popular support. Their pragmatic opposition to laissez-faire was entirely consistent with their belief in a fair electoral process. What they wanted, in short, was democratization.

Although the Progressives were open-minded about economic and social policy, they had very rigorous ideas about what it would mean for the public to exercise its sovereignty. First of all, the political system had to be unbiased. Everyone had to be able to vote, and every vote had to count equally. Consequently, the Progressives opposed unequal electoral districts and property qualifications, and they favored women's suffrage. "Co-suffrage," La Follette wrote, "like co-education, will react not to the special advantage of either men or women, but it will result in a more enlightened, better balanced citizenship, and in a truer democracy."[13] He was proud that he had appointed women to high positions in government, which "strengthened" state institutions.[14]

No political injustice rivaled the disenfranchisement of African Americans, and the Progressives did too little to secure political rights for people of color. However, La Follette and his closest allies believed in racial equality as an integral part of democratic reform. For this reason, W. E. B. Du Bois and the National Association for the Advancement of Colored People (NAACP) endorsed La Follette for president in 1924. Among La Follette's many honors was the title "arch enemy of the nation," bestowed on him by the Imperial Wizard of the Ku Klux Klan (KKK).[15]

As well as seeking the vote for all adult Americans, Progressives also sought to extend the principle of representative democracy to primary elections and party conventions, where national policy often originated. Once an election was over, they wanted politicians to remain accountable to voters and not to wealthy interests. Hence they favored campaign-finance reform, conflict-of-interest rules, and lobby regulation; and they tried to prevent public officials from receiving private gifts or income. Congress passed campaign-finance legislation in 1907, 1910, 1911, and 1925, forbidding contributions from banks and corporations, requiring disclosure, and establishing spending limits. Especially after hostile courts had reviewed these laws, they were full of loopholes and lacked enforcement mechanisms; but stronger statutes passed in some states.[16] To ensure that voters would be able to assess the performance of their elected representatives, Progressives also fought for press freedom, open-meeting laws, and roll-call votes. And—in case politicians still violated the voters' will—they favored initiative, referendum, and recall provisions to enhance direct democracy.

La Follette's program in Wisconsin was especially sweeping. At his urging, the legislature restricted campaign contributions and forced the railroads to end their tradition of giving politicians free passes. Lobbyists were required to register and forbidden to have any private contact with legislators; if they communicated with elected officials in writing, they had to file copies in a public office, "so that any citizen or body of citizens shall have the opportunity, if they desire, to answer such arguments."[17] Wisconsin also passed initiative and referendum provisions to give its citizens more direct control over policy.

In 1910, William Allen White wrote:

> to have told the campaign managers of '84 or '88 that within a quarter of a century the whole nation would be voting by secret ballot, the candidates nominated in two-thirds of the American states by a direct vote of the people, without the intervention

of conventions or caucuses, and that further than that every dollar spent by a candidate or by a party committee would have to be publicly accounted for, would have set . . . the managers of those days to cackling in derision until they were black in the face. . . .

By making the party a legalized state institution, by paying for the party primaries with state taxes, by requiring candidates at primaries to file their expense accounts and a list of their contributors (as is done in some states), by limiting the amount to be spent (as is done in certain states), and by guaranteeing a secret vote and a fair count, the state has broken the power of money in politics. Capital is not eliminated from politics, but it is hampered and circumscribed, and is not the dominant force it was ten years ago. It is safe to say that the degree of divorce between business and politics will be absolute within a few years.[18]

The Progressives' obsession with corruption has been criticized by those who believe that bribes, gifts, campaign contributions, and lobbying efforts are not the most important ways for corporations to gain power. These critics claim that the government is "structurally dependent" on the market to produce jobs and wealth, so politicians will discriminate in favor of moneyed interests as long as we have a capitalist economy. This argument was implicit in works like Beard's *Economic Basis of Politics* (1916), with its dictum that, "in the absence of military force, political power *naturally and necessarily* goes into the hands which hold the property."[19] As far as I can tell, the original Progressives did not respond effectively to Beard's hypothesis, but the recent literature is illuminating. Therefore, I will consider the structural-dependence thesis while outlining a modern Progressive agenda (see chapter 4).

In addition to promoting procedural reforms, the Progressives sometimes argued that extremes of wealth and poverty were inherently bad for democracy. Thus, for instance, the National Child Labor Committee worked to reform conditions in Southern cotton mill towns, arguing that these were "the poorest place[s] in the world for training the citizens of a democracy."[20] Certain levels of income, education, and leisure, it seemed, were necessary for full and active citizenship. Consequently, democratic values might require economic reform to bring everyone to a baseline level of affluence.[21] Meanwhile, almost every Progressive book, article, letter, and speech contained some variation of the theme here expressed by Herbert Croly: "the prevailing abuses and sins, which have made reform necessary, are all of them associated with the prodigious concentration of wealth, and of the power exercised by wealth, in the hands of a few men." From an economic point of view, Croly explained, "I am far from believing that this concentration is wholly an undesirable thing."[22] It might be efficient to put wealth in the hands of large corporations and skilled capitalists. The danger was not economic but political: people who controlled extraordinary amounts of capital might also gain disproportionate political power, thus endangering democracy. For this reason, Progressives often advocated modest economic changes, such as the minimum wage and antitrust laws, as integral parts of political reform. They also stood prepared to accept more radical changes, should these emerge from a re-formed political system.

DELIBERATION

So far, I have described Progressivism as a movement to enhance majority rule by strengthening both representative and direct democracy. This was the motivation for many of the Progressives' good-government initiatives, from referenda to campaign-finance reform. They believed in democratic government, and they wanted to make elections fair so that privileged special interests would not wield disproportionate power. However, their concept of citizenship included much more than voting; and their notion of good government meant something quite different from majority rule.

Some people think of democracy as a mere system for registering popular preferences in periodical elections: the ballot-box theory. But there are several important reasons to be unsatisfied with this theory, most of them apparent to the Progressives. First, majorities are not necessarily wise. Certainly, people who are distant from politics are unlikely to know much about issues, nor will they have thought very carefully about other people's interests and values or the ramifications of their own ideas. They may demand short-term, narrowly self-indulgent, or utterly unrealistic policies from the politicians who represent them. Majority rule does not necessarily reflect what White sought: "an enlightened public conscience."

Second, voters who belong to electoral minorities have no weight in a ballot-box democracy, except insofar as they can threaten to form part of some future majority. It is easy to imagine situations in which majority rule can bring about patently unjust results. Citizens who clearly and permanently fall outside of a democratic majority might fare just as well under a monarchy.

Third, a ballot-box democracy gives—even to members of the political majority—little opportunity to exercise the arts and skills of government, which are valuable in themselves. Hannah Arendt wrote that the founders of the United States "knew that public freedom consisted in having a share in public business, and that the activities connected with this business by no means constituted a burden but gave those who discharged them in public a feeling of happiness they could acquire nowhere else."[23] A representative democracy reserves these "feelings of happiness" for the few who hold public office. Even if voters can address some issues through referenda—thereby governing directly—they still have an extremely modest and sporadic role to play in public life.

Fourth, the theory behind a ballot-box democracy assumes that people possess clear and ordered preferences that the government can implement. Some political theorists view ends, goals, and preferences as given; they define a good political process (or an efficient market) as one that satisfies as many preferences as possible. But often we lack opinions until we talk to other people. For example, most of us don't automatically know how we would weigh tax cuts against spending priorities; we must *discuss* this question in order to formulate our own views. Senator Edmund Muskie once said of Senate proceedings, "The debate didn't change my mind. It made up my mind."[24] Without talking and listening (or reading and writing), we may never formulate clear, ordered positions, and then no democratic government can possibly implement our wishes.[25]

Thus politics is not simply a matter of aggregating private preferences (as a proponent of majority rule might say); it is also a process of generating and shaping opinions. If one aspect of politics is negotiation, competition, or compromise among groups that have pre-established goals, another aspect is persuasion about ends.[26] And because healthy democracies encourage deliberation, they can sometimes choose between two solutions to an unmet demand. One is to give the dissatisfied citizens what they want, but the other is to persuade them that they should change their goals and values.

Ballot-box democracy presents another problem that was not as clear to the Progressives (although their contemporary, Walter Lippmann, dimly perceived it). If we favor a system of majority rule, we will face intractable dilemmas as we design the electoral system. Voters can be asked to choose among candidates, parties, *or* issues. There can be one-stage elections or runoffs, proportional representation or single-member districts (whose borders can be drawn in innumerable ways). Finally, there are many methods for selecting the items, candidates, packages, or slates that are included on the ballot. Thanks to Kenneth Arrow, we know that the same group of people may resolve the same question differently if the voting system changes, and that no electoral system can satisfy all desirable standards of fairness and rationality. William Riker concludes: "there is no fundamental reason of prudence or morality for preferring the amalgamation produced by one [voting] method to the amalgamation produced by another."[27]

It is a mistake, then, to interpret a majority vote as an expression of support for any particular proposition. Perhaps the outcome would have been different if there had been other choices on the ballot, or if people had been able to express separate opinions about each issue and each attribute of each candidate. Lippmann wrote:

> We go into a polling booth and mark a cross on a piece of paper for one of two, or perhaps three or four names. Have we expressed our thoughts on the public policy of the United States? Presumably we have a number of thoughts on this and that with many buts and ifs and ors. Surely the cross on a piece of paper does not express them. It would take hours to express our thoughts, and calling a vote the expression of our mind is an empty fiction.[28]

A related problem endemic to democratic systems is the "voting cycle," in which majorities prefer policy or candidate A to B; B to C; *and* C to A. For example, perhaps social liberalism would beat social conservatism in a current election, but social conservatism might defeat economic liberalism, and economic liberalism might prove more popular than social liberalism. When this kind of situation arises, the public can be said to support each of the three alternatives, depending on what binary choice they are given. Some observers detect this pattern in the confused ideological climate of the late 1990s, when the same voters seem to shift between liberal and conservative candidates, depending on the structure of the campaign debate. As Tony Fabrizio, a Republican pollster, said in 1998, "politics is no longer linear." [29] In such cases, election results are particularly ambiguous, and politics is especially subject to manipulation by skillful tacticians. However, if everyone arranges the available options on a single spectrum—say, from right to left—then no cycle can arise, even if people disagree about the ideal outcome. [30] Thus another advantage of deliberation is that we may be able to agree about the *dimensions* of the political debate, thereby solving the problem of voting cycles. There is some evidence, for example, that the intense political debate of the 1960s temporarily organized American public opinion into a coherent continuum. [31]

For all these reasons, a democracy can hardly function without public conversation. If leaders want to know what "the people want," they cannot simply look at votes and polls; they also have to listen to public discourse. Meanwhile, if we citizens are to develop views that are practical, specific, and coherent enough for our government to represent, we must talk among ourselves. Even then, our conversations may be ill-informed, superficial, or narrow, and the outcomes may be foolish or unjust. Thus we should be concerned about the quality, not just the amount, of political discussion.

Dewey aptly summarized the Progressives' view of majority rule:

> The ballot is, as often said, a substitute for bullets. But what is more significant is that counting of heads compels prior recourse to methods of discussion, consultation, and persuasion, while the essence of appeal to force is to cut short resort to such methods. Majority rule, just as majority rule, is as foolish as its critics charge it with being. But it is never *merely* majority rule. . . . The strongest point to be made in behalf of even such rudimentary political forms as democracy has already attained, popular voting, majority rule and so on, is that to some extent they involve a consultation and discussion which uncover social needs and troubles. [32]

When politicians want to appear democratic and friendly to "the common people," they often assert that average Americans automatically know what is the best policy for their country. But citizens usually disagree among themselves about important political issues. Besides, it is patronizing—and in most cases, insincere—to applaud whatever opinions a majority of people happen to hold at a particular instant. An opinion is not worth much unless the people who express it have informed themselves about the issue and reflected carefully, and unless they are willing to discuss their views with open minds. In our private lives, we do not automatically assent to majority opinion; and there is no reason for us to do so in public affairs. The soul of democracy is not a reflex admiration for popular opinion but rather a belief that all citizens can deliberate about public policy. But very few of us in any class or community actually discharge this fundamental civic duty. Dewey wrote: "The essential need, in other words, is the improvement of the methods and conditions of debate, discussion and persuasion. That is *the* problem of the public."[33] Anyone who is truly committed to democracy should be dissatisfied with standards of civic responsibility and competence—but hopeful that they can be improved.

Deliberative democracy thus steers a safe course between two serious errors. One is to endorse whatever the majority appears to say through polls, votes, or market decisions. The other is to try to impose one's own views on the public. Some moral positions (for example, abhorrence of torture) are clearly right and are as important as democracy itself. Nevertheless, it would a mistake to dictate these positions, even if one were king for the day. Unless moral principles enjoy broad public support, they will not last for long or be reliably enforced. Moreover, a political system that is subject to manipulation by an honorable minority can also be manipulated by a selfish or misguided few. Thus we should always seek deliberative public support for our views, even the ones that seem obviously right. Furthermore, as soon as we move away from clear moral issues and start making everyday decisions about economic and social policy, public discussion becomes indispensable. To make good policy, we need information about everyone's needs, goals, and capacities, and most people are the best judges of their own situations.

Although Woodrow Wilson had elitist ideas that I will criticize further on, his campaign speeches of 1912 accurately reflected Progressive ideas about deliberation. "The whole purpose of democracy," he said, "is that we may hold counsel with one another. . . . For only as men are brought into counsel, and state their own needs and interests, can the general interests of a great people be compounded into a policy that will be suitable to all." Unfortunately, he thought, large-scale economic forces had undermined the autonomy of small towns, thereby robbing Americans of natural forums in which to deliberate, such as town meetings and country stores. "For a long time there has been no sufficient opportunity of counsel among the people; no place and method of talk, of exchange of opinion, of parley. . . . It is partly because citizens have foregone the taking of counsel together that the unholy alliances of bosses and Big Business have been able to assume to govern for us." By no means all Progressives shared Wilson's program, which called for the destruction of large trusts and a return to "the locality, the community, the self-contained town." But they all shared his ideal. "What we need," he wrote, "is a universal revival of common counsel."[34]

The Progressives were political realists, so their reform ideas were rarely utopian or romantic. But they had a utopian ideal in mind, and they measured their progress in terms of the distance traveled toward that end. Their goal (in short) was a perfectly deliberative democracy, which would function much like an idealized jury but enlarged to include the whole public. Public opinion, wrote the Progressive journalist Lincoln Steffens, is a "jury that can not be fixed."[35] According to traditional civics textbooks, juries consist of twelve diverse but equal members, not personally involved in the case before them, who discuss it until they arrive at a unanimous verdict. Threats and bribes are forbidden. There is little scope for quid-pro-quo agreements or other forms of bargaining. Jurors can express personal beliefs and values and refer to their own experiences, but ultimately they must persuade all of their colleagues. Under these conditions, it is rarely effective to demand special treatment, to repeat slogans, or to offer private deals. The best way to achieve consensus is to defend a view about what is *right* in terms that everyone might be able to accept. Unless the whole panel can agree, everyone remains locked together in the jury room.

Even ordinary juries do not operate according to this ideal theory. Bargaining sometimes takes place (for example, when some jurors favor very harsh penalties and others prefer to be more lenient). Jurors who have plenty of time on their hands—and no aversion to mistrials—can opt out of deliberation altogether, ignoring their colleagues' arguments. Finally, differences in power and status among jurors may distort the results of deliberation.

All of these problems would grow far more severe if a whole society tried to function like a jury. Apart from anything else, it would take a prohibitively long time to achieve unanimous consent on a national scale; and minorities could always filibuster. Since it is usually impossible to create a national consensus, all societies must resolve some of their differences coercively—by majority votes, executive decisions, court rulings, and other exercises of power. Majority rule satisfies more people more of the time than any other system; but to prevent majorities from abusing smaller groups, the Constitution reserves rights to individuals and political minorities. These rights also encourage deliberation, because they prevent majorities from simply ignoring those whom they happen to outnumber. In short, a healthy democracy approaches the ideal of a national jury deliberation, although it can never achieve that ideal.

In deliberation, people must rank their preferences and balance conflicting values. Furthermore, in order to persuade others, they must develop positions that have a chance of achieving consensus, and these positions cannot be openly selfish, irrational, or unrealistic. If you say, "I demand lower taxes because I don't like paying them," you will persuade no one; so you must justify your position by arguing that you *deserve* more money in your pocket for some specific reason—or that a tax cut for you will help another group that deserves aid. Whether this position is *true* can then be tested by other participants in the debate.

Thus deliberation demands general justifications or reasons for private preferences. In fact, it is remarkable how rarely anyone in public life makes an overtly selfish or private claim. They know that they must offer persuasive arguments, and that persuasion requires general principles. The more people are persuaded by good arguments, the less they have to be coerced. While deliberation rarely achieves perfect consensus, at least it encourages participants to articulate and defend testable conceptions of the public interest. In the process, they are sometimes forced to abandon utterly indefensible positions. So, for example, in a genuinely public debate, demands for narrow tax breaks might have to be dropped in favor of *general* tax relief, and proponents would have to explain why the economy would benefit from their proposals.

The ideal of deliberation is as firmly rooted in American traditions as the concept of representation. When James Madison first drafted a Bill of Rights, he included the following phrase: "the people shall not be restrained from peaceably assembling and consulting for their common good."[36] Clearly, his goal was to protect and encourage public deliberation. The actual Bill of Rights did not include Madison's language, but La Follette's friend Louis Brandeis correctly interpreted the Founders' general intentions: "Those who won our independence believed that . . . the deliberative forces should prevail over the arbitrary; . . . that the greatest menace to freedom is an inert people; that public discussion is a political duty; and that this should be a fundamental principle of the American government."[37]

Lippmann thought that our representatives had to do our deliberating for us.[38] Elected officials, after all, are interested in public issues, well served by expert advisers, and accountable; and they can all gather in one place to discuss public business. They are therefore better equipped to deliberate than most members of the public, who are only casually acquainted with the complex issues that come before government. On the other hand, there are serious drawbacks to official deliberation, which were mostly overlooked by Lippmann. Because the political environment is necessarily competitive, politicians must put distance between themselves and their opponents, so consensus is difficult to attain. Everything that politicians say can be used against them for years to come. A casual remark can be interpreted as a sign of weakness or a change of bargaining position. Furthermore, only certain types of people choose to become politicians and succeed in that business, which means that their deliberations will never be perfectly representative. Dewey defined "the democratic method" as "persuasion through public discussion carried on not only in legislative halls, but in the press, private conversations, and public assemblies."[39] In his view, as many people as possible should participate.

If the public deliberates, then the votes that people cast each November will be relatively wise. Not only will citizens choose relatively good policies at the polls, but they will be able to select skilled deliberators to represent them in the legislatures, for they will have personal experience with deliberation.[40] A good legislator is someone who can (among other things) talk coherently, assimilate information, act on principle, make concrete moral judgments, and offer rationales for

his or her votes. Unless we have participated in collective decision-making ourselves, we won't be able to recognize these qualities.

Citizens can also participate in public life in many ways that go beyond voting.
Our choices about what jobs to take, what voluntary organizations to join, what
consumer goods to buy, what communities to live in, what charitable contributions to make, and how to educate our children may all be influenced by serious
deliberation. Finally, the legislators and bureaucrats who govern us always begin
as members of the public, and they remain parents, children, neighbors, and
friends of ordinary citizens. Therefore, they will be heavily influenced, not only
by the votes that we cast on election day, but also by the ideas, values, and arguments that circulate in public dialogue. In short, public deliberation is not fruitless; we have many opportunities to implement our deliberative judgments.

WHAT THE PROGRESSIVES DID TO
ENCOURAGE DELIBERATION

In 1914, Margaret Woodrow Wilson, the president's daughter, wrote that the
mass of citizens were still too disorganized to reach deliberative judgments. "No
wonder that [politicians] do not always know what the people want. Let us get
together so that we may tell them. All of our representatives are organized into
deliberative bodies. We, whom they represent, ought also to be organized for deliberation. When this happens, and then only, shall we vote intelligently." This
was standard Progressive rhetoric: La Follette printed it on the front page of his
Weekly.[41] Dewey made the same point a few years later, when he wrote, "The
government, officials and their activities, are plainly with us. . . . But where is
the public which these officials are supposed to represent?" Dewey denied that
there were "publics" wherever there were human populations. On the contrary,
"opinions and beliefs concerning the public presuppose *effective and organized*
inquiry. . . . For public opinion is judgment which is formed and entertained by
those who constitute the public and is about public affairs. Each of the two phases
imposes for its realization conditions hard to meet."[42]

Dewey meant, I think, that authentic public judgment required both broad participation and a serious focus on matters of social and political importance. It was
not enough for some people to discuss politics, nor for everyone to talk together:
everyone had to talk together about politics. Although public judgment could
only emerge under these stringent conditions, the Progressives set out to encourage it.

Margaret Wilson, for example, favored making public school buildings available to informal social clubs of all kinds. As strangers gathered in such public
settings, they could talk together about social and political issues. This idea had
originated with Mary Parker Follett, a Boston Progressive, around 1900. (Parker
later developed a powerful theory of deliberation, arguing that it was preferable

to both conflict and compromise, because it alone could reveal unforeseen solutions that would benefit all parties.)[43] By 1911, a National Community Center Association worked to turn schools into social venues, and all three of the 1912 presidential candidates endorsed the idea.[44] On the campaign trail, Wilson said, "Why not insist everywhere that [school buildings] be used as places of discussion, such as of old took place in the town-meetings to which everyone went and where every public officer was freely called to account? The schoolhouse, which belongs to all of us, is a natural place in which to gather to consult over our common affairs."[45]

Meanwhile, some settlement houses supported diverse social and cultural clubs in their neighborhoods. Mary Simkhovitch, the Progressive founder of the Greenwich Settlement in New York City, explained that such clubs fostered cooperation and discussion. "The object of clubs," she wrote, "is training in self-government and in the art of group accomplishment." She conceded that "organization alone does not produce harmony. A man may enjoy singing in the same chorus with a man he must oppose when it comes to election time." However, participating in a chorus would at least encourage people to talk about issues; they might also develop the mutual trust upon which a lasting consensus could be built. She concluded: "conflicts tend to dissolve also in the light of a more civilized and searching understanding."[46] In the 1990s, scholars have argued that common activities create "social capital"—habits of trust, cooperation, communication, and discussion that are essential to democracy.[47] The Progressives anticipated this argument.

People occasionally talk about public issues when they meet on the street, but lasting, structured discussions can only occur within the institutions of "civil society"—schools, clubs, community associations, journals, and civic groups. One contributor to *La Follette's Weekly* stressed "the necessity of citizenship *organization* for deliberation as the prerequisite to voting." In order to become good citizens, people did not primarily need information—handed down from above—but rather opportunities to communicate among themselves. If they did talk about political issues, then they would become active and eager consumers of information. Voluntary associations, according to this writer, offered "equipment whereby citizens may go to school to each other in preparation for the examination of our intelligence at the ballot box."[48]

Jane Addams recalled the Working People's Social Science Club that used to meet at Hull-House in Chicago during the 1890s:

> At eight o'clock every Wednesday night the secretary called to order from forty to one hundred people; a chairman for the evening was elected, a speaker was introduced who was allowed to talk until nine o'clock; his subject was then thrown open to discussion and a lively debate ensued until ten o'clock, at which hour the meeting was declared adjourned. The enthusiasm of this club seldom lagged. Its zest for discussion was unceasing, and any attempt to turn it into a study or reading club always met with the strong disapprobation of the members.[49]

Immigrant laborers organized these meetings, but Addams (who called herself a Progressive after 1912) gave them space at Hull-House and personally participated in their deliberations. At about the same time, rural Progressives encouraged the Chautauqua movement, a national program of educational meetings and discussions that were organized for—and by—farmers. La Follette called Chautauquas "truly an educational force in the life of the country," because participants "not only listen to, but also they demand, the serious discussion of public questions."[50] "The composite judgment," he explained, "is always safer and wiser and stronger and more unselfish than the judgment of any one individual mind."[51] Putting these ideas into practice, La Follette personally attended at least 300 Chautauqua conventions, at which a total of 240,000 people were present.[52]

Meanwhile, the University of Wisconsin (a Progressive redoubt) formed a Department of Debating and Public Discussion that lent 80,000 background papers every year to citizens who wanted to discuss such topics as the income tax, women's suffrage, and simplified spelling.[53] *La Follette's Weekly* endorsed the role of "Civic Secretary" in small Midwestern cities; this person typically organized public discussions, maintained a file of newspaper clippings, and coordinated the activities of local civic groups.[54]

When women won the federal franchise in 1920, the leading suffragists, most of whom were self-described Progressives, immediately tried to encourage deliberative citizenship. The mere right to vote was not enough, they thought; women would also have to learn how to discuss public policy. Along these lines, the new League of Women Voters devised an "experiment in political education"—discussion groups that were open to all citizens. The League's first president, Belle Sherwin, believed (according to a modern historian) that "the experience of viewing all sides of public issues would develop habits of fairness and sagacity as well as the capacity to perceive relationships; individuals would be enabled to do their own thinking and possess their own viewpoints, would be inducted into the civil culture by internalizing a self-conception as participants within the larger society."[55]

For similar reasons, the Progressives introduced deliberation into public-school classrooms. School newspapers and student governments were largely invented by Progressive reformers, who also devised a new kind of civic education that aimed to teach students how to talk freely and rationally about politics. For example, the State of Wisconsin encouraged public schools to host political discussions for their communities, and some 500 schools had joined this effort by 1915.[56] The same year, the U.S. Bureau of Education officially endorsed an approach called "community civics," which stressed public discussion.[57]

Whether or not people deliberate depends in part upon practical considerations. In a state of anarchy or widespread violence, the weak do not dare to discuss public issues with their opponents, and the strong do not have to. Thus peace and the rule of law are essential ingredients of a deliberative civil society. So is political fairness. If some citizens wield disproportionate power because of their wealth, then they are unlikely to seek consensus with their less-fortunate fellow citizens; they can simply purchase the policies they want. If small numbers of people make crucial decisions behind closed doors, then they have little reason to seek public consensus before they act. In general, the more fair and open the political system, the more attractive deliberation becomes for all its citizens. Thus the Progressives fought corruption as much to encourage deliberation as to achieve political equity.

They also took direct steps to make political institutions more deliberative, even when these institutions were already fair and open. For example, La Follette criticized party conventions in 1901: "If it were possible to eliminate all bargains and deals and dickers and corruption, if the delegates were controlled by the purest motives, and desired only faithfully to represent the voters, whose agents they are,—even then the nominating convention is under no circumstances a fit place to transact the most important business in a representative government. A political convention is never a deliberative body." La Follette went on to criticize conventions for being too hurried and unstructured to permit rational discussion. Their "business is rushed through under pressure for time. Excitement and impatience control, rather than reason and judgment. Noisy enthusiasm outweighs the strongest argument."[58] As governor of Wisconsin, he abolished conventions altogether and changed the legislature's rules and structure to enhance deliberation.

The Progressives' commitment to deliberation also helps to explain their quarrel with laissez-faire. In defense of a capitalist economic system, we could note that public decisions are made collectively by many agents, not by a tiny elite, and there is considerable scope for deliberation. Once we have reached deliberative judgments by discussing issues with other people, we can select our economic transactions accordingly. For instance, some people choose to become schoolteachers instead of bond traders; others swear off insecticides, sweat-shop products, or meat.

Nevertheless, it would be a serious mistake to limit public choices to the marketplace alone. For one thing, economic power is distributed unequally, so aggregate results are often unfair. Besides, public discussion can be distorted by capitalism, for the mass media ignore some voices, paid advertising influences public opinion, and the rich enjoy high status. Finally, in a market transaction, I can only control my own actions and must make my decisions one at a time. Through the democratic process, on the other hand, I can advocate general rules that will bind me *and* all of my fellow citizens permanently. It should at least be possible for a public to consider such rules.

A 1990 *Wall Street Journal*/NBC poll asked: "Sometimes the laws that are designed to protect the environment cause industries to spend more money and raise their prices. Which do you think is more important: protecting the environment or keeping prices down?" Eighty percent favored environmental protection over low prices.[59] Nevertheless, consumers often select products that harm nature in order to save money. The difference between private behavior and public attitudes could be seen as evidence of hypocrisy. If all consumers acted according to their stated values, then there would be no need for government regulation. But consumers cannot control the choices that are put before them, nor can they be sure how their fellow citizens will behave. To buy an expensive product when everyone else chooses the cheaper alternative is futile; and companies won't sell environmentally friendly products if most people think this way. This logic does not prevent some people from making altruistic consumer choices in line with their deliberative judgments; but it does make such choices inherently frustrating unless the government can act as well.

As a nation, we have decided to delegate many decision-making functions to the market. It decides, by and large, what is produced and consumed and who is hired and fired. Its decisions are efficient—in some respects—and they contribute to economic growth and certain kinds of personal freedom. But market decisions are rarely deliberative, because they do not represent a joint discussion about the common good. For the most part, they are aggregates of private interest. The same can be true of majority votes, unless voters deliberate before they go to the polls. Nevertheless, the Progressives favored democratic political institutions because they thought that voting would encourage deliberation. In the end, if the public chose to give capital free reign, at least it should make that decision deliberatively.

THE PUBLIC INTEREST

The word *progressive,* as used around the turn of the century, was so ambiguous as to be virtually indefinable. However, practically all self-described progressives shared at least one commitment. They believed that there was a "national interest" or "public good," superior to special interests and market outcomes. For them, "the moral and the general were synonymous, and that which was unworthy [was] the private, the partial, interest."[60]

But how could the national interest or common good be known? La Follette's answer was reasonably clear. Ordinary people knew best what ailed them, and everyone had a right to participate in self-governance. Technical experts who promised to solve public problems without public participation were just another powerful special interest. Only in a broad discussion could private desires turn into a true public good.[61] One could, however, believe in the national interest and not care much for public deliberation. Herbert Croly, for example, thought that the best way to accomplish the public good was to elect a strong, charismatic leader who would set a course for the nation, employing expert advisers to implement his policies. It is only a slight exaggeration to say that the citizen's role, according to Croly, was to elect Theodore Roosevelt.

Some of Croly's contemporaries believed that the public good *could not* emerge from a democratic process that included everyone, because too many people lacked sufficient virtue and knowledge. Elitist reformers who called themselves progressives imposed voter registration rules and literacy tests, often for the first time, and often for the express purpose of reducing the working class vote in the name of "good government." Partly as a result, voter turnout (as a percentage of the total number of citizens who were legally eligible to vote) declined steadily from 79 percent in 1896 to 49 percent in 1924.[62]

But a more genuinely democratic species of reform also flourished during the same period. For example, Frederic Howe, a Progressive activist and close associate of La Follette, began his political career as a Mugwump reformer in Cleveland, opposed to the Democratic machine. In his maiden speech before the City Council, he described his machine opponents as "men who have substituted corruption for discussion, and ours is a government by discussion." This was classic Progressive rhetoric. But Howe soon discovered that his fellow Mugwumps did not care much about the interests of poor Cleveland citizens, whereas the "bad men in the council rallied to the children. They knew better than I did where the children lived and where they had to play. On measures where there was no money moving they voted right; while representatives from the [wealthy] east end wards often voted wrong."[63] Howe gradually decided that "the public good" could emerge only from inclusive, democratic politics. Other prominent Progressives reached similar conclusions, among them Governor Hiram Johnson of California, Cleveland mayor Tom Johnson, Detroit mayor Hazen Pingree (later governor of Michigan), and five-time Chicago mayor Carter Harrison, Jr.[64] This type of democratic reformer often ended in the orbit of Senator La Follette, to whom Hiram Johnson once wrote: "A humble admirer and follower congratulates the PIONEER in the great progressive movement. . . . You have been our inspiration."[65]

Even if we choose to define the public good as the product of broad, inclusive deliberation, we could still ask: Why should we value it? Isn't the very idea of a "common interest" a myth—and a hypocritical or even dangerous one at that? President Wilson often spoke in a way that invited such criticism:

> So, at this opening of a new age, in this its day of unrest and discontent, it is our part to clear the air, to bring about common counsel; to set up the parliament of the people; to demonstrate that we are fighting no man, that we are trying to bring all men to understand one another; that we are not the friends of any class against any other class, but that our duty is to make classes understand one another. Our part is to lift so high the incomparable standards of the common interest and the common justice that . . . a new day of achievement may come for the liberty we love.[66]

Here Wilson aptly summarized progressive attitudes (or platitudes) about the public interest. But his ideal of a nation united could be dangerously hostile to values like cultural diversity and personal autonomy. If all Americans were to accept one set of values and goals, then ethnic minorities would surely have to adjust far more drastically than Wilson's WASP brethren.

Furthermore, Wilson's distinctions between public and special interests, consensus and division, have struck many critics as mere hypocrisy. A "special interest," these critics say, is just a faction that other groups happen to dislike. Wilson's rhetoric implies that even a poor minority cannot agitate on its own behalf—because that would be special pleading—whereas bourgeois civic reformers can amass great influence, as long as they advance what they choose to call the public interest. The very notion of a calm, national discussion aimed at consensus (Wilson's "parliament of the people") often seems irrelevant or unfair. Why should the industrial workers of Wilson's time have sought to "understand" the rapacious robber barons who exploited them? Why not strike, boycott, form a labor party, or use other divisive tactics, rather than deliberate about "common justice" with their oppressors?

For that matter, consider Wilson's own racial policies. In 1914, after he agreed to segregate the federal work force, the president told black visitors to the White House that "discrimination may not be intended against anybody, but for the benefit of both [groups]. . . . If you take it as a humiliation, which it is not intended as, and sow the seeds of that impression all over the country, why the consequences will be serious."[67] In other words, Wilson wanted African Americans to accept that his racist policies served the public interest and not to sow discord by criticizing him in public. To complain would have meant special pleading. On another occasion, he said, "I hope . . . that by the slow pressure of argument and persuasion the situation may be changed and a great many things done eventually which now seem impossible. . . . I appeal to you most earnestly to aid at holding things at a just and cool equipoise until I can discover whether it is possible to work out anything or not." Once again, Wilson favored calm, rational deliberation, even though it would have been much more appropriate and effective for the president to denounce racism.[68]

Wilson's fault was to declare himself the sole arbiter of the public interest and to demand acquiescence rather than real consensus. This was possible because black citizens had been largely disenfranchised, and in many parts of the country they had been terrorized into silence. (A Memphis newspaper had openly editorialized that Teddy Roosevelt's "negro appointees will be killed.")[69] In general, Wilson assumed that his own beliefs and values epitomized the national interest. As a political scientist, he had favored a strong presidency because he thought that any duly elected president would embody the public will: "The voices of the nation unite in his understanding in a single meaning and reveal to him a single vision so that he can speak . . . the common meaning of the common voice."[70] Unfortunately, many of America's "voices" did not agree that Woodrow Wilson spoke for them.

However, leaving aside Wilson's arrogance and racism, there is much to be said for the distinction between special interests and the public good. Certainly, all Americans have the right to petition government for the redress of their own grievances. But there are two ways to seek beneficial policies from the state.

Some groups simply make demands; and when their opponents disagree, they threaten to use votes, influence, or money to get their way. Regardless of the merits of their case, this approach exemplifies special-interest politics. There is no reason to believe that the aggregation of such demands will yield good policy. But the alternative is to support a desired policy by articulating some notion of the public interest or by describing a general principle of justice. This is the deliberative approach favored by La Follette and his allies.

In 1960, E. E. Schattschneider proposed a rough-and-ready test for distinguishing between public- and private-interest groups.[71] Public-interest organizations are generally defined by some end or principle. Anyone who agrees with their credo can join, although membership may require a modest fee. Thus, for example, members of Common Cause, the Christian Coalition, and the Sierra Club do not necessarily share anything except a set of political beliefs. Organizations that so readily admit members usually interpret their ends in general terms: reforming politics, renewing morality, or saving the earth. Not everyone agrees with their specific agendas, but their aspirations are framed in (formally) universal language. Furthermore, their methods and proximate—if not ultimate—goals are usually subject to modification by their members.

By contrast, the National Association of Manufacturers (NAM) permits only industrial corporations to join. What defines the NAM is not a principle or end, but rather an identity and the interests that follow from it. In more than a century of effective lobbying, the NAM has changed its positions, arguments, and methods many times, but always as a tactic to advance the interests of manufacturers. If the NAM had an open-admissions policy, then millions of unionized laborers and environmentalists might join, subverting its purpose. Its special-interest character, then, is revealed by its rules of admission. People are asked to join because of their identities, not because of their beliefs about what is right for America. The same is true of the AFL-CIO and the Nation of Islam, but not of the NAACP or the Moral Majority.

Of course, it is necessary and proper to form special-interest groups, especially on behalf of the disadvantaged. But by themselves such organizations probably will not generate a civil society in which the common good is clearly debated. To that end, the Progressives founded such classic "public-interest" associations as the League of Women Voters, the National Civic League, the National Consumers League, and the American Civil Liberties Union. They also tried to reform politics so that the least savory methods of special-interest politics would be circumscribed, and a principled debate could occur in Congress, the parties, and the press.

It is very difficult, however, to organize a political movement around such abstract concepts as political reform and the public good. Any concrete social or economic proposal is bound to favor some people over others, so we cannot say (without being controversial and divisive) that it serves "the public interest." According to Jean-Jacques Rousseau, it should be possible to achieve consensus about matters of institutional design, but "as soon as a question of particular fact or right arises . . . the matter becomes contentious. It is a case in which the individuals concerned are one party, and the public the other."[72] Yet no political movement can gain power or change society if it *fails* to take positions on the important questions of the day, including the divisive ones.

This dilemma was evident in La Follette's career. As a Progressive, he said that he did not want to promote any particular economic ideology or interest: his goal was to enhance democracy. Until the last phase of his career, he spoke about little except political reform and generic rights for all consumers and taxpayers. Repeatedly, he promised that a fair and deliberative democracy would benefit everyone except the shadowy special interests who refused to discuss their privileges. However, he also thought that the public should choose politicians on the basis of specific platforms. Candidates should pledge to implement policies, so that elections would be opportunities for serious and focused debate.[73] Thus, he was obliged to explain exactly what he would do about the concrete problems of the day. To make matters even more difficult, he knew that most people wouldn't vote for purely procedural reforms unless they could also expect tangible benefits.

La Follette solved this problem on his way to the Governor's Mansion by emphasizing a proposal—the equal taxation of railroads—that seemed to follow *automatically* from pure political reform. The railroads, a powerful special interest, had persuaded Wisconsin to tax them at a uniquely low effective rate. There was no good reason for this inequity (since railroads were highly profitable), so political corruption seemed the obvious cause of their favorable treatment. Local rumor held that the state capitol had been built facing the train depot "just to remind the legislators of the true source of power."[74] When La Follette succeeded in taxing railroads at the general rate, he thereby moved the state budget from a deficit to a substantial surplus. Such neat solutions were not always available, but at least he had an appropriate economic issue for his gubernatorial campaign.

When La Follette campaigned for tax fairness, he emphasized the taxpayers' interest against a special interest. In the same way, he often defended consumers against the industries that exploited them. We all pay taxes and we all purchase consumer goods. Therefore, La Follette's defense of the consumer/taxpayer was formally an appeal to *everyone*.[75] In 1912, the Progressive theorist Walter W. Weyl wrote that the role of "consumer is most universal, since even those who do not earn wages or pay direct taxes consume commodities. In America to-day the unifying economic force, about which a majority, hostile to the plutocracy, is forming, is the common interest of the citizen as a consumer of wealth."[76]

Although corporations are not citizens, their owners are, and capitalists can argue that tax breaks for their enterprises would help the whole public. They can thereby join the political debate with an alternative view of the consumer's authentic interests. The railroads in Wisconsin had no such argument to make. But even if they had argued effectively against new taxes, La Follette would still have succeeded in making the public interest the sole topic of debate. By 1910, the whole nation had begun to discuss what was best for consumers, as sectional and partisan loyalties temporarily faded.[77] Spurred by La Follette and his allies, a consumer revolt brought down President Robert Taft in 1912 and precipitated a presidential race between two men, Wilson and Roosevelt, who each vied to appear the tougher advocate of consumer interests.

Even when La Follette took the side of a particular occupation, he still tried to assert the whole community's interests. For instance, railroad workers wanted their shifts limited to a maximum of sixteen hours. As a senator, La Follette supported them by arguing that long shifts were responsible for 60,000 annual railroad fatalities; thus a shorter workday would benefit *everyone*.[78] La Follette could be criticized for emphasizing one aspect of human nature (consumption) over the equally important aspects of work and production. He did, however, take the side of workers—but generically, not one occupation at a time. Thus he enthusiastically supported the legal right to unionize, but he treated each union as a special interest.[79]

At the peak of La Follette's power, consumer-consciousness was the dominant force in American politics, campaigns were national debates about the common good, and Progressives often won. But the movement for consumers and taxpayers could not sustain its momentum for long. It was rational for special interests to spend money gaining information and leverage on specific issues that mattered greatly to them. But the average citizen would see too small a return from such an investment, especially since each citizen could expect most other people to remain apathetic. It made much more sense either to ignore politics altogether or to join a narrow, organized faction.[80] Here, then, was another dilemma: La Follette stood for diffuse public interests that had a natural disadvantage against organized special interests.

While he was president, Theodore Roosevelt observed that consumers never complained about the cost of railroad travel, although firms complained about freight charges—so passengers must not mind the price of their tickets. But La Follette better understood the cause of the consumer's silence: "He cannot organize and come before a legislative committee and make himself heard. . . . Nor has he the means of knowing, when he buys his coal, his supplies, his food, his lumber, his hardware, how much the price he has to pay is due to excessive freight charges."[81] Industries possessed relevant information and the means to lobby effectively on specific issues; but taxpayers and consumers had no such advantages. In 1914, La Follette wrote in his magazine: "It is impossible for the people to maintain perfect organization in mass. They are often taken unawares and are liable to lose at one stroke the achievements of years of effort."

Thus La Follette well understood the advantages enjoyed by well-organized, well-financed factions in a complex, pluralist society: "Their resources are inexhaustible. Their efforts never relax. Their political methods are insidious." Nevertheless, he placed hope in democratic institutions that had popular support, for "the united power of the people expressed directly through the ballot can over-throw the enemy."[82] But it was difficult to construct a popular majority when people identified with their own professions, economic interests, and ethnic and cultural groups. After the First World War, as Americans discovered that political action by narrow factions was particularly effective, they signed up to join one new pressure group or another, from the National Association of Manufacturers to the American Federation of Labor, from the NAACP to the KKK. By 1924, most Americans saw themselves as mine workers or Daughters of the American Revolution, as Irish Catholics or steel executives—but not primarily as citizens and taxpayers.[83]

In this new political environment, La Follette's personal sympathies were clear: he stood with the disadvantaged. He now sought to combine needy interest-groups into a ruling coalition. In 1920, he became a leader of the Citizens' Legislative Service, a new lobbying organization that still spoke the language of Progressive political reform but basically stood for workers' and farmers' interests. In 1924, La Follette's attention shifted to the Conference for Progressive Political Action (CPPA), which supported his independent bid for the presidency. Despite its name, the CPPA epitomized coalition politics, not democratization or consumer/taxpayer interests. It consisted of delegates from various organized groups, such as the League of Women Voters and the NAACP, unions and farmers' associations. Each organization cast votes in proportion to its official membership, and the CPPA struggled to devise a platform that could satisfy all of its diverse constituencies. Arthur Garfield Hays recalled, "Marxists, single-taxers, vegetarians, theosophists, radicals of all shades of opinion, gathered under La Follette emblems to preach their diverse religions. Our emblem was the Liberty Bell, and as Allen McCurdy remarked, 'The crack is getting larger every day.'"[84] La Follette, never fond of factions, believed that "the only way to organize a new progressive party was on the basis of individual membership with the states as the units of organization."[85] But his preference was ignored.

Accepting the CPPA nomination, La Follette rehearsed classic Progressive themes: the urgency of political reform, the curse of corruption, and the need to turn party platforms into substantive contracts with voters.[86] His supporters agreed, but their main concerns were narrower economic and social issues.[87] In many cases, their demands were justified; but each faction clashed with another, and no one was willing to put political reform ahead of economic issues. As La Follette told a supporter in 1925, the CPPA had faltered because it was "made up of various economic and political groups whose primary purpose were other than progressive political action."[88] This fact partly explained why the Progressives failed to advance a civil rights agenda. A movement for democratic reform would have battled Jim Crow; but a coalition of enfranchised special-interest groups refused to sacrifice anything for Southern blacks.[89]

In a New Progressive Era, we must again seek to reform the political system so that it deliberates fairly about the common good. But we will inevitably encounter the problem that people identify with narrow groups (and sometimes for good reasons). We will therefore need the functional equivalent of La Follette's railroad taxation bill to galvanize mass support for Progressive reform. Otherwise, we may repeat the experience of another Progressive Wisconsin senator, Russell Feingold, who nearly lost his 1998 reelection race because he failed to connect his signature good-government issues, especially campaign-finance reform, to the "grittier problems that immediately affect people's lives."[90]

CENTRALIZATION, ORDER, AND EXPERTISE

La Follette's career illustrates another problem that is endemic to Progressivism. In Wisconsin, political reform produced a stronger, more efficient, and more representative government. La Follette's successor, Governor Francis E. McGovern, then passed legislation on workman's compensation, factory safety, work hours for women and children, a state income tax (the first in the country), a highway commission, waterpower conservation, a forest reserve, a state life insurance fund, farm cooperatives, and agricultural extension.[91] Theodore Roosevelt wrote: "Thanks to the movement for genuinely democratic popular government which . . . La Follette led to overwhelming victory in Wisconsin, that state has become literally a laboratory for wise experimental legislation aiming to secure the social and political betterment of the people as a whole."[92]

Indeed, by establishing a powerful regulatory state, McGovern was doing just what La Follette had promised: asserting popular control over the economy. But the resulting bureaucracy was complex and technical, and it often dealt with narrow issues that seemed to concern only special interests. McGovern was defeated in the 1914 gubernatorial election by a conservative Republican, Emanuel Philipp, who criticized the new Wisconsin bureaucracy as elitist and wasteful. He derided more than fifty "useless commissions" run by university "experts."[93] Philipp invoked taxpayer interests and populist values, thereby appropriating some of the Progressives' traditional rhetoric. In fact, La Follette (who was now a U.S. senator) endorsed Philipp's complaints.[94] As a result, the Wisconsin Progressive movement split into factions, divided on both philosophical and personal grounds.[95] But as much as La Follette might complain about the elitism and complexity of McGovern's administration, he could not entirely escape responsibility. Once he had made government genuinely representative and sovereign over the economy, the state apparatus naturally grew in power and complexity. Here, then, was a true dilemma: popular reform seemed to generate elite institutions.

In 1912, Thomas McCarthy, an adviser to the Wisconsin legislature, pointed out that any private corporation "[has] an accounting system that shows every item of the cost of its business. It has scientific experts, technical engineers and a general concentration of intelligence and ability and scientific knowledge; it has a central administrative office. It has also in its employ experts on the legal side of the question."[96] If such a corporation came into conflict with the state, how could the latter prevail, unless it, too, deployed lawyers, scientists, accountants, statisticians, surveyors, and other experts?

For McCarthy, democratic principles required a massive increase in the powers of government, which (in turn) necessitated the use of expert administrators. He conceded that appointed commissions were "seemingly contrary to our idea of democracy."[97] But, he wrote, "the people are slowly working toward a distinction between those who determine policy and those who are chosen for administrative or technical skill—as servants merely to carry out the will of the people as expressed in the law. Thus the appointive commission is an aid to democracy. There is no inconsistency in these two principles."[98] Based in part on McCarthy's book, one historian writes: "Perhaps to a greater degree than any other contemporary political leader, it was La Follette who adopted the cult of expertise, science, and rationality."[99]

This is an exaggeration, resulting from a cursory reading of Wisconsin Republican politics. McCarthy, an ally of Governor McGovern, criticized La Follette's primary reform bill and expressed considerable reservations about the initiative and referendum, which La Follette had endorsed. He used elitist rhetoric that would have made La Follette uneasy—as, for example, when he wrote "that it is just as ridiculous to elect a railroad commissioner as it would be to elect, on a state-wide ballot, a professor of comparative literature." Central to *The Wisconsin Idea* is a parable about a German prince who realizes that his realm is bankrupt. A wise counselor persuades him to cut unnecessary expenses, rationalize the tax code, invest in public infrastructure and education, and punish usury. As a result the realm flourishes.[100] Conspicuously absent is any discussion of democratic participation or public deliberation—nor is La Follette's name used anywhere in the book.[101]

Compared to McCarthy, La Follette was much more ambivalent about the role of expertise in a democracy. In 1913, he seems to have supported a Wisconsin Senate bill that would have allowed the recall of all state commissioners by public vote.[102] Nevertheless, there is no denying that experts and professionals gained power in Wisconsin and Washington while La Follette held public office.

In part, this was the culmination of deep historical trends. At the turn of the century, medicine, public health, nursing, law, academic research, teaching, journalism, and accounting were rapidly turning into "professions," complete with recognized credentials, advanced degree programs, periodicals, associations, and accepted standards of behavior. The number of professionals per 100,000 citizens almost doubled between 1870 and 1890.[103] Lawyers formed their first professional association in 1878; social workers started theirs in 1874. More than 200 learned societies were founded between 1870 and 1890. Doctors became not only professionals but often specialists as well: ophthalmologists, orthopedists, pediatricians, and many others formed their own organizations between 1864 and 1888.[104] As a result, practically every occupation now coveted the term "professional," so that a plumber in 1891 could state with a straight face: "Plumbing is no longer merely a trade. Its importance and value in relation to health, and its requirements regarding scientific knowledge, have elevated it to a profession. It is clothed in the responsibilities of the learned professions and the dignity of the sciences."[105]

Some might have doubted that plumbers deserved to be called "scientists," but that honor was generally granted to economists, sociologists, and psychologists. These disciplines had only recently emerged as cumulative, empirical research programs, but they quickly attained great prestige. By 1900, many people in universities and industry believed that science could definitively explain, and potentially control, all social phenomena. Specifically, some reformers hoped to make government more efficient and effective by introducing both scientific methods and professional credentials into public management. Such ideas were not the Progressives' alone; they also inspired American robber barons, French socialists, Prussian aristocrats, and British imperial administrators. European sociologists, such as Robert Michels, were the first to suspect that modern life required complex organization and that complexity undermined democracy.[106] As Leonard White wrote in 1927, "What the *whole world* is witnessing is the emergence of government by experts, by men and women who are trained technicians highly specialized to perform some service by scientific methods."[107]

Nevertheless, according to some historians, American Progressivism epitomized the era's enthusiasm for technical expertise. In his classic book on the Progressive Era, Robert H. Wiebe writes: "Scientific government, the reformers believed, would bring opportunity, progress, order, and community."[108] Samuel P. Hays argues that the progressives sought "a rational and scientific method of making basic technological decisions through a single, central authority," such as the Department of the Interior.[109] The widespread use of experts in government always requires a bureaucracy. Therefore, Wiebe writes, "The heart of progressivism was the ambition of the new middle class to fulfill its destiny through bureaucratic means."[110] Both Wiebe and Hays have revised their accounts of the Progressive Era, but their earlier view remains influential.[111] According to this view, "progressivism" was a complex of related ideals: expertise, professionalism, technical rationality, administration, order, centralization, and bureaucracy. No account of the Progressive Era is complete without a discussion of these values, for they colored all the debates of the day.

This is an important topic for more than historical reasons. In the Progressives' alleged enthusiasm for expertise and science, some conservatives see an attractive point of attack. Progressivism, they think, is the beginning of a long, liberal, largely Democratic tradition that also produced the New Deal, the New Frontier, and the Great Society—each of which increased the power of bureaucrats and experts. Progressives gave their name to an era in American history, the period during which professional expertise and scientific rationality finally became dominant. It does not follow that Progressives were *responsible* for this development. But conservatives argue that "the core of progressive thinking was the goal of the scientific management of society."[112]

For instance, Michael Joyce and William Schambra quote the Progressive-Era sociologist Charles Horton Cooley, who said that he favored "a comprehensive 'scientific management' of mankind, to the end of better personal opportunity and social function in every possible line."[113] Hardly anyone today—neither liberals nor conservatives, college professors nor unskilled laborers—will like the sound of *this*. In fact, the current conservative critique echoes an older, leftist view of progressives as "paternalistic and bureaucratic."[114] The New Right is heavily indebted to radical historians of the 1960s, who first depicted progressivism as an arrogant, elitist effort to control ordinary people.

However, Joyce and Schambra choose to quote Cooley instead of anyone who was particularly prominent in progressive circles. Even Cooley harbored serious doubts: "Exact prediction and mechanical control for the social world I believe to be a false ideal inconsiderately borrowed from the provinces of physical science." He added: "The opinion sometimes expressed that social science should set forth a definite, tangible criterion of progress is also, I think, based on a false conception of the matter, derived, perhaps, from mechanical theories of evolution." Instead of scientific management, Cooley favored "democracy, in the sense of an active participation of the common people in the social process." In the paragraph that Joyce and Schambra quote, Cooley espoused "scientific management" as a concession to popular opinion. "But," he immediately added, "inseparable from this is the whole question of democratic development through the state and other institutions." His guiding ideal was "deliberative self-government." This meant not just a strong, democratic state, but also a vibrant, independent civil society. "Democracy should not mean uniformity, but the fullest measure of differentiation, a development everywhere of special spirits—in communities, in occupations, in culture groups, in distinctive personalities."[115]

So, unless Cooley's words are torn out of their original context, he cannot be made to fit the conservative stereotype of a progressive: i.e., someone who believes that "Government is responsible for the scientific management of society."[116] Certainly, that stereotype does not apply to Dewey, Addams, or La Follette—nor to Presidents Wilson and Roosevelt. We can criticize the progressives' ideas about technical management in a democracy, but it is important to get the facts straight first. In my view, they wrestled with unavoidable and persistent problems. We may not admire all of their answers, but their values were diverse, and we can learn much from them.

The debate about "scientific management" illustrates the full range of Progressive-Era opinion. Frederick Winslow Taylor was famous as an "efficiency expert," someone who advised managers on better ways to organize their manufacturing plants. He used to stand near workers with a stopwatch, trying to determine how much labor they could accomplish in a given amount of time. The "best management," he wrote, "is a true science, resting upon clearly defined laws, rules, and principles, as a foundation."[117] In his view, efficient industrial management required the services of professional experts.

Thanks to Taylor, an "efficiency craze" began in 1911.[118] Conferences and congressional hearings were held, successful books appeared, and a Taylor Society was formed.[119] The popular press ran stories about efficient household management. Taylor's ideas appealed to some pro-business conservatives who believed that industry could improve its performance (and image) without government regulation. The National Association of Manufacturers supported Taylorism in Congress. President Taft, the bane of the Progressives, created a President's Commission on Economy and Efficiency to implement Taylorite ideas.

From the Progressive camp, Brandeis agreed that industry could become more efficient if it adopted scientific management. But he saw these potential savings as a good reason for the state to demand lower railroad fares and other pro-consumer outcomes. While Brandeis envisioned Taylorites in the employ of regulated private enterprise, other Progressives saw Taylorism as a way to organize the government's own activities. Woodrow Wilson used Taylorites—including that brilliant engineer and administrator Herbert Hoover—to manage the United States' war effort.[120] Robert Moses studied municipal management with members of the Bureau of Municipal Reform, a Taylorite association in New York City. He later created an authoritarian fiefdom that comprised the Triborough Bridge and Tunnel Authority, the City Planning Commission, and the Parks Commission. He hired engineers, lawyers, and accountants to build the modern infrastructure of the New York metropolitan area, virtually without democratic oversight and on allegedly scientific principles. Often these principles justified bulldozing whole neighborhoods.

Nowhere were professional ideals and bureaucratic methods more evident than in the conservation movement of the Progressive Era. Hays writes: "Its essence was rational planning to promote efficient development and use of natural resources." Conservationists were committed to the Gospel of Efficiency, which "molded the policies which they proposed, their administrative techniques, and their relations with Congress and the public. . . . Since resource matters were basically technical in nature, conservationists argued, technicians, rather than legislators, should deal with them." Foresters, engineers, and agronomists on the payroll of the Department of the Interior could manage federal lands efficiently in the public interest, whereas businessmen were venal and congressmen were logrolling ignoramuses. But this was one of many points on which La Follette disagreed with his more technocratic contemporaries.[121]

Indeed, La Follette denounced Taylor on the Senate floor: "I care not whether the stop watch be held over the operative or whether men are tempted by a bonus system to strive for prizes and drive their competitors, their fellow workmen to the breaking-down point. Mr. President, it is nothing but a 'sweating system.'"[122] La Follette's own suggestion for increasing "efficiency" echoed the unions' demand: an eight-hour day.[123] His friend and adviser John R. Commons held that Taylorism meant "government by experts." It turned workers into "objects to be investigated, not investigators," and thereby reduced any "goodwill" that might otherwise form between management and labor.[124]

Most reformers felt considerable ambivalence about professionalism, bureaucracy, and scientific management. During the 1912 campaign, for instance, Wilson accused Roosevelt of favoring "a government of experts."[125] Wilson wanted to split large corporations into pieces rather than submit them to expert oversight: this was the difference between his New Freedom and Roosevelt's New Nationalism. The Democratic Party, he later recalled, had promised "to set up a government in the world where the average man, the plain man, the common man, the ignorant man, the unaccomplished man, the poor man had a voice equal to the voice of anybody else in the settlement of the common affairs, an ideal never before realized in the history of the world."[126] On Labor Day 1912, Wilson said explicitly, "God forbid that in a democratic country we should resign the task and give government over to experts. What are we if we are to be taken care of by a small number of gentlemen who are the only men who understand the job? Because if we don't understand the job, then we are not a free people."[127]

On the other hand, Wilson signed bills creating the Federal Reserve, the Federal Trade Commission, and the Tariff Commission—all expert regulatory bodies. In effect, he implemented his opponent's New Nationalism once elected. Roosevelt, meanwhile, sometimes argued for expert management, but he also said that "the majority of the plain people will day in and day out make fewer mistakes in governing themselves than any smaller body of men will make in trying to govern them."[128] On these grounds, he called for the removal of federal judges when they blocked the people's will. He expressed his own credo in an oxymoron: "scientific popular self-help."[129] Apparently, he believed that democratic, technocratic, *and* individualistic ideals could be comfortably combined.

Finally, La Follette established boards and regulatory bureaus that employed professional experts. When he created a state railroad commission, he said that he "felt that the state should always have the best experts in the country for these positions, whether residents of Wisconsin or not, for much would depend upon the way in which our new law was administered. . . . I have always advocated the appointive method for filling all places requiring the services of trained experts."[130] Yet La Follette maintained: "It is the essence of republican government that the citizen should act for himself directly whenever possible."[131] He stated his fundamental beliefs in a speech delivered almost at the end of his career:

> The Progressives believe that the machinery of government should be so completely in the hands of the electorate that the deliberate popular will may be reflected alike in the making of laws and in their administration and execution.
>   Our opponents, hostile to self-government, declare that this doctrine is dangerous and revolutionary, and that the machinery of government must be of such character

or so far removed from the people as to yield, if at all to the popular will, very slowly and after long delay.[132]

The fact is that Progressives and other democratic reformers faced a genuine dilemma. They saw that any democracy worthy of the name had to take active measures to regulate the economy and to protect the environment. Otherwise, the public would cede its sovereignty to private corporations. Moreover, popular control could not be exercised exclusively at the neighborhood or township level. The only effective counterweights to huge corporations were large political units, such as city and state administrations or even the federal government. Indeed, issues like unemployment and the depletion of natural resources *had* to be addressed on a national scale, because the economy was national. As La Follette said, "No power other than the government itself is equal to that of these industrial combinations."[133] But large-scale regulation, oversight, and enforcement required a professional government work force.

Today, some management theorists argue that discipline and specialization were needed under the special conditions of capitalism around 1900, but not any more. As long as demand for commodities was fairly stable, firms and state enterprises that were large, centralized, and disciplined had competitive advantages. Their size won them economies of scale; their discipline allowed them to prevent uncooperative behavior by individuals; and their stability permitted their workers to specialize. Seeing the effectiveness of such firms, unions and government agencies adopted similar bureaucratic structures—at considerable cost to democracy. But after World War II, consumer goods became more important than commodities like steel and coal, demand ceased to be stable and predictable, and size and discipline became liabilities. Taylorite corporations were too rigid to adjust to rapid changes; they had invested too much in hardware and bureaucratic procedures. They began to lose market share to more loosely structured corporations in which interdisciplinary teams of workers were able to deliberate about goals and strategy. In today's economy, the tradeoff between democratic participation and Taylorite efficiency may vanish—with lessons for the public sector as well as industry.[134]

Dewey would greet this news with joy. He searched all his life for workable alternatives to bureaucratic regulation in both the government and industry. He wrote:

> No government by experts in which the masses do not have the chance to inform the experts as to their needs can be anything but an oligarchy managed in the interests of the few. . . . The man who wears the shoe knows best that it pinches and where it pinches, even if the expert shoemaker is the best judge of how the trouble is to be remedied. . . . It is impossible for high-brows to secure a monopoly of such knowledge as must be used for the regulation of common affairs. In the degree in which they become a specialized class, they are shut off from the knowledge of the needs which they are supposed to serve.[135]

For Dewey, true democracy required broad public participation and face-to-face discussions about concrete problems. He wanted people to govern themselves in local units, for, "unless local communal life can be restored, the public cannot adequately resolve its most urgent problem: to find and identify itself." The "home" of democracy, he thought, was "the neighborly community." Dewey concluded his book *The Public and Its Problems* with a paean to grassroots, decentralized, participatory democracy: "We lie, Emerson said, in the lap of an immense intelligence. But that intelligence is dormant and its communications are broken, inarticulate and faint until it possesses the local community as its medium." This was stirring language, but Dewey recognized a basic obstacle: communities had lost their autonomy as they became part of an international marketplace. A town meeting could handle garbage collection, but it would be impotent if a faraway corporation decided to remove the local plant or strip-mine the countryside.

Dewey's political ideal was "the Great Community"—not a powerful state, but an environment in which communities could govern themselves safely. It "will do its final work," he wrote, "in ordering the relations and enriching the experience of local associations."[136] Unfortunately, he was never able to develop a concrete plan for the Great Community. His own strongest commitments were to experimental schools and Progressive settlement houses. For instance, he served on the first board of Addams's Hull-House and then worked closely with Lillian Wald at Henry Street and Mary Simkhovitch at Greenwich House.[137] Some settlements were basically Christian missionary societies, and some existed to "Americanize" recent immigrants. But the Progressive settlements that Dewey loved were early experiments in community organization and participatory democracy. They tried not to treat poor people as passive clients, as recipients of expert advice and service. Dewey wrote:

> The vice of the social leader, of the reformer, of the philanthropist and the specialist in every worthy cause of science, or art, or politics, is to seek ends which promote the social welfare in ways which fail to engage the active interest and cooperation of others. The conception of conferring the good upon others, . . . which is our inheritance from the aristocratic civilizations of the past, . . . dies hard.[138]

To enlist the "freely cooperative activities of others" was, for Dewey, "the root principle of the morals of democracy." Similarly, Simkhovitch noted that "the idea of the Neighborhood Center [or settlement house] has shifted from being a leaven in a lump—the service idea—to the conception of arousing the neighborhood to a sense of its capacities and responsibilities." Her method involved "bringing to bear upon neighborhood problems expert knowledge while building up neighborhood democratic associations." Ultimately, she wrote, "the purpose of the Settlement is to act as a stimulus for community organization. The House is not an agency for putting over a program. It is only incidentally a center of enlightenment for the community. But it is an attempt to arouse all the latent forces of the neighborhood and bring them into play. It is an expression of confidence in the unplumbed possibilities of individuals and society."[139] The heirs of Greenwich House and the other Progressive settlements were not the bureaucratic programs of the New Deal (which Dewey later opposed), but the grassroots activities of the Civil Rights Movement, Saul Alinsky's Industrial Areas Foundation, and Students for a Democratic Society (SDS) during the early 1960s.

In 1919, Wilbur Phillips tried an experiment called the Social Unit Plan in Cincinnati. Under his plan, a bicameral legislature would be created to govern each district within the city. One house would represent people as consumers, with every 100 families electing a member. The other house would represent people as producers, with each vocation sending a representative. Members of the consumers' house would canvass their districts, deliberate about public needs, and decide priorities. Members of the vocational house would provide information and skills, each according to his or her special training. Thus "each member of the Citizens' and Occupational Councils was to be at one and the same time a teacher and a student—now instructing all of the others, now learning from them; now informing the citizens, now informed by them."[140]

Although the Social Unit idea seems rather fanciful, it actually got off the ground in Cincinnati. Residents decided to focus on health care, and after two years they "had established one of the most comprehensive, efficient, and cooperative public health programs in the nation." The Social Unit Organization only fell apart during the Red Scare of 1919, when Mayor John Galvin called it "one step away from Bolshevism." Neighborhood residents were invited to vote their opinion of Phillips's organization: they supported it, 4,000 to 20. However, the charge of radicalism frightened away funders and the plan fell apart.[141]

The Social Unit Plan died quickly, but the fact that leading Progressives embraced it tells us something about their values. Croly and the *New Republic* enthusiastically backed it, Gifford Pinchot served as honorary president, and Margaret Wilson sent money.[142] Felix Frankfurter also contributed, and Wilson's interior secretary chaired its board in 1919.[143] These, then, were not people who reflexively favored big bureaucracies and professional experts. Instead, they began to struggle with the perennial problem of expertise in a democracy. Any New Progressive Movement will have to face the same dilemmas.

NOTES

1. "Amid Wild Hurrahs a Third Party Is Born," *New York Herald*, February 25, 1892, p. 5; "Furious Free Fight," *Chicago Tribune*, February 24, 1892, p. 2; Barton C. Shaw, *The Wool-Hat Boys: Georgia's Populist Party* (Baton Rouge, 1984), p. 54.

2. Quoted in John P. Diggins, *The American Left in the Twentieth Century,* by John P. Diggins (New York, 1973), p. 65.

3. Karl Marx, comments on Bakunin's *Statehood and Anarchy,* 1874–75, in *The Marx-Engels Reader,* 2d ed., by Robert C. Tucker (New York, 1978), p. 547.

4. Robert M. La Follette, Sr., "Official Statement," reprinted in *Politics: The Citizen's Business* (New York, 1924), p. 317.

5. Quoted in Irving Howe, *Socialism and America,* by William Allen White (New York, 1985), p. 70.

6. John Chamberlain, *Farewell to Reform: The Rise, Life and Decay of the Progressive Mind in America,* 2d ed. (New York, 1932), p. 81.

7. Robert M. La Follette, *La Follette's Autobiography,* 1911, with a foreword by Allan Nevins (Madison, Wis., 1960), pp. 116–117 (La Follette's italics).

8. John Dewey, *The Public and Its Problems* (New York, 1927), pp. 74, 202. Compare Teddy Roosevelt's admission that he was "rather an agnostic" on the most burning issue of the day, the tariff. Quoted in *The Warrior and the Priest: Woodrow Wilson and Theodore Roosevelt,* by John Milton Cooper, Jr. (Cambridge, Mass., 1983), p. 80.

9. William Allen White, *The Old Order Changeth* (New York, 1910), p. 241.

10. Ibid., p. 71.

11. Charles A. Beard, *The Economic Basis of Politics,* lectures originally delivered in 1916 (New York, 1945), p. 5.

12. Speech at Chicago, May 10, 1905, in Cooper, *The Warrior and the Priest,* p. 83.

13. La Follette, *Autobiography,* p. 136.

14. La Follette, *Autobiography,* pp. 14, 134–135.

15. David P. Thelen, *Robert M. La Follette and the Insurgent Spirit* (Madison, Wis., 1985), p. 188. See also Gilbert Osofsky, "Progressivism and the Negro: New York, 1900–1915," *American Quarterly* 16 (Summer 1964): 153–168.

16. See Larry J. Sabato and Glenn R. Simpson, *Dirty Little Secrets: The Persistence of Corruption in American Politics* (New York, 1996), pp. 11–12. *No one* was prosecuted for federal campaign-finance violations between the passage of the Corrupt Practices Act of 1925 and the post-Watergate reforms, embodied in the Federal Election Campaign Act of 1974.

In 1904, almost no states had yet regulated the role of private money in politics; but in a period of just two years, 1907–1908, 10 states passed lobbying laws, 19 banned corporate political contributions, 14 prohibited private entities from giving state officials free transportation passes, and 18 established direct primaries. Secret ballots were introduced in most states, and laws were passed to prevent citizens from being paid to vote. See Richard L. McCormick, "The Discovery That Business Corrupts Politics: A Reappraisal of the Origins of Progressivism," *American Historical Review* 86 (April 1981): 266; and Arthur Link and Richard McCormick, *Progressivism* (Arlington Heights, Ill., 1983), pp. 32, 40, 50, 52, 54.

17. La Follette, *Autobiography,* p. 128.

18. White, *The Old Order Changeth,* pp. 49–50; 52–53.

19. Beard, *The Economic Basis of Politics,* p. 103, italics added. This quotation appears in the 1945 addendum (i.e., chapter 5) as a summary of Beard's 1916 lectures.

20. Alexander J. McKelway, "Child Labor and Its Attendant Evils," *Sewanee Review* 16 (April 1908): 222. For background on the NCLC, see Dewey W. Grantham, *Southern Progressivism: The Reconciliation of Progress and Tradition* (Knoxville, Tenn., 1983), pp. 190–192.

21. See, e.g., Herbert Croly, *The Promise of American Life*, ed. Arthur M. Schlesinger, Jr. (1909; reprint Cambridge: 1965) p. 205.

22. Ibid., p. 23.

23. Hannah Arendt, *On Revolution* (New York, 1963), p. 115.

24. Quoted by Joseph Bessette, *The Mild Voice of Reason: Deliberative Democracy and American National Government* (Chicago, 1994), p. 55.

25. See Bernard Manin, "On Legitimacy and Political Deliberation," trans. Elly Stein and Jane Mansbridge, *Political Theory,* vol. 15, no. 3 (August 1987): 350.

26. For a succinct statement of this position, see Cass B. Sunstein, "Constitutions and Democracies: An Epilogue," in *Constitutionalism and Democracy,* ed. Jon Elster and Rune Slagstad (Cambridge, Mass., 1988), pp. 333–334; and Robert B. Reich, introduction to *The Power of Public Ideas* (Cambridge, Mass., 1988), pp. 1–12.

27. William H. Riker, *Liberalism against Populism: A Confrontation between the Theory of Democracy and the Theory of Social Choice* (Prospect Heights, 1982), p. 234. The classic text is Kenneth J. Arrow, *Social Choice and Individual Values,* 2d ed. (New Haven, Conn., 1963).

28. See Walter Lippmann, *The Phantom Public* (New York, 1925), p. 56.

29. Jackie Calmes and John Harwood, "Gingrich Gone, GOP Is Still Left Struggling to Craft Its Message," *Wall Street Journal,* November 10, 1998, p. A6.

30. Riker, *Liberalism against Populism,* p. 128.

31. An index of average ideological consistency rose from .15 in 1960 to a plateau of .4 between 1964 and 1972. See Samuel P. Huntington, "The United States," in Michel Crozier, Samuel P. Huntington, and Joji Watanuki, *The Crisis of Democracy* (New York, 1975), p. 77.

32. Dewey, *The Public and Its Problems,* pp. 207, 206.

33. Ibid., p. 208.

34. Woodrow Wilson, *The New Freedom: A Call for the Emancipation of the Generous Energies of a People* (New York, 1913) pp. 105, 90–91, 239, 100. This book is actually a medley of Wilson's campaign speeches, edited by William Bayard Hale.

35. Steffens to Francis J. Heney, June 1, 1908, quoted in "The California Progressive and His Rationale: A Study in Middle Class Politics," by George E. Mowry, *Mississippi Valley Historical Review* 36 (September 1949): 247. Cf. Walter Rauschenbusch, *Christianity and the Social Crisis,* 1907 (New York, 1991), p. 261: "If [citizens] are purposely misled by distorted information or the suppression of important information, the larger jury before which all public cases have to be pleaded is tampered with, and the innermost life of our republic is in danger." Similar quotations could easily be multiplied.

36. Madison's Amendments to the Constitution, drafted June 8, 1789, quoted in *Framed for Posterity: The Enduring Philosophy of the Constitution,* by Ralph Ketcham (Lawrence, Kans., 1993), p. 100.

37. *Whitney v. California* (1927), 274 U.S. 375.

38. Since Lippmann was a skeptic about rationality and morality, he actually shunned the word *deliberation* altogether, for it implies a rational effort to decide what is right. In his view, government officials could *negotiate*; private citizens could only watch.

39. Dewey, *Freedom and Culture* (1939; reprint, New York, 1963), p. 128.

40. I owe this point to Stephen Elkin.

41. "Our Need," *La Follette's Weekly,* vol. 6, no. 25 (June 20, 1914): 1.

42. Dewey, *The Public and Its Problems,* pp. 116–117 (italics added), 177.

43. Mary Parker Follett, *Creative Experience* (New York, 1924), pp. 156–178. (Her characteristic term is not "deliberation" but "integration.")

44. Allen F. Davis, *Spearheads for Reform: The Social Settlements and the Progressive Movement, 1890–1914* (New York, 1967), pp. 79–81.

45. Wilson, *The New Freedom,* p. 96.

46. Mary Kingsbury Simkhovitch, *The Settlement Primer: A Handbook for Neighborhood Workers* (1926; reprint, New York, 1936), pp. 27–44.

47. See, e.g., Robert D. Putnam, "Bowling Alone: America's Declining Social Capital," *Journal of Democracy,* vol. 6, no. 1 (January 1995): 65–78; and Putnam, "The Strange Disappearance of Civic America," *The American Prospect* (Winter 1996): 35–48.

48. J. W. McMullen, "Unifying School House and City Hall," *La Follette's Weekly,* vol. 6, no. 24 (June 13, 1914): 5 (italics added).

49. Jane Addams, *Twenty Years at Hull-House* (1910; reprint, New York, 1961), pp. 134–135.

50. La Follette, *Autobiography,* pp. 130–131.

51. Quoted in *Midwestern Progressive Politics: A Historical Study of Its Origins and Development, 1870–1958,* by Russel B. Nye (New York, 1965), p. 186.

52. Jesse Lyman Hurlbut, *The Story of Chautauqua* (New York, 1921), p. 390. A typed schedule shows that La Follette was booked to appear at fifty-one Chautauquas in July and August, 1905. These meetings were scheduled to take place in Indiana, Iowa, Kansas, Nebraska, Illinois, Minnesota, Ohio, Kentucky, and Missouri. See "Governor Robert M. La Follette's Chautauqua Dates," La Follette Family Collection, Series B, box 153, Library of Congress.

53. Charles McCarthy, *The Wisconsin Idea* (New York, 1912), pp. 133, 135.

54. *La Follette's Weekly,* vol. 5, no. 5 (February 1, 1913): 9; vol. 6, no. 25 (June 20, 1914): 1.

55. Louisa M. Young, *In the Public Interest: The League of Women Voters, 1920–1970* (New York, 1989), p. 82. See also Sara Barbara Brumbaugh, *Democratic Experience and Education in the National League of Women Voters* (New York, 1946), pp. 24–27. On the connections between suffragists and Progressives, see, e.g., Young, *In the Public Interest,* pp. 17, 21.

56. Thelen, *Robert M. La Follette and the Insurgent Spirit,* pp. 108–109.

57. Arold W. Brown, *The Improvement of Civics Instruction in Junior and Senior High Schools* (Ypsilanti, Mich., 1929), p. 32: quoting U.S. Bureau of Education Bulletin, 1915, no. 23. See also Clyde B. Moore, *Civic Education: Its Objectives and Methods for a Specific Case Group: A Study in Educational Sociology* (New York, 1924), pp. 78, 51.

58. "Message of Governor Robert M. La Follette to the Senate and Assembly of Wisconsin, January 10, 1901," in *La Follette* ed. Robert S. Maxwell (Englewood Cliffs, N.J., 1969), p. 24.

59. Barbara Rosewicz, "Friends of the Earth: Americans Are Willing to Sacrifice to Reduce Pollution, They Say," *Wall Street Journal,* April 20, 1990, p. A1.

60. Otis L. Graham, Jr., *An Encore for Reform: The Old Progressives and the New Deal* (New York, 1967), p. 70.

61. See p. 30–31.

62. Frances Fox Piven and Richard A. Cloward, *Why Americans Don't Vote* (New York, 1988), pp. 54, 86–88; Link and McCormick, *Progressivism,* p. 53.

63. Frederic Howe, *Confessions of a Reformer* (New York, 1925), pp. 104, 109.

64. See John D. Buenker, *Urban Liberalism and Progressive Reform* (New York, 1973).

65. Quoted by Thelen, *Robert M. La Follette and the Insurgent Spirit,* p. 78.

66. Wilson, *The New Freedom,* pp. 109–110.

67. See Lewis L. Gould, *Reform and Regulation: American Politics from Roosevelt to Wilson* (New York, 1986), pp. 178–179.

68. Quoted by Nancy J. Weiss, "The Negro and the New Freedom: Fighting Wilsonian Segregation," *Political Science Quarterly* 84 (March 1969): 148–149.

69. Gould, *Reform and Regulation,* p. 59.

70. Quoted by Michael S. Joyce and William A. Schambra, "A New Citizenship, a New Civic Life," in *The New Promise of American Life,* ed. Lamar Alexander and Chester E. Finns, Jr. (Indianapolis, 1995) p. 143.

71. E. E. Schattschneider, *The Semisovereign People* (Hinsdale, Ill., 1960), p. 25.

72. Jean-Jacques Rousseau, *The Social Contract,* trans. G. D. H. Cole (London, 1913, new edition, 1993), book 2, chapter 4, p. 206.

73. See, e.g, speech on accepting the Republican nomination for governor, 1902, in Ellen Torelle, ed., *The Political Philosophy of Robert M. La Follette, as Revealed in His Speeches and Writings* (Madison, Wis., 1920), p. 58.

74. Thomas Dreier, *Heroes of Insurgency* (Boston, 1910), p. 21. See also Clay Mc-Shane, *Technology and Reform: Street Railways and the Growth of Milwaukee, 1887–1900* (Madison, Wis., 1974), pp. 46–47.

75. In 1906, La Follette declared that "the welfare of all the people as consumers should be the supreme consideration of the Government" (Thelen, *Robert M. La Follette and the Insurgent Spirit,* p. 56). He even gave a consumer-oriented *justification* for opposing margarine, although his *motive* may have been to protect Wisconsin dairy farmers.

76. Walter E. Weyl, *The New Democracy,* rev. ed. (New York, 1914), pp. 248–250.

77. Thelen, *Robert M. La Follette and the Insurgent Spirit,* p. 71 (citing Walter Lippmann and Walter Weyl), and p. 76 (quoting Albert Beveridge); see also Richard Hofstadter, *The Age of Reform* (New York, 1955), pp. 172–173.

78. Senate speech, April 23, 1906, in Maxwell, ed., *La Follette,* p. 43. Cf. Senate speech of July 26, 1916, in Torelle, *The Political Philosophy of Robert M. La Follette,* p. 133.

79. See further on, chapter 7.

80. The classic discussion of such issues appears in Mancur Olson, *The Logic of Collective Action: Public Goods and the Theory of Groups* (Cambridge, Mass., 1965).

81. La Follette, *Autobiography,* p. 172 (the order of the sentences is reversed.)

82. *La Follette's Magazine,* October 17, 1914, in Torelle *The Political Philosophy of Robert M. La Follette,* p. 173.

83. Thelen, *Robert M. La Follette and the Insurgent Spirit,* p. 160 and passim.

84. Arthur Mann, *La Guardia: A Fighter against His Times, 1882–1933* (Chicago, 1959), p. 174, quoting Garfield Hays, *City Lawyer* (New York, 1942), p. 270.

85. Belle Case La Follette and Fola La Follette, *Robert M. La Follette* (New York, 1953), vol. 2, p. 1153.

86. La Follette, "Official Statement," in White, *Politics,* pp. 307–308.

87. The Progressive platform led with economic issues and said nothing about campaign-finance reform, civil rights, or obstacles to voting. It did call for national referenda and initiatives and the election of federal judges. See White, *Politics,* pp. 322–330.

88. La Follette to William Rawleigh in 1925, quoted by Thelen, *Robert M. La Follette and the Insurgent Spirit,* p. 192.

89. W. E. B. Du Bois endorsed La Follette in 1924 but then justly complained about the Progressive's record on race. See Manning Marable, *W. E. B. Du Bois: Black Radical Democrat* (Boston, 1986), p. 126; Du Bois, "A Negro Nation within the Nation," from *Current History* (1930), in Philip S. Foner, ed., *W. E. B. Du Bois Speaks: Speeches and Addresses, 1920–1933* (New York, 1970), pp. 77–78.

La Follette's 1924 presidential campaign claimed: "The colored American . . . may safely place his destiny in the hands of Senator La Follette, whose past record relative to colored citizens stands unblemished." The campaign cited La Follette's appointment of the first African-American officeholder in Wisconsin; his support for black soldiers unjustly discharged by Teddy Roosevelt; his editorial defense of blacks after race riots in East St. Louis and Washington; his belief that Southern representation should be cut to reflect black disenfranchisement; and his legislative support for Howard University. See "Senator Robert M. La Follette's Stand on Issues Vital to the Negro's Interest," La Follette Family Collection, Series B, box 206.

90. Peter Beinart, "Fussy Russ," *The New Republic,* November 23, 1998, pp. 14–15.

91. See Robert C. Nesbit, *Wisconsin: A History,* 2d ed. (Madison, Wis., 1989), pp. 425–426.

92. Introduction to McCarthy, *The Wisconsin Idea,* p. vii.

93. La Follette, extended dictation on the Administration of Emanuel Philipp, pp. 64–65, La Follette Family Collection, Series B, box 217. La Follette wrote an almost book-length attack on Philipp. It was never published, but it reveals that La Follette was deeply troubled by the conservative attack on Progressivism.

94. "Exclusive Responsibility," *La Follette's Weekly,* vol. 6, no. 30 (July 25, 1914): 1 (signed editorial). La Follette argued that McGovern alone was responsible for controlling government spending and that excessive spending could ruin the Progressive movement.

95. McGovern supported Roosevelt against La Follette for the Republican presidential nomination that year; La Follette's supporters possibly tried to sabotage McGovern's next administration. See Nesbit, *Wisconsin,* pp. 430–431; Gould, *Reform and Regulation,* p. 157; and Herbert F. Margulies, "The Background of the La Follette-McGovern Schism," *Wisconsin Magazine of History* 40 (Autumn 1956): 21–29. On May 30, 1913, Nell D. Commons, John Commons's wife, wrote to La Follette, describing the "intolerable situation here," with attempts being made to "embarrass McGovern." "All this is going on in your name, in spite of the letters you wrote Mr. Beck and others." La Follette Family Collection, Series, B, box 73.

96. McCarthy, *The Wisconsin Idea,* p. 68.

97. Thelen, *Robert M. La Follette and the Insurgent Spirit,* p. 117, quoting McCarthy's defense of *The Wisconsin Idea.*

98. McCarthy, *The Wisconsin Idea,* p. 172. See also Croly, *The Promise of American Life,* p. 169.

99. Gabriel Kolko, *The Triumph of Conservatism: A Reinterpretation of American History, 1900–1916* (Chicago, 1963), p. 213.

100. McCarthy, *The Wisconsin Idea,* pp. 88, 116, 46, 12.

101. McCarthy wrote to "Senator R. M. La Follette" (April 25, 1913), describing "utter chaos" in the legislature as a result of the La Follette/McGovern schism. He wrote:

"You may be sore at me and I care not. If you are fighting under the battle [sic] of progress, fighting the people's battle, it matters little what you think of me. I will be with you. . . . I feel as I grow older an increasing admiration for you and the great work you have done in this state. That admiration is not uncritical, but it recognizes the big, craglike personality which has done so much for this state and this nation." This letter suggests that McCarthy belonged to McGovern's faction; that he did not know La Follette well; that he had been no great supporter of La Follette's administration; but that he admired the senator for his personal qualities. (La Follette Family Collection, Series B, box 74.)

102. Bill 1100A. John R. Commons, La Follette's constant adviser, sent him the bill with a letter suggesting that La Follette favored it: see Commons to La Follette ("Dear Bob"), April 24, 1913, La Follette Family Collection, Series B, box 73. In McGovern's defense, it should be noted that he passed campaign-finance legislation, a critical element of Progressive political reform.

103. Robert L. Buroker, "From Voluntary Association to Welfare State: The Illinois Immigrants' Protective League, 1908–1926," *Journal of American History* 57 (December 1971), in Mann, *La Guardia,* p. 133.

104. Burton Bledstein, *The Culture of Professionalism* (New York, 1976), pp. 84–86.

105. Address to the American Public Health Association, quoted in Bledstein, *The Culture of Professionalism,* p. 35.

106. See, e.g., Robert Michels, *Political Parties: A Sociological Study of the Oligarchical Tendencies of Modern Democracy,* trans. Eden and Cedar Paul (Glencoe, 1915), pp. 37–41. Cf. Lippmann, *The Phantom Public,* p. 180.

107. Leonard D. White, *The City Manager* (Chicago, 1927), p. 295 (italics added).

108. Robert H. Wiebe, *The Search for Order, 1877–1920* (New York, 1967), p. 107.

109. Samuel P. Hays, *Conservation and the Gospel of Efficiency: The Progressive Conservation Movement, 1890–1920* (Cambridge, Mass., 1959), p. 271.

110. Wiebe, *The Search for Order,* p. 166.

111. See Robert H. Wiebe, *Self-Rule: A Cultural History of American Democracy* (Chicago, 1995), pp. 162–165. And compare the two editions of Hays's *The Response to Industrialism* (1957 and 1995). In the first edition, Hays depicts reform as a series of attacks on parties, launched by disaffected interests, technocrats, suffragists, and corporations. In the second edition, he attributes reform enthusiasm to a widespread fear of corporate power. He now thinks that anti-party activity was just one version of reform, favored above all by industrial leaders and conservatives. The parties survived, nevertheless, because they alone could "express the varied demands of the entire society" and "express skepticism about the alleged perfect wisdom of a managerial and technical elite." The relevant part of the first edition, entitled "The Attack on Party Politics," is now called more neutrally, "Political Reform." See Hays, *The Response to Industrialism, 1884–1915,* 1st ed. (Chicago, 1957), pp. 152–158; 2d ed. (Chicago, 1995), pp. 192–199.

112. Robert Nelson, "In Memoriam: On the Death of Progressivism and the 'Market Mechanism,'" paper prepared for the 69th Annual Meeting of the Western Economic Association, June 29–July 3, 1994, p. 2.

113. Joyce and Schambra, "A New Citizenship, A New Civic Life," p. 142, quoting Cooley, *Social Process* (New York, Charles Horton, 1918), p. 347.

114. David Bouchier, *Radical Citizenship: The New American Activism* (New York, 1987), p. 58.

115. Cooley, *Social Process*, pp. 398, 405, 248, 347, 148.

116. Nelson, "In Memoriam," p. 3.

117. Taylor, *The Principles of Scientific Management* (1911; reprint New York, 1967), pp. 7, 9.

118. Samuel Haber, *Efficiency and Uplift: Scientific Management in the Progressive Era, 1890–1920* (Chicago, 1964), p. 52.

119. See, e.g., *Addresses and Discourses of the Conference on Scientific Management Held October 12, 13, 14, 1911* (Hanover, N.H., 1912).

120. Joan Hoff Wilson, *Herbert Hoover: The Forgotten Progressive* (Boston, 1975), pp. 39, 90.

121. Hays, *Conservation and the Gospel of Efficiency*, pp. 2–3. For La Follette's position, see pp. 85–86.

122. Senate speech on the Taylor System, July 27, 1916, in Torelle, *The Political Philosophy of Robert M. La Follette,* pp. 131–132.

123. *La Follette's Magazine*, 1915, quoted in Torelle, p. 137.

124. John R. Commons, *Industrial Goodwill* (New York, 1919), p. 19. See also Robert Westbrook, *John Dewey and American Democracy* (Ithaca, N.Y., 1991), pp. 176–177.

125. Gould, *Reform and Regulation,* p. 172.

126. Arthur Stanley Link, *Wilson: The Road to the White House* (Princeton, 1947), p. 518. The day before, Link notes, Wilson had "paid a memorable tribute to La Follette, who was by now throwing the full weight of his influence to the Democratic cause." Wilson's short-term interest in attracting La Follette's voters may partly account for his views on popular sovereignty in October 1912.

127. Quoted by Joyce and Schambra, "A New Citizenship, a New Civic Life," p. 146.

128. Quoted by Benjamin R. Barber, *Strong Democracy: Participatory Politics for a New Age* (Berkeley, Calif., 1984), p. 151.

129. Introduction to McCarthy, *The Wisconsin Idea*, p. x.

130. La Follette, *Autobiography*, p. 149.

131. Message to the Legislature, 1901, in Torelle, p. 39.

132. Madison Square Garden Address, reprinted as press release number 34 from the La Follette-Wheeler Progressive Campaign Headquarters, released September 19, 1924, in the La Follette Family Collection, Series B, box 206.

133. Message to the Wisconsin Legislature, 1904, in Torelle, p. 86.

134. See Michael C. Dorf and Charles F. Sabel, "A Constitution of Democratic Experimentalism," *Columbia Law Review*, vol. 98, no. 2 (March 1998): 292–314.

135. Dewey, *The Public and Its Problems*, pp. 208, 207, 206.

136. Ibid., pp. 213, 215, 216, 219, 211.

137. Davis, *Spearheads for Reform*, pp. 58–59.

138. *Ethics*, p. 276, in Westbrook, *John Dewey and American Democracy*, p. 185, citing Dewey and James A. Tufts, *Ethics* (1908), p. 276.

139. Simkhovitch, *The Settlement Primer,* pp. 46, 48, 43. For a list of settlements and their activities, see Robert A. Woods and Albert J. Kennedy, eds., *Handbook of Settlements, 1911* (New York, 1970).

140. Wilbur Phillips, *Adventuring for Democracy* (New York, 1940), pp. 149–153.

141. Robert Fisher, *Let the People Decide: Neighborhood Organizing in America* (Boston, 1984), p. 25.

142. Haber, *Efficiency and Uplift*, p. 88; Phillips, *Adventuring for Democracy,* p. 148.

143. Fisher, *Let the People Decide,* pp. 23, 25.

2

The Emergence of Modern Politics

I have devoted considerable attention to the ideals of Robert La Follette and his allies, because I believe that they ought to inspire a new Progressive Movement. But it would not be wise to adopt La Follette's platform verbatim. The country, after all, has changed greatly in the last seven decades. We still need political reform before we can expect good social policy; and real reform still means increasing both fairness and deliberation. But the rules of American politics have evolved, as have our habits of association, our attitudes toward politics, and our ways of communicating. In addition, Americans have tried numerous experiments in government reform and participatory democracy, from which there is much to learn. This chapter surveys some of the most important developments in formal government and politics. Then chapter 3 covers our behavior and attitudes as citizens. We need at least an outline sketch of contemporary politics and civil society before we can develop a sensible agenda for the New Progressive Movement.

THE RISE OF FEDERAL REGULATION AND
INTEREST-GROUP LIBERALISM

Many people have seen Roosevelt's New Deal as a revival and consummation of Progressive ideals, and there is something to this view. But it is instructive that of 204 prominent, self-described "progressives" who survived until 1937, just 40 supported the New Deal.[1] Since progressives were a diverse and unruly lot, it is not surprising that they split on an issue as contentious as FDR's first administration. Furthermore, some of them could have changed in the decade after 1924, moving toward conservatism or socialism in their old age. But it is striking how classically Progressive they sounded when they attacked the second President Roosevelt.

Insofar as La Follette's old friends embraced the New Deal, it was because they and Roosevelt shared some common enemies. The Progressives believed that a democratic government could legitimately interfere with private contracts, if voters decided deliberatively that laissez-faire would not serve the public interest. Many conservatives disagreed. They argued that a free market maximized prosperity, and—more important—that government had no legal or moral authority to restrict private property. Whatever Progressives thought about economics, they all opposed this libertarian political theory as an unwarranted constraint on democracy.

FDR was not elected on any particular economic platform, but he promised "bold, persistent experimentation" to ease people's suffering during the Depression.[2] The surviving Progressives differed in their reactions to Roosevelt's experiments—LaGuardia and Howe liked them; Brandeis, Dewey, and White didn't— but they generally thought that the federal government had a right to act if it wanted to. They must have felt a familiar sense of despair in 1935 and 1936, when the Supreme Court struck down a New York State minimum-wage law for women, plus the very heart of the New Deal: railroad pensions, price-fixing legislation, the Agricultural Adjustment Act, and the National Industrial Recovery Act. Roosevelt's ultimate victory over the Court vindicated Progressive ideas about popular sovereignty.[3] Since then, libertarians have continued to argue their case, but such New Deal programs as Social Security have enjoyed broad and consistent support since the 1930s. Only on the fringe do people deny the federal government's right to tax, spend, and regulate the economy. The defeat of political libertarianism was a victory for Progressivism, and it explains Roosevelt's support among surviving Progressives.

On the other hand, the New Deal's way of responding to laissez-faire violated core Progressive principles. It epitomized a style of politics that Theodore Lowi has called "interest-group liberalism." This ideology is defined by several major tenets: that there is no knowable "public good"; that everyone belongs to a faction; that factions have permanently conflicting interests; that government can (at most) help groups to resolve their differences by peaceful bargaining; and that justice is served by giving weak factions support in the bargaining process. Interest-group liberals deserve the "liberal" label because they are enthusiastic about state power, and they want to increase social justice. They pursue fairness by organizing unrepresented people into groups and then inviting these organizations to sit at the bargaining table. Although factions may be willing to negotiate with competing groups, they are never expected to change their goals in response to moral arguments.

Interest-group liberalism began as early as the Wilson administration, when Herbert Hoover (then secretary of labor) convened representatives of "organized labor and organized agriculture" to negotiate a mandatory price for wartime wheat. Anticipating the doctrines of interest-group liberals, John R. Commons argued that it would have been "autocratic" for Congress to have set the price, "bureaucratic" for Hoover to have done so, and sheer "dictatorship" if the unions' will had prevailed—but bilateral negotiations could produce an "equilibrium of capital and labor" that would represent "the public interest" *just because* both factions would sign the agreement.[4] Although Commons was La Follette's friend, the senator strongly objected to any plan that would strip Congress of its deliberative role and empower "special interests of tremendous power" (or any "one man" in the executive branch) to set prices.[5] But La Follette lost the battle.

Notwithstanding this early example, John Kenneth Galbraith has identified the New Deal as the moment when the government's main job became the management of interest-group negotiations. New Dealers assumed that factions such as labor and capital would be permanently at odds. Under these circumstances, they tried to create new negotiating arenas in which disadvantaged groups would have power. This was the primary function of the National Recovery Act, the National Labor Relations Board, the National Bituminous Coal Commission, and most of the New Deal's "alphabet soup" of agencies. Liberals no longer proposed general principles of justice or the national interest; now their role was "the buttressing of weak bargaining positions."[6]

Since it is not necessary to please everyone in a democracy, interest-group liberalism encourages politicians to assemble *majority* coalitions. To build majorities, leaders may appeal to common values and ideals, using public arguments to attract new members. But interest-group liberalism rewards a less principled approach, in which leaders invite all available groups to join their side in return for specific, ad hoc advantages. The coalition that results may have no coherent justification or guiding philosophy, in which case uncommitted citizens cannot deliberate about whether to support or oppose it. To be sure, Franklin Roosevelt used idealistic arguments to win over voters. But he also used plenty of horse-trading, compromising, and logrolling. For instance, the New Deal coalition included both white Southerners (who were spared federal action against Jim Crow and the sharecropping system), and African-American Northerners (who were included in the new welfare programs). The surviving Progressives disliked this approach. Irvine Lenroot, an important Wisconsin politician, said that he had no objection to Roosevelt's redistributive policies, because he considered himself an economic radical. But he lamented: "We are largely a nation of groups, with little thought of the general welfare. Organized capital, organized labor, organized farmers, organized wets and organized dries." In 1943, he wrote privately: "I was for old Bob La Follette and I have not changed in any way my views that I held then concerning abuses in our economic life. But I have always believed that a thing that was wrong when committed by capital and industry did not become right if committed by large groups who were able to swing elections." Ray Stannard Baker, Wilson's biographer and an old Progressive, voted for FDR in 1936, but he complained in his diary: "everywhere group demands for special favors, and career politicians promising to grant them."[7]

Interest-group liberalism (a style of politics) has encouraged the growth of administrative rule making (a method of governance). Although bargaining certainly occurs in legislatures, they are not perfectly designed to manage negotiations among interest groups. A legislature's power lies in its ability to pass bills. If a law reflects a negotiated deal, then the underlying agreement must fall apart as soon as the balance of power shifts or new parties enter the game. This is a serious practical problem, because legislatures do not have the time to amend statutes regularly. Besides, laws are general, so they may inadvertently hurt groups that have bargaining power. Finally, since a statute is binding, there is no room for appeal (other than a constitutional challenge). A clear and simple law leaves nothing for lobbyists, interest groups, and lawyers to do.

Consequently, interest groups usually find it more satisfactory to settle their disputes before regulatory bodies or courts, which can issue whole bodies of complex, adjustable, even inconsistent, law. For its part, Congress often prefers to delegate its referee function to administrative rule makers. When regulatory agencies were created after the Civil War, they were usually ordered to identify and punish specific abuses, defined by statute. This changed with the New Deal, when agencies were told, in effect, "Here is the problem: deal with it."[8] In 1948, the sociologist C. Wright Mills (a fan of La Follette) observed that New Deal policies had helped to integrate "real, and more particularly, potential democratic forces into the apparatus of the political state." But as a result, representative bodies, such as Congress, had lost power to administrative bureaucracies. Mills warned: "Often in this situation, politics becomes a battle between various pressure organizations, represented by lawyers and technicians, not understood by the masses of people."[9]

Regulatory discretion also allows Congress to evade its deliberative responsibilities. Consider just one typical example. In 1970, Congress began to debate whether any toxic chemicals should be permitted in industry if they impaired workers' health, functional capacity, or life-expectancy. Senator Jacob Javits (R-NY) warned that the proposed law "might be interpreted to require absolute health and safety in all cases, regardless of feasibility." He and his colleagues thus faced a profound philosophical question: whether safety should ever be balanced against efficiency, prosperity, employment, equity, or other economic values—and if so, how the balance should be struck. But Congress refused to deliberate on this topic, thereby avoiding its responsibility as the national legislature. Instead, in response to Javits's question, the Senate Committee on Labor and Public Welfare adopted an amendment ordering the secretary of labor to "set the standard which most adequately and feasibly" prevents harm to workers. The statute was, in Justice Rehnquist's words, "completely precatory, admonishing the Secretary to adopt the most protective standard if he can, but excusing him from that duty if he cannot."[10] Congress surely envisioned a permanent process in which corporations, unions, and consumer groups would negotiate safety issues under the eye of the secretary of labor, with constant appeal to federal courts. The result would be an elaborate and evolving body of rules that would reflect the balance of power in each industry. Meanwhile, Congress would be excused from its duties under Article 1, Section 1, of the Constitution, which baldly states: "All legislative powers herein granted shall be vested in a congress of the United States."

Since the New Deal, government by regulatory agencies has been the norm. It has had a deeply malign influence, I believe, on the democratic values of accountability, political equality, access, and deliberation. Since administrative rule making was still nascent in the Progressive Era, the Progressives could ignore its defects—but we cannot. The case for radical reform will be made in chapter 6.

CIVIL RIGHTS

American politics has changed in another fundamental way since the Progressive Era. While winning political power for African Americans, the Civil Rights Movement also expanded our notion of human and political rights; and it added new styles of popular political action to our repertoire.

The connection between Progressivism and racial justice is, unfortunately, ambiguous. C. Vann Woodward writes that the original progressive movement "coincided paradoxically with the crest of the wave of racism. Still more important to the association of the two movements was the fact that their leaders were often identical. In fact, the typical progressive reformer rode to power in the South on a disenfranchising or white-supremacy movement. . . . Racism was conceived by some as the very foundation of Southern progressivism."[11] Southern progressives were mainly affluent whites, interested not in enlarging but in "improving" the electorate. They borrowed Northern progressive ideas about efficiency and expertise, but they ignored the radically egalitarian strand of Progressivism represented by La Follette, who had no Southern following.

Furthermore, the credit for ending segregation belongs not to Progressive reformers or other federal politicians but primarily to Southern blacks. Civil rights initiatives succeeded only after valiant, well-publicized grassroots struggles had provoked white racist violence that embarrassed the national government. For example, the Civil Rights Act of 1964 passed when Bull Connor trained his fire hoses on black children in Birmingham; the Voting Rights Act passed when Colonel Al Lingo's state troopers beat peaceful marchers on the Edmund Pettus Bridge near Selma. Furthermore, legal guarantees of rights meant nothing until civil rights workers actually registered voters, ran for election, and took office amid violence. Where the largely white Progressives had failed to bring democracy to people of color, the black-led civil rights crusade largely succeeded, using methods of nonviolent resistance.

The ideas that inspired such leaders as Martin Luther King, Jr., mostly came from sources other than Progressivism. King, for example, drew on the Exodus story and the Hebrew prophets, the New Testament, the rhetoric of the abolitionist church, the long tradition of African-American solidarity and resistance, and the struggle against European imperialism, especially in India.[12] James H. Cone

particularly stresses the influence of the black church on King's thought, concluding: "References to the tradition of Western philosophy and theology were
primarily for the benefit of the white public so King could demonstrate that he
could think as well or better than any other seminary or university graduate."[13]
It would, however, be a serious mistake to ignore King's explicit arguments and
his achievements as a theorist within the "Western" tradition. In particular, King
learned a great deal from two theologians who had actively supported La Follette
and who had moved within the Progressive orbit. King's political theory was an
advance on Progressivism, but it began with Progressive principles.

One Progressive who influenced him deeply was Walter Rauschenbusch, the
chief exponent of the Social Gospel doctrine. Rauschenbusch had sent fan letters
to Robert La Follette, and his *Christianity and the Social Crisis* (1907) was generally considered a Progressive text.[14] King recalled that he read it in the early
1950s, and it "left an indelible imprint on my thinking."[15] Rauschenbusch
showed himself a typical Progressive when he denounced corruption, arguing
that those who wanted to do God's work on earth ought to get money out of
politics. But he was more famous for emphasizing personal redemption: "The
fundamental contribution of every man is the change of his own personality. We
must repent of the sins of the existing society."[16]

King admired Rauschenbusch, but he came to see the Social Gospel doctrine
as naive. He reached this conclusion under the influence of Reinhold Niebuhr,
another theologian who had considered himself a Progressive. (Indeed, Niebuhr
began his political career working on La Follette's last presidential campaign.)[17]
"I became so enamored of [Niebuhr's] social ethics," King once wrote, "that I
almost fell into the trap of accepting uncritically everything he wrote."[18] Niebuhr
took seriously the idea of original sin, believing that force or greed governed all
large-scale human institutions and that consensus was utopian. Individuals, who
were created in God's image, could be moral in their personal relationships; but
human beings also had to live in society, and no society would cohere except
under threat of force. Niebuhr accused Rauschenbusch of overestimating the
power of moral suasion and "the community-building capacities of human sym-
pathy." Politics, for Niebuhr, was largely a clash of economic interests, and society could become just only if powerful interests were curbed by force.[19]

Despite his "realism," Niebuhr shared the Progressives' ideal of a democratic
society, governed by discussion rather than coercion. Like his Progressive colleagues, he thought that the point of a democratic state was to "arbitrate conflicts
from a more impartial perspective than is available to any party in a given conflict."[20] A true democracy was not merely a system of private rights but a community in which "rights and liberties [are] exercised with a higher sense of responsibility for the common good."[21] All of this sounded like conventional
Progressivism, but Niebuhr was hard-nosed enough to think that the struggle for
community and justice often required *force*. For example, he argued that American whites would never renounce their privileges without a struggle. However,

black Americans faced very long odds if they resorted to violence; and force had a tendency to spin out of control.[22] Under these circumstances, Niebuhr advocated Gandhian methods of nonviolent resistance. Beginning in 1947, the Civil Rights Movement used just such methods to achieve racial justice that had eluded the Progressives. Thus King and his colleagues moved beyond Progressivism by embracing radical, confrontational, extra-legal means to achieve a Progressive end. Such means might have frightened reformers like La Follette, but they proved necessary—for reasons that Niebuhr understood.

The Civil Rights leaders also enriched the Progressives' ideal of a democratic community. For many Progressives, the basic goals of reform were negative: to protect the people *against* corrupt politicians and predatory special interests. They knew what they opposed but not exactly what they stood for. La Follette once wrote: "Mere passive citizenship is not enough." But the alternative that he favored was a defensive struggle against anti-democratic forces: "Men must be aggressive for what is right if government is to be saved from those who are aggressive for what is wrong."[23] Once corrupt lobbyists were chased out of the Capitol, the only advice La Follette had for citizens was to do "right." In 1914, Croly argued:

> This conception of democracy, precisely because it fails to associate democracy with the conscious realization of a social ideal, always assumes a negative emphasis. Its dominant object is not to give positive momentum and direction to popular rule. It seeks, above all, to prevent people from being betrayed—from being imposed upon by unpopular policies and unrepresentative officials. But to indoctrinate and organize one's life chiefly for the purpose of avoiding betrayal is to invite sterility and disintegration.[24]

Like the Progressives, King demanded concrete changes in the rules of American politics. But the goal of his movement was far more ambitious and compelling. For him, the point was to love one's neighbor. Disinterested love, agape, was an active, consuming ideal. "When I am commanded to love, I am commanded to restore community, to resist injustice, and to meet the needs of my brothers."[25] Love was possible even under oppressive conditions, but it would never govern a whole society until force and corruption had been banned by law. For example, whites would never listen to blacks until blacks had the vote; legal segregation encouraged intimidation and fear. The purpose of political reform was to create conditions under which people could cooperate lovingly. In fact, members of a truly democratic community would be required to discuss issues cooperatively, because they would have no opportunity to exclude or threaten one another. They would *need* "understanding good will."[26]

In short, King's ideal was the "Beloved Community," a place governed by agape instead of greed or fear. Agape was not only a political good, encouraged by fair democratic procedures, but also a fundamental moral and spiritual virtue.

Jesus himself had commanded it. Thus, for King, the point of such Progressive reforms as the Voting Rights Act was to enact God's will on earth. Democratic laws could "uplift human personality" by requiring people to act with love, thus overcoming original sin to the degree possible on earth.[27] Such laws could only be achieved by a movement that itself exemplified democratic and Christian virtues: a movement that was peaceful, consensual, voluntary, and nonhierarchical. And this movement would have to change attitudes and habits as well as laws. The resulting transformation would be basic—spiritual and psychological as well as legal and political.

Two reporters who followed the Civil Rights Movement recalled:

> Negroes who were involved directly in direct action experienced something not quite like anything we know normally in American life and history, something of mysticism and exaltation, and thus perhaps something more akin to early Christianity than to Western democracy. Part of this was the finding of a belief and courage at mass meetings that, individually, they might not have been able to muster. It is not likely that those who participated will lose in a lifetime what they had found. Whites like the police who struggled with marchers and the jailers who confined them, whether they would ever admit it, were touched by the experience too, not unlike, it seems fair to say, the Roman persecutors of early Christians; and there are some few tales of white toughs who encountered the spirit of non-violent love and resistance and came away changed.[28]

In a fairly short time, the Civil Rights Movement splintered into competing factions, and spiritual revival transformed into ordinary politics. White hatred found ways, both blatant and subtle, to reassert itself. The ecstatic moment was gone, if only because African Americans could now participate in the quotidian, contentious business of self-government. But if the moment of democratic exaltation was gone, it was not forgotten. Women, Native Americans, gays, and migrant workers all learned to play politics in a new key. Their goals were often classically Progressive—to increase fairness and to improve the public dialogue. But their methods were more radical and their ethos was more spiritual than the Progressives could have imagined.

EXPERIMENTS WITH PARTICIPATORY DEMOCRACY

As the Civil Rights Movement transformed the South, a creed variously called the New Left, campus radicalism, the counterculture, or simply "Movement" politics attracted the support of some radicals, especially young, Northern whites. The New Left was similar to the old Progressivism in its commitment to political critique and democratic reform, but otherwise it seemed a completely different phenomenon. At the Yippie Congress in July of 1970, conferees could only agree to a program of "drugs, rock, and public fornication."[29] The top-hatted, mustachioed lawyers who had backed La Follette in 1912 would have summoned the police at the first sight of a Yippie. They would have been utterly bewildered by the mix of Eastern mysticism, Black Power, Maoism, anarchism, post-structuralism, and countercultural lifestyles that passed for radical politics around 1970.

Looking back at the New Left, it is difficult to see through the late-60s haze of incense, pot, tear gas, and burning cities. But if the "Movement" began at any identifiable moment, it was when Students for a Democratic Society (SDS) published their Port Huron Statement in 1962. This document popularized the phrases "new left" and "participatory democracy" for the decade to come. It was written at a conference organized by Robert Alan Haber, whose parents had named him after Robert La Follette, Sr.[30] The SDS itself grew out of the John Dewey Discussion Society at the University of Michigan.[31] Its founders still thought in the tradition of Midwestern Progressivism; La Follette could easily have signed their Statement.

Far from demanding social revolution or Marxist economic policies, the Port Huron Statement advocated conventional political reform. The SDS authors claimed that the seniority system in Congress gave too much power to racist "Dixiecrats." The major parties were incoherent coalitions, so voters lacked clear choices on election day. Blacks and migrant workers were disenfranchised; gerrymandering hurt the cities. Politicians "respond not to dialogue, but to pressure: and knowing this, the ordinary citizen feels even greater inclination to shun the political sphere." An "enormous lobby force, composed predominantly of business interests, [spends] hundreds of millions each year."[32]

The SDS authors also argued that civil society needed renewal, in order to remedy the "loneliness, estrangement, isolation" that "describe the vast distance between man and man."[33] They opposed big bureaucracies, for, in a participatory democracy, "decision-making of basic social consequence [would be] carried on by public groupings."[34] Therefore, they argued: "Mechanisms of voluntary association must be created through which political information can be imparted and political participation encouraged." To counter special interests, citizens should organize into participatory groups, and the government should distribute "objective materials on all public issues."[35]

The SDS authors wanted to enlarge the public sector so that economic activity could be "debated and planned," which was impossible in a market. But they wanted this state sector to be truly "public, and not the arena of a ruling bureaucracy of 'public servants.'" This would require "steadfast opposition to bureaucratic coagulation." More important, it would demand "experiments in *decentralization.*" Although they didn't use his name, they endorsed Wilbur Phillips's Social Unit Plan for "community decision-making and participation."[36]

From 1962 to 1965, SDS members tried to put their theory into practice by organizing poor residents of Northern cities. At the same time, the most radical of the Civil Rights groups, the Student Nonviolent Coordinating Committee (SNCC), organized blacks in the rural South. Both groups considered themselves "nonideological," believing that the people they organized should set their own political agendas. They saw themselves as catalysts, not as leaders in the traditional sense. They encouraged poor people to talk about social issues, taught them political skills, formed loosely structured organizations, and established "free spaces"—offices, shelters, and union halls—where people could meet to talk.[37] Jane Mansbridge recalls, "In the late 1960s, every major American city and every rural area to which young people had migrated could claim a host of free schools, food co-ops, law communes, women's centers, hot lines, and health clinics organized along 'participatory' lines." For the most part, they followed "the unwritten rules of unitary democracy: face-to-face, consensual decision making and the elimination of all internal distinctions that could encourage or legitimate inequality."[38]

Most of this was happening without SNCC or SDS, whose organizers had encountered difficulties by the middle of the decade. Their privileged backgrounds caused them to stand out uncomfortably in the poor neighborhoods where they worked. They discovered intimidating obstacles to even modest social change, and their resistance to authority made them hesitant to adopt leadership roles. In one extreme example—the SDS "nonproject" in Hoboken, New Jersey—the "organizers" decided to take no action beyond finding blue-collar jobs and waiting for the working class to mobilize itself.[39]

As the sixties progressed, frustrated SDS members renounced their own Port Huron Statement as "bourgeois" and began endless debates about the nature of the Marxist revolution to come. However, parts of the statement were implemented when Lyndon Johnson began the Great Society initiative in 1964. Johnson certainly paid no attention to the SDS or SNCC, but ideas about participatory democracy were in the air, thanks to John Dewey and the Progressive Settlement Houses, C. Wright Mills and Saul Alinsky, organized labor and the mainstream Civil Rights organizations, sociologists like Richard Cloward and Lloyd Ohlin, and the Ford Foundation.[40] The Kennedy administration had put some of these ideas into practice when it began a juvenile-delinquency program, but the Kennedys were more interested in expertise and efficiency than grassroots democracy. Then urban America started to burn, and the Johnson administration had to respond somehow to the new militancy of Northern blacks. In 1964, Johnson announced a War on Poverty.

The main weapon in this "war" was the Economic Opportunity Act, which introduced the idea of "community action" to end poverty in the United States. A community action program had to be "developed, conducted, and administered with the *maximum feasible participation* of the residents of the areas and members of the groups served."[41] Johnson explained: "This program asks men and women throughout the country to prepare long-range plans for the attack on poverty in their own local communities. These are not plans prepared in Washington and imposed upon hundreds of different situations. They are based on the fact that local citizens best understand their own problems and know best how to deal with those problems."[42]

In the same vein, the Model Cities bill of 1966 required "widespread citizen participation."[43] Under the authority of these statutes, the federal government began Head Start, the Public Health Service, the Legal Services program, public housing and urban renewal assistance, community mental health centers, the New Careers Program, and scores of other welfare initiatives. These new programs, plus much of the existing welfare state, came under the "maximum feasible participation" mandate. Community Action Associations, or CAAs, were established in poor and disadvantaged areas—theoretically, to oversee all federal services and to give citizens opportunities to influence the welfare bureaucracy. After eighteen months, 1,000 CAAs had begun operation and were experimenting busily. They created citizens' advisory committees; held open hearings; organized "unions" of people who received government services; established community corporations with actual control over services; developed poor peoples' political skills; and otherwise tried to generate an "urban community based on small, self-contained, self-maintaining, self-directing neighborhoods."[44]

The idea of community action quickly ran into trouble. Many local politicians, threatened by direct federal intervention in their cities, began making patronage appointments to CAA boards. Often, when politicians or bureaucrats selected community representatives, residents came to distrust the entire process. Some local politicians actually preferred to hold elections, since independent candidates lacked the money necessary to wage effective campaigns. In general, turnout in CAA elections was low, and professional politicians controlled the outcome. For example, federal officials set up 154 polling places in the Watts area of Los Angeles, chartered 25 buses, and mailed 100,000 leaflets to residents, but fewer than 1 percent of eligible voters participated, at a cost of $22.94 a vote. When Los Angeles stopped trying to achieve community representation, the federal grants kept flowing.[45] Meanwhile, "poor," "citizen," and "community" all gradually became code-words for "black." Therefore, even well-meaning white politicians assumed that they could fulfill the community participation mandate if they merely talked to established African-American leaders, such as the local head of the NAACP.[46]

Perhaps no one in power had ever meant to cede real authority to welfare recipients. Johnson's promise of broad public participation may have been a rhetorical flourish. However, the promise itself had a powerful motivational effect. Across the country, poor people demanded the right to participate in CAA governance. In at least twenty cities, they gained control of their local boards, usually after a bitter struggle. Once aroused, they took the same fight to school boards, police oversight bodies, city counsels, and state legislatures. A whole generation of poor and minority leaders matured during the War on Poverty—although not exclusively because of it.

Through Neighborhood Legal Services, they filed class-action lawsuits on behalf of poor people. They demanded participation not only in government agencies, but also in all the bureaucracies they encountered, including colleges, hospitals, foundations, and the United Way. CAA directors hired as many as 180,000 workers and created thousands of independent organizations to manage federal programs or to agitate politically; most of these groups were staffed by black people from poor backgrounds. Community-action workers duplicated some of the habits of the old political machines, dispensing patronage and trading favors. However, the beneficiaries were people who had never been able to participate in politics before. In many cases, CAA directors gradually abandoned their militant styles and became traditional politicians or bureaucrats during the 1970s. Radical critics complained that these minority leaders had been "coopted into the system," and leftist historians have since echoed that complaint. It is true that no revolution occurred, but War on Poverty workers organized themselves into insurgent political movements that captured City Hall in Detroit, Atlanta, Cincinnati, Los Angeles, and many smaller communities.[47] Majority rule in the nation's great cities was no small achievement.

During the Kennedy administration, the first experiments in community action were deliberately designed to encourage political reform. The idea was to give federal money to grassroots groups of poor people, bypassing state and local governments that were controlled by affluent majorities or by white-ethnic political machines. Once poor people became organized and politically "competent," they would begin to vote, run for office, and otherwise force their local governments to represent them.[48] SDS, SNCC, and other private organizations on the Left also tried initially to organize the poor so that they could gain more influence over official government institutions; participatory democracy was supposed to complement and improve representative democracy, not replace it.[49]

But mayors and governors were predictably upset when federal money began supporting grassroots institutions controlled by independent black leaders. They fought back, winning some battles and losing others. As the conflict grew bitter—even violent—everyone had to take sides. Johnson, the epitome of a professional politician, lined up with local elected officials. He once asked Sargent Shriver, the War on Poverty's general, whether his office was being "run by a bunch of kooks, commies, and queers."[50] In fact, many poverty activists had completely lost interest in traditional political reform, arguing—as the popular slogan put it—that "democracy is in the streets." They now believed that authentic democracy was participatory, *not* representative. The democratic spirit was alive on picket lines, in union halls, in communes, even during riots—but not in the dry business of legislation and administration. New Leftists instinctively resisted all kinds of formal authority. In 1971, Crosby, Stills, and Nash sang in protest against the mayor of Chicago, Richard J. Daley: "Rules and regulations, who needs them? Throw 'em out the door!"[51]

This attitude was not necessarily democratic. After all, a standard theory of democracy holds that citizens are best represented by *elected* officials who sit in deliberative bodies. Nor is it only the Left that resists state authority—Ronald Reagan and Newt Gingrich have also denounced regulation, bureaucracy, and government intervention. It was true in 1964, as it is today, that local governments ignored some of their citizens, but the proper response was to enfranchise nonvoters, redraw electoral districts, delegate power to local elected bodies, experiment with proportional representation, and revamp campaign-finance systems. Unless local governments were reformed, they would inevitably try to suppress poor people. If radicals succeeded in bypassing or subverting government, then citizens would lose their chance to be represented democratically. Ironically, however, the most lasting impact of the War on Poverty was fairly conventional political reform. Poor people, especially African Americans, gained political skills through community action and then demanded changes in state and local politics. As a result, institutions from school boards to state legislatures became more open, fair, and representative.

The Great Society embodied a liberal social philosophy: it redistributed wealth from the rich to the poor and created new positive economic rights or entitlements. These values did not follow from pure Progressive principles. A democratic people may decide collectively to *reject* liberalism, as many Americans had by 1980. However, there was more to the Great Society than liberal economics: it also strengthened democracy by building fair, participatory, deliberative institutions at the local level. This aspect of the War on Poverty followed from classic Progressive ideas about citizenship and self-government. An independent study published in 1970 took into account all the failures of community action but concluded: "Federally supported programs have created the ground for a remarkably rich, complex, exciting communal life for a growing number of people."[52] When modern conservatives attack "big government," they overlook this aspect of the Great Society—as do many liberals when they defend the welfare state. By themselves, the experiments in participatory democracy were not hugely expensive, so they could be implemented by fiscal conservatives of either party.[53] At a minimum, the War on Poverty provides a worthy point of departure for people who hope to involve more citizens in self-government. Chapter 6 contains suggestions on how to improve on the participatory models of the 1960s, guided by Progressive ideas about deliberation.

POLITICAL REFORM AFTER WATERGATE

Although the Johnson and Nixon administrations tried to support democratic institutions in poor neighborhoods, they did nothing to fight corruption in Washington.[54] On the contrary, the evils that had troubled the Progressives seemed to grow worse every year. Successive presidents indisputably lied to the American people about the Vietnam War. The CIA and the FBI were caught interfering in private citizens' business, sometimes for partisan purposes. Meanwhile, lobbyists wielded conspicuous power in the nation's capital. In 1972, the Nixon campaign raised $63 million, mostly from wealthy individuals and corporations, including $2.14 million from one man, W. Clement Stone. The Watergate scandal revealed numerous corrupt arrangements with contributors. A $600,000 donation from the Milk Producers was a quid pro quo for federal price supports, and a $400,000 contribution by ITT probably influenced the Justice Department to drop a $2-billion antitrust suit against the company.[55]

The time was ripe for Progressive reform. In fact, starting in the late sixties, a new type of insurgent started winning election to Congress. These people were mainstream politicians, not New Left radicals. Many were liberal Democrats, but a significant number belonged to the Republican Party. Although they typically opposed the war in Vietnam and supported the War on Poverty, they were most successful in their efforts to reform government procedures. They often defended oppressed minorities, but they spoke most comfortably about general consumer and taxpayer rights. In 1973, John Gardner, the founder of Common Cause, wrote:

> Effectiveness, access, responsiveness, accountability—these are the attributes that we have a right to expect of our instruments of self-government. They do not characterize government today. Under present conditions, our political and governmental machinery cannot serve *anybody*—neither poor people nor the middle class, neither black nor white, neither young or old. . . .
>
> It is not a question of efficiency for efficiency's sake. Government and politics will never be genuinely efficient; but when they are no longer responsive, when they can no longer be held accountable, then we all suffer.[56]

Gardner's agenda closely followed La Follette's. It included campaign-finance reform, open-meeting laws, democratic primaries, civil rights, tough ethics rules, freedom of information, and regulation of lobbying. Many of these goals were achieved after a few years' struggle.

Even before Nixon resigned, Congress passed new "sunshine" rules that made closed meetings much less common. The War Powers Act of 1973 reasserted congressional control over the military—a modest victory for Progressive values, since Congress had avoided accountability during the Vietnam conflict. As Watergate revealed seamy details about Republican finances, Congress passed major campaign-finance legislation, which will be discussed further on. Then, in the 1974 election, numerous congressional incumbents were replaced by challengers who promised further reform—the so-called Watergate Babies.

Just before this new class was sworn in, the House voted to reduce the power of committee chairs, who had owed their seats to pure seniority. Caucus leaders gained at the chairs' expense, but they were made accountable to the rank-and-file members who elected them. Congress also increased the accountability of the budget process and passed the amended Freedom of Information Act (FOIA), which gave citizens the right to see most government documents.[57] When the class of 1974 arrived in Washington, they immediately broke with sixty years of tradition by unseating powerful committee chairmen: Wilbur Mills of Ways and Means, Wright Patman of Banking Committee, W. R. Page of Agriculture, and Edward Hebert of Armed Services. Hebert blamed that "insidious organization," Common Cause, for his fall.[58] The new Congress also abolished the notorious House Un-American Activities Committee (HUAC), which had harassed suspected (or former) Communists since the late forties, and started hearings into the behavior of the CIA and FBI. Out of those hearings came the modern system of congressional oversight.[59]

But the most important reform of the era was the Federal Election Campaign Act (FECA), which President Gerald Ford signed into law just days before the 1974 election in an effort to appropriate the Democrats' good-government campaign theme. The FECA set spending and contribution limits for all federal races. Donations and expenditures had to be disclosed so that opponents and constituents could spot signs of undue influence. A Federal Election Commission was created and given powers to enforce election law. Finally, FECA provided matching grants for presidential primary candidates in return for their agreement to limit their spending, and full public financing for general-election presidential candidates who agreed not to accept any private money. The presidential elections of 1976 and 1980—conducted under the FECA regime—were almost universally praised as clean. Former Senator Paul Laxalt (R-NV), who ran President Reagan's 1980 campaign, said of public financing: "It was anathema to me . . . but in my experience with the presidential campaigns, it worked, and it was like a breath of fresh air."[60]

La Follette would have embraced these reforms without hesitation, since he had advocated them himself. But he and his contemporaries had responded to a regime of laissez-faire, whereas by 1970 the prevailing ideology was interest-group liberalism. For better or worse, the state was now a powerful and pervasive force. Under these circumstances, it was necessary to regulate the regulators in order to ensure more fair and accountable outcomes. To this end, reformers emphasized conflict-of-interest regulations, revolving-door provisions, open-meeting laws, and public-comment periods. During the Progressive Era, regulators had not yet possessed enough authority to warrant such careful oversight.

To some extent, the new generation of reformers can themselves be seen as interest-group liberals, for they accepted the idea of constant negotiation, but they sought to bring previously overlooked groups into the bargaining process. Consider, for example, the founding of the Mexican American Legal Defense and Education Fund (MALDEF) in 1968. Chicano leaders wanted to appear in court and before regulatory agencies on behalf of their neglected community. They approached the Ford Foundation, which had supported Progressive-style political reforms. Ford gave them $2.2 million, and a new organization was born.[61]

Although this initiative can be defended as a way to increase fairness, it did nothing to overturn a system of negotiation and litigation that had undermined public deliberation. But reformers also founded an array of lobbying groups that purported to represent the *public* interest in legislative and regulatory battles. The very names of Common Cause, Public Citizen, Citizen Action, and the Public Interest Research Group signified a commitment to core Progressive values. These organizations closely resembled the Citizen's Legislative Service, a public-interest lobby that La Follette had directed in the last years of his life. Their other models were such venerable Progressive associations as the League of Women Voters and the National Consumers League. These groups did not make campaign contributions, nor could they mobilize narrow voting constituencies to support their agendas. Thus they would be impotent and irrelevant unless the government began to respond to moral arguments and information instead of money and raw power.

According to Robert Wiebe, the original Progressives had believed that

> The interests thrived on secrecy, the people on information. No word carried more progressive freight than *publicity:* expose the backroom deals in government, scrutinize the balance sheets of corporations, attend the public hearings on city services, study the effects of low wages on family life. Mayor Tom Johnson of Cleveland held public meetings to educate its citizens. Senator Robert LaFollette of Wisconsin heaped statistics on his constituents from the back of a campaign wagon. Once the public knew, it would act; knowledge produced solutions.[62]

Sixty years later, Gardner, Ralph Nader, and their allies agreed. They filed FOIA requests, sued corporations to force disclosure of their records, and barraged the media with statistics. Thanks to their efforts, William Greider has argued, "information, not dirty money, is the vital core of the contemporary governing process."[63] Greider may underestimate the role of money, as arguments in the following sections will testify. But even if he is right that information is the main currency of power, we still do not have a fair political system. A system dominated by pure data and arguments will not necessarily produce just public policy.

In the early 1970s, public-interest groups wielded considerable power in Washington, just as consumer advocates had influenced Congress around 1912. Nearly 100,000 households gave "at least $70 a year to three or more of the following: Common Cause, Public Citizen, ACLU, public television and public radio, and environmental lobbying groups." Senator Abraham Ribikoff (D-CT) observed, "instead of the big lobbies of the major corporations dominating the hearings process, you have had practically every committee in Congress according 'equal time' to public interest people." In 1969–72, David Vogel writes, "Congress enacted the most progressive tax bill in the postwar period, transferred the primary authority for the regulation of both pollution and occupational health and safety from the states to the federal government, established the Consumer Product

Safety Administration, and banned the advertising of cigarettes from radio and television." Most of these changes were advocated by "Nader's Raiders," the hundreds of volunteers and lawyers who staffed the Center for the Study of Responsive Law.[64]

But the dominance of public-interest groups could not last for long. Vogel writes: "It took business about seven years to rediscover how to win in Washington." With their enormous advantages of wealth and discipline, they appropriated the tactics of the public-interest movement, including the "sponsorship of research studies to influence elite opinion, the attention to the media as a way of changing public attitudes, the development of techniques of grassroots organizing to mobilize supporters in congressional districts, and the use of ad hoc coalitions to maximize political influence."[65] Industry lobbyists were as successful in 1978–81 as public-interest activists had been a decade before.

For every Common Cause or MALDEF, there were now scores of trade groups, professional associations, and corporate PACs, each with a large budget. By 1980, public-interest groups were able to attend only half of all federal regulatory proceedings, and when they were present, they constituted less than 10 percent of the witness lists. There is no evidence that they have gained influence since 1980, but their enemies have.[66] Today, almost one-fourth of the 15 million businesses in America belong "to some kind of business, professional, or trade association." Five of the richest counties in America are Washington suburbs, in part because of all the legal, political, and technical experts who are employed by economic interests. Meanwhile, conservative think tanks have increased their budgets as much as tenfold, their research supported by large corporate grants.[67]

It is helpful to distinguish here between technical information and moral argument. Everyone can develop values, goals, and ideas about the good society. It is much more difficult to acquire statistical data, to make cost/benefit calculations, or to master a body of law. In a political system dominated by information and argument, the rich will prosper only if the debate concerns means and costs, not ends and values. Unfortunately, our political discourse is heavily technical. Participants in policy debates tend to share values, such as maximizing GNP, controlling risk at an acceptable cost, or adhering to mainstream constitutional doctrine. Since everyone assumes these ends, the debate raises questions that only expensive research can answer. The bargaining process of interest-group liberalism has survived, but today's negotiators use statistics and legal citations as additional sources of leverage.

The cost of technical information is one reason for the overall failure of Progressive reforms in the 1970s. Another reason is that these reforms undermined the very institutions that had been most loyal to ordinary people. In the interest-group liberal regime of 1940 or 1960, there was little deliberation about the common good; political strength and money usually carried the day. Nevertheless, workers had considerable influence, because the Democratic Party and labor unions were powerful negotiating blocs. By and large, rank-and-file members of

these huge organizations trusted their leaders to tell them how to vote and when
to strike. Although this trust could be misplaced, it was often salutary. To acquire
political information is difficult, time-consuming, and expensive, so most people
don't participate at all unless they are guided by trusted institutions.[68]

One set of institutions, political parties, suffered when the campaign-reform
and civil-service bills of the early 1970s struck at their main sources of power:
fundraising and patronage. Meanwhile, unions lost members rapidly as a result
of mechanization, foreign competition, and weak labor laws. Workers and middle-class consumers did gain the support of lobbies such as Common Cause and
Public Citizen, but these groups had far less power than the old party structures.
In 1994, just 2.8 percent of the population said that they were members of "some
group like the League of Women Voters, or some other group which is interested
in better government." By contrast, almost one-third of nonagricultural workers
had belonged to unions in 1953, and 47 percent of voting-age Americans had
identified themselves as Democrats. The rise of organizations like Public Citizen
could hardly compensate for a 50-percent drop in union membership or a 25-
percent decline in support for the Democratic Party.[69] Given their low levels of
public support, the new representatives of workers, citizens, and consumers did
not have much clout.

Finally, the Progressive reforms of the 1970s failed because they did not complete the job that reformers set themselves: getting money out of politics. Congress exempted itself from the system of partial public financing that it imposed
on presidential candidates. Also, private groups could establish political action
committees, or PACs, that could collect money and pass it on to candidates. This
meant that corporations could make legal campaign contributions for the first
time since the Progressive Era, albeit using PACs as intermediaries.[70] To make
matters worse, the Supreme Court overturned much of FECA in its *Buckley v.
Valeo* decision of 1976. The Court found that campaign spending and political
contributions were forms of expression that enjoyed First Amendment protection.
Therefore, a limit on campaign spending would violate constitutional rights. Citizens also had the right, according to *Buckley,* to spend unlimited sums on their
own campaigns. However, the Court upheld two kinds of limits: on the amount
that each person or PAC could contribute to any candidate, and on the total annual
contributions by each citizen or PAC. The Court found that these provisions were
justified, since they prevented corruption and the appearance of corruption without unduly reducing free expression.[71]

When the dust settled, presidential campaigns were covered by a stringent set
of rules, but congressional candidates had to contend only with disclosure provisions and contribution limits: they could raise and spend as much as they wanted.
Since special-interest money could no longer flow into presidential races, contributors formed PACs and turned their attention to congressional campaigns. Between 1974 and 1976, there was a five-fold increase in the number of business

PACs. Unions also increased their contributions, but at a more modest rate: from $6.3 million to $8.3 million.[72]

The new campaign-finance regime struck a final, fatal blow at political machines. Everything that party bosses had done to accumulate power had cost them money, which they had raised from special interests. With stringent limits on party fundraising, the earmarks of the old system quickly disappeared: gone were most of the old smoky back rooms, party hacks, ward heelers, powerful partisan clubs, and slush funds. In 1950, city bosses had hand-picked congressmen, and national party leaders had chosen their presidential nominees. By 1990, there were hardly any bosses left, and party chairs were figureheads. However, candidates could still raise money from private sources and spend it in the marketplace. As a result, the traditional cast of political characters was soon replaced by a new one: PAC directors, political consultants, independent pollsters, fundraising experts, and incumbent politicians with huge personal war chests.

I will return to a detailed critique of the new system in chapter 4, but its unsavory features are not hard to spot. Above all, money still undermined the basic principle of fairness. Organized workers and corporations both wielded substantial influence through their PACs. In 1974, Ben Albert, an AFL-CIO public relations director, said: "we are having no problem with the law. We function very comfortably with it."[73] However, consumers, tenants, and patients had no PACs, so they had very little clout compared to manufacturers, landlords, and hospitals. The poor and unemployed certainly had no way to make large campaign contributions. Finally, rich individuals, unlike unionized workers, could make personal contributions to supplement business PAC money.

Progressives, faced with this situation, would have demanded basic reform, aimed at replacing all large private contributions with small donations and public matching funds. However, the Watergate Babies had learned to thrive under the new system. They enjoyed reelection rates of close to 100 percent, in part because of a huge advantage in fundraising. Starting in the early 1980s, they became the chief defenders of the status quo. Led by Representative Tony Coehlo (D-CA), the head of the Democratic Congressional Campaign Committee, House Democrats approached business with the following argument. They pointed out that they were the majority party, having controlled the House for all but a few of the past fifty years. Therefore, business was wasting its money giving to Republicans. Business PACs would be foolish not to contribute to Democrats as a way of increasing their access, goodwill, and influence.[74] The PACs complied, and money gradually eroded the lines of ideological demarcation, precluding real debate about many economic issues. As Robert Reich wrote before he became secretary of labor:

> The Democrats . . . lost their identity not because Americans became more respectful
> of wealth and power or more convinced trickle-down economics would actually
> work (polls show widespread opposition to capital gains breaks for the rich), but

because Democrats became dependent on the rich to finance their campaigns. . . . It is difficult to represent the little fellow when the big fellow pays the tab. . . . Democrats have come to sound like Republicans because they rely on the same funders to make the same contacts as the GOP.[75]

To make matters worse, after 1984 private money returned to presidential campaigns with a vengeance, thanks to both parties' exploitation of a loophole in FECA. Starting in 1976, general-election candidates who received public funding were supposed to accept no private money at all. But the Federal Election Commission ruled that individuals and PACs could contribute to *parties,* which could spend their money on generic, "party-building" activities that would benefit their candidates. By the mid-nineties, this so-called soft money, laundered through party organizations, flowed at the rate of hundreds of millions of dollars in every election cycle. When this book went to press, Republicans were expecting to collect a total of $500 million in soft money for the 2000 elections, including $1 million each from one hundred especially generous donors.[76]

REFORM IDEAS IN THE 1990S

By 1992, there were clear signs that the American public was again deeply dissatisfied with the rules of the political game. That year, the public's fundamental distrust of the political system manifested itself in 20-percent approval ratings for Congress, stunning electoral support for Ross Perot, bursts of enthusiasm for antiestablishment politicians such as Pat Buchanan and Jerry Brown, millions of votes cast for measures that would throw *all* incumbents out of office, and even the Los Angeles riots, which among other things revealed a near-total despair about the established political process as a means of solving social problems.

There was now a good deal of evidence that "Americans, particularly those from blue collar and working class backgrounds, think the interests of average people simply are not being heard in Washington" because of the excessive power of wealthy special interests and other flaws in the political system.[77] For decades, citizens have been asked whether they think that government "is run for the benefit of all the people" or "for a few big interests looking out for themselves." In 1964, just 31 percent doubted that their government had the public's interest at heart. Throughout the 1990s, however, at least 70 percent of those polled have said that they believe government is run for "a few big interests." According to a *Washington Post* poll taken during the 1992 campaign, 75 percent of those polled worried either a "great deal" or a "good amount" about the problem that "special interest groups have too much influence over elected officials."[78] And participants in focus groups now consistently blame bad federal policies on defects in the electoral and political system.[79]

In 1992, Perot won his 19 million votes in part by focusing on procedural questions such as the budget process and campaign reform, and in part by seeming to embody an alternative way of conducting politics. Bill Clinton, who beat him, also took a strong line on campaign-finance reform, government ethics, voting rights, and other Progressive issues. In fact, he was more Progressive than either Perot or Governor Jerry Brown (who made political corruption his leading issue during the Democratic primary), because Clinton alone had the courage to favor partial public financing of elections—the only way to reduce the power of private money. However, once elected, Clinton chose to emphasize a substantive issue, health-care reform, instead of trying to change the political process.

The Clinton health-care bill was defeated for many reasons, probably including poor design, bad tactics, and lukewarm support from a public of whom 85 percent already had health insurance. Perhaps achieving universal health insurance is not even a worthwhile goal: that is a matter for the public to decide deliberatively. However, it was certainly unfair that special interests spent roughly $100 million to defeat the Clinton bill. Nor was the general political atmosphere conducive to constructive legislation. The way that difficult issues are debated in the mass media, during political campaigns, and on the floor of Congress promotes polarization and misinformation, not illumination or consensus. The following chapters will demonstrate that our discussion of policy is marred by the rules of the political game, which we can change. Therefore, procedural reform should have come first, and major policy changes could have followed.

However, congressional Democrats resisted reform, clinging to their privileges, and the Clinton administration failed to challenge them. The administration refused to disclose the size of the intelligence budget and delayed releasing classified documents. Campaign-finance reform, lobby regulation, and new ethics rules all died in Congress. Clinton's first chair of the Democratic National Committee (DNC), David Wilhelm, tried to raise money in a populist fashion, soliciting small donations from a wide base. He raised $9 million in contributions of less than $200 each, but the fundraising campaign cost the committee $8 million. Shaken by the Democrats' defeat in the 1994 House elections and the "Harry and Louise" commercials that had helped to sink his health-reform bill, Clinton listened to his consultant, Dick Morris. Morris planned a massive polling and broadcast campaign, which would cost the DNC $1.5 million every week. But the party had almost no funds.[80] Top administration officials scrambled to raise money, using disreputable intermediaries, offering nights in the Lincoln Bedroom, and accepting illegal contributions from foreign donors.

In 1994, the Democrats finally lost control of the House, not because they had failed to pass political reform, but because they had achieved little meaningful change of any kind. This failure, in turn, resulted from the sordid political system that congressional Democrats had permitted to flourish. Moreover, Republicans successfully portrayed the Democratic majority as corrupt, mostly by dwelling on relatively trivial issues such as the House Bank scandal. By refusing to change their ways, the Democrats left the Republican charges unanswered. Turnout among core Democratic constituencies was extremely low in 1994, because poor people and minorities saw nothing worth defending in Washington. However, wealthy people voted in unprecedentedly high numbers, perhaps fearful of the Democrats' health agenda.[81] The result was a stunning victory for Representative Newt Gingrich and his House Republican acolytes.

The insurgent Republicans ran on economic and social issues popular with their core constituencies—tax cuts, school prayer, and so on. But they also needed a blueprint for procedural reform, because large segments of the electorate wanted a new political system, not just changes in federal policy. However, the Republicans' reform agenda was not Progressive, despite the party's strong Progressive heritage. Instead, they emphasized term limits for members of Congress, a balanced-budget amendment, new obstacles to raising taxes, limits on "unfunded mandates," the line-item veto (subsequently struck down), and devolution of power to the states. Taken together, these provisions would have undermined basic Progressive values, if they had become law.

Term limits (first of all) would restrict the right of citizens to reelect incumbent candidates whom they continue to support. Limiting access to the ballot is logically incompatible with full popular sovereignty. At best, it is a misguided method of unseating incumbents whose tenure is secured by their lock on campaign money. Not only did congressional Republicans fail to pass term limits, but they also squelched campaign-finance reform. Their plan was to raise enormous sums once they controlled Congress, thus becoming as entrenched as their Democratic predecessors had been. Indeed, they raised $267 million in the first two years of Gingrich's speakership, while their collective popularity sank to abysmal levels. The public's demand for reform remained unsatisfied.

Like term limits, a balanced-budget amendment would limit popular sovereignty, for it would prevent elected leaders from adopting a policy—deficit spending—that some people favor under appropriate circumstances. It would write a particular economic theory into the Constitution, foreclosing debate about it. Some versions of the proposed amendment would have allowed Congress to ignore the balance requirement if 60 percent of both houses agreed to waive it. In that case, whenever a balanced budget appeared unattainable, congressional leaders would have to seek broad support for a waiver motion. They might have to offer targeted appropriations or tax cuts to minority coalitions in return for their votes, thus further increasing the deficit and encouraging special pleading. If Congress failed to pass a balanced budget, then federal courts would intervene, so unelected judges would gain legislative powers and responsibilities—hardly a Progressive outcome.

The Gingrich Congress also restricted "unfunded mandates": rules that Congress imposes on state and local governments without paying the cost of their implementation. If Congress believes that something should be done, then it should normally raise and spend the necessary money, so that voters can hold it accountable. If it transfers the cost to another government entity, then voters may praise Congress for taking action but blame local officials for spending money. Therefore, Progressives should be wary of unfunded mandates. On the other hand, there are times when the federal government is right to force local authorities to solve problems that they have created through their own negligence. For instance, a city that built racially segregated schools and public housing should have to bear the cost of desegregation. Except by analyzing a particular bill, it is difficult to decide whether an unfunded mandate is justified. In the end, Clinton signed legislation that simply requires Congress to take a separate vote on any unfunded mandate of over $50 million, after the relevant agency has done a cost-benefit analysis. The rule does not apply to anti-discrimination laws, nor does it cover business regulation.[82] It will probably do no harm, and it may even increase accountability—but it was no great Progressive achievement.

Finally, Republicans began a wholesale transfer of federal programs to the states. Most prominently, they replaced most federal welfare entitlements with block grants. They had economic motivations for these changes, which William Kristol described candidly. Block grants, he explained, were not the ultimate goal, since they might make "state and local governments . . . ever more dependent extensions of the federal octopus." Instead, conservatives wanted "*real* federalism, understood as part of a general program of relimiting government." This meant transferring power from the states to private citizens and corporations, once the federal government had "devolved" its authority to the states.

Thus, for conservatives, devolution was not just a way to reorganize government functions, shifting them from one level to another in the name of efficiency or accountability. It was rather a tactic in their war against the state. For fifty years, voters had supported a large federal government that, according to Kristol, had become self-perpetuating and "pathological." Conservative candidates had often won national elections, but they seemed unable to destroy this beast. In fact, an assertive national government had remained broadly popular: for example, voters revolted whenever politicians talked of trimming Medicare and Social Security. But Kristol wanted to kill the welfare state once and for all by changing the rules of politics. Indeed, this was his justification for the whole Republican reform agenda, including "a balanced budget amendment, term limits, tax and spending limitation at several levels of government, . . . and the privatization of government functions."[83]

But why would devolution undermine the welfare state? Why wouldn't each state and locality ultimately increase its taxes to make up for reduced federal aid? In short, why would giving power to the states produce the laissez-faire economic policy beloved of conservatives? Kristol argued that the federal government was unpopular but entrenched—that liberals won reelection only because powerful interest groups supported them. If the federal system were destroyed, no new welfare state would arise to replace it. This argument ignored the deep and abiding popularity of middle-class entitlements. But Kristol did not state another, more plausible argument. The smaller the unit of government, the less power it has to distribute wealth from rich to poor. Many affluent citizens already live across jurisdictional lines from the people who need government services the most. Those who still reside in states with large poor populations and traditions of social welfare would be free to move away if federal taxes dropped and states tried to pick up the burden. It is no accident that state income taxes are much less progressive than the federal system; indeed, the poorest fifth of the population pays 12.5 percent of their income in state and local taxes, whereas the richest percentile pays only 7.9 percent.[84]

Thus there were conservative economic reasons to favor devolution. But transferring power to the states also has a Progressive rationale. State governments, some people believe, are "closer to the people." State legislators represent smaller districts than federal legislators; state capitals are physically closer than Washington; and state governments are smaller and easier to understand than the federal bureaucracy. Therefore, a welfare program administered by the states might be more accountable than the federal program it replaced. On the other hand, the federal government undergoes much more scrutiny than state governments do. The Washington press corps far outnumbers the reporters in any state capital. Perhaps, as power flows to the states, they will receive more critical attention, but it is inherently difficult to keep track of fifty separate governments. National television cannot begin to do the job; neither can news magazines or the *New York Times.* Thus it is by no means certain that devolution to state governments will produce more accountable politics. What is certain is that poor areas will receive less aid from wealthy ones.

The Republicans' effort to transfer federal welfare programs to the states was so popular that Clinton and about half of the congressional Democrats supported it in 1996. However, their other procedural reforms did not produce the kind of change that voters had demanded in 1994. The House Republicans, and especially Newt Gingrich, became widely despised figures. In their second year of power, having failed to pass term limits and a balanced-budget amendment, they belatedly adopted two ideas from Common Cause and the Democratic leadership. In November of 1995, the House voted 422–6 to prevent representatives from accepting gifts other than free travel and campaign contributions. Just two weeks later, the same body unanimously passed a bill to require most lobbyists to register and disclose their expenditures. This legislation certainly improved the existing statute of 1946, which had resulted in very little disclosure. About $1.2 billion is now being disclosed each year, although estimates of real lobbying expenses range as high as $8.4 billion.[85] However, more disclosure and fewer gifts will not satisfy the mass of citizens who yearn for decent, fair, responsive, constructive politics. If anything, new information about lobbying is likely to increase the demand for regulation, just as disclosure of campaign finances has undermined the legitimacy of the election system.

In 1997 and 1998, the parties set a new record for soft money collected in a nonpresidential cycle: $192.3 million.[86] Republican moderates forced the House to pass modest reform legislation whose main goal was to end this practice. Their tactical success against their own leaders' determined opposition showed that corruption remained a motivating issue for some voters, editorial writers, and conscientious representatives of both parties. But the bill died in a Senate filibuster.

Meanwhile, Congress became embroiled in Bill Clinton's moral, financial, and legal problems. Even if we view one man's alleged adultery, perjury, and obstruction of justice as serious issues worthy of congressional action—and even if we blame him for the ensuing investigations—these scandals were a distraction from the more prevalent problems of government. As this book goes to press, the most likely consequence appears to be a repeal of the Independent Counsel Act. No harm will be done if an adequate substitute is found.[87] But it would be a shame to lose a mechanism for investigating high executive-branch officials just because the Whitewater investigation was handled so badly.

The Republicans' loss of seats in 1998 showed that their version of "good government" had little popular appeal. Their emphasis on Clinton's personal immorality had won few them converts, and their campaign to limit the powers of Congress and the federal government appeared to have faltered. Now that Whitewater and the Monica Lewinsky affair seem basically closed, the future lies with the party that embraces genuine political reform, aiming toward a fair and deliberative democracy.

NOTES

1. Otis L. Graham, Jr., *An Encore for Reform: The Old Progressives and the New Deal* (New York, 1967), p. 192.

2. Quoted, e.g., by Richard Hofstadter, *The Age of Reform* (New York, 1955), p. 316.

3. See William E. Leuchtenburg, *The Supreme Court Reborn: The Constitutional Revolution in the Age of Roosevelt* (New York, 1995), p. 220. One historian who sees more continuity than revolution in the Court's rulings is Richard A. Maidment, *The Judicial Response to the New Deal: The US Supreme Court and Economic Regulation, 1934–1936* (Manchester, 1991).

4. John R. Commons, *Industrial Goodwill*, (New York, 1919) pp. 39–43. Another early proponent of interest-group liberalism was Arthur F. Bentley, whom I discuss at the beginning of chapter 6.

5. La Follette's remarks of July 21, 1917, in the *Congressional Record*, vol. 55, part 5 (65th Congress, first session), p. 5351. His frequent ally, Senator George Norris of Nebraska, made the opposite case (pp. 5347–5348).

6. John Kenneth Galbraith, *American Capitalism: The Concept of Countervailing Power* (Boston, 1956), pp. 136, 151.

7. Irvine Lenroot, speech of July 4, 1935, in Graham, *An Encore for Reform*, p. 70; Lenroot to E. D. Parsons, August 28, 1943, Library of Congress MS, in Graham, *An Encore for Reform*, p. 44; Baker, notebook entry, November 3, 1936, in Graham, *An Encore for Reform*, p. 70.

8. Theodore Lowi, *The End of Liberalism: The Second Republic of the United States* (New York, 1979), pp. 92–99, quoting Kenneth Culp Davis.

9. C. Wright Mills with Helen Schneider, *The New Men of Power: America's Labor Leaders* (New York, 1948), p. 229. See also Robert Reich, "Policy Making in a Democracy," *The Power of Public Ideas*, pp. 123–56.

10. *Industrial Union Department, AFL-CIO v. American Petroleum Institute*, 448 U.S. 607, at 647 (citing the Legislative History); 675. The Supreme Court overruled the Labor Department's regulations at issue in this case, but not on the grounds that the statute had given the Department unconstitutional powers.

11. C. Vann Woodward, *The Strange Career of Jim Crow* (New York, 3d rev. ed., 1974), p. 91.

12. On the unique political/theological tenets of the African American church, see Garry Wills, *Under God: Religion and American Politics* (New York, 1990), pp. 195–255.

13. "Martin Luther King, Jr.,—Black Theology, Black Church," in *Martin Luther King, Jr., Civil Rights Leader, Theologian Orator*, ed. David J. Garrow (Brooklyn, N.Y., 1989), vol. 1, pp. 203–214.

14. Rauschenbusch to La Follette, March 6, 1917, and May 21, 1917. La Follette Family Collection, Series B, box 81. Rauschenbusch also sent La Follette a copy of his book.

15. Martin Luther King, Jr., *Stride toward Freedom: The Montgomery Story* (New York, 1958), p. 90.

16. Walter Rauschenbusch, *Christianity and the Social Crisis* (1907; New York, 1991), pp. 254 and passim, 412.

17. Richard Wightman Fox, *Reinhold Niebuhr: A Biography* (New York, 1985), p. 92.

18. King, *Stride toward Freedom*, p. 97.

19. Reinhold Niebuhr, "Coherence, Incoherence, and Christian Faith," *Journal of Religion*, vol. 31, no. 3 (July 1951): 162. For Niebuhr on original sin, see *Moral Man and Immoral Society* (New York, 1932), p. 6. I believe that Niebuhr was unfair to Rauschenbusch, who actually shared most of his views. See, for example, *Christianity and the Social Crisis*, pp. 400–401: "idealists alone have never carried through any great social change. In vain they dash their fair ideas against the solid granite of human selfishness." Cf. Winthrop S. Hudson, ed., *Walter Rauschenbusch: Selected Writings* (New York, 1987), p. 68.

20. Reinhold Niebuhr, *Nature and Destiny of Man* (New York, 1941), vol. 2, p. 260.

21. Reinhold Niebuhr, "A Living Process," *The Nation* 161 (November 17, 1945): 526–527, quoted in *Niebuhr and His Age: Reinhold Niebuhr's Prophetic Role in the Twentieth Century* by Brown (Philadelphia, 1992), p. 130.

22. Ibid., p. 252.

23. La Follette's introduction to *The Making of America*, 1905, in Ellen Torelle, ed., *The Political Philosophy of Robert M. La Follette, as Revealed in His Speeches and Writings*, p. 111.

24. Herbert Croly, *Progressive Democracy* (1914; reprint, New York, 1915), pp. 213–214.

25. King, *Stride toward Freedom* pp. 105, 106.

26. Martin Luther King, Jr., "Facing the Challenge of a New Age," *Phylon* 18 (April 1957): 30.

27. "Letter from a Birmingham Jail," 1963, in *I Have a Dream: Writings and Speeches That Changed the World*, by Martin Luther King, Jr., ed. James M. Washington (Glenview, 1992), p. 89

28. Pat Watters and Reese Cleghorn, *Climbing Jacob's Ladder: The Arrival of Negroes in Southern Politics* (New York, 1967), pp. 51–52.

29. Edward J. Bacciocco, Jr., *The New Left in America: Reform to Revolution, 1956 to 1970* (Stanford, Calif., 1974), p. 251. "Fornication" was not the Yippies' term.

30. James Miller, *"Democracy Is in the Streets": From Port Huron to the Siege of Chicago* (New York, 1987), p. 23.

31. Alan Ryan, "Dream Time," *New York Review of Books*, October 17, 1996, p. 40.

32. *Port Huron Statement*, June 15, 1962, reprinted as an appendix in Miller, *Democracy Is in the Streets*, p. 336.

33. Ibid., p. 332. ("Civil society" is not one of their terms.)

34. Ibid., p. 333.

35. Ibid., p. 362.

36. Ibid., pp. 363–364, 366.

37. This term is best described in Sara M. Evans and Harry C. Boyte, *Free Spaces: The Source of Democratic Change in America* (New York, 1986), pp. 17–25.

38. Jane J. Mansbridge, *Beyond Adversary Democracy* (New York, 1980), pp. vii, 21.

39. Robert Fisher, *Let the People Decide: Neighborhood Organizing in America* (Boston, 1984), pp. 99, 100–101, 107.

40. For background, see James A. Morone, *The Democratic Wish: Popular Participation and the Limits of American Government* (New York, 1990), pp. 221–222.

41. Quoted in ibid.

42. Johnson's 1964 State of the Union Message, in Marvin E. Gettleman and David Mermelstein, *The Great Society Reader: The Failure of American Liberalism* (New York, 1967), p. 184.

43. Melvin B. Mogulof, *Citizen Participation: A Review and Commentary on Federal Policies and Practices* (Washington, D.C., 1970), p. 69.

44. Fisher, *Let the People Decide*, p. 114; Mogulof, *Citizen Participation*, p. 5.

45. David Stoloff, "The Short Unhappy History of Community Action Programs," in Gettleman and Mermelstein, *The Great Society Reader*, by Gettleman and Mermelstein pp. 234–236; Morone, *The Democratic Wish*, p. 231; Daniel C. Kramer, *Participatory Democracy: Developing Ideals of the Left* (Cambridge, Mass., 1972) p. 96.

46. Mogulof, *Citizen Participation*, p. 2; Morone, *The Democratic Wish*, p. 219.

47. Morone, *The Democratic Wish*. pp. 230, 237, 239, 245, 248.

48. See Allen J. Matusow, *The Unraveling of America: A History of Liberalism in the 1960s* (New York, 1984), pp. 111, 116–118.

49. Miller, *Democracy Is in the Streets*, pp. 94–95.

50. Morone, *The Democratic Wish*, p. 241.

51. Quoted—for much the same purpose—in *Why Americans Hate Politics*, by E. J. Dionne, Jr. (New York, 1991), p. 31.

52. Melvin Mogulof, *Citizen Participation*, p. 165.

53. For an example of a successful program, consider the Child Development Group in Mississippi in 1964, described in Morone, *The Democratic Wish*, p. 236. The Community Action Program spent just $395 million on nonpackaged programs in 1966: see Stoloff, "The Short Unhappy History of Community Action Programs," p. 233, note 5.

54. Lyndon Johnson proposed campaign-finance reform and lobby regulation bills, but they were generally weak and in some respects they would have turned the clock back.

See James McGregor Burns, ed., *To Heal and to Bind: The Programs of Lyndon B. Johnson* (New York, 1968), pp. 425ff.

55. David Vogel, *Fluctuating Fortunes: The Political Power of Business in America* (New York, 1989), pp. 115–117. The dairy quid pro quo was not proved until the release of White House tapes in 1997: see "President Nixon on a Political Shakedown: Linking Dairy Price Supports to Donations, President Wanted Treasury Secretary to 'See If We Can Get More,'" *Washington Post*, October 30, 1997, p. A19. The ITT charge also gained credibility with the release of the tapes: see George Lardner, Jr., "On Tape, Nixon Outlines 1971 'Deal' to Settle Antitrust Case against ITT," *Washington Post*, January 4, 1997, p. A3.

56. John W. Gardner, *In Common Cause*, rev. ed. (New York, 1973), p. 17.

57. *Congressional Quarterly*, January 11, 1975, p. 81; December 7, 1974, p. 3247; November 9, 1974, p. 3058; November 23, 1974, p. 3151.

58. *Congressional Quarterly*, January 18, 1975. p. 115. Mills was ousted after the 1974 election but before the new class took office, in large part because of personal sex scandals.

59. *Congressional Quarterly*, January 18, 1975, p. 117; February 1, 1974, p. 240.

60. Source: Common Cause.

61. "The Founding of MALDEF," on the Internet at http://www.azteca.net~maldef/founding.html. (This is an official MALDEF document).

62. Robert H. Wiebe, *Self-Rule: A Cultural History of American Democracy* (Chicago, 1995) p. 163.

63. William Greider, *Who Will Tell the People? The Betrayal of American Democracy* (New York, 1992), p. 46.

64. Vogel, *Fluctuating Fortunes*, pp. 97–98, 93, 13, 101.

65. Vogel, *Fluctuating Fortunes*, pp. 10–11.

66. See Cornelius M. Kerwin, *Rulemaking: How Government Agencies Write Law and Make Policy* (Washington, D.C., 1994), pp. 196–197.

67. Vogel, *Fluctuating Fortunes*, p. 12; Greider, *Who Will Tell the People*? pp. 48–49.

68. See, e.g., Samuel Popkin, J. Gorman, C. Phillips, and J. Smith, "Comment: What Have You Done for Me Lately? Toward an Investment Theory of Voting," *American Political Science Review*, vol. 70, no. 3 (September 1976): 795. See also chapter 3, on trust and participation.

69. In 1994, only 2.7 percent of adults actually worked for any political party. See Roper Surveys (for group membership and party work); Robert D. Putnam, "Bowling Alone: America's Declining Social Capital," *Journal of Democracy*, vol. 6, no. 1 (January 1995): 69 (for unions); and G. Calvin MacKenzie, *The Irony of Reform: Roots of American Political Disenchantment* (Boulder, Colo., 1996), p. 41 (for party identification).

70. A widespread rumor holds that Common Cause deliberately created PACs as part of the 1971–74 reforms, only to denounce them later. On the contrary, PACs had existed since 1943, when the CIO formed one; and the first umbrella business PAC was founded as a counterweight to labor in 1963. But FECA defined and recognized PACs, limiting their contributions while allowing corporations to pay their overhead costs. Reform groups vehemently opposed this approach. Then the Federal Election Commission ruled that corporations could each form more than one PAC and solicit contributions from employees as well as from shareholders. These decisions led to the boom in corporate-connected political action committees.

71. 424 US 29.

72. Common Cause data.

73. *Congressional Quarterly Almanac*, 1977, p. 802.

74. See John Barry, *The Ambition and the Power* (New York, 1990), p. 186.

75. Robert B. Reich, "Have the Democrats Lost Their Soul? Yes: Blame Election Funds," *New York Times*, October 12, p A29.

76. See Don van Natta, Jr., "Republicans' Goal Is $1 Million Each from Top Donors," *New York Times,* August 9, 1999, p. A1.

77. Peter D. Hart and Doug Bailey, *Centel Public Accountability Project* (based on focus group interviews), October 1991.

78. ABC News/*Washington Post* poll, conducted on October 27, 1992. *Washington Post,* November 3, 1992.

79. See, e.g., *Centel Public Accountability Project*, "People versus Politics," October 1991.

80. Jane Mayer, "Inside the Money Machine: How the Democrats Went Wild," *The New Yorker*, February 3, 1997, pp. 35–37; John Kifner, "Clinton Ad Plan Led to Asian-American Donors," *The New York Times*, April 14, 1997, p. A16.

81. Peter Levine, "In this Election, G.O.P. Won Because More Rich People Voted" (letter), *New York Times*, November 25, 1994.

82. *Congressional Quarterly*, March 25, 1995, p. 871.

83. William Kristol, "The Politics of Liberty, the Sociology of Virtue," in *The New Promise of American Life*, ed. Lamar Alexander and Chester E. Finns, Jr. (Indianapolis, 1995), pp. 122–123.

84. Citizens for Tax Justice, "State & Local Taxes Hit Poor and Middle Class Far Harder than the Wealthy," press release, June 26, 1996.

85. Lobbyists (under a very strict definition of the term) must register with the clerk of the House and the secretary of the Senate. Based on a random sample of disclosure forms, their aggregate expenditures were roughly $1.26 billion in 1997. But no disclosures were filed for Vernon Jordan, George Mitchell, or Robert Dole, all famous and powerful lobbyists. See Allan Shuldiner and Tony Raymond, "Who's in the Lobby? A Profile of Washington's Influence Industry," available from the Center for Responsive Politics (CRP) or at http://www.crp.org/pubs/lobby/lobbyindex.htm. It appears that Dole and Mitchell did not register by name, but their firm (Verner, Liipfert) billed its lobbying clients $19 million in 1997. See Jill Abramson, "The Business of Persuasion Thrives in Nation's Capital," *New York Times*, September 29, 1998, p. A1, and the CRP lobbying database at http://www.crp.org/lobby/. Thus the disclosure reports may give an accurate picture of aggregate spending, even though they do not reveal the lobbyists' names.

The estimate of $8.4 billion comes from "Washington's Lobbying Industry: A Case for Tax Reform," a Tax Foundation study prepared for Representative Dick Armey (R-TX) on June 19, 1996 (http://flattax.house.gov/stlobby.htm). This study compares the percentage of people employed in legal services, membership, accounting, auditing, bookkeeping, and public relations in Washington, D.C., with the comparable figures in five other cities. After various adjustments are made, the unusual composition of Washington's private-sector work force is attributed to the lobbying industry. This study makes numerous disputable assumptions, but its overall estimate may actually be too low, since it ignores those who work in suburban Virginia and Maryland.

According to one estimate, for every dollar that is contributed to a politician's campaign, ten are spent to lobby federal officials (*USA Today*, June 19, 1991). If this is true, then lobbying expenditures probably exceeded $1 billion per year by the mid-1980s. The *New York Times* already estimated in 1979 that lobbying by the oil industry cost "hundreds of millions of dollars" (Richard Halloran, "Capital's Diverse Oil Lobbyists: Much Criticized, Often Effective," *New York Times*, August 9, 1979, pp. A1, D14). The *Wall Street Journal* (David Rogers, "Firm Gets $1 Million In Fees From Institutions Seeking Federal Grants," *Wall Street Journal*, May 30, 1991, p. A16) has estimated that some 80,000 people are employed in lobbying the federal government; their salaries alone would consume well over $1 billion. The estimate of 80,000 lobbyists was provided by Professor James Thurber, who later told The *New York Times* that it came "Off the top of my head" ("80,000 Lobbyists? Probably Not, but Maybe . . ." *New York Times*, May 12, 1993, p. A13). However, competing estimates by officials of the American League of Lobbyists are almost certainly too low, and Thurber's figure does not seem implausible, given what we know about lobbying on specific legislative issues. (Armey's report finds that a comparable 70,000 people work in the federal lobbying industry.)

86. Common Cause press release, February 22, 1999.

87. For example, the assistant attorney general in charge of the Justice Department's Criminal Division could be given various protections against interference by the attorney general and president. See "Common Cause Proposes New Plan for Ensuring Integrity in Criminal Investigations of High-Ranking Federal Officials; Would Replace Independent Counsel Act," press release, March 10, 1999.

3

Trends in Civil Society

Chapter 2 surveyed the emergence of modern politics, on the assumption that we cannot devise an appropriate reform agenda until we have understood our current condition. The same is true if we hope to improve public attitudes and behavior or to revitalize nongovernmental institutions. The Progressives considered these goals as important as political reform, but we cannot borrow their program, because we live in a different culture. Before we can formulate a sensible plan of action, we must evaluate contemporary "civil society"—a task that requires both facts and moral principles.

TOWARD A THEORY OF CITIZENSHIP

The Progressives tried to make government more democratic and accountable. But they realized that political reform would never come until Americans knew—and cared—enough about government to demand change, and the quality of reform would depend upon citizens' wisdom and public-spiritedness. Then, if ordinary people succeeded in democratizing their political system, their virtues and abilities would only become more important.

Worried that many Americans were not yet equal to the task of self-government, Progressive reformers promoted civic and democratic education in schools and settlement houses. They also created associations, such as the League of Women Voters, to improve citizenship; and they constantly exhorted Americans to be active, informed, and responsible. Their sermonizing has struck many observers as sanctimonious. But La Follette and his closest allies respected ordinary Americans. They knew that political injustice was often the cause of public apathy and ignorance—but an alienated public might also permit corruption to flourish. In short, there was an essential relationship between good citizenship and political reform.

As well as advocating civic virtues in their speeches and publications, the Progressives developed what Michael Sandel has called a "political economy of citizenship."[1] That is, they recognized that legal and economic factors could influence civic ideals and habits, and vice versa. For instance, Teddy Roosevelt said, "The prime problem of our nation is to get the right type of good citizenship, and to get it, we must have progress, and our public men must be genuinely progressive."[2] By "progress," TR meant state regulation of the economy as well as civic rhetoric and anti-corruption measures. Thus an ambitious economic program was a key to civic renewal. Powerful federal agencies, he thought, would make active citizenship possible in an age of inevitable corporate concentration. Likewise, some Progressives advocated the minimum wage because people who were reduced to "wage slavery" made bad citizens; antitrust laws because corporate monopolies had robbed individuals of their political power; Prohibition because alcohol had undermined civic virtue; public schools because a heterogeneous population needed civic instruction; eugenics because citizenship required breeding; and war because it gave people discipline and a common end. The aim of urban planning, some Progressives thought, was to build "a new sense of citizenship." They even saw municipal playgrounds as "the womb from which a new urban citizenry—moral, industrious, and socially responsible—would emerge."[3]

There certainly are potential connections between the economic and social environment (on one hand) and the capacity of ordinary people to be effective citizens (on the other). However, when the Progressives defended their favorite social, economic, and foreign policies on the grounds that these ideas would improve *citizenship*, their rationale often seemed rather artificial and convoluted. Perhaps they wanted to avoid revealing their substantive commitments—which might be unpopular—and that is why they emphasized civic virtue.

For instance, *McClure's* magazine, a Progressive organ, maintained that American participation in World War I would restore citizens' toughness and discipline and make them truly capable of self-government. "Wallowing in physical luxury, we have become spiritually so loose, so lax and so lazy that we have almost lost the capacity to act."[4] As it turned out, the war had some positive civic effects. Wilson's rhetoric about global democracy was skillfully appropriated by women's suffragists, who pursued the vote while American troops fought in France. Some recruits broadened their perspectives, raised their personal aspirations, and came to expect more from the state as a result of their service. But the war also had negative effects, especially when censorship laws discouraged public discussion. Calling it a patriotic act, two copper companies even rounded up 1,118 striking workers, loaded them into cattle cars, and dumped them in the New Mexico desert.[5] Even if no such abuses had occurred, "good citizenship" would have been a weak justification for sacrificing 100,000 American lives in a dubious cause.

The Progressives sometimes implied that no true democracy could exist unless their policies were implemented. But a democratic state should be able to decide *against* the very programs that the Progressives considered essential for citizenship. A government that cannot abolish antitrust laws (for example) has been shorn of its sovereignty, no matter how beneficial such laws may be. Indeed, the Progressives themselves argued heatedly about the wisdom of antitrust policy.

To make matters worse, some reformers seemed to suggest that individuals were incompetent to serve as citizens unless they had received the blessings of Progressive social programs, from the minimum wage to eugenics. It is one thing to note the deleterious effects of poverty on civic life, but it is quite another thing to view poor people or immigrants as politically unfit. The Progressives have been seen as elitists, in part because some of them committed this serious error.

Finally, the original Progressives' arguments about the "political economy of citizenship" were marred by a telling omission. Reformers might suggest, for example, that people could not become good citizens if they toiled in mill towns or came of age in tenement houses. Therefore, certain kinds of government intervention were necessary. This argument omitted an essential step: a definition of citizenship. We can only assess the civic effects of slum clearance or industrial reform once we have agreed how citizens should behave and what capacities they should possess. But most Progressives lacked convincing answers to these questions.

Michael Schudson writes, "Progressive Era politics instructed people in a citizenship of intelligence rather than passionate intensity. Political participation became less a relationship to party than a relationship to the state, less a connection to community than to principles and issues. . . . The new model of citizenship called for a voter more intelligent than loyal."[6] If Schudson is right, then the Progressives had an unduly thin account of citizenship, implying that Americans merely had to read nonpartisan newspapers and vote independently. This would be a ballot-box theory of democracy, which I criticized in chapter 1. On the other hand, Progressive authors and politicians often called for something more demanding: they defined "citizenship" as patriotic virtue, moral integrity, and broad participation in public life. But their ideas on this score tended to be frustratingly vague. Theodore Roosevelt, for example, proposed a rather vacuous triad of honesty, courage, and common sense to define "The Good Citizen."[7]

A more promising source is Alexis de Tocqueville, who observed that Americans of his time had a remarkable propensity to create associations—"of a thousand kinds, religious, moral, serious, futile, general or restricted, enormous or diminutive." For example, Tocqueville observed, "if a stoppage occurs in a thoroughfare and the circulation of vehicles is hindered, the neighbors immediately form themselves into a deliberative body; and this extemporaneous assembly gives rise to an executive power which remedies the inconvenience."[8]

By forming associations to manage even trivial or parochial matters, Americans acquired "facility in prosecuting great undertakings in common." Members of associations, Tocqueville observed, constantly "meet together in large numbers, they converse, they listen to one another, and they are mutually stimulated to all sorts of undertakings." In the process, they might refine their beliefs and improve their morals, moving from selfishness toward "self-interest rightly understood." Tocqueville argued that "feelings and opinions are recruited, the heart is enlarged, and the human mind is developed only by the reciprocal influence of men upon one another." For him, civic virtue meant above all a willingness to cooperate voluntarily, which in turn required a reasonable level of mutual trust, an ability to deliberate, and a sense of enlightened self-interest. In democratic countries, he thought, all this "can only be accomplished by associations." Groups were valuable not only as schools of "morals and intelligence" but also as instruments for distributing power and ensuring the free circulation of ideas.[9]

Today, Tocqueville is widely admired for having analyzed "civil society," although he did not invent the phrase. Civil society has been defined in several contradictory ways, but modern theorists most often use it to describe nongovernmental institutions, including nonprofit groups, the family, and (sometimes) corporations. According to leading conservatives, such associations are the seedbeds of civic virtue, and they are threatened by state power. George F. Will writes approvingly: "Conservatives who worry about the 'sociology of virtue' and the 'ecology of liberty' believe that swollen government, which displaces other institutions, saps democracy's strength. There is, these conservatives believe, a zero-sum transaction in society. As the state waxes, other institutions wane."[10] This is a "political economy of citizenship," but it precisely inverts the Progressives' doctrine. Conservatives propose government *retrenchment* as a precondition for healthy democracy and good citizenship.

Anyone who holds this view must face some awkward facts. First of all, the bigger a country's government, the *more* of its citizens tend to belong to private voluntary associations. There is also a strong correlation between the strength of nonprofit groups and the degree of government intervention in the economy. Even taxes are positively correlated to group membership.[11] I suspect that these correlations emerge because people who are protected from economic ruin by Social Security and health insurance are relatively free to join private associations, and those who enjoy short working hours because of government intervention can spend more time in voluntary groups. These are not sufficient reasons to embrace welfare, but they do refute the conservative theory that government and civil society are at odds.

In any event, there is no reason to suppose that private associations are the only seedbeds of virtue. Indeed, Tocqueville did not stress the distinction between state and private sectors. What he admired about America was its abundance of small, deliberative, autonomous bodies that people could freely join. If this is what we call "civil society," then it must encompass all organizations that encourage cooperative and deliberative behavior—state-run institutions as well as private groups. In fact, there may be more grassroots participation and deliberation in a school board or a neighborhood advisory council than in any large, bureaucratic philanthropy. We would not want all groups to be controlled by the state, because then diversity would suffer and organizations would be unable to exercise true self-government. However, state-funded institutions can be autonomous, and private ones can be dominated by higher powers. Thus, in the following pages, I will discuss the advantages of voluntary, participatory, associational life—"civil society"—without drawing an invidious distinction between the public and private sectors.

Abroad, we have seen that the transition from communism to democracy requires vibrant civil society (in this sense) and appropriate personal habits. These are not *sufficient* conditions for peace and good government. Michael Ignatieff notes, for example, that Yugoslavia "enjoyed one of the most vigorous revivals of an independent civil society anywhere in the communist world in the 1960s and 1970s," yet the country broke into warring and despotic fragments as soon as political circumstances changed.[12] Badly designed institutions and unscrupulous politicians can be deadly, even where civil society is strong. Nevertheless, civil society and democracy tend to go together. Presumably, they reinforce one another: democratic regimes help people to cooperate voluntarily, and voluntary cooperation helps to sustain democratic institutions.[13]

At home, meanwhile, there is new evidence that certain associations are crucial to the health of our democracy—yet they are declining. Robert Putnam, a Harvard political scientist, has made this case most prominently. He and his allies adopt Tocqueville's theory more or less wholesale, but they add certain modern refinements. First, from the sociologist Jane Jacobs and the economist James Coleman, they borrow the idea of "social capital." Putnam writes, "By analogy with notions of physical capital and human capital—tools and training that enhance individual productivity—'social capital' refers to features of social organizations such as networks, norms, and social trust that facilitate coordination and cooperation for mutual benefit."[14]

Social capital helps to sustain healthy democratic politics. If people belong to associations, they can develop coherent political ideas and values and learn to speak publicly. Only by cooperating can ordinary citizens put much pressure on the government: thus associational life is a source of political *power* that can partially counterbalance the influence of money. To the extent that people cooperate voluntarily, they do not have to legislate or litigate to solve their problems, so they can reserve their political energies for necessarily contentious issues. And citizens who participate in voluntary associations may develop a moral concern for others, a public-spiritedness that is normally cultivated neither by private economic behavior nor by solitary voting. Both the political system and the market are intensely competitive. Cooperation occurs much more easily in the sphere of civil society; and once people have cooperated as members of a voluntary group, they may be less antagonistic in the political realm.

As well as contributing a new theoretical concept (social capital), the neo-Tocquevillians also bring sophisticated analytical tools to bear. Tocqueville was fond of causal arguments. He wrote, for example, that "there is a necessary connection between public associations and newspapers: newspapers make associations and associations make newspapers."[15] Statistical data cannot definitively establish cause-and-effect relationships, but they can reveal correlations. Social scientists have used survey research to demonstrate correlations among most of the following variables: trust in government, trust in other people, membership in associations, volunteering, knowledge of politics, willingness to serve on juries, and voting. Thus Tocqueville's general impressions now have empirical support. If you belong to several clubs, you are more likely to trust your fellow human beings, to read the newspaper, to recognize the names of political leaders, to discuss elections, and to vote. What's more, according to Putnam, these mutually connected aspects of good citizenship have all suffered measurable declines since 1970. A discussion of each one follows.

ASSOCIATIONAL LIFE

Tocqueville considered Americans the world's experts on voluntary cooperation. They had, he said, "carried to the highest perfection the art of pursuing in common the object of their common desires."[16] This may still be true; only Iceland, Sweden, and the Netherlands have higher rates of membership, and just 18 percent of Americans belong to no associations at all.[17] Tocqueville relished Americans' tendency to form futile organizations, so he would be glad to learn that there is now a Benevolent and Loyal Order of Pessimists and a Procrastinators Club of America (with 4,000 members who actually got around to joining).[18] Apparently, the spirit of voluntary association is not dead. On the other hand, the United States is comparatively weak in some aspects of civil society. For instance, America has a lower rate of union membership than most other industrialized democracies, and we spend less time socializing than people in other wealthy nations do.[19]

No one believes that Americans' propensity to join organizations has increased lately, even though we are better educated and more affluent than ever before. I have argued elsewhere against Putnam's claim that membership has actually *declined* over the last twenty-five years.[20] But this thesis is not of overwhelming importance here. Even if we had stronger and larger associations today than we had in 1975 (or in 1910), we would still need more of them. In the following sections, I will describe the civic virtues that they foster, arguing that there is no better way to nourish democracy than to encourage the growth of voluntary groups. If our political institutions become more democratic, then the demands on citizens will increase, and we will rely more heavily on the civic virtues that associations foster. Therefore, there is no reason for complacency, even if Putnam is wrong about the recent trends.

In any case, the debate provoked by Putnam's initial work concerns group memberships per person, which is a very coarse measure of social capital. Scholars still debate the significance of these aggregate figures, but one fact is certain: people have *shifted* their memberships from certain kinds of association to others. Civil society may have waxed or waned; but it has definitely altered its composition. In 1953, the rate of union membership was almost twice what it is today. Fraternal organizations have shrunk by similar margins; and the PTA now enjoys much lower support per student than it did in past decades. But professional associations have swelled at about the same rate that unions have waned. And groups as diverse as the Sierra Club, the National Organization for Women, and the American Association of Retired Persons (AARP) have grown impressively.[21] Fewer people bowl in leagues today, but more play organized soccer (although not nearly enough to compensate). There has been a mass migration from mainline Protestant denominations to evangelical churches. Finally, whole new categories of association have appeared, so that people may now join the Christian Coalition, the Michigan Militia, Habitat for Humanity, or Gamblers Anonymous.

If we value voluntary groups because they build civic virtue, help people to cooperate, and distribute political power, then not all types of association are equal. For instance:

Unions

Unions not only give economic power to working people; they are also potential sources of solidarity, political information, efficacy, and community support. Compared to other Americans, members of union households are 8 percent more likely to vote.[22] Unionized workers also join more voluntary organizations and make more charitable contributions than other people do.[23]

The dramatic decline in union membership has probably been caused by factors that do not directly affect other associations, such as automation, international competition, the relocation of factories to Southern states, and revisions in federal labor law. Therefore, unions must be considered separately, but they cannot be ignored in a discussion of civil society. It is worth emphasizing that the rate of union membership in the United States (less than 9 percent of adults) is paltry compared to that in some other industrialized democracies.

Fraternal Organizations

Fraternal organizations, such as the Lions and Elks, have lost even more of their membership since 1974.[24] These groups are advocates for their communities, places where local issues are discussed, and sources of voluntary and charitable labor. While they encourage involvement in local matters, they also have national and international meetings and programs that can promote a broader dialogue. Although some of their activities have traditionally been segregated by sex, they have often developed powerful women's auxiliaries and counterparts. According to Theda Skocpol, they have offered people of different classes an opportunity to talk and cooperate as rough equals. In all these respects, they are preferable to professional associations, which have grown as the fraternals have shrunk.[25] Without returning to the segregated patterns of the past, we need something to replace the cross-class, local organizations that flourished through most of American history.

Church-Based Associations

Church-based associations account for the relative strength of civil society in the United States. They have attracted almost half of the U.S. population, compared to just 13 percent of people in the average industrialized democracy.[26] All the classic activities of civil society—debating issues, collecting money, recruiting volunteers, signing petitions, making contacts, and raising consciousness—occur with special frequency in church basements. Like fraternal organizations, church-based groups have national conventions, policies, and lobbying arms that are linked to their local bodies. They successfully recruit people with little income or education, who tend to be overlooked by other groups.[27] And membership in church-based associations correlates with voting, volunteering, charity, and political activity.[28]

Fundamentalist Denominations

Fundamentalist denominations are no exception. They aggressively recruit people of all backgrounds and motivate them to participate politically. Since most evangelical churches are managed by lay people, they are especially likely to offer their members political experience and to cultivate strong interpersonal ties. For example, as part of their church activities, Baptists are much more likely to plan meetings and make presentations than Catholics are.[29] (Not all Baptists are fundamentalists, but all fundamentalists belong to Protestant denominations that teach civic skills.) It is true that fundamentalists join considerably fewer groups than people who call themselves religious moderates or liberals do. They are also less likely to vote, to trust other people, and to read a daily newspaper.[30] However, fundamentalists have lower-than-average family incomes. If we control for income, most of the differences between fundamentalists and religious moderates and liberals disappear. For example, adjusting for income, fundamentalists belong to about the same number of associations as average Americans do and are actually more likely to vote in some years.

Although fundamentalist denominations build communities of mutual support, they also promote suspicion of outsiders.[31] However, political participation does not suffer as a result. If anything, people seem to be motivated to vote by a belief that many of their compatriots are immoral.[32] In short, the results of successful evangelization probably include more civic participation by some poor and low-status people, but also more generalized distrust and ideological division.

Mailing-List Associations

Mailing-list associations existed before 1970, but the last thirty years have been their golden age. Whether you want to save the rain forest, fight gun control, or cure cancer, there is a group for your ideology and interest. Such organizations ask their members for financial support, but they rarely request time, effort, or initiative. Most members never collaborate or discuss their shared interests; they may not even know the names of other supporters in the area. It would be surprising if people gained much political experience or developed deep social bonds from mailing an occasional check.

Furthermore, raising money by direct mail is a competitive business in which ideological groups sometimes try to outdo one another by inciting anger in their likely donors. For instance, a mailing from the National Rifle Association called federal agents "jack-booted government thugs" in "nazi bucket helmets and black storm trooper uniforms."[33] This letter became notorious because it coincided with the Oklahoma City bombing: the murder of innocent federal agents (and others) by an opponent of gun control. However, many equally inflammatory letters of all ideological hues have escaped broad public notice, because they are sent to targeted mailing lists of potential supporters. This practice is not likely to increase deliberation, cooperation, or trust.

On the other hand, it is important not to stereotype mailing-list organizations. Putnam originally included the Sierra Club on his list of "tertiary associations"—those in which members merely write checks and read newsletters.[34] This seems to be false. In one May weekend, the Los Angeles chapter alone organized thirty-nine events, from classes to camping excursions, that were cooperative and participatory; they seemed almost calculated to increase social capital.[35] Besides, Skocpol argues that the voluntary associations praised by Putnam—such as the PTA and the American Legion—originally flourished because they had effective federal lobbying arms; they were quite similar to today's Sierra Club.[36] Even pure mailing-list organizations do not necessarily reduce social capital, because they can produce efficient results, thereby freeing members to perform other civic tasks. And writing a check to a lobbying group requires a kind of interpersonal trust, which is an ingredient of social capital. Nevertheless, a major shift from participatory groups to membership organizations would be grounds for concern.

TRUST

Trust is an attribute of citizenship, a civic virtue. Of course, it is possible to trust too much; mere complacency may result if we place unwavering faith in people and institutions. Even when trust is socially helpful, its cost to the trusting individual can be unreasonably high. For example, the Jews of Weimar Germany trusted and served their country; their political activism probably improved German democracy, but not enough to save it or themselves. Nevertheless, there are good reasons to think that *warranted* trust is helpful to democracy and civil society. It may even be good to trust somewhat beyond what the evidence warrants—to give the benefit of the doubt. I call this state of mind "reasonable trust."

Reasonable trust permits a healthy division of political labor. For instance, I allow mainstream environmental organizations to speak for me on their issues, reserving my time for other political matters that I understand better. This would be impossible, however, if I believed that the government was a vast conspiracy, impervious to civil persuasion; or if I thought that all nonprofit organizations were hypocritical and corrupt; or if I doubted everything that the mass media told me. A citizen who fundamentally distrusts these institutions may lapse into alienated apathy or else join with a few like-minded conspiracy theorists to oppose the authorities wholesale. Complacent trust is not much preferable to paranoia; but distrust has to be targeted and warranted if it is to produce effective political action.

A certain level of trust is necessary, too, if deliberation is to occur. I don't have to agree with other people in order to discuss political issues with them, but I must believe that they are susceptible to persuasion, sincere in their commitments, and reliably nonviolent. Fifty-one percent of trustful people say that they have tried to influence other citizens' voting, compared to 42 percent of distrustful people.[37] Of course, one can deliberate about matters other than elections. We lack data on deliberation in general, but we know that trust correlates with participation in many civic and social activities.[38] Eric Uslaner has even shown a correlation between social trust and the passage of "major laws" at the federal level. He suggests that Congress can legislate effectively only when most citizens are willing to credit others with honorable motives, and when electoral minorities accept political defeats in the belief that they will be treated fairly. A profound lack of trust simply paralyzes Congress.[39]

The ability to cooperate politically is especially important for the poor and disenfranchised, who are weak as individuals. Thus, for example, the success of the Civil Rights Movement required remarkable levels of mutual trust. If one African-American citizen went to the courthouse to register and no one else showed up, the lone protester was doomed. Since no one could compel (or even expect) everyone else to act, it seemed irrational for individuals to defy the racist authorities. Two years after the Montgomery bus boycott began, Martin Luther King recalled: "Many of the Negroes who joined the protest did not expect it to succeed. When asked why, they usually gave one of three answers: 'I didn't expect Negroes to stick to it,' or 'I never thought we Negroes had the nerve,' or 'I thought the pressure from the white folks would kill it before it got started.'"[40] Still, despite reasonable doubts, each of these people took the terrible risk of protesting segregation. They had been persuaded to trust one another. At the same time, they believed that America's political institutions and its white majority had some potential for justice—that the nation was subject to redemption. When members of poor minority groups believe that America is irredeemably unjust and hostile, they may abandon political action altogether.

As a statistical matter, those who trust other people are most likely to vote, to work on community problems, to serve on juries, and to give money and time to charity. Also, trusters belong to more private organizations than non-trusters do.[41] According to one study, people do not gain much trust by participating in groups; rather, trustful people tend to join associations. However, a rival study finds just the opposite: that "the effect of civic engagement on interpersonal trust [is] much stronger than the reverse effect."[42] Despite this disagreement, no one doubts that there is a positive reciprocal relationship between trust and participation in civil society. The fact that trust has declined suggests that associations have shrunk (in the aggregate), *or* that they are delivering fewer psychological benefits to their members than they did in the past, *or* that they have been unable to overcome external factors, such as crime, that have undermined trust.

The proportion of Americans who tell pollsters that "most people can be trusted" has oscillated, but the general trend is down—from 58 percent in 1960 to 34 percent in 1994.[43] Trust in government has fallen much more precipitously. The proportion of people who agree that "You can trust the government in Washington to do what is right just about always, or most of the time" has fallen from

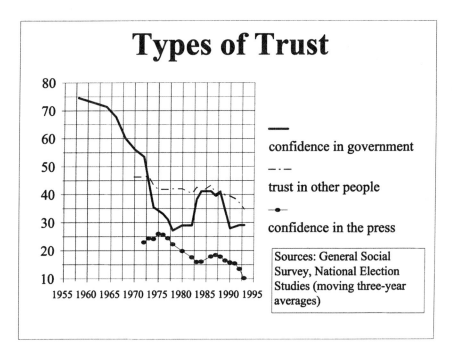

Types of Trust

— confidence in government

—·— trust in other people

—•— confidence in the press

Sources: General Social Survey, National Election Studies (moving three-year averages)

72 percent in 1960 to about 22 percent today. This decline has been continuous except for a modest rebound during the Reagan years.[44] Trust in people is conceptually different from trust in government, but they correlate statistically and have fallen more or less in tandem.[45]

Finally, reported trust in the press has plummeted in recent years. The proportion of Americans who said that they had "a great deal of confidence" in television news dropped from 55 percent in 1988 to 25 percent in 1993. In the same period, confidence in newspapers fell from 50 percent to 20 percent, and confidence in magazines declined from 38 percent to 12 percent.[46] Only 10 percent of Americans now say they have "a great deal of confidence" in the press overall (down from 29 percent in 1976).[47]

To make matters worse, those who need to trust most, actually trust least. Although African Americans' attitudes toward the government are similar to those of whites, they have consistently distrusted other people at a very high rate.[48] This is not surprising, given the long history of discrimination and mistreatment. In addition, household income, self-reported class, education, marital status, sex, and job security all correlate with trust.[49] A wealthy, economically secure, college-educated, white, married man is much more likely to trust his fellow citizens than a single, poor, African-American woman is—yet she needs both interpersonal trust and trust in (certain) institutions if she is going to cooperate with others to improve her situation. On the other hand, it is clear why disadvantaged people often distrust others: they are particularly vulnerable to exploitation.

Why has the level of self-reported trust declined in the United States? There is certainly no consensus answer, nor has any scholar proposed a fully convincing theory. The following, then, are partial hypotheses, each inadequate to explain the trends.

First, our loss of trust in government could be warranted. Corruption is probably no worse today than it was in 1960, but the government has failed spectacularly on several occasions: consider Vietnam, the War on Poverty, and supply-side economics. Furthermore, disclosure of campaign-finance data and other government information increased in the 1970s, when Congress passed the Federal Election Campaign Act and the Freedom of Information Act. It is much harder today for political leaders to conceal potentially embarrassing facts. Repeated exposés of government waste have been particularly effective in shaping public attitudes. In one poll, respondents estimated (on average) that 48 cents of each tax dollar is wasted.[50] What's more, politicians and government agencies assume responsibility for macroeconomic performance. Therefore, the "uniquely poor" growth in productivity since 1973 could have gradually eroded faith in government.[51]

The drop in trust among people could also be warranted. The relevant poll question asks whether you can trust most people most of the time, or whether "you can't be too careful." The dramatic increase in crime since the 1960s has given Americans reason to choose the latter option. Indeed, recent victims of robbery report heightened suspicion about other people, but their attitudes cannot account for the general deterioration of trust.[52] Instead, Robert Wuthnow blames our changing attitudes toward government officials. His data show that every time citizens are disappointed in politicians because of a scandal or a gross mistake, they lose faith in strangers generally.[53]

If citizens are empirically correct to distrust their fellow citizens and government, then the only ways to raise trust would be to reduce crime, cut waste, and reform the political system. These are not modest objectives, and they can be made even more difficult by high levels of public distrust. For example, crime flourishes where people are too mutually fearful to cooperate. A vicious circle results, in which mistrust breeds crime and crime undermines trust. As for campaign-finance reform, this has proved elusive—in part—because voters do not believe that any particular proposal is genuine. Why should incumbent politicians give up their huge fundraising advantages by passing reform legislation, if most citizens assume that it's a sham?

In any case, trust may have waned for reasons unrelated to government corruption and incompetence or individual misconduct. One obvious culprit is divorce, since breaking one's marriage vows is a good way to induce cynicism in a spouse and children alike. In fact, divorced and separated people trust less than married people, but even the latter group has reported a marked decline in interpersonal trust, from 50 percent in the 1970s to 39 percent in the 1990s.[54]

Another plausible reason for declining trust is the increasing complexity of our lives. In the technologically sophisticated, globally integrated modern economy, we have relationships—direct or mediated—with millions of people. Therefore, it is now difficult (perhaps even irrational) to trust most people most of the time. As Americans migrated from small towns to big cities, and then to huge metropolitan areas, we might expect interpersonal trust to have waned.

In addition, meager growth in family incomes could have contributed to faltering trust. Senator Daniel Patrick Moynihan (D-NY) has stated that the period 1970–1986 was "the longest stretch of 'flat' income in the history of the European settlement of North America."[55] If a rising tide lifts all boats, then I can trust even those who are more successful than I. But if my situation declines in real terms while others prosper, then I may begin to believe that anyone else's gain must come at my expense. In that case, I may view with suspicion all welfare recipients, government employees, union bureaucrats, and/or corporate executives; and overall interpersonal trust may decline accordingly.

Yet another factor is suburbanization. In 1961, Jane Jacobs described the community life of safe and heterogeneous urban neighborhoods. She observed that people were able to trust one another because certain residents kept their "eyes on the street," enforcing an "intricate, almost unconscious, network of voluntary controls and standards."[56] The most dedicated defenders of urban neighborhoods were homeowners, small-business people, and resident landlords: the petit-bourgeoisie.

What happened to these people? In a word, they *left*—bound for the suburbs, where they felt that they didn't have to keep their eyes on the street, because their neighborhoods were ethnically and economically homogeneous. Since residential segregation by wealth is growing, many middle-income Americans no longer live near those who are most likely to commit violent crimes: the poor.[57] Furthermore, those who can afford private security services prefer to spend money protecting themselves, rather than fighting crime in their broader communities. This is economically rational policy: why act as an unpaid crime-fighter in a potentially dangerous neighborhood when you can move far away from most of the potential lawbreakers? And why pay taxes for police and schools when you can hire a specialist to keep criminals away from *your* house? In fact, three times as many people are now employed by private protective services as by police forces; and private security consumes $52 billion a year, 73 percent more than public law enforcement (up from 57 percent more in 1980). As the National Institute of Justice reported in 1990, "Private security is now clearly the nation's primary protective resource."[58]

If we succeed in protecting ourselves against crime by keeping our eyes on the street—knowing our neighbors and cooperating voluntarily—then we have good reason to trust most of the people we encounter most of the time. If, on the other hand, we seek security by moving away from mixed neighborhoods and hiring guards, then we not only exhibit distrust, but we also perpetuate it. Poor urban neighborhoods become genuinely dangerous, and suburban enclaves are hostile to poor and minority visitors.

The epitome of suburban life may be a development like Bear Creek in Washington State, where "there are no pesky doorbellers, be they politicians or Girl Scouts. . . . A random encounter is the last thing people want here. There is a new park, every blade of grass in shape—but for members only. Four private security guards man the entrance gates 24 hours a day, keeping the residents of Bear Creek in a nearly crime-free bubble. And should a dog try to stray outside its yard, the pet would be instantly zapped by an electronic monitor."[59] Bear Creek is a civil society: a well-ordered, nongovernmental association. Residents probably trust one another; they certainly share resources and delegate impressive powers to their community association. However, Bear Creek is exclusive and inward-looking; its walls signify a deep mistrust of the society beyond. About four million Americans now live in "gated communities."[60]

The social and economic factors discussed so far may be the most significant causes of diminished trust. However, it is also tempting to suspect a favorite modern culprit: the media. Chapter 5 offers a detailed criticism of modern journalism. For now, it is enough to note the two reliable correlations that have emerged from survey research. Regular newspaper readers trust the government at an unusually high rate; and heavy television viewers overwhelmingly distrust other people.[61] However, we shouldn't jump to conclusions about the direction of causality. Uslaner, for instance, believes that "Television doesn't cause mistrust or pessimism, but the people who watch a lot of television are the sorts of folks who are pessimistic and don't trust others."[62] Similarly, those who begin by trusting the government may choose to read newspapers, rather than vice versa.

This debate concerns the putative effect of viewing and reading habits on trust, but there is also the question of what appears on TV and in daily newspapers. The message, not just the medium, may count. The effect of different kinds of programs on trust has not been studied adequately, but it is intriguing to note that people who watch the television news are modestly *more* likely to vote and to join organizations than people who don't. Viewers of public-affairs programs such as *The Newshour* with Jim Lehrer are even more likely to participate civically. Nevertheless, total hours in front of the TV set correlate negatively with civic participation and trust.[63] It seems, then, that not all television programs have equal effects on citizenship.

Furthermore, any given type of broadcast may change over time. Between 1988 and 1995, "the number of minutes devoted to crime on the nightly news" quintupled. Crime reporting has fallen since 1995, but a third of the average local news broadcast is still devoted to it.[64] In a community of several million people, there may be a heinous outrage every week, even if the crime rate is low. The worse the horror, the more we can expect the television news to give us a riveting, prurient, vicarious experience of it. A decline in interpersonal trust seems almost predictable under these circumstances. Summarizing various studies, Putnam concludes that "heavy watchers of TV are unusually skeptical about the benevolence of other people—overestimating crime rates, for example."[65]

If shows like *Cops* and *HardCopy* reduce trust in other people, then they may harm civil society—and therefore democracy. When it comes to political news, however, the question of trust is more problematic. Journalists have often seen themselves as public watchdogs, obligated to reveal all manner of government malfeasance and incompetence. If citizens lose trust in government because of what the watchdog press discovers, so much the worse for politicians.

But the press often covers politics in a way that undermines public trust without good reason. In particular, journalists frequently insinuate that politicians act out of naked self-interest. This claim is usually irrefutable—but also unverifiable and largely irrelevant. Motives are always difficult to assess, and in any case the important question is not why a politician votes in a particular way, but whether this position is right. If we assume that politicians are hypocrites, guided by self-interest instead of arguments, then we may view politics as a sport: horse racing is the usual metaphor. In a horse race, the contestants are entirely self-interested and there is no normative difference between the sides. The same is true of political campaigns as they are portrayed in the media.

Amy Gutmann and Dennis Thompson argue that it is a fallacy to interpret an opponent's position as a reflection of his or her political self-interest. This, they write, is an all-purpose argument which can be used to discredit any position, whatever its moral merits. What all such arguments have in common is a refusal to give moral reasons for rejecting the position. Contrary to the practice of imputing ulterior motives, we manifest mutual respect by joining with our fellow citizens in serious and sustained moral discussion on the substance of the issues that divide us. In such discussions we not only state publicly our reasons for rejecting an opponent's position but also invite and consider responses to our objections.[66]

Most journalists are not comfortable engaging in (or even covering) "sustained moral discussion," because they think that they should keep their values out of their writing. At the same time, they believe that they can write "objectively" if they interpret politicians' statements as mere expressions of political self-interest. But to make cynical insinuations is itself a moral argument. It is an argument against every moral view in the public arena—indeed, against public deliberation per se.

In practice, coverage of politics as a sport may well reduce public trust in government. Kathleen Hall Jamieson and Joseph N. Capella tested this hypothesis experimentally. They asked volunteers in cities other than Philadelphia to read about that city's mayoral race. Half of the volunteers were give horse-race stories and articles about "character." The other participants were shown stories that explained the candidates' positions on public issues. Members of the first group were much more likely to conclude that the "candidates were posturing, deceptive, self-interested, and unconcerned with the welfare of the city"; they were correspondingly less likely to believe that there was any point to civic involvement.[67]

In addition to horse-race coverage of politics and grisly footage of crime victims, viewers are now treated to political advertisements that are often extremely negative. The caustic, scathing "attack ad" is a staple of modern campaigns. Especially since most commercial advertising is cheerful and self-congratulatory, we might expect negative political ads to cause a decline in trust toward government.

Unfortunately, candidates have good reasons to favor negative advertising. In a commercial market, the more customers who buy a firm's products, the better. If one company attacks another, customers may either switch to a third brand or else lose faith in the commodity altogether. It is much wiser, therefore, to use positive advertising to increase general demand as well as market share. If one company's advertising happens to benefit its competitors as well, no harm is done. An election, on the other hand, is a zero-sum game with (in general) just two players. The winner is the candidate with the most votes, even if turnout is extremely low. If I attack my opponent effectively, citizens may vote for me or else drop out altogether—and either result is satisfactory. I can instead try to improve my own reputation, but that is often much more difficult than using select charges to undermine my opponent. Only in a genuine multi-candidate race is it unwise to "go negative."

Trust is valuable because it encourages group membership and civic engagement, but it is not a variable that we can tinker with directly. According to Wuthnow, a loss of confidence in government leaders probably caused the drop in interpersonal trust, so perhaps political reform would ultimately persuade Americans to place a bit more faith in one another. Meanwhile, we ought to support associations, for at least some of them cultivate generalized trust. The following sections will demonstrate that associational membership also has advantages for knowledge, participation, deliberation, and solidarity.

POLITICAL KNOWLEDGE AND PARTICIPATION

In January 1996, the *Washington Post* published a lead article to announce the results of an extensive poll. The headline proclaimed, "Who's in Control? Many Don't Know or Care." Indeed, only 52 percent of respondents could say correctly whether the Democrats or the Republicans were the more conservative party; about a third could name their U.S. representative; 27 percent were aware (or guessed) that the federal government spent more on Medicare than foreign aid, and 6 percent could name the chief justice. People who knew a great deal were likely to vote, no matter how interested they were in politics. But those with little knowledge generally believed that they were powerless—and abstained from voting. If they did vote, their choices at the polls were so unconnected to their stated priorities that "it was as if their vote was random," according to Michael Delli Carpini, a political scientist.[68]

Anyone who was alarmed by these findings would have been further distressed when fewer than half of eligible adults voted in the 1996 elections, the lowest turnout in a presidential election since 1924. Nor did matters improve in 1998, when participation was the worst in an off-year election since 1942, and a record number of citizens did not vote.[69] The United States always has extremely low levels of participation compared to other countries; only Switzerland is obviously worse among the industrialized democracies.

This is due, in part, to our constitutional structure. Voters in a European parliamentary system have just one opportunity every few years to cast a single vote in an election that will decide which party governs—without checks or balances—until the next election is called. If all elected positions in the United States were filled in one quadrennial election, and voters simply had to pull a lever that would give unchecked power to either the Democrats or the Republicans, then turnout would doubtless soar. However, our Constitution divides power among the branches and levels of government and staggers elections. Since change is incremental, each vote seems to lack urgency and many people stay home.

Still, we should not be satisfied with current levels of turnout, because participation has fallen steadily and steeply since 1960, with only a modest rebound in

1992. Thus we know that we can do better. On the other hand, Americans are no worse informed about official politics today than they were when polling began in the 1940s.[70] In fact, public ignorance and alienation have been the topics of debate since at least the Progressive Era, when Lippmann gathered anecdotal information and concluded:

> The random collection of bystanders who constitute a public could not, even if they had a mind to, intervene in all the problems of the day. They can and must play a part occasionally, I believe, but they cannot take an interest in, they cannot make even the coarsest judgments about, and they will not act even in the most grossly partisan way on, all the questions arising daily in a complex and changing society. Normally, they leave their proxies to a kind of professional public consisting of more or less eminent persons. Most issues are never carried beyond this ruling group; the lay publics catch only echoes of the debate.

Lippmann did not present himself as a moral critic of ordinary citizens. Dismissing the theory that people were "competent to direct the course of affairs," he wrote: "I think it is a false idea. I do not mean an undesirable ideal. I mean an unattainable ideal, bad only in the sense that it is bad for a fat man to try to be a ballet dancer."[71]

Although Dewey tried to answer Lippmann in *The Public and Its Problems*, he did not deny Lippmann's anecdotal information. He conceded that citizens were unprepared to understand political and social issues, but he thought that they could be *made* competent by educational and political reform. Lippmann and Dewey represented two influential positions in the Progressive-Era debate. Diehard skeptics favored professional management, doubting the capacities of the public, while reformers hoped that more and better schooling could produce an informed electorate.

Neither side had much hard information with which to support its case. But during and after the Second World War, public opinion became a subject of statistical measurement. Polling data, George Gallup predicted, would show that "the case against the common man has frequently proceeded on the basis of the flimsiest circumstantial evidence." Gallup admitted that his polls were just the "early returns," but he was sure that further data would only confirm his faith in the "honesty and common sense" of most citizens. Ordinary people grasped the "broad principles" of policy and adjusted "themselves to the ever-changing movement of events."[72]

He was wrong. When academic researchers began to poll people scientifically, all their results seemed to confirm Lippmann's anecdotal evidence about public ignorance. A group of political scientists associated with the Survey Research Center at the University of Michigan conducted the first large-scale longitudinal studies, from which they concluded that "the average citizen is very much less involved in politics than is often imagined. His awareness of political events is limited and his concern with ideological problems is only rudimentary."

Most students of democracy had assumed that citizens could make rational choices among policy alternatives, and that professional leaders offered people such choices at election time. But the Michigan researchers drew "a portrait of an electorate almost wholly without detailed information about decision making in government." The public, they argued, "knows little about what government has done . . . or what the parties propose to do. It is almost completely unable to judge the rationality of government actions; knowing little of particular policies and what has led to them, the mass electorate is not able to appraise either its goals or the appropriateness of the means chosen to serve these goals." Consequently, election results were less meaningful than most politicians had believed, and leaders ought to make decisions without heeding so-called public opinion.[73]

One member of the Michigan School was Philip E. Converse, who found that most people's opinions on given issues did not remain stable, nor did their attitudes evolve in response to events. Rather, a typical individual's responses over time were "statistically random." Nevertheless, most Americans had deep partisan loyalties. Thus, although they might randomly change their minds about issues such as school desegregation, they would vote reliably for one party and its candidates. This was putting the cart before the horse, Converse thought, because a party was supposed to be "an instrument to further particular policy preferences."[74]

It seemed, too, that answers to opinion polls were extremely sensitive to the exact phrasing and ordering of questions. As a result, pollsters struggled (with some success) to devise questionnaires that would draw consistent and meaningful answers. But their difficulties suggested that citizens had a rather shallow acquaintance with important issues. If, for example, most people had thought about school desegregation by 1960, they wouldn't have been influenced by subtle changes in question-order. Apparently, the Progressives' ideal of an independent and rational voter was a fantasy.[75]

As information about scanty public knowledge came to light, Anthony Downs wrote a classic book explaining *why* most people didn't seek more information. "In general," he wrote, "it is irrational to be politically well-informed." All information had a price; even acquiring "free" news and opinion took time, which could be used for other purposes. Information relevant to people's work was comparatively valuable, since it could raise their incomes. But political information could only make their votes more intelligent. Given the large number of people voting, this was not particularly important to each person or to anyone else. Unless people gained pleasure or satisfaction from acts of citizenship, it was irrational for them to go to the polls—let alone inform themselves about candidates and issues. Downs noted, further, that poor people had a harder time paying the costs of information and voting, so they were especially likely to opt out of politics.[76] We know today that people at the bottom of the economic ladder are distressingly ill-informed about political matters that may directly affect them. For instance, two out of three of the poorest Americans cannot describe the political parties' attitudes toward government spending, whereas most wealthy Americans know exactly how the Democrats differ from the Republicans.[77] This information gap helps to explain the difference in voter participation between rich and poor, because it makes no sense to vote if you lack information about the issues.

While members of the Michigan School were analyzing poll data, a small group of students on the same campus read Dewey and adopted his moral stance. The public *had* to become competent, they thought, or else the transformative potential of democracy would be wasted. In particular, the poor and dispossessed had to participate, or else policy would continue to be set by a satisfied bourgeoisie. These students deplored rampant apathy and the "withdrawal from public life." For instance, they denounced "the faceless ones polled by Gallup who listed 'international affairs' fourteenth on their list of 'problems' but who also expected thermonuclear war in the next few years."[78] For them, inconsistent answers to poll questions were a source of moral outrage.

Thus SDS was born; and soon a whole movement aimed to bring political awareness to an apathetic public. The radicals were not entirely unsuccessful. Individuals' opinions became strikingly more consistent between 1960 and 1964, and they stayed both consistent and polarized throughout the decade of Johnson and McGovern, Goldwater and Wallace.[79] Leaders on the extreme right and left offered people distinct political choices, clarifying their opinions. Participation generally rose and Americans' reported interest in government and politics was relatively high in the decade after 1964.[80] Almost half the population could name their own U.S. representatives in 1974, the highest level ever recorded.

Nevertheless, voter turnout began its long decline in 1960, and the gains in knowledge and participation receded during the 1970s. Today, most people do not know basic information about the official political system, such as who represents them in Congress or whether the Republicans are more conservative than the Democrats. We could argue that these facts don't matter. There is, after all, hardly any difference between the two parties, and the names of politicians could be considered trivia. But in practice there is usually a link between factual knowledge and habits of deliberation. As Richard Niemi and Jane Junn write, "One can live one's daily life without knowing that the president is the commander-in-chief of the armed forces or, for that matter, without knowing the name of the president. But how many political discussions and how many news reports would be incomprehensible without this information?"[81] What's more, people who do know such facts tend to vote; and this active, informed minority is disproportionately wealthy, educated, and white.[82] After the 1998 election, news reports suggested that the Democrats had performed unexpectedly well because of comparatively high turnout among poor people (two-thirds of whom voted Democratic). But the poorest fifth of the population still represented just 8 percent of the electorate.[83]

If those who participated in politics somehow came to reflect the racial, economic, regional, and sexual composition of the overall population, then elections would be fair. But even if the electorate were representative, it would still be disappointing if most Americans knew little about government and abstained from voting. The Progressives dreamed of a national dialogue about moral and political questions that aimed toward consensus. Elections are opportunities for such discussion, but if half of the population opts out of the conversation, then there is no hope for consensus, and little reason to believe that a truly popular opinion has formed. Nor can we assume that the people who abstain from politics are satisfied with the status quo: they are so poorly informed about the government's behavior that their passive acquiescence does not signify support.

American democracy has muddled along for decades—perhaps since its inception—with low levels of information and participation. But there seems to be reason for special concern today. The best-educated people are the most likely to vote and to learn about politics. However, Americans are less politically engaged than ever, despite massive increases in schooling. In 1940, less than 40 percent of the population had progressed past sixth grade; today, that many people have spent at least two years in college.[84] Therefore, we would expect much higher turnout and a more informed electorate in the 1990s than in the 1940s. In fact, fewer people know who represents them in Congress, and turnout has dropped dramatically. In 1940, 59 percent of adult citizens voted. That fraction approached two-thirds in the fifties and early sixties; and even more people would have participated if they hadn't been thwarted by racist authorities. In short, voting was the norm, but today this is true only for a generally wealthy and well-educated minority.

The correlation between education (i.e., years spent in school) and political engagement is "the best documented finding in American political behavior research."[85] But this correlation does not prove that schools make people better citizens. It turns out that what really correlates with civic and political engagement is the amount of time that one has spent in school compared to other people in the same community and age cohort.[86] If *relative* levels of education are what correlates with good citizenship, then it is most likely that education is really a proxy for something else, such as wealth, social status, initiative, discipline, or intelligence. I suspect that people with high status gain (or are given) prominent positions in government, the market, and private associations. In turn, participation encourages political learning and voting. This means that raising the average level of education would not produce a higher average level of citizenship. So we should not be concerned to see that voter participation and knowledge have not improved despite improvements in education.

But turnout has actually fallen, and the fragmentary data about political knowledge suggest that it may have declined as well. Turnout fell most dramatically between 1968 and 1976. Part of the reason is that campaigns changed dramatically. Imagine two types of election. In the first, political parties encourage people to vote by persuading them face-to-face. This requires a huge, pyramid-shaped structure that extends from ward-level volunteers to the president. Since human labor is valuable, the parties try to mobilize people. Party officials meet immigrants at dockside and recruit vagrants to serve as ward-heelers. Meanwhile, the two parties have distinct constituencies, so they differ dramatically in their positions, at least within any given jurisdiction. In short, citizens are *asked* to vote, and they have good reason to comply.

In the second system, politicians communicate with the electorate en masse, using broadcast commercials and mailings. Unskilled labor is not particularly valuable; just a few consultants can create a TV spot, and a computer can generate mailing labels. Experts analyze the broadcast audience and buy the addresses of active voters, so that they won't waste their resources on citizens who haven't voted before. Candidates need money to pay for all this technology and air time, and they can raise funds efficiently only from a small class of wealthy individuals and lobbying organizations. Since all potential donors have fairly similar interests, the candidates' positions tend to converge. No one encourages people to vote for the first time; and even interested citizens can hardly see any difference between the parties.

We shouldn't romanticize the campaign system that fell apart in the late 1960s: party machines could be corrupt, and they frequently discriminated against racial minorities. However, their replacement, the system described in the last paragraph, demobilizes voters. According to one study, 54 percent of the drop in voter

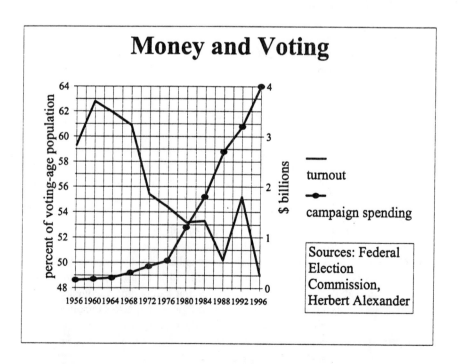

participation was caused by the "decline in mobilization" that occurred when parties ceased to be powerful, broad-based, labor-intensive institutions.[87]

We know that people who are asked to participate in politics tend to comply, but less than half are ever asked. Those who are approached tend to be wealthier than average.[88] If people do not vote, then they have little reason to seek political information. And since they cannot screen the political material out of their newspapers and public-affairs programs, they may lose interest in the news generally.[89] As a result, they have only vague ideas about social problems, and they are completely oblivious to any positive projects that are going on around them. I suspect that for some people, political demobilization has reduced interest in the news, which has discouraged them from joining community organizations.

This is a vicious cycle, but the opposite process could occur. We could, I think, broaden political participation and knowledge if we increased the rate of membership in voluntary associations. Certainly there is a clear correlation between membership and political engagement. For instance, members of church groups are 11 percent more likely to be able to name their U.S. representative than other people are. The gap widens to 18 percent when they are asked to name the head of their local schools. Members of church groups are also 10 percent more likely than other people to read the newspaper every day. Belonging to a fraternal group, a veterans' organization, or a hobby club has similar effects. Even sports leagues, which seem totally unconnected to politics, correlate with political knowledge. Members of sports clubs are 9 percent more likely than other people to know the name of their governor. Although group members tend to be well educated compared to others, those who belong to associations are much more knowledgeable than non-members with the same levels of income and education.[90]

The relationship between group membership and political engagement may be causal and not a mere correlation. As an individual, your vote hardly counts, and it's not worth reading the newspaper just so that you can vote wisely. But if you belong to an association—even a sports club—you will meet people who may persuade you how to vote, and others whom you can persuade in turn. If you bring several people around to your point of view, then your political power has been multiplied. People who are affiliated with groups are more likely than others to be asked to vote.[91] They also tell their fellow members *how* to vote. For instance, participants in sports clubs are 13 percent more likely than nonparticipants to try to persuade someone else about an election; the same is true for fraternal associations and church groups.[92]

Second, people who know one another through organizations often trust one another, so they can cooperate. Members of church groups are 23 percent more likely than nonmembers to "work with others to solve community problems." They may raise money, volunteer time, write letters, and lobby local officials. Once people have done several of these things, they may decide to vote as well. Voting makes sense as part of an overall strategy for solving social problems.

Third, politicians do not have time to contact individuals, but they often talk to groups. They may approach organizations, looking for bodies of active citizens to impress; or they may be approached by voluntary associations that want help in dealing with the government. In either case, such personal contacts encourage further communication between citizens and politicians. Fully 69 percent of the people who wrote or called their mayor's office said that they knew the mayor personally.[93] In many cases, I suspect, they had met His Honor as part of a group activity.

Finally, voters often feel that the messages they send to politicians are rather cryptic. Elected officials may not know *why* citizens voted as they did: was it because of a single issue, party loyalty, ideology, the candidates' characters, or their styles of campaigning? The ambiguous nature of a vote reduces its value. But if you vote *and* belong to an organization, then you can send a clearer message. You are not just a voter, but an N.R.A. voter, a Baptist voter, or a union voter. Groups often trumpet their own electoral clout, which increases the significance of their members' individual votes.

In theory, everyone could be involved in associations. But political participation, unlike group membership, is typically a struggle for limited goods. If a political leader meets with me, she may not have time for you. If the number of citizens who called their U.S. representatives doubled, then the Capitol switchboard would be jammed and no call would count for very much. Thus, as more citizens participate in politics, each participant will realize smaller returns, and it may not make sense for everyone to become involved.[94] It is not sufficient to increase associational membership and interest in public affairs. We must also make government more responsive, increasing the number of people to whom our leaders are willing and able to listen. This is a theme for the following chapters.

DELIBERATION

I believe that the single most important civic activity that occurs in associations is deliberation. This was not a significant theme for Tocqueville. He knew that participation in civil society could help citizens to sharpen and refine their beliefs, but he presumed that people created organizations because they already shared certain values or ideas that they wanted to propagate.[95] In contrast, I argue that collective reasoning and mutual persuasion often occur within associations, and that deliberation of this kind is critical to democracy.

Just talking about political issues—even in homogenous groups and without much information—allows us to develop preferences and values that can guide us as we vote and make decisions in the market. Without this simplest kind of deliberation, we are incapable of democratic citizenship, because we have no views for the government to reflect. Therefore, simply talking (or reading and writing) about political issues is essential. But if we only talk to relatives or old friends, then we won't be exposed to many new ideas and values. Talking in diverse groups is better; it may expose us to a broader range of perspectives and make our judgments both wiser and less selfish. Finally, a conversation that is serious, civil, fair, and inclusive creates the potential for *consensus,* which is the ideal outcome, because it renders coercion unnecessary. This is another reason that associations are crucial to the health of a democracy.

To get a rough measure of the state of deliberation in America, I have constructed an index of seventeen variables. These include various activities that tend to promote or reflect discourse about public issues, whether local or national. All of the components have been weighted equally; this was an arbitrary decision. But I have also generated 5,000 *random* weighting schemes, 80 percent of which produce strikingly similar results. (They fall between the 10th percentile and 90th percentile lines on the following chart.) The results cluster tightly because the component variables all follow similar trajectories: evidence that the index is meaningful. The result is a 25-percent decline in deliberation over two decades. One of the purposes of the following chapters is to develop concrete and practical proposals to reverse this trend.[96]

It is impossible to continue the index past 1992, because several of the survey questions on which it is based have been dropped or changed. Besides, the growth of the Internet after 1992 has encouraged on-line deliberation, the extent of which is difficult to quantify. Still, we know that there have been significant recent improvements in the following index components: local-meeting attendance, committee service, making speeches, working for political parties, belonging to reform groups, and attending political meetings. At the same time, Americans have become somewhat *less* likely to serve as club officers, attend rallies, sign petitions, read a newspaper regularly, and write letters-to-the-editor or articles. But the improvements have outweighed the declines and would have raised the index above 86 by 1996 (assuming that the unknown variables remained at least constant). We cannot know why certain aspects of deliberation improved in the 1990s, nor whether the trend will last. But it is possible that the reform efforts described in subsequent chapters have already begun to pay dividends.

These data tell us something about the quantity of political talk in America (both over time and in absolute terms), but it is equally important to analyze what topics we discuss. Consider, first of all, Americans' discussion of "identity politics"—the relationships among races and ethnic groups and between the sexes. When pollsters ask people whether they frequently talk about politics, some respondents may overlook their own conversations about these issues; they may think that "politics" is just a matter of laws and elections. In fact, racial and sexual topics seem to provoke widespread discussion. All kinds of ideas and proposals are considered, reflecting values that range from open bigotry to integrationism and radical separatism. Many people have opinions about these ideas; legislatures, courts, businesses, churches, talk shows, and informal groups constantly discuss them. Clearly, no national consensus has developed. On the con-

Index of Deliberation

tenth percentile

index

ninetieth percentile

Components: belonging to at least one group or attending church services (GSS); attending a local
meeting (Roper Starch International); serving as an officer of an association (Roper); serving on a local
committee (Roper); belonging to a reform group (Roper); attending a rally (Roper); reading the
newspaper daily (GSS); writing a letter to the newspaper (Roper); making a speech (Roper); writing an
article (Roper); being generally interested in politics (NES); influencing other people's vote during
campaigns (NES); signing a petition (Roper); writing to Congress (Roper); attending political meetings
(NES); working for a political party (Roper); wearing a button or displaying a sticker (NES). NES figures
are 4-year moving averages. Roper figures are annual moving averages.

trary, the discussion is heated and angry, and it frequently ends in litigation or
even violence. Moreover, the conversation is usually fragmented: whites talk to
whites about blacks, women discuss men with other women, and so on. Partly
for this reason, stereotypes abound and perspectives are often narrow and selfish.
However, at least the first advantage of deliberation has been achieved: most
Americans have developed opinions about race and gender that guide them as
they vote, choose their careers, hire their employees, and buy or rent their
homes.[97] And in the best cases, the second level of benefit has emerged as well.

Despite the persistence of racism and sexism, it seems clear that many people have changed their attitudes and behavior for the better in the last forty years.

One reason for the prominence of identity politics in our public discourse is that minorities and women have developed self-conscious and assertive movements. The Civil Rights Movement, feminism, and other deliberate campaigns have put race and gender on the table for discussion. Even sexists and racists cannot avoid discussing these issues, although they may never listen to their opponents. At the same time, the rules of discussion have been made more fair by the legal assault on segregation and discrimination. Hardly any deliberation about race was possible under Jim Crow, because whites and blacks were not allowed to mingle, certainly not on terms of equality. Legal fairness permits deliberation, and the resulting conversation has (in turn) convinced a broad majority of Americans to support legal fairness. Finally, many of us now have peers of different races and of the opposite sex. In the classroom and the workplace, we must confront the demands of diversity. Sometimes we respond by complaining privately to other people of our own background, but at least we respond.

Compare the issue of class. Most people never seriously discuss the distribution of wealth, status, and power between workers and management, professionals and laborers, the middle class and the poor. The status quo seems almost natural: it is part of the immutable backdrop before which life is played. People complain about abusive employers, but mainly because of their personal failings; and they lament general unfairness, but much as they might deplore inclement weather. Proposals for radical change are discussed mainly in academic circles. Average Americans don't so much disagree with such proposals as ignore them; for no one raises them in conversation.

More discussion of class interests would produce more controversy. Tension always increases when leaders like Patrick Buchanan and Jesse Jackson invoke class distinctions. The ultimate aim of a civil society is not conflict but consensus. As Theodore Roosevelt said in 1904, "No republic can permanently exist when it becomes a republic of classes, where the man feels not the interest of the whole people, but the particular class to which he belongs, or fancies that he belongs, as being of prime importance."[98] Many of Roosevelt's contemporaries, including Woodrow Wilson, also deplored class rhetoric. But Americans' general silence about class does not reflect true consensus. What Rauschenbusch wrote in 1907 could be said as well today: "We hear passionate protests against the use of the word 'class' in America. There are no classes in our country, we are told. But the hateful part is not the word, but the thing."[99]

Why do Americans shy away from discussions of class? One possible reason is ideology—in particular, the widely held view that we all belong to one economic class, although race and gender divide us. There is no question that many Americans believe this ideology, but that does not explain their silence about class: we want to know *why* alternative views are so rarely heard. American classes lack the self-consciousness and assertiveness of ethnic and sexual groups.

But our lack of class-consciousness could result from the dearth of conversation, rather than vice versa. In any case, only 60 percent of Americans describe themselves as "middle-class," which means that at least 40 percent of the population acknowledges class differences.[100]

Perhaps the underlying cause of the silence is that true deliberation only occurs among peers, and our peers (almost by definition) do not belong to our class. Black and white workers, male and female colleagues are forced to listen to each other to some degree, however biased they may be, because officially they are equals. But employers and employees are officially *un*equal, so deliberation about economic issues is almost impossible in the workplace. If workers complain about the distribution of profit between labor and management, they risk being fired. No one expects the firm's ownership to try to reach consensus with its workers on terms of equality, unless the workers happen to belong to a strong union: now a rare circumstance. Fraternal organizations (such as the Elks and Masons) often permitted middle-class people and workers to talk as equals. However, their membership levels have fallen dramatically. The shift in membership from fraternal organizations to professional associations suggests that class differences have worsened even as other barriers have lifted.

PUBLIC-SPIRITEDNESS IN AN AFFLUENT SOCIETY

The Progressives constantly exhorted people to rise above class or group interest, to embrace the public good. Some critics have responded with a cynical (but plausible) theory: people on average always vote their economic self-interest. If this is true, then repeated calls for altruism are irrelevant—even harmful. At worst, such rhetoric might discourage the poor and weak from agitating on their own behalf, while the rich continue to run the country. Thus, for example, the Progressives' attacks on Franklin Roosevelt contained a strong element of elitism. How *could* he pit working people against economic aristocrats? The idea of a common good was much more congenial to them.

FDR won significant victories by championing the bread-and-butter interests of working people. However, his success depended on an important fact: more than half of the electorate was poor. This is no longer true, and the changing composition of the American population should make us reconsider the debate between Progressives and New Dealers. In our current situation, we may need some pure public-spiritedness, after all.

Democratic administrations from FDR to LBJ transferred wealth from a small number of rich people to the mass of ordinary citizens, allowing them to afford adequate transportation, health, and education without government help. More democracy meant more power for the majority, and that in turn implied economic redistribution. But America was sufficiently wealthy by the 1960s that a majority of citizens no longer needed government aid, except in restricted areas. A New

Deal slogan had been: "If you want to live like a Republican, vote Democratic." But in recent decades, many traditional Democrats have actually begun to live as Republicans used to live in the 1930s—in affluence—and so they have begun to vote like Republicans. In 1993, a 41-percent plurality of adults favored cuts in government services (and not just in spending) if this would permit lower taxes; only 20 percent favored more services and more taxes.[101]

How many people we call "affluent" depends on our definition of the word. But the median household income—roughly $37,000 in 1997—is remarkably high by global and historical standards.[102] It puts more than half of the population in the bourgeoisie, an unprecedented phenomenon. Also, three-fifths of American families have accumulated at least $30,000 in assets; and by the time they reach retirement age, people in this group have saved a median of $138,000. Almost two-thirds of the population own their own home (with median equity of almost $47,000); and four-fifths own at least one car. About half of the rising generation is educated beyond high school.[103] Nevertheless, some Americans remain in poverty, and the actual quality of life of the urban poor may have declined since World War II.

According to John Kenneth Galbraith, the activist government of the New Deal and the Great Society seemed at first to be a "permanent revolution." But in reality, the welfare state was "a self-liquidating political movement." He writes:

> With the spread of well-being, more and more people have a comfortable satisfaction with their own economic position. Once thus blessed, they find, as in all past times, a suitably persuasive reason for separating themselves and their consciences from the still-persisting poverty of the now less numerous poor. . . . Those who are financially secure are the people who are most likely to vote in elections and who are best able to contribute to the high cost, especially in the United States, of modern political campaigns. So endowed, they vote out of power those who made the revolution on behalf of the insecure and the poor and who would continue efforts on behalf of the smaller number of the underprivileged who remain.[104]

The health-care crisis illustrates Galbraith's thesis. In 1991, with health-care reform rising quickly on the national agenda, 66 percent of Americans still rated their own health insurance as "excellent" or "good."[105] And on the eve of President Clinton's announcement of a health-reform package in 1993, polls showed that more than 80 percent of adults were satisfied with their own medical benefits and services.[106] These people could not be expected to support national health insurance with much enthusiasm, unless it somehow brought them lower health bills. Forty-three million uninsured people constitute a vast human tragedy, perhaps the worst social disaster in the developed world; but uninsured people do not cast very many votes in a nation of 250 million.[107] Most people with family incomes under $30,000 predicted that the Clinton plan would make health care better, while wealthier people thought that it would make things worse.[108] But only one-third of voters belonged to the under-$30,000 income category.[109] Thus a majority of American voters may have been basically happy when health-care reform stopped at the point it had reached in 1968: with Medicare for the elderly (because everyone gets old), Medicaid to provide minimal support for the very poor, and $65 billion a year in tax deductions for middle- and upper-income tax-payers who buy their own health insurance.[110]

In general, the existing balance of power has prevented most kinds of social intervention, including the establishment of a public health-care system or any aggressive action against unemployment, poverty, or homelessness. However, government action has been possible in restricted areas. For example, 86.3 per-cent of all American families own a car, but none can afford their own high-ways.[111] Federal aid for road construction has therefore remained popular, al-though support for mass transportation—which is used by a generally poor minority—has been weak. And most Americans remain committed to public higher education, because private universities are so expensive that only a wealthy minority can afford them without subsidy. But most people are not inter-ested in redistributing funds to poor public school districts; they would rather raise funds for their schools within their own communities, where everyone usu-ally enjoys a similar income level. For example, a proposed Texas amendment to force wealthy school districts to share funds with poor ones was defeated in a 1993 referendum, two-to-one.[112]

Opinions in favor of redistribution have consistently correlated with income. For example, a 1939 Roper poll asked: "Do you think our government should or should not redistribute wealth by heavy taxes on the rich?" Thirty-four percent more poor people than "prosperous" people said yes. The same kind of correla-tion has shown up in polls ever since. Many middle-class Americans have gener-ous feelings toward their less-fortunate compatriots, but they express these feel-ings at the donation box, not the ballot box. A government cannot survive for long as a charity, spending taxpayers' money on purely altruistic goals, if only because private, nonprofit organizations are better equipped to fulfill people's charitable priorities. Therefore, a population with a middle-class majority will probably lack widespread support for income redistribution.

In a host of suburban communities across the country, people essentially get what they pay for from local government—little more, little less. In an economi-cally homogeneous area, such as the typical suburb (where a majority of voters now lives), everyone pays a roughly equal share of the cost of police protection, schools, and roadworks, and everyone benefits from these amenities to a roughly equal degree.[113] There are few free-riders, because the poor are safely closeted away across political boundaries in the inner cities or countryside. In a few sub-urbs, all children are excluded by zoning laws, thereby obviating the need for *any* school taxes. On the other hand, the people who live in this kind of community get *less* than they pay for from federal domestic programs, because the beneficia-ries of health, employment, and welfare programs have less-than-average incomes. Therefore, middle-class suburbanites no longer need or want many traditional kinds of federal programs.

Clearly, liberals have not thrived in a nation with both an affluent majority and lingering poverty. But the demise of the welfare state does not show that *democracy* has failed: citizens should be able to support conservative policies if they so choose. Indeed, a core tenet of Progressivism (as I have defined it) is the right of democratic publics to choose any outcomes they like. How, then, can I criticize Americans for trying to dismantle the welfare state?

Progressives have two reasons to object to recent policies. First, democracy does not mean majority rule; at its heart, it suggests government by consent. But people who live in trailer parks, buy dry milk, and can't afford to take their children to the doctor may not "consent" to the existing economic arrangements. Some of them vote for liberal Democrats; many more abstain in disgust or alienation.[114] Year after year, they are defeated in national elections. To be severely harmed by a majority of one's fellow citizens is hardly better than being oppressed by a despot. It is true that we can almost never attain unanimous consent in a large and diverse society. But when a substantial minority is repeatedly and seriously harmed by a more affluent majority, then democracy has not fully succeeded.

If a poor majority were to tyrannize the rich by seizing some of their assets, this, too, would violate the ideal of consent. According to libertarians, forced redistribution of property is always a crime, whereas government inaction can never be wrong. But a sin of omission by the government is little better than a sin of commission. Progressives do not accept the naturalness of market outcomes; for them, only democracy is sovereign. A truly democratic society must examine itself critically, not tolerating some people's suffering just because the market has caused it. To refuse to provide medical care for poor workers is a serious moral omission, since we can clearly afford universal insurance. Wealthy Americans should not be bullied (any more than poor ones), but they should have to negotiate a mutually acceptable arrangement with the less advantaged. Instead, they dominate the electoral process and hardly care what the minority thinks.

Progressives should also object to antigovernment policies because they reflect a general retreat from the public sphere. Citizens are free to decide how big the private and public sectors should be. There is nothing in Progressivism that requires intrusive government or high taxes. But beyond a certain point, the decision to solve problems privately is harmful to democracy. Consider, for example, the current fashion for gated communities, malls with private security forces, and professional guards for homes and offices. By hiring a security service and posting its logo on our front lawn, we hope that we can persuade criminals to stay away—even if that means that they will rob someone else who lacks such protection. At the same time, many of us withdraw our financial support from the city and state governments that provide general law enforcement, education, and employment programs. As a result, we may no longer deliberate together about an issue that has traditionally been considered public: crime and punishment. The scope of civil society and democratic government has narrowed frighteningly. Civilization itself implies joint action against violence; taking care of one's own is the law of the jungle.

The House majority leader, Dick Armey (R-TX), was asked what functions the government should perform. He said, "Defend our shores, build a system of justice and construct some infrastructure." He paused to think, then remarked: "Gee, I'm running out of other suggestions."[115] This is a recipe—not only for low taxes and unintrusive government—but also for minimal democracy.

Still, if what I have said about majority interests is true, then it will be difficult to persuade the affluent majority to support government programs, even ones that are well designed. As long as trust in government remains low, it will be especially hard to generate this support. But three factors suggest that it may be possible. First, the affluent majority is not huge—it constitutes no more than 60 percent of the population. Thus a few defections from the upper-middle class can change the balance of power. Under these circumstances, Teddy Roosevelt's bully pulpit may be a significant force after all. Appeals to public-spiritedness would be most effective if people frequently talked to others of different classes, but this happens only in certain types of association. Here, then, is a final reason to support civil society.

Second, it is possible to design effective programs that benefit many and yet cost the remainder of the population only modestly. For example, it would be a political mistake—and also a moral one—to ask working-class families to finance the medical care of the poor. But a well-designed national health insurance program could benefit middle-class people as well as those at the bottom of the income scale, while costing wealthy individuals and corporations a reasonable amount.

Finally, if one reason for the decline of government is majority self-interest, another is political bias. Wealthy people may outnumber the poor: that depends on how we define wealth and poverty. They certainly out-vote and out-contribute everyone else. It should be impossible for some people to wield more political influence than others, simply because they have more money. To prevent this, we need effective political reform as well as civic virtue. Above all, we must reform the way that campaigns are conducted, and that is the subject of chapter 4.

NOTES

1. Michael Sandel, *Democracy's Discontent: America in Search of a Public Philosophy* (Harvard, 1996), p. 221

2. Speech at Sioux Falls, September 3, 1910, speech at Osawatomie, August 31, 1910, both in *The New Nationalism*, by Theodore Roosevelt, ed. William E. Leuchtenburg (1910; reprint Englewood Cliffs, N.J., 1961), pp. 93, 39

3. John Ihlder, "The Development of Civic Spirit" (1909), quoted by Paul Boyer, *Urban Masses and Moral Order in America, 1820–1920* (Cambridge, Mass., 1978), p. 269; Boyer, p. 242.

4. Porter Emerson Browne, "We'll Rally 'round the Flag, Boys!" *McClure's*, vol. 49 (October 1916): 81, quoted in Hofstadter, *The Age of Reform*, (New York, 1955), p. 278.

5. David P. Thelen, *Robert M. La Follette and the Insurgent Spirit* (Madison, Wis., 1985), p. 140.

6. Michael Schudson, *The Good Citizen: A History of American Civic Life* (New York, 1998), p. 182.

7. Speech at the Milwaukee Auditorium, September 7, 1910; speech at Pueblo, August 30, 1910, in ibid., pp. 141–146

8. Alexis de Tocqueville, *Democracy in America*, trans. by Henry Reeve, rev. Francis Bowen and Phillips Bradley (New York, 1954), vol. 2., p. 114; vol. 1, p. 198.

9. Tocqueville, *Democracy in America*, vol. 2., pp. 123, 127, 129, 117, 116–117.

10. George F. Will, "Look at All the Lonely Bowlers," *Washington Post*, January 5, 1995, p. A29.

11. For a sample of twenty-three countries—mostly industrialized democracies—I have compared the following variables: the percentage of people who belong to at least one group (World Values Survey, 1990–1991); the government's share of GDP (Penn World Tables, 1992), and the Heritage Foundation's five-point indices of taxation and government intervention. The correlation between associational membership and government size is .5501; between membership and taxation, it is .0476; and between membership and intervention, it is .5054.

12. Michael Ignatieff, "On Civil Society: Why Eastern Europe's Revolutions Could Succeed," *Foreign Affairs*, vol. 72, no. 2 (March/April 1995): 135.

13. Ronald Inglehart, "Trust, Well-Being and Democracy," paper presented at the Georgetown Conference on Democracy and Trust, November 7–9, 1996, table 3, p. 19. (This and the other Georgetown conference papers cited further on will be published in *Democracy and Trust* ed. Mark Warren [Cambridge, 1999]. Warren's volume was not yet available when *The New Progressive Era* went to press.) Inglehart notes that the effects of associational membership on democracy are not statistically significant when he controls for variables such as trust, well-being, GNP, and education. However, he considers Robert Putnam's theory plausible: i.e., that trust boosts associational membership, which supports democracy.

14. Robert D. Putnam, "Bowling Alone: America's Declining Social Capital," *Journal of Democracy*, vol. 6, no. 1 (January 1995): 67.

15. Tocqueville, *Democracy in America*, vol. 2, p. 120.

16. Tocqueville, *Democracy in America,* vol. 2, p. 115.

17. World Values Surveys, 1990–1991, analyzed by the author. The parts of Germany that were formally Communist also had slightly higher rates of membership than the United States in 1990–1991.

18. "Brotherhoods of Oddballs: America's Strange Clubs," *The Economist* (December 23, 1995): 29–30.

19. For the percentage of employees who are unionized, see "Workers of the World" (chart), in The *Washington Post*, August 30, 1997; for the percentage of adults who say

they're in unions, see the World Values Survey; and for social time, see OECD, *Living Conditions in OECD Countries* (Paris, 1986), table 18.2. See also James E. Curtis, Edward G. Grabb, and Douglas E. Baer, "Voluntary Association Membership in Fifteen Countries: A Comparative Analysis," *American Sociological Review* 57 (April 1992): 139–152, which argues that America's comparative advantage results largely from our high level of church membership. That, in turn, may arise from "extensive sectarianism" and "the comparatively aggressive 'marketing' of religion to the American populace" (pp. 148, 149). I have also heard Seymour Martin Lipset suggest that Protestants are more likely than Catholics to say that they belong to a church "organization"; Catholics do not consider the Body of Christ to be an organization. This hypothesis can be tested to a degree. In 1987, the General Social Survey (GSS) asked people: "You said you were a member of a church-affiliated group. Is that group or organization the church (synagogue) itself, or some other group related to the church?" Protestants were most likely to say that they had counted their congregations as "groups" (at 56.5 percent), followed by Catholics (47.2 percent) and Jews (37.5 percent). This difference in definitions could partially account for high levels of reported group membership in Protestant countries.

20. See an article written with William A. Galston, "America's Civic Condition: A Glance at the Evidence," *The Brookings Review*, vol. 15, no. 4 (Fall 1997): 23–26. This article is reprinted in *Community Works: The Revival of Civil Society in America*, ed. E. J. Dionne, Jr. (Washington, D.C.: Brookings Institution Press, 1998), pp. 30–36.

21. GSS data on organizational membership, analyzed by the author; Putnam, "Bowling Alone," pp. 69–72.

22. Eric Uslaner, "Faith, Hope, and Charity: Social Capital, Trust, and Collective Action." Excerpt from book in progress, circulated at conference sponsored by the Pew Charitable Trusts, the National Commission on Civil Renewal and the Brookings Institution, November 25, 1996, table 2.

23. Eric Uslaner, "Social Capital, Television, and the 'Mean World': Trust, Optimism, and Civic Participation," *Political Psychology,* vol. 19, no. 3 (1998): 459; Uslaner, "Faith, Hope, and Charity," table 5. Note, however, that compared to other types of participation, union membership is a relatively weak predictor of overall associational membership. The relative contribution ("standardized loading") of union membership to associational membership is just 0.04. See John Brehm and Wendy Rahn, "Individual Level Evidence for the Causes and Consequences of Social Capital," *American Journal of Political Science,* vol. 41, no. 3 (July 1997): 1007.

24. Robert Putnam, "Tuning In, Tuning Out: The Strange Disappearance of Social Capital in America," *PS: Political Science and Politics,* December 1995, fig. 1.

25. See Theda Skocpol, "The Tocqueville Problem: Civic Engagement in American Democracy," presidential address for the Social Science History Association, October 12, 1996, p. 29.

26. World Values data.

27. Sidney Verba, Kay Lehman Schlozman, and Henry E. Brady, *Voice and Equality: Civic Voluntarism in American Politics* (Cambridge, Mass., 1995), pp. 18, 282–283.

28. Uslaner, "Faith, Hope, and Charity," pp. 9–10.

29. Verba et al., *Voice and Equality,* p. 327. Episcopalians—a nonevangelical group—use even more civic skills in their churches than Baptists do, but they have considerably higher incomes and educational levels. Controlling for socioeconomic status, membership in a Baptist church seems to increase civic skills dramatically.

30. Source: GSS.

31. GSS data show that fundamentalists distrust "most people" at a 10 percent higher rate than moderates, and at a 24 percent higher rate than liberals—even adjusting for income. According to Uslaner, the link between pride in one's own group and general distrust is high for fundamentalists: "Faith, Hope, and Charity," p. 50, note 5.

32. Uslaner, "Faith, Hope, and Charity," p. 18.

33. Eric Eckholm, "The Dark Science of Fund-Raising by Mail," *New York Times*, May 28, 1995, p. E6.

34. Putnam, "Bowling Alone," p. 71.

35. George Pettinico, "Civic Participation: Alive and Well in Today's Environmental Groups," *The Public Perspective* (June/July 1996): 27.

36. Theda Skocpol, "Unravelling from Above," *The American Prospect* (March/April 1996): 21–22.

37. Source: GSS.

38. Eric Uslaner, "Democracy and Social Capital," paper presented at the Georgetown Conference on Democracy and Trust, Washington, D.C., November 7–9, 1996, p. 14.

39. Eric Uslaner, *The Decline of Comity in Congress* (Ann Arbor, Mich., 1993), p. 149.

40. Martin Luther King, Jr., "Our Struggle," *Liberation* 1 (April 1957): 3–6, in James M. Washington, ed., *I Have a Dream: Writings and Speeches That Changed the World*, ed. James M. Washington (Glenview, Ill., 1992), p. 6.

41. Uslaner, "Faith, Hope, and Charity," tables 2, 4, 5, 6, and 7; Brehm and Rahn, "Individual Level Evidence," pp. 1012–1013.

42. Uslaner, "Social Capital, Television, and the 'Mean World,'" p. 449; Brehm and Rahn, "Individual Level Evidence," p. 1017.

43. Source: GSS. For the 1960 figure, see Putnam, "Bowling Alone," p. 73.

44. University of Michigan National Election Studies, cited in Inglehart, "Trust, Well-Being and Democracy," figure 9.

45. GSS data.

46. Poll by Yankelovich Partners, cited in *Getting the Connections Right: Public Journalism and the Troubles in the Press*, by Jay Rosen (New York, 1996), p. 22.

47. Source: GSS.

48. Since 1972, 80 percent of African-American respondents have stated that most people *cannot* be trusted most of the time, compared to 51 percent of whites. Part of the cause may be African Americans' warranted distrust for whites; only 7 percent report that they trust "most" white people. African Americans' attitudes toward government institutions are more polarized than whites' attitudes. (Source: GSS.)

49. Orlando Patterson, "Liberty against the Democratic State: On the Historical and Contemporary Sources of American Distrust," unpublished paper. pp. 23–24.

50. Derek Bok, "Measuring the Performance of Government," in *Why People Don't Trust Government*, ed. Joseph S. Nye, Philip D. Zelikow, and David C. King (Cambridge, Mass., 1997), p. 62. Bok provides no source, but he may be citing a *Washington Post* poll of August 10, 1993.

51. Robert Z. Lawrence, "Is It Really the Economy, Stupid?" in ibid., p. 125.

52. GSS data; cf. Brehm and Rahn, "Individual Level Evidence," p. 1013.

53. Robert Wuthnow, "The Role of Trust in Civic Renewal," in *Civil Society, Democracy, and Civic Renewal*, ed. Robert K. Fullinwider (Lanham, Md., 1999), p. 212.

54. Patterson, "Liberty against the Democratic State," p. 24.

55. Quoted in Kevin Philips, *Boiling Point: Democrats, Republicans, and the Decline of Middle-Class Prosperity* (New York, 1993), p. 47.

56. Jane Jacobs, *The Death and Life of Great American Cities* (New York, 1961), pp. 35, 32

57. See *Confronting the Nation's Urban Crisis: From Watts (1965) to South Central Los Angeles (1992)* (Urban Institute, 1992), p. 5.

58. Ralph Blumenthal, "Private Guards Cooperate in Public Policing," *New York Times*, July 13, 1993, p. B1.

59. Timothy Egan, "Many Seek Security in Private Communities," *New York Times*, September 13, 1995, p. A1.

60. George Cantor, "Searching for New Living Arrangements," *The Detroit News*, April 26, 1998, p. B5.

61. GSS. See also Thomas M. Guterbock and John C. Fries, "Maintaining America's Social Fabric: The AARP Survey of Civic Involvement" (Washington, D.C., December 1997), pp. 93–96.

62. Uslaner, "Democracy and Social Capital," p. 29; Patterson, "Liberty against the Democratic State," figure 12. The negative correlation between television watching and trust was confirmed by Guterbock and Fries's 1997 poll (p. 94).

63. Pippa Norris, "Does Television Erode Social Capital? A Reply to Putnam," *PS: Political Science & Politics* (September 1996): 476, table 1; p. 479, appendix A1. Norris uses the American Citizen Participation Survey (1990), but I found substantially the same results using GSS data. However, for a skeptical view, see Uslaner, "Social Capital, Television, and the 'Mean World,'" pp. 460–461. Two recent surveys discover a strong connection between TV watching and distrust, but none between viewing hours and civic participation: see the Pew Research Center for Public Life and the Press, "Trust and Citizen Engagement in Metropolitan Philadelphia: A Case Study" (1997); and Guterbock and Fries, "Maintaining America's Social Fabric," pp. 23, 94.

64. The Tyndall Report (headed by Andrew Tyndall), as reported in The *Washington Post*, August 10, 1997, p. C5. In 1992, the Center for Media and Public Affairs found that 1,846 episodes of violence were shown on broadcast and cable television between 6 A.M. and midnight on one day in Washington, D.C. Violent events were most common during prime time (165.5 per hour). R. S. Lichter, and D. Amundson, "A Day of Television Violence" (Washington, D.C.: Center for Media and Public Affairs, 1992).

65. Putnam, "Tuning In, Tuning Out," p. 679. However, see Uslaner, "Social Capital, Television, and the 'Mean World,'" pp. 450–455.

66. Amy Gutmann and Dennis Thompson, *Democracy and Disagreement* (Cambridge, Mass., 1996), p. 83.

67. Kathleen Hall Jamieson and Joseph N. Capella in the *Atlanta Journal and Constitution* (September 15, 1994), quoted in *Breaking the News: How the Media Undermine American Democracy*, by James Fallows (New York, 1996), p. 204.

68. Richard Morin, "Who's in Control? Many Don't Know or Care," *Washington Post*, January 29, 1996, pp. A1, A6. Delli Carpini's comments are presumably based on the book he wrote with Scott Keeter, *What Americans Know about Politics and Why It Matters* (New Haven, Conn., 1996), pp. 230–267. See also: League of Women Voters press release, August 26, 1996, "Survey Indicates Nonvoters Lack Information, Recognition of the Consequences of Elections" (poll conducted in March of 1996).

69. See notes 1 and 2 to the introduction.

70. The percentage of people able to identify their own U.S. representative has fluctuated from 38 in 1947, to 46 in 1973, to 37 in 1987, to 29 in 1989, to 33 in 1995. The last figure comes from the *Post* survey; the rest are reported in *The Rational Public: Fifty Years of Trends in Americans' Policy Preferences*, by Benjamin I. Page and Robert Y. Shapiro (Chicago, 1992), p. 11. See also Delli Carpini and Keeter, *What Americans Know about Politics*, p. 117.

71. Walter Lippmann, *The Phantom Public* (New York, 1925), pp. 125, 38–39. He reached this conclusion after having presented more specific evidence—but a less radical thesis—in *Public Opinion* (New York, 1922).

72. George Gallup and Saul Forbes Rae, *The Pulse of Democracy: The Public-Opinion Poll and How It Works* (New York, 1968) pp. 284, 289, 287.

73. Angus Campbell, Philip E. Converse, Warren E. Miller, and Donald E. Stokes, *The American Voter* (New York, 1960), pp. 151, 542, 543, 544.

74. Philip E. Converse, "The Nature of Belief Systems in Mass Publics," in David E. Apter, ed., *Ideology and Discontent* (New York, 1964), pp. 240–242.

75. For a more optimistic reinterpretation of the same and other data, see Page and Shapiro, *The Rational Public*.

76. Anthony Downs, *An Economic Theory of Democracy* (New York: 1957), pp. 259, 267, 274

77. Delli Carpini and Keeter, *What Americans Know about Politics*, pp. 214–215.

78. "The Port Huron Statement," reprinted in Miller, *Democracy Is in the Streets: From Port Huron to the Siege of Chicago* (New York, 1987), p. 335. See p. 25 for a discussion of the Michigan School and SDS.

79. See Samuel P. Huntington, "The United States," in *The Crisis of Democracy*, by Michael Crozier, Samuel Huntington, and Jaji Watanuki (New York, 1975).

80. Source: NES cumulative datafile. These data do not permit comparisons to earlier decades, but the fraction of the people who followed politics and government "most of the time" rose from 20 percent in 1960 to 30 percent in 1964, then hovered between 30 percent and 40 percent until 1976, after which political interest declined again.

81. Richard G. Niemi and Jane Junn, *Civic Education: What Makes Students Learn* (New Haven, Conn., 1998), p. 11.

82. The most recent GSS data that permit us to analyze these correlations date from 1984–1987. At that point, the correlation between income and political knowledge (i.e., correctly naming one's U.S. representative) was 0.8; between income and voting, it was .83; between education (i.e., the highest degree received) and political knowledge, it was .93; and between education and voting, it was .98. Whites were 9 percent more likely to say that they had voted than blacks were, and 30.2 percent more likely than members of other races. Also, whites were 14 percent more likely to name their U.S. representatives than blacks were, and 6 percent more likely than members of other races. See also Delli Carpini and Keeter, *What Americans Know about Politics*, pp. 157,

83. U.S. Bureau of the Census, Current Population Reports, pp. 60–200, *Money Income in the United States: 1997 (with Separate Data on Valuation of Noncash Benefits)*, Washington, D.C., 1998, Table B; "A Look at Voting Patterns of 115 Demographic Groups in House Races" (reporting Voter News Service data), *New York Times*, November 6, 1998, p. A20.

84. Huntington, "The United States," p. 110; GSS.

85. Norman H. Nie, Jane Junn, and Kenneth Stehlik-Barry, *Education and Democratic Citizenship in America* (Chicago, 1996), p. 31.

86. Nie et al., *Education and Democratic Citizenship,* p. 48, fig. 3.4; p. 55, fig. 3.5.

87. Steven Rosenstone and John Mark Hansen, *Mobilization, Participation, and Democracy in America* (New York, 1993), p. 215

88. Verba, Schlozman, and Brady, *Voice and Equality,* pp. 135, 150.

89. Guterbock and Fries found ("Maintaining America's Social Fabric," p. 23): "Those who read the newspaper every day have a much higher social involvement score (6.8) than those who read the paper less than once a week."

90. GSS data show that the more types of membership you have, the more likely you are to be able to name your own governor (r = .814), your U.S. representative (r = .756), and your local school head (r = .863). Only 25 percent of people with no memberships can recognize their representative, compared to 69 percent of people with eight types of membership. Membership correlates with knowledge even controlling for education and income. For example, lower-middle class people (i.e., those with family incomes between $15,000 and $25,000 in 1986) who belong to hobby clubs are 23 percent more likely than nonhobbyists of the same class to know the name of their representative. College graduates are 19 percent more likely to recognize their governor's name if they belong to a church group than if they don't. If we look only at people near the median income, those who belong to church groups are 20 percent more likely to work on community problems than those who don't. Similarly, participation in a church association can compensate for a lack of college education. Church-group members who have not attended college are more likely to be able to name their U.S. representative than people with four years of college who don't participate in church associations. Only the very poor do not seem to gain much information from the organizations they join, perhaps because they rarely become group leaders.

91. Verba, Schlozman, and Brady. *Voice and Equality,* p. 147.

92. GSS data.

93. Verba, Schlozman, and Brady, *Voice and Equality,* p. 57.

94. See Nie et al., *Education and Democratic Citizenship,* p. 102.

95. "When an opinion is represented by a society," he writes, "it necessarily assumes a more exact and explicit form." See Tocqueville, *Democracy in America,* vol. 1, p. 199.

96. It is also worth noting that the proportion of first-year college students who said that they "discuss[ed] politics frequently" dropped to its lowest recorded level in 1995: 14.8 percent. Even in 1968, when protesters were occupying campus buildings, cities were burning, and college graduates were subject to a wartime draft, just under 30 percent of college freshmen said that they often talked about politics. See UCLA's Cooperative Institutional Research Program, press release, "1995 Freshman Survey Results Released," January 1996.

97. Donald Kinder and Lynn M. Sanders argue that Americans may lack stable and consistent political opinions generally, but they have such opinions about race—yet their views of race are deeply divided, and little interracial discussion occurs. See Kinder and Sanders, *Divided by Color: Racial Politics and Democratic Ideals* (Chicago, 1996), p. 33.

98. John Milton Cooper, Jr., *The Warrior and the Priest: Woodrow Wilson and Theodore Roosevelt* (Cambridge, Mass., 1983), p. 84.

99. Walter Rauschenbusch, *Christianity and the Social Crisis* (1907; reprint, New York, 1991), p. 250.

100. According to an NBC News/*Wall Street Journal* poll taken in December 1998, 46 percent of Americans described themselves as "middle class"; 16 percent, "upper middle class"; 29 percent, "working class"; 6 percent, "poor"; and 2 percent, "well-to-do."

101. *USA Today* poll of 1,003 adults, March 26, 1993.

102. U.S. Bureau of the Census, Current Population Reports, pp. 60–200, *Money Income in the United States: 1997*, table B.

103. Census Bureau figures for 1993.

104. John Kenneth Galbraith, *The Affluent Society* (New York, 1984), pp. xxvi–xxvii.

105. *New York Times*/CBS poll, reported September 25, 1991.

106. David S. Broder and Richard Morin, "The Public Wants a Revolution, Unsure of which Faction to Join," *Washington Post*, September 12, 1993, p. A28.

107. The figure is for 1997: see Census Bureau press release, "Number of Americans without Insurance Coverage Increases in 1997," September 28, 1998.

108. *New York Times* poll reported on March 15, 1994, p. B8.

109. "Portrait of the Electorate," *New York Times*, November 13, 1994, p. 24 (chart).

110. Eli Ginzberg in the *New York Times*, November 12, 1992. Medicaid provided coverage for 7.4 percent of the population in 1988, according the *Statistical Abstract of the United States*.

111. *Statistical Abstract.*

112. Sam Howe Verhovek, "Texans Reject Sharing School Wealth," *New York Times*, May 3, 1993, p. A12.

113. Michael Barone, David Gergen, and Kenneth T. Walsh, "The Rebel Yell Of America's Suburbs," *U.S. News and World Report*, vol. 111, no. 21, p. 44.

114. Of voters in the poorest third of the population, 30 percent are Democrats and 11 percent are Republicans (NES). But most of them don't vote. Another way of describing the same phenomenon is to say that voters in the lowest quintile have been 28.5 percent more Democratic and 24 percent less likely to vote than average Americans since 1980; those in the highest quintile have been 27.5 percent more Republican and 17 percent more likely to vote than average. See Warren E. Miller and J. Merrill Shanks, *The New American Voter* (Cambridge, Mass.: 1996), pp. 532–533, tables B5.1, B5.3. The gap in partisanship widens if we exclude 1984, when Reagan drew unusually strongly from low-income voters.

115. David E. Sanger, "Republicans Want to Renew Vision of Reagan (Then Redo His Math)," *New York Times*, January 15, 1995, section 1, p. 18.

PART TWO

REFORM PROPOSALS

4

Elections

GENERAL PRINCIPLES

Elections should serve two vital functions. First, they should ensure that government is *fair* by allowing citizens to choose their leaders, with each voter granted equal weight at the ballot box. A duly elected government must pay careful attention to public needs and values, or else it will be unseated at the next election. Second, any election worthy of the name must be preceded by a political campaign, which is an opportunity for broad public deliberation. The "counting of heads," wrote Dewey, "compels prior recourse to methods of discussion, consultation, and persuasion."[1] An election is a private registering of preferences, but the campaign season is a time for inquiry, reflection, and discussion.

If "deliberation" means an effort to reach agreement, then we cannot expect candidates to deliberate with each other, because they have to show why they are better than their opponents. An election is—and ought to be—a competition. However, we might hope that candidates would engage in constructive dialogues with *voters* during campaigns. At the same time, the debate among candidates should enlighten the public's conversation about values, ends, and priorities. Our need to cast votes at the end of the process may force us to turn, at least for a time, to public issues. With the raw material of platforms, speeches, advertisements, debates, and journalistic commentary before us, we should be able to discuss issues collectively and constructively. In fact, without campaigns and elections, it is doubtful that public opinion would form—even to the limited extent that it exists in America today.

By these standards, however, our election system is a failure; it is neither fair nor very deliberative. The majority of adults don't vote at all. Most who do participate find the political debate unilluminating. Rarely does anyone's opinion about the issues change as a result of campaign rhetoric—although sometimes we lower our estimates of the candidates' characters. Nor are the results of elections remotely fair. In order to run for high public office, any potential candidate needs enormous funds. Unless he or she is personally rich, these funds must come from individuals or groups that have compelling political interests. And since the bulk of campaign contributions go to incumbent politicians, they can win reelection even when their behavior and decisions have been basically unpopular.

In total, candidates spent about $10 billion of private money to gain office between 1988 and 1996.[2] Those who pay for the broadcast advertisements, publications, mailing lists, airplane rentals, and phone banks of a modern campaign determine to a significant degree what is said and who wins. These contributors are, by any measure, an extremely affluent slice of the American population. Less than 1 percent of Americans give the vast majority of political contributions. In 1996, 95 percent of the people who contributed at least $200 to congressional campaigns were white; 81 percent were male; 87 percent were older than 45; and 81 percent made over $100,000 per year. More than half made over $250,000; and more than half belonged to "high status mainline Protestant churches."[3]

Under these conditions, citizens do not have equal weight; candidates have grossly unequal resources; the campaign dialogue is distorted; and true deliberation is rare. On election day, the wheels of public opinion are supposed to interlock with the apparatus of government, so that citizens can control the whole mechanism. However, in privately funded campaigns, a different kind of coupling occurs. Public opinion hardly forms on most issues; it certainly doesn't direct the course of political events. Instead, the market manipulates the political system.

A democracy gives each of its citizens one vote; but a market assigns power in proportion to wealth. In a democracy, majorities pass general, binding rules; but in a market, individuals register immediate, concrete, personal preferences. Since these two mechanisms are fundamentally different, their outcomes often conflict. Those who admire the market should be able to vote against government regulation and taxation, and they can argue for their beliefs in public. But they should not have disproportionate political power as a result of their wealth, or else democracy will be swamped by the marketplace. A privately funded election is not fully democratic; to a large extent, it is a financial transaction.

Some theorists reject the emphasis on campaign finance, arguing that corporations do not have to influence government in any deliberate way. The state is "structurally dependent" upon big business, because capitalists tend to lose confidence when the government threatens to harm their interests. When market confidence drops, the economy falters, and incumbent politicians suffer at the polls.[4] For example, a Democratic president may be elected with support from poorer-than-average people, but he cannot raise corporate taxes without upsetting the bond market, thereby reducing tax receipts, worsening the national debt, slowing growth, and requiring budget cuts. If all this is true, then large companies hardly need to make PAC contributions; their interests are automatically protected. Without necessarily meaning to, capitalists hold workers and consumers hostage. Charles Lindblom argues that we need "no conspiracy theory of politics, no theory of common social origins uniting government officials and business officials, no crude allegation of a power elite established by clandestine forces. Business simply needs inducements, hence a privileged position in government and politics, if it is to do its job," which is to generate prosperity. In short, "to make the [economic] system work government leadership must often defer to business leadership."[5]

Structural dependence is a serious intellectual threat to Progressivism. Progressives argue that the government, if protected from specific corrupt influences, can implement fair economic policies. But if businesses inevitably control the state—even without taking any deliberate action—then the Progressive ideal is utopian. No government elected under capitalism will even seriously *try* to change the economic system, and political reform is pointless.

Some versions of the structural-dependence thesis are testable. If the government could never thwart the selfish interests of big business, then it would not matter which party held power. Election results would have no effect on corporate tax rates. However, since 1955, Democratic governments have taxed corporations considerably more heavily than Republican administrations have. Likewise, if the government were structurally dependent on business, then we would expect corporate taxes to be at their lowest during recessions, because then the state would be especially reliant on businesses to produce wealth and jobs. In fact, firms are taxed most heavily during lean years, because the public demands more from its government at those times.[6]

These data seem to rebut the structural-dependence thesis. But proponents can respond as follows. Structural dependence is a matter of unintentional, uncoordinated market behavior, so no one should expect it to determine the *nuances* of federal policy. Of course, businesses must use PACs and lobbyists if they want to persuade the government to make fine adjustments in tax rates. But perhaps the broad outlines of American politics are determined by structural dependence. In that case, we can blame the political power of capital for a generally unfair economy.

Put this way, structural dependence is closer to an ideology than a theory: it cannot be tested against concrete evidence. It seems to me that there is a more plausible explanation for America's faithfulness to capitalism: no comprehensive alternative enjoys significant popular support. Some Americans are socialists, anarchists, radical environmentalists, neofascists, Christian communitarians, or Moslem fundamentalists, but their total numbers probably do not exceed one million. This does not mean that the free market is a consensus ideal; rather, our mixed economy seems better than any speculative and ill-defined alternative. Proponents of structural dependence can respond that we should *ignore* popular opinion, because public discourse and beliefs are shaped by capital. But anyone who dismisses the majority view as "inauthentic" must have an extremely high estimation of his or her own independence and wisdom.

If we reject the structural-dependence thesis, then how should we react when politicians seem terrified to take any action against the rich and powerful, for fear of harming the overall economy? First, we should observe that taxes and regulations cannot be imposed without cost, as long as we have a basically capitalist system. To some extent, therefore, it is rational to coddle the securities markets. We should also note, however, that politicians frequently overestimate the costs and underestimate the benefits of taxing wealthy interests. The reason is not structural dependence, but rather the specific and deliberate influence of money on politics. And this influence is strongest during campaigns.

The problem is not that too much money is spent to elect candidates. It is expensive to communicate to huge audiences, especially when everyone else with a product, service, or idea also wants to tell the world about it. The total cost of all 1996 campaigns—about $20 per voting-age person—does not seem excessive, especially considering that thousands of uncoordinated races were run.[7] Television time, mass mailings, and campaign travel are expensive commodities. But if we are not concerned about the *amount* of campaign funds, we should worry about their *source, distribution,* and *destination.* Although money tends to flow to capable candidates (thereby cementing some foreordained outcomes), it also affects the results of elections, measurably improving the chances of politicians who have wealthy supporters.[8] These donors usually have interests that they want to promote in government. Most of their money goes to powerful incumbent politicians; very little reaches insurgents and outsiders. Finally, their funds too often buy forms of communication that are harmful to democracy.

A CORRUPT SYSTEM

The money that is used in federal elections has been disclosed since the 1970s. Most states also have adequate reporting requirements. However, disclosure has not satisfied the majority of Americans. A system of disclosed but basically unregulated donations is unstable, because it constantly suggests that our election system is corrupt. Virtually all incumbents and serious challengers file long lists of wealthy contributors: organizations, trade groups, and individuals. Every time a politician acts in the interests of one of these donors, it is plausible to suspect undue influence. Since candidates from both major parties disclose similar lists, voters cannot punish the recipients of campaign money at the polls. This is one reason for the precipitous decline in political trust since 1970. In turn, low trust discourages public engagement and makes public service unattractive.

According to a national poll taken in 1997, three-quarters of Americans believe that "many public officials make or change policy decisions as a result of money that they receive from major contributors."[9] Most ordinary citizens suspect that wealthy donors exert disproportionate influence; in fact, four out of five say that the government is run "for a few big interests looking out for themselves" and not for "the benefit of all the people."[10] Under these circumstances, the high-minded rhetoric of politicians often rings false, since their views on any particular issue may be calculated to maximize campaign funds. Because the current system seems to many Americans to violate basic moral principles of equity and integrity, large majorities support fundamental reform.

Public dismay at the campaign-finance system has been caused, in part, by anecdotes about wealthy lobbyists who appear to wield unseemly power. Reformers often point to the example of Charles H. Keating, Jr., owner of the now-defunct Lincoln Savings & Loan, who arranged for more than $1.3 million in contributions and financial benefits to flow to the reelection campaigns of five U.S. senators. These senators summoned the government's chief thrift regulator, Edwin Gray, to a private meeting on Capitol Hill and demanded to know why Lincoln S & L was being investigated. Instead of being sanctioned, Lincoln was granted new federal loans—only to fail, thereby costing taxpayers at least $2 billion. When Keating was asked whether his contributions had influenced the senators to help him, he responded: "I want to say in the most forceful way I can: I certainly hope so."[11]

Despite such anecdotes, academic experts caution that donors do not hold all the power in their exchanges with elected officials. Firms and organizations may feel compelled to contribute to powerful incumbents. For their part, legislators have so many potential sources of funds that they can choose their positions with considerable freedom. As Representative Barney Frank (D-MA) has said, "There's money any way you vote."[12] Most social scientists who have analyzed the statistical data believe that contributors "buy" relatively little influence from elected officials. A task force on campaign finance reform, composed of leading experts, argues that special-interest contributions have only a slight impact on "the roll-call behavior of legislators." The task force cites "a long line of empirical research" to bolster its case.[13]

The academic literature has indeed concentrated on the relationship between money and roll-call votes. But it is precisely the emphasis on voting that has led scholars to underestimate the impact of contributions. Compared to other legislative acts, votes are the easiest to analyze, but also the least susceptible to special-interest pressure. Since they are public, they can be assessed by party leaders, journalists, constituents, and potential challengers. A vote can be counted, categorized, and compared to previous behavior. Inconsistencies can be unmasked; broken promises can be challenged. Thus candidates are heavily constrained when they vote, and they cannot easily do their contributors' bidding.

If votes are relatively safe from financial pressures, however, they are also relatively unimportant. The House of Representatives passes no more than one of every six bills introduced. We have detailed statistics for 1989–90, when only 15 percent of House bills were even reported to committee; just 4 percent became law—and half of those were uncontroversial "commemorative resolutions."[14] Legislation that failed after being reported to committees almost always died for lack of scheduled hearings: actual defeats on the floor of Congress were rare. Thus powerful representatives who wanted to kill legislation could easily do so without risking a recorded vote. Most votes were formalities that House leaders permitted only once they could predict a satisfactory outcome.

There is a second reason not to overemphasize voting. Congress passes more than 7,000 pages of legislation in any two-year period.[15] Only a handful of members help to draft or amend each of these pages; hardly anyone else can say what was in them, let alone influence their details. Particularly in the House of Representatives (where floor amendments are generally prohibited), a vote cannot affect the content of legislation.

In order for a specific provision to be included in a bill, to reach a committee, to receive hearings, to survive a floor vote, and to pass unscathed through a conference committee, it must have active sponsors who are either exceptionally dedicated and focused or else powerful. In some cases, writes Richard Hall, "a standing committee of reputed legislative specialists reduces to only two or three players, who bargain among themselves with relative impunity on significant (though not necessarily salient) matters of public policy."[16] What lobbyists need, therefore, is the active and careful attention of a few members who are willing to draft language, move bills through the committee process, and conduct negotiations. In addition, they want their potential opponents in Congress not to interfere until the formality of a final vote.

This is why lobbyists give most heavily to well-placed incumbents who are either especially friendly or else deeply hostile to their concerns. As Hall and Frank Wayman put it, donors want to "mobilize legislative support and demobilize opposition, especially at the most important points in the legislative process."[17] And they apparently get what they pay for. Hall and Wayman found that PAC contributions correlated with participation in three major legislative battles of the early 1980s. In general, friendly incumbents who received PAC money attended hearings, offered substitute bills, and negotiated deals. Those opponents who received PAC funds refrained from active participation.[18]

Despite studies showing that money has a weak effect on legislative votes, the journalist Philip M. Stern has produced several charts like the following.

Donations Received from the Dairy Lobby, 1979–1986	Votes for the Dairy Subsidy in 1985
More than $30,000	100 percent
$20,000–$30,000	97
$10,000–$20,000	81
$2,500–$10,000	60
$1–$2,500	33
Zero	23

This one illustrates the relationship between contributions from the dairy lobby and votes in favor of a dairy subsidy in 1985—a subsidy that (Stern says) cost taxpayers $1 billion a year and added up to 60 cents to the price of a gallon of milk.[19]

These raw figures give an obvious impression of corruption. However, Stern does not perform the kind of statistical analysis that the experts on the task force recommend; he does not weigh the relative importance of money compared to legislators' ideologies, their party identities, and the composition of their districts. Even the most sophisticated analysis cannot peer into politicians' minds to determine their motivations. But, presumably, some members of Congress who vote with the dairy industry (and receive its PAC money) support agricultural subsidies as a matter of principle; and some represent districts that depend on dairy farming.[20]

Public officials typically deny that they ever vote based on promises of campaign money—not even when all the donations come from one side. Rather, they vote their consciences, and then friendly interests reward them financially. Mary Crawford, a spokesperson for the Republican National Committee, explained that donors who paid $250,000 to sit at a head table with congressional leaders did not hope to buy access or influence; instead, they wanted to support the party's historical principles, especially low taxation.[21]

Lobbyists often say the same thing, even within their own organizations. For instance, according to a private General Electric Company memorandum, GE gave $93,000 to members of Congress who had previously "contributed to the company's success in saving us over $300 million" in taxes. One representative's efforts to "protect" a $20-million contract "alone justifies supporting him," the memo said.[22] Likewise, an official at the National Education Association's PAC claimed that representatives "behave as they would anyway, and the money comes after."[23]

Even if this is true, it offers little comfort to ordinary citizens. Those candidates who favor moneyed interests—whether out of a sincere commitment or a desire for campaign funds—generally raise enough money to win reelection; but those who consistently fight special interests are defunded and defeated. Newcomers to politics who lack either personal wealth or affluent friends cannot win office in the first place. In the long run, Congress fills up with members who support the interests of large contributors over the needs of underfinanced or unorganized constituencies. Money doesn't influence votes so much as it screens out troublesome politicians, determining who can hold public office in the first place.

There are, of course, exceptions: candidates who win without generous donors. For the most part, however, these are either politicians with personal fortunes; incumbents who were first elected decades ago and have remained popular; or representatives from politically uncompetitive districts in which churches and unions are springboards to public office. These exceptions account for just a few percent of the total membership of Congress. All the other legislators have survived "screening" by the campaign-finance system, which partially explains why our major parties are so similar and so reliably pro-corporate.[24]

Sometimes, wealthy contributors are able to buy specific action or inaction with their political donations. More frequently—and, in a way, more insidiously—special-interest money alters the nature of the political debate. The need to raise campaign funds (and to prevent one's opponent from doing so effectively) discourages politicians from broaching controversial questions on the campaign trail in ways that might offend well-funded interests. Most candidates are willing to run afoul of some special-interest groups whose views they oppose on principle. But when any policy idea that a politician articulates carries a risk of offending a well-funded lobby, there is a powerful incentive not to deal concretely and specifically with most issues. And if many issues are ignored in campaigns, then members of Congress arrive in Washington without a mandate or a clear sense of the public's wishes.

It is difficult for candidates who disagree with certain high-profile groups, such as the National Rifle Association (NRA), to avoid tangling with them: the NRA often forces politicians to support or oppose gun control publicly, and attacks those with whom it disagrees. Other groups operate more discreetly, yet provide at least as much money to candidates. Organizations such as the National Association of Realtors sometimes contribute to as many as 540 congressional candidates in a single year. Most of these candidates do not take strong public stands in support of the realtors, but neither do they adopt positions that would harm their donors' interests. It is true that the PACs for realtors, developers, builders, and construction workers have conflicting interests, and all give widely. Thus, when these groups find themselves divided on an issue, their money may not carry the day. But there is no PAC for homeowners, renters, or the homeless. Thus candidates have good reason not to invoke their interests in any specific and binding way.

Regulation of savings and loans is an example of an issue that was ignored until it became a disaster. During the 1980s, Congress quietly deregulated the troubled industry without reducing federal insurance liabilities or creating an adequate insurance fund. By 1988, insiders knew that a huge bailout would be necessary. The Democratic presidential nominee, Michael Dukakis, had good reasons to make this scandal a campaign issue. However, his running mate, Lloyd Bentsen, Democratic Speaker Jim Wright, and House Banking Committee Chair Fernand J. St. Germain (D-RI) had all received savings-and-loan money and had voted to deregulate the industry. Between 1981 and 1990, S & L PACs and owners gave nearly $12 million to members of Congress, funding all but two of the seventy-one senators and representatives who sat on banking committees. Early in the eighties, the U.S. League of Savings Institutions had spent more than $2,000 a month on meals, entertainment, and travel for St. Germain, who cowrote the main deregulation act.[25] Bentsen and Wright told Dukakis to drop the issue, and St. Germain silenced most of the House Democrats. As a result, the

1988 campaign dealt with flag burning and the ACLU, the death penalty and Willie Horton, but not with an economic issue of vast public importance.

John Barry, the author of a highly sympathetic book about Speaker Wright, has argued that Wright only helped Texas savings and loans in their dealings with regulators because he did not understand the nature of the crisis. If this account is accurate, then Wright was less venal than some of the other key players, notably St. Germain. But Barry concedes that Wright's information about S & Ls came almost exclusively from thrift owners and lobbyists, which must have distorted his perspective considerably. Here, then, is a final explanation for the influence of money on politics. As well as preventing dissident politicians from winning office, affecting who participates behind the scenes, and keeping certain issues out of the public debate, campaign contributions also distort the flow of information to political insiders. Senator Robert Torricelli (D-NJ) said that he raised money over the telephone for about three hours every day between August 1995 and November 1996. During that time, he also attended more than 300 fundraising events.[26] For the 2000 presidential campaign, it is widely expected that competitive campaigns will raise $25 million. Since the maximum contribution from any individual is $1,000, and since large donors usually want to talk personally to the candidates, would-be presidents will have to hold 25,000 successful conversations with $1,000 contributors over a two-year period, or 34 every day. There won't be much time left to speak to anyone else.

Special interests provide incumbents with much more money than they need to beat their impoverished challengers. The last year for which we have aggregate data on campaign spending is 1992. This was supposed to be a competitive election; incumbents would have to spend every available penny to hold on to their seats. Yet House incumbents still had $67 million when the campaign was over, and senators had $23 million. More than half of their expenditures went to purposes unrelated to traditional campaigning. For example, House candidates spent just 27 percent of their money on TV and radio.[27] Incumbents used a substantial portion of their campaign money to improve their styles of life and to gain the goodwill of constituents and colleagues through gifts and contributions. In 1990, Senator Alan Simpson (R-WY) bought a $4,000 ticket to Australia for his wife; then Representative Robert Torricelli (D-NJ) spent $7,400 on meals in at least four countries; and Representative Tom Lantos (D-CA) paid his daughter $25,000 for "consulting fees."[28] Many members of Congress channel excess campaign funds to their peers when they seek preferment within Congress and to state legislators to ensure friendly treatment when their districts are redrawn. Some use campaign funds to buy cars, take constituents to ball games, endow scholarships, and send thousands of dollars' worth of Christmas cards and flowers.

Large campaign war chests serve the same function that political machines used to serve: they make incumbent politicians rich and turn them into dispensers of favors. No longer does Tammany Hall send Christmas turkeys into poor Irish neighborhoods. Instead, members of Congress buy flowers, meals, or even Super Bowl tickets for their constituents, using special-interest money.

When a virtually unchallenged incumbent asks a PAC for thousands of dollars, the PAC can only conclude that the incumbent wants the money for himself. For instance, when lobbyists gave money to Representative Bud Shuster (R-PA), who spent $178,000 from his campaign account on *meals* between 1988 and 1992, they could not have thought that they were saving him from electoral defeat.[29] Rather, they were giving a member of Congress extra spending money, which is generally called a bribe.

There are defenders of the current campaign-finance system who see it as evidence of healthy political participation and competition. For instance, Senator Mitch McConnell (R-KY) says that the current system is not "a scandal at all. . . . I think it ought to be applauded and encouraged."[30] He writes, "The campaign finance reform debate . . . is advanced on the premise that special interest influence is pervasive, corrosive, and must be abated at all costs. But the cost of the alleged reforms in terms of constitutional freedoms for all Americans is high. And the special interest premise is deeply flawed." The phrase "special interest," McConnell argues, is just a pejorative way to describe groups that exercise their right to petition government.[31]

The Task Force on Campaign Finance Reform also depicts organized donors as legitimate participants in civil society. "We do not share the animus to PACs that is commonplace among reformers," the members write:

> Rather than rejecting PACs as tools of "special interests," we view them in the context of the larger stream of American political life which, as Alexis de Toqueville [sic] observed in the 1830s, has often witnessed the creation of new forms of association to further people's interests and goals. We take the view that such activity inevitably comes with a vibrant democracy. PACs represent an aspect of American pluralist democracy which we must accept, and not solely because the rights of association and speech are protected by the First Amendment.[32]

In this passage, we see the distilled essence of what Theodore Lowi called "interest-group liberalism." Interest-group liberals defend a system of competition if everyone has an equal right—or, according to some, an equal capacity—to participate, and if no faction is so strong that it can overwhelm the others. Thus Frank Sorauf is glad to report that the "countervailing controls of American pluralism constrain even the most determined PACs," at least when their issues have public visibility.[33] For the sake of argument, imagine that everyone contributed money to political campaigns and that all the contributions canceled each other out. Then the system would be ideal in the terms of interest-group liberalism. But even under these unlikely conditions, consider what would happen to the basic values and principles of democracy—what Lowi calls "the very ethic of government."[34] A policy would be "legitimate" and would serve "the national interest" if statistics showed that campaign money was evenly balanced on all sides of the issue. "Participation" would mean check writing or other activities of comparable market value. "Equality" would imply that everyone had an equal capacity to send a check. "Civil society" would be composed of registered political action committees. "Transparency" and "openness" would mean full disclosure of all campaign money. The "rule of law" would require that actual bribery be punished and that violations of spending and contribution limits be prosecuted. "Principle" would become largely irrelevant.

Finally, under such a system, words like *discussion* and *debate* would gain new and disturbing definitions. "Ours is a government by discussion," said the Progressive reformer Fred Howe optimistically, when he first joined the Cleveland City Council.[35] But consider a letter that Tom DeLay, the House majority whip, wrote to PACs that had previously supported Democrats, offering them a chance to build "a positive future relationship" with Republicans by sending money immediately. The staff member who drafted this letter explained, "we wanted to send a very clear message that we're very serious about winning this debate. The Republican majority of the House needs to be preserved."[36] Note what "debate" has come to mean: a partisan victory engineered by efficient fundraising, with issues and values left utterly unmentioned. That would be true even if principled politicians had the upper hand in their exchanges with PACs—which is a highly optimistic way to read the statistical data.

HOW THE MONEY IS SPENT: POLITICAL CONSULTANTS

Incumbents receive such a large share of the available campaign money that they are able to use some of it to improve their standard of living and to buy influence over other politicians. Another substantial fraction of campaign money purchases just what we would expect: broadcast advertisements and mass mailings. These forms of communication are virtually inevitable, because television, radio, and computerized mailing lists are essential parts of most modern publicity efforts— commercial and religious as well as political. But the fact that they are effective and ubiquitous does not imply that they are good for democracy.

On the contrary, since broadcasts—and, especially, mailings—can be targeted efficiently at likely voters, they do nothing to encourage new participation. Nor do they produce a real dialogue among the candidates. Campaigns sometimes use advertisements or letters to respond to their opponents' charges; but there is rarely a genuine exchange of views. To the extent that dueling advertisements produce a debate, it generally involves ad hominem charges and refutations. Candidates rarely probe their opponents' positions on the issues. Of course, it is legitimate to criticize an opponent's personal behavior and character, but the campaign system arbitrarily favors this kind of discussion over matters of policy.

Broadcast advertisements tend to be short and uninformative. Since politicians need not appear in their TV spots or flyers, they are able to make scurrilous attacks without seriously affecting their own reputations. Finally, both mailings and advertisements travel only one way: *from* candidates *to* voters. Of course, politicians try to learn what the public thinks, but mainly through polls instead of direct encounters that might permit mutual persuasion. Most of their direct encounters have to be with potential campaign donors. It is unfortunate that debates, personal contacts, and sustained written or spoken arguments do not play more important roles in modern campaigns.

A third, very substantial, portion of campaign money flows to professional political consultants, who now constitute an industry of their own. In 1992, consultants charged federal candidates $249 million in fees and expenses: this was 46 percent of all congressional campaign expenditures.[37] Some House candidates spent close to $1 million on consultants; Senator Jesse Helms (R-NC) once spent $10 million.[38] Experts estimate that at least 5,000 people now work full-time in the for-profit campaign industry; about 30,000 individuals are paid for consulting during peak periods.[39]

In past generations, political party officials played a major role in electoral campaigns: they chose candidates, raised money, and provided expertise, labor, and voter lists. Today the parties play a diminished role, but political consultants often operate in their place. Consultants design and produce broadcast advertisements and mass mailings; they conduct fundraisers and contact donors; they maintain lists of voters and contributors; they manage campaign logistics; and they write speeches and position papers. They are major repositories of political experience and employers of skilled labor.

Consultants sometimes imply that they could elect a fence post to Congress if they were paid enough money.[40] However, it is difficult to verify the claim that they profoundly influence election results. Granted, victorious campaigns usually employ consulting firms, and campaigns that do not employ consultants are generally defeated. But the more decisive fact may be that victorious campaigns are often many times *wealthier* than unsuccessful ones. In 1998, the average successful House candidate had raised three-quarters of a million dollars before election day. Since these campaigns generally bought broadcast advertising, produced professional mass mailings, and conducted elaborate polls, they almost always employed consultants. On the other hand, more than 127 defeated candidates spent less than $25,000 each.[41] In this spending range, consultants are often unaffordable—but so are broadcast advertisements, mailings, and polls. Thus, the figures do not prove that consultants are an important cause of victory. It is even conceivable that well-funded campaigns would be better off spending *less* on consultants.

Still, the fact that consultants are widely employed by winning candidates suggests that they have a great influence on the *character* of elections, whether or not they affect outcomes. Victorious campaigns pay consultants a great deal of money for guidance and services—often more than half of their total budgets. The consultants' dearly bought advice presumably carries weight; their products certainly fill our airwaves and clutter our mailboxes during election season. Moreover, candidates act as if consultants are central figures in the electoral process. When a campaign hires a famous consulting firm, it may announce this triumph with a press conference, because the signing of a celebrated expert can seem as important as a party nomination or a major endorsement. In some cases, consultants actually recruit citizens to run for office, confident that the individuals whom they select will be able to raise money and attract votes.

The profound influence of consultants invites us to ask whether we should blame them for the rise of certain kinds of campaign tactics that alienate American voters. Admittedly, few of the disturbing aspects of modern campaigns were invented by consultants. Personal attacks, lavishly funded advertising campaigns, the reliance on divisive "hot-button" issues, and similar tactics were all present before the first consulting firm was founded in 1934, and they are still employed even when consultants are absent.[42] It is also true that every form of political organization has disadvantages. The parties that once dominated politics were famous for smoky back rooms, patronage deals, financial corruption, and racial discrimination. Nevertheless, it appears that consultants have reasons to favor and encourage certain unsavory tactics that are endemic to the current political system. In part, this is because for-profit political experts have their own interests, distinct from those of candidates, activists, parties, and voters.

For example, one would like to think that many politicians are motivated by strongly held beliefs and policy commitments, and not only by the ambition to win elections. Though candidates often try to evade politically difficult questions, some will risk defeat rather than ignore or finesse the issues that prompted them to run in the first place. But the subculture of professional consultants is famous for a general lack of interest in ideology or the legislative process.[43] When consultants are asked what motivates them, more cite money or the thrill of competition than political beliefs as a major factor.[44] Some consultants express contempt for lawmaking; others state that they have chosen to work in campaigns rather than government because they find legislation baffling, tedious, or esoteric.[45] Although consultants sometimes have ideological commitments, they focus on other factors. More than half admit that when they are deciding whom to take as a client, a candidate's financial condition is a very important factor. They also care about their clients' chances of winning, because their careers depend upon their ratio of wins to losses. One firm boasts: "Breit Strategies' 72% win ratio is even better than it sounds when you know that we're always willing to take on the tough ones."[46] They protest too much. If consultants deliberately supported underdogs, their "win ratios" would fall to unsustainable levels; and if they were overly fussy about the platforms of their potential clients, they would have difficulty finding work.[47] Forty-four percent said that they had helped to elect candidates whom they were sorry to see in office.[48]

The fact that consultants rarely care much about issues would not matter much if candidates set the agenda. But 44 percent of consultants agree that, "when it comes to setting issue priorities, candidates are neither very involved nor very influential."[49] If many candidates eschew leadership in choosing issues, then consultants presumably fill that role—but most admit that they are fairly uninterested in issues except as a means of attracting uncommitted voters.[50] Having selected a theme on the basis of polls and focus groups, they concentrate on wooing the swing vote with broadcast advertisements and mass mailings.[51]

Unfortunately, this approach to issues militates against any careful, broad-based discussion of public concerns during an election campaign. In ideal cases, the process of public discussion can cause citizens to modify their initial beliefs as they exchange ideas and weigh pros and cons, instead of expressing visceral preferences. However, public discussion of this kind is the last thing that most consultants want to see. After they have identified a divisive "wedge issue" on which their candidate happens to agree with the majority, they often want to *prevent* any shift in public opinion. Thus they are adept at using rhetorical formulas that discourage reflection and discussion, that freeze public opinion in place, and that polarize and inflame voters.

Because consultants have little time to get to know the communities where they work, they often rely on themes and rhetoric that they have found effective elsewhere. Their national experience may compensate for their lack of familiarity with regional issues and values, but the result is a certain standardization of political discourse. The consultants' superficial knowledge of particular communities also makes it difficult for them to design positive campaigns, because a positive agenda often involves local issues and interests. However, consultants are adept at discovering weaknesses in opponents' voting records and resumés—so-called opposition research. The result is a heavy emphasis on negative campaigning, which consultants consider effective.[52]

Several factors that sometimes work to keep politicians and parties honest do not apply to consultants. For instance, campaigns have traditionally relied on volunteers, whose motives tend to be principled and even idealistic, and for whom winning a particular election is not always the most important goal. Volunteers can be overzealous at times, but usually they expect campaigns to maintain high ethical standards. Consultants, however, do not rely on volunteers. For one thing, they lack the local connections and reputations that would enable them to recruit free labor. Instead, their major assets are money, national connections, expertise, and technology. James Severin, a consultant who worked for George Bush, has said that it is important to project the *appearance* that a campaign has volunteer support, but volunteers actually have no substantive role in modern elections.[53] Even if Severin is wrong, his comment reveals a great deal about consultants' attitudes.

An effective strategy for local parties and politicians is to build a core of support among activists and then broaden it into a majority. Although this approach does not rule out exclusive politics (and even bigotry), at least it encourages a long-term perspective. But consultants lack the time to recruit activists and new voters, to court community leaders, or to change local opinion. Instead, they typically use sophisticated technology to target a small group: habitual voters who are uncertain about whom to support. Sometimes, a poll or "focus-group" interview of these voters reveals that a particular issue holds the key to victory. In such cases, short-term tactical considerations may determine the whole message of a campaign, and there are no lasting benefits for the community.

A typical consulting firm proclaims its expertise in "Targeting Contributors, Targeting Voters, Targeting Issues, and Automated Dialing to Targeted Homes." The firm explains, "Automated dialing can be used both to identify supporters and key issues, and . . . on election day to maximize key voter turnout. Sophisticated databasing techniques including desktop mapping are used to deliver mail and voice messages to specific constituency groups."[54] "Targeting," "tailoring," and "focus," are among consultants' favorite words—along with "aggressive," "hard-hitting," and "creative."

According to polls, most people thought that the Republican Party had overplayed the Monica Lewinsky sex scandal by November 1998. But two Republican consultants, William Dalbec and Michael Dabadie, recalled "a simple rule: you don't have to appeal to everyone to win. It's a waste of resources. What you need to do is secure your base—make sure core supporters turn out and vote—and appeal to swing voters, those who often split their tickets."[55] They explained that the Republican base was composed of Christian conservatives, while the relevant "swing voters" were politically independent married women. Both of these groups would appreciate advertisements that directly criticized the president. Perhaps Dalbec and Dabadie gave poor tactical advice in 1998, but their approach usually works. It is also a recipe for low turnout, because targeted commercials motivate people who are *already* likely to vote, alienating everyone else. But consultants aren't paid to enhance democracy. They are paid to win.

One of their main jobs is to inject such worldly realism into campaigns. Four out of five consultants report that when campaigns turn negative, it is usually because they have recommended it—not because the candidates wanted to attack one another.[56] Consultants also remind candidates to raise money, to heed poll data, and to keep their messages simple and popular.[57] Although cynical advice is often valid, cynics do not make good politicians. People who conspicuously lack ideals have trouble appealing to voters, and they usually lack the stomach for public service. Nevertheless, there is money to be made by standing on the sidelines, reminding candidates not to be too idealistic. Thus consultants often serve as moral thermostats, switching off their clients' idealism when it threatens to ruin their electoral prospects. Dick Morris, President Clinton's Svengali in 1996, was only an extreme example of this phenomenon.

Politicians may be cautious about using obviously disreputable campaign tactics because they wish to retain the loyalty and respect of their constituents over the course of their careers. In the heat of battle, they may be able to get away with distortions, exaggerations, divisive rhetoric, unrealistic promises, or efforts at suppressing the vote. But once elected, they can to some extent be held accountable for these sins. The local media, for example, can investigate them. Adverse publicity may hurt their effectiveness in office and their chances of reelection; it may also besmirch their personal reputations in the communities where they (and their families) live. Consultants, on the other hand, move on soon after election day, so they are not usually interested in building local reputations for integrity. On the contrary, they may try to mislead the electorate or the local media, to suppress overall turnout by alienating select groups of voters, or to divide communities along convenient fault-lines, such as those of race and class. They sometimes even use such dubious practices as "push polling," in which alleged "opinion researchers" call likely voters to ask questions like the following: "Would you reelect Congressman X if you knew that he was a sex offender who had voted to subsidize pornography?" The insinuations in this question may not be based on any evidence whatsoever. About a fifth of political consultants say that they know of some or many campaigns that used "push-polling" in 1996.[58]

Of course, politicians are supposed to be the bosses of their own campaigns; they hire the consultants and establish standards of behavior. However, if candidates believe that they can win by listening to consultants, then it is difficult for them to ignore this advice. It is all very well to run an issue-oriented, grassroots, positive, low-budget campaign; but if such campaigns are almost always defeated by teams of pollsters and media consultants, then they can begin to seem rather quixotic.

The professional skills that consultants employ during campaigns are also effective after election day. Some consultants work as lobbyists between campaigns, using their skills to influence legislation and benefiting from their relationships with former clients who now hold office.[59] Several consulting firms have adapted election strategies—and even specific computer software—to lobbying efforts.[60] One of the most impressive efforts, organized by Americans for Fair Taxation, has employed Richard Wirthlin, who polled for Ronald Reagan; Don Sipple, Bob Dole's media adviser; Fred Steeper, a Michigan pollster; Charles B. Sewell, a Democratic strategist; and two lobbying firms, Arter & Hadden and the Argus Group.[61]

The success of political consultants creates an apparent paradox. Their methods seem to work: voters elect politicians who use consultants and usually reject candidates who do not. Whatever the precise impact of consultants on election results, clearly voters do not punish candidates for employing consultants to manage their campaigns. At the same time, however, most Americans view elections in general as shameful exercises in mudslinging, obfuscation, and demagoguery.[62] As individual voters, they apparently respond to the tactics of professional consultants; but as a public, they are alienated by the political culture that consultants have helped to create.

This phenomenon is not altogether surprising. In the economy at large, the individual choices of consumers often produce aggregate results that they dislike; and in such cases we often resort to government regulation. In the political arena, too, our private choices cannot control what the marketplace produces, so we may call for state action. We could establish binding rules of conduct for consultants; we could even try to ban the industry. But regulation of campaign practices always raises constitutional questions, because candidates and their supporters have the right to express themselves without official restraint. Besides, unforeseen consequences could easily result if we tried to put consultants out of business by statute. If, for example, we made it illegal to pay campaign workers, then no one but rich, unemployed, or retired people would be able to participate in electoral politics. If, on the other hand, we tried to prevent the use of specialized expertise in campaigns, then we might just reward bumbling amateurs. Besides, consultants are not the only political experts: some candidates, staff members, and even volunteers bring considerable skills and experience to campaigns.

Many people assume that candidates should come alone before the bar of public opinion to be judged as fit or unfit for political office. This seems to be the purest concept of electoral democracy—the ideal that is taught in civics class. But in a mass society, it is impossible for candidates to win elections literally on their own. They need at least some of the following: donors, parties, volunteers, the media, interest groups, other politicians, a personal fortune, public financing, and/or professional advisers.

It is not surprising, then, that whenever one form of political organization declines or is suppressed, another always seems to take its place. For example, the dissolution of traditional party structures created a vacuum that has been filled by entrepreneurial politicians who use campaign money to provide expertise and support to candidates in other states or districts. One fairly typical incumbent congressman spent $270,000 to defeat an opponent with a budget of $2,498. The incumbent spent less than half of his resources on consultants ($109,750), since his challenger posed no threat to him. However, he maintained a permanent campaign organization and hired qualified election specialists on a full-time basis, assigning these employees to help other candidates during election season.[63] In effect, he ran his own consulting service, exacting political influence (rather than money) as his price. If we banned private consultants, well-funded politicians might replace them as purveyors of professional services.

All these observations suggest that it would probably be futile to regulate or proscribe consultants as a discrete class. Even constructing a legal definition of the industry might prove impossible. But consultants are creatures of the current funding regime, in which individual politicians collect money from special interests in order to pay independent, profit-seeking political experts. Any campaign system reflects the way that money is raised and spent, and our system is a bad one. It reflects the values of the marketplace, not the ideals of a democratic polity. What we need, then, is a financial regime that promotes fairness and deliberation. A properly reformed system would discourage the kind of tactics that have given consultants a bad reputation.

APPROACHES TO REFORM

The most straightforward approach to campaign-finance reform—limiting expenditures—was ruled unconstitutional in *Buckley v. Valeo.* The Supreme Court found that spending was a form of expression that could not be restricted, at least not given the evidence about corruption that reformers had presented before 1974.

Although the Court's equation of money with speech was dubious,[64] it did no serious harm, because spending limits are not the key to reform. If Congress could limit spending, then incumbents might deliberately set the limits so low that challengers would be unable to finance viable campaigns. Besides, there is not too much total spending in campaigns. If anything, more dialogue with voters would be a good thing, but television time, mailings, and travel all cost money.

Although *Buckley* struck down spending limits, the Court allowed Congress to restrict the size of donations as a way of preventing corruption and the appearance of corruption. In subsequent decades, contribution limits have made life relatively difficult for wealthy special interests. Thus they should be maintained, contrary to the arguments of Senator Trent Lott (R-MS) and other Republican incumbents who call unrestrained donations "the American way."[65] But contribution limits are not the key to reform, any more than spending limits are. There are enough wealthy special interests to finance incumbents lavishly, even if each PAC and individual operates under severe financial constraints. And contribution limits can be circumvented. Ban large donations to candidates, and donors will give to parties. Ban this kind of "soft money," and donors will produce independent advertisements that influence elections. The latter are very difficult to regulate within the limits of the First Amendment, but they have become a significant factor, consuming as much as $150 million in 1995–96.[66] Donors may also form multiple PACs so that each can give to its limit; and they may coordinate their donations, either formally or informally.

The key to reform is to provide new methods of campaigning that help democracy, that are accessible to all, and that are free of corruption. It would be easy to take the first baby steps in this direction. Since the Progressive Era, California, Oregon, and Washington State have mailed voter guides to all citizens. These booklets contain statements by every qualified candidate. They cost politicians nothing, so they are equally accessible to all campaigns. To the extent that they affect the outcome of elections, they reduce the marginal value of each campaign dollar. And since candidates are given space to write substantial essays, voters gain useful information with a minimal expenditure of time and money. The cost of acquiring information is a major barrier to voting (especially for poor people), so we would expect more political participation if voter guides were widely used.[67]

Politicians must sign their own statements in these booklets. If they write mean-spirited attacks, this tends to reflect badly on their own characters. And candidates who lie in voter guides can be prosecuted. Former Representative Wes Cooley (R-OR) was successfully prosecuted for claiming that he had served in the "Special Forces" in Korea, although he had not actually fought in that conflict at all.

The federal government could print voter guides, or it could offer free postage to jurisdictions that issued their own. Various levels of government could also establish Internet sites with information provided by the candidates. A private organization called Project Vote Smart now provides a site at which citizens can enter their zip codes and receive information about their elected officials, from state legislators to the president. With the click of a mouse, they can see their officials' addresses, committee status, biographical data, campaign-finance statistics, and voting records.

An extremely interesting format for television has been pioneered by James Fishkin, whose experiments in Deliberative Polling[68] have worked well in the United States and Britain. With government support, similar events could become much more common. Fishkin writes:

> The idea is simple. Take a . . . random sample of the electorate and transport these people . . . to a single place. Immerse the sample in the issues, with carefully balanced briefing materials, with intensive discussions in small groups, and with the chance to question competing experts and politicians. At the end of several days of working through the issues face to face, poll the participants in detail. The resulting survey offers a representation of the considered judgments of the public.[69]

One such gathering was held in Texas during the 1996 presidential primary, with a nationally representative sample of 460 people. The experiment lasted for an entire weekend, and for the whole time, the participants labored hard to assimilate information and share viewpoints. The national press corps attended in force, and ten million people watched some of the event on PBS, which broadcast it for more than nine hours.[70] Such events could not be covered regularly on commercial television at any comparable length. However, broadcasters could be encouraged—or even required—to televise the period when the informed citizens interviewed the political candidates. Then viewers would be able to watch the interchange between politicians and people who were just like themselves demographically—except that the questioners would have studied the issues and exchanged ideas. Both candidates and citizens would learn the direction of an enriched or deepened public opinion, and everyone would witness a model of deliberation that might prove infectious. Participants in the Texas experiment, although randomly selected and diverse, agreed that the experience was very worthwhile and inspiring.[71]

It is difficult to dispute the merits of voter guides or Deliberative Polling. The next few steps are more controversial, but they are also more important. All levels of government should provide free television and radio time to qualified candidates, requiring them to address the audience in person for periods of at least one minute. Such proposals have generated a debate about whether broadcasters can be *forced* to provide free time. Proponents note that the industry is granted use of the spectrum in return for serving the "public interest, convenience, and necessity."[72] In response, broadcasters invoke their First Amendment rights and flex their lobbying muscle to prevent meaningful reform. If necessary, the government should subsidize political broadcasts—a reasonable price to pay for real democracy. In any case, the state should buy time on cable television, which is not subject to the same regulations as broadcast media but which attracts a large share of the viewing audience. The government could also buy time for broadcast debates and/or deliberative sessions with voters. After all, nothing is more instructive than a sustained, face-to-face interaction among the candidates.

Some people have objected to free-time proposals that require politicians to appear in person without expensive video presentations. Indeed, this is not a neutral provision: it discriminates in favor of good speakers and reduces the power of media consultants. It rewards positive presentations and discourages personal attacks. Candidates who lack personal charisma may suffer as a result, and some capable people may be kept out of public office.[73] But no campaign system is neutral, and effective speaking is a worthy skill in a deliberative democracy. In any event, it is better to have good speakers than skillful fundraisers in Congress. As Woodrow Wilson wrote, "It is natural that orators should be the leaders of a self-governing people."[74] Still, candidates have a First Amendment right to opt out of any particular forum, so they should not be required to attend deliberative sessions or to use publicly funded broadcast time.

In addition to free broadcast time, qualifying candidates could be given free postage to mail campaign letters written over their own signatures. Currently, members of Congress have this privilege (known as "the frank"), which helps to protect their incumbency. The House Republicans cut the average frank allowance to $216,000 per two-year term, but this amount still exceeds the entire budget of an average major-party challenger in 1998.[75] The frank should be granted to both sides, not just to incumbents.

These ideas have limited value—they are just components of a definitive solution. Sooner or later, we will have to offer full (but optional) public financing to all qualified candidates. This is already done in presidential general-election campaigns—now marred by soft money—and in Maine's legislative and gubernatorial races. Public funding could be combined with more modest ideas like voter guides and government-sponsored Internet sites and debates. This is not an unrealistic goal. In 1997, 50 percent of Americans agreed that "public financing of campaigns would reduce the influence of special interests."[76] To qualify for public funds, candidates would file petitions signed by a specified number of registered voters. The signature requirement should be set high enough to exclude marginal candidates, but low enough that teams of volunteers could manage petition drives. Campaigns would be able to use their public funds to buy any combination of broadcast advertisements, mailings, travel, and printing. In addition, they could spend limited sums on rent, salaries, telephone charges, lawyers and accountants, outside contracts, and miscellaneous expenses. But they would not be able to raise or spend a penny of private money.

As a result, two kinds of candidate would compete in American elections. One type would continue to use private donations to buy professional campaign services. Such candidates would no doubt attack their opponents for receiving public funds, and voters would be free to agree with them. On the other hand, they would have to spend time and money raising contributions, and they would be beholden to their contributors. Politicians with large personal fortunes would be able to avoid fundraising burdens, but very few millionaires have political ambitions and are acceptable to the electorate.

The other type of candidate would use public funds to run truly independent campaigns. These candidates would have to defend their use of tax money, but they would owe nothing to special-interest donors, so they could freely choose their themes and agendas. Although their spending would be limited, they would be given sufficient funds to compete. Beyond a certain point, campaign spending hardly affects election results, so publicly funded candidates would fare reasonably well against opponents with very large war chests. Candidates who accepted government money could not spend much on professional advice. If they were successful, then the political consulting industry would shrink—perhaps below sustainable levels.

Some people object to public financing of campaigns by arguing that it is "welfare for politicians," a waste of taxpayers' money. But imagine the most expensive possible outcome: that all campaigns from school board to president were covered, all eligible candidates participated, the broadcast industry bore none of the expense, and current spending patterns were sustained. Even then, the total cost of public financing would be about $20 per capita. That is not a high price to pay for democracy. In any case, billions of dollars might be saved if lobbyists were not able to purchase government subsidies and tax breaks.

There is a more serious objection to full public financing: it slights political parties. Although the current system is centered around candidates, parties have won a role for themselves as fundraising coordinators. Their darkest hour occurred during the 1970s, after the Watergate-era reforms but before the Republican National Commission invented soft money. If Congress banned this invention and offered full financing to individual candidates, then parties would be reduced to coalitions of independent politicians. And if the public financing regime were extended to primaries, then party establishments would not even be able to choose their own representatives. In a few years, the party would be over.

In principle, strong parties have advantages. Since they stand to suffer from criticism of any particular campaign, they may try to avoid disreputable tactics. In order to appeal to majorities, they must develop coherent national agendas. Their endorsements help people to decide how to vote, thereby reducing a significant cost of participation—the need to acquire information. Because they have to think about long-term strategy, they may labor hard to persuade people to vote and volunteer for the first time. Parties sometimes recruit talented newcomers and train them for public service, just like baseball organizations that rely on farm teams instead of free agency. Finally, parties have an incentive to allocate money to the candidates who need it most, because they want to win as many seats as possible. In contrast, private donors generally favor incumbents, who are also the favorite clients of political consultants. Thus a party-centered system might prove more competitive than a candidate-centered one.

However, the parties' power was curtailed for good reason. Traditionally, the main source of their authority was their ability to raise and spend money. This power was reduced after Watergate because of evident and systematic corruption in party fundraising. Corruption—or at least the appearance of corruption—is inevitable whenever parties solicit and allocate large sums of private money. Besides, the single most efficient way to promote competition is to offer full public financing to all qualified candidates.

Even if the parties were given clean public money to allocate, their control of the purse strings would raise issues of fairness. Party officials would have to make crucial decisions about whom to support, thereby becoming a kind of shadow government. Although parties are sometimes praised for improving competition, their leaders often use money for their own private purposes, while slighting the needs of challengers. Consider, for example, Senator Alphonse D'Amato, who used Republican Senatorial Campaign Committee (RSCC) money to influence state campaigns and ballot initiatives in New York State, even though several Senate races were in doubt. Two years later, Senator McConnell poured RSCC money into Wisconsin to punish Russ Feingold (D-WI), a supporter of campaign-finance reform, but he withheld funds from Linda Smith, the Republican nominee in Washington State, because she favored reform. Even if McConnell were on the right side, his control of funds would give him disproportionate power. To avoid cases like this, party officials could be made directly accountable to the rank and file. But then they would have to conduct campaigns for office, complete with contributors and consultants. This would only shift financial scandals to a new domain.

Before devising an appropriate role for parties, we should distinguish their beneficial functions from their harmful ones. When the parties debate matters of policy, this helps to sustain a deliberative democracy. For instance, citizens benefit if they can compare party platforms or watch the national chairs arguing on television. Similarly, when parties sponsor internal debates, this promotes deliberation within the main currents of American politics. Finally, when parties offer free information, recruit volunteers, register voters, and "get out the vote," they lower the cost of becoming informed and thereby make politics more participatory and fair. On the other hand, when party institutions act as conduits for wealthy groups that want to give money to powerful people, they harm both deliberation and fairness.

Thus the parties should be granted public funds for advertising, research, and voter registration and mobilization efforts. (The federal government already finances their national conventions.) These funds would supplement, not replace, the larger grants made to individual candidates. In return for federal support, parties would agree to accept no private gifts. This seems to me the best approach, even though party leaders might sometimes distribute their funds inequitably and inefficiently. But if taxpayers balked at major subsidies to parties, then the government could match small private contributions instead.

Regardless of the approach that we choose for financing parties, their heyday may be over. Traditional parties were labor-intensive enterprises, capable of conducting politics at both the retail and the wholesale level. Presidential candidates needed volunteers in every ward to get out the vote, and local politicians relied on the national ticket to inspire their troops. But vacuum cleaners are no longer sold door-to-door, and it may be anachronistic to elect candidates that way. Broadcast advertisements and mass mailings are simply more effective than grassroots labor in any reasonably large electoral district. This implies that concerns about the viability of the parties should not prevent us from reforming campaign finances—for the parties' decline may be inevitable. It also means that we should expect other organizations to do some of the work that parties used to handle.

For example, the Christian Coalition began as a grassroots, volunteer-driven campaign to elect a presidential candidate, Pat Robertson. But retail politics was not effective at the national level, where money is crucial and the best strategy is to use mass advertising to persuade centrist voters. Robertson's defeat in 1988 persuaded him and his allies that they ought to fight local battles in friendly districts—campaigns to control school boards, for example. Their story shows that grassroots mobilization no longer has much influence on federal elections, although it can make a difference in other contexts. To the extent that the Christian Coalition has tried to influence federal campaigns since 1988, its activities have violated the spirit (if not the letter) of campaign-finance laws. But the Coalition's work at the grassroots level—organizing citizens and electing local candidates in low-budget races—is good for democracy. This approach should have imitators on both the right and the left, and the imitators will probably not be parties.

States, localities, and the federal government must all wrestle with the curse of money in politics, but they should not be asked to adopt precisely the same solution. No single approach will work equally well in a presidential race and in a rural campaign for local office. Besides, states have some autonomy under the Constitution, and it is good for them to try diverse experiments. My purpose in this chapter has not been to devise a precise blueprint for campaign reform at all levels of government but rather to propose some principles that would apply in virtually any circumstances. The twin goals of reform should be fairness and deliberation. Both ends have one solution: public financing of beneficial campaign practices—those that draw people into politics and promote debate. If public money is distributed equitably, it will increase competition; and if it is dispensed wisely, it will help to create a deliberative democracy.

NOTES

1. John Dewey, *The Public and Its Problems* (New York, 1927), p. 207.

2. Source: Herbert Alexander, University of Southern California.

3. Paul Herrnson et al., "Individual Congressional Campaign Contributors: Wealthy, Conservative and Reform-Minded" (June 1998), pp. 2, 11, available at http:/george town.edu/wilcox/donors.htm or from the Joyce Foundation. In periodic polls taken since 1952, no more than 14 percent of American adults have ever said that they make political contributions; just 7.2 percent contributed in 1988. (*Campaign Practice Reports*, September 30, 1991, citing polls by the Survey Research Center, the Center for Political Studies, and Gallup.)

4. See Claus Offe, "European Socialism and the Role of the State" (1978) in *Contradictions of the Welfare State*, ed. John Keane (Cambridge, Mass., 1984), p. 244.

5. Charles Lindblom, *Politics and Markets: The World's Political Economic Systems* (New York, 1977), p. 175.

6. Dennis P. Quinn and Robert Y. Shapiro, "Business Political Power: The Case of Taxation," *American Political Science Review*, vol. 85, no. 3 (September 1991): 861, 863, 866–867. I am using "recession" to mean a time of low private-sector investment and low GNP growth.

7. I have divided Herbert Alexander's estimate of total spending in 1996—$4 billion—by the FEC's count of voting-age population.

8. See, e.g., Alan I. Abramowitz, "Explaining Senate Election Outcomes," *American Political Science Review* 82 (June 1988): 385–403; and Gary C. Jacobson, "The Effects of Campaign Spending in House Elections: New Evidence for Old Arguments," *American Journal of Political Science*, vol. 34, no. 2 (May 1990): 334–362. Levitt argues that studies like Abramowitz's underestimate the importance of incumbents' spending and overestimate the effect of challengers' finances. I am not persuaded that he has refuted Abramowitz, but both scholars concur that campaign spending matters. See Steven D. Levitt, "Policy Watch: Congressional Campaign Finance Reform," *Journal of Economic Perspectives*, vol. 8, no. 1 (Winter 1995), p. 188.

9. *New York Times*/CBS poll of adults, reported in the *New York Times,* April 8, 1997, p. A14.

10. R. W. Apple, Jr., "Poll Shows Disenchantment with Politicians and Politics," *New York Times,* August 12, 1995, section 1, p. 1.

11. FDIC, "The S & L Crisis: A Chrono-Bibliography" (http://www.fdic.gov/publish/slchron.html); David J. Jefferson, "Keating of American Continental Corp. Comes Out Fighting," *Wall Street Journal,* April 18, 1989.

12. Quoted by Frank Sorauf, *Inside Campaign Finance: Myths and Realities* (New Haven, Conn., 1992), p. 172.

13. "New Realities, New Thinking: Report of the Task Force on Campaign Finance

Reform," Citizens' Research Foundation, University of Southern California (http://www.usc.edu/dept/CRF/DATA/newrnewt.htm). The task force does not provide a bibliography, but presumably the "long line of empirical research" includes: Henry W. Chappell, Jr., "Campaign Contributions and Congressional Voting: A Simultaneous Probit-Tobit Model," *Review of Economics and Statistics* 64 (1982); John R. Wright, "PACs, Contributions, and Roll Calls: An Organizational Perspective," *American Political Science Review*, vol. 79, no. 2 (June 1985); Janet M. Grenzke, "Candidate Attributes and PAC Contributions," W*estern Political Quarterly*, vol. 42, no. 2 (June 1989); Grenzke, "PACs and the Congressional Supermarket: The Currency Is Complex," *American Journal of Political Science* 33 (February 1989); Sorauf, *Inside Campaign Finance*; and Levitt, "Congressional Campaign Finance Reform."

14. Norman J. Ornstein, Thomas E. Mann, and Michael J. Malbin, *Vital Statistics on Congress, 1995–96* (Washington, D.C., 1996), table 6–1; Mary Cohn, ed., *Congressional Quarterly's Guide to Congress*, 4th ed. (Washington, D.C., 1991), p. 419.

15. Ornstein, et al., *Vital Statistics on Congress*, table 6–4.

16. Richard L. Hall, *Participation in Congress* (New Haven, Conn., 1996), p. 8.

17. Richard L. Hall and Frank W. Wayman, "Buying Time: Moneyed Interests and the Mobilization of Bias in Congressional Committees," *American Political Science Review*, vol. 84, no. 3 (September 1990): 800–801, 803. Grenzke finds that PACs prefer to support members with "agenda power," i.e., those who belong to relevant subcommittees or hold committee leadership posts: see Grenzke, "Candidate Attributes and PAC Contributions," p. 249.

18. It has been common in the literature to concede that money might influence committee behavior; but this hypothesis was not tested until Hall and Wayman's joint work. See, e.g., Chappell, "Campaign Contributions and Congressional Voting," p. 79; Grenzke, "PACs and the Congressional Supermarket," p. 18.

19. Philip M. Stern, *Still the Best Congress Money Can Buy* (Washington, D.C., 1992), p. 166.

20. One of the three cases analyzed by Hall and Wayman involved the dairy industry, but it took place in 1982. They found that the two biggest influences on participation in committee deliberations were: (1) whether each representative held a leadership position; and (2) the number of dairy cows in his or her district. PAC contributions from the dairy industry followed very close behind. (Hall and Wayman, "Buying Time," table 1, p. 810.) Thus, enough money could make the whole of Congress act like representatives from rural Wisconsin. By coincidence, Chappell also analyzed a dairy-subsidy vote—this time from 1975—finding a statistically insignificant influence of money on votes.

21. Katharine Q. Seelye, "G.O.P. Blithely Seeks Big Donors," *New York Times*, April 17, 1997, p. A23. See also Don van Natta, Jr., "Republicans' Goal is $1 Million Each from Top Donors," *New York Times,* August 9, 1999, p. A1 (citing "several fundraisers").

22. Quoted by Charles R. Babcock, "GE Files Offer Rare View of What PACs Seek to Buy on Capitol Hill," *Washington Post*, June 1, 1993, p. A10.

23. Grenzke, "PACs and the Congressional Supermarket," p. 8.

24. The Republican analyst Kevin Phillips argues that the Republicans and Democrats are the two most pro-business parties in the world. See Kevin P. Phillips, *The Politics of Rich and Poor: Wealth and the American Electorate in the Reagan Aftermath* (New York, 1980), p. 32.

25. Jack Anderson, "PACs Guide Hill with Reins of Green," *Washington Post,* January 13, 1992.

26. Guy Gugliotta, "For Torricelli, Fund-Raising Started at Home," *Washington Post,* May 18, 1997, p. A11.

27. Dwight Morris and Murielle E. Gamache, *Handbook of Campaign Spending: Money in the 1992 Congressional Races* (Washington, D.C.: 1994), p. 100.

28. Morris and Gamache, *Handbook of Campaign Spending: 1992,* p. 100, pp. 35, 36.

29. Sara Fritz and Dwight Morris, *Handbook of Campaign Spending: Money in the 1990 Congressional Races* (Washington, DC, 1992), p. 35; Morris and Gamache, *Handbook of Campaign Spending: 1992,* p. 33. (The figure for Rep. Shuster's meals comes from adding up numbers from these two books.)

30. Francis X. Clines, "A Free-Speech Senator Fights Limits on Donations," *New York Times,* August 21, 1997, p. A26.

31. Mitch McConnell, "Just What Is a Special Interest?" *Washington Post,* February 21, 1996, p. A19.

32. "New Realities, New Thinking," p. 20.

33. Sorauf, *Inside Campaign Finance,* p. 172.

34. Thëodore J. Lowi, *The End of Liberalism: The Second Republic of the United States.* 2d ed (New York, 1979).

35. Howe, *Confessions of a Reformer* (New York, 1925), p. 104.

36. Richard L. Berke, "G.O.P Seeks Foes' Donors, and Baldly," *New York Times,* June 17, 1995, p. A1.

37. Morris and Gamache, *Handbook on Campaign Spending: 1992,* p. 83.

38. Fritz and Morris, *Handbook of Campaign Spending: 1990,* p. 46.

39. Nicolas J. O'Shaughnessy, *The Phenomenon of Political Marketing* (New York, 1990), p. 128. The number of political consultants has increased from about 100 to about 5,000 in the last thirty years, according to Bradley O'Leary, chair of a consultants' professional organization. See James P. Sterba, "Democracy Inc.: Politicians at All Levels Seek Expert Advice, Fueling an Industry," *Wall Street Journal,* September 1, 1992. Walter de Vries estimates that 12,000 people earn at least part of their living as political consultants: "American Campaign Consulting: Trends and Concerns," *PS: Political Science & Politics* (March 1989): 21.

40. In a 1998 poll conducted by the Pew Research Center for the People and the Press, 42 percent of consultants "said it is relatively easy to sell a 'mediocre candidate.'" See "Don't Blame Us: The Views of Political Consultants," at http://www.people-press.org/con98rpt.htm.

41. Common Cause data.

42. On the first consultants, see David Lee Rosenbloom, *The Election Man: Professional Campaign Managers and American Democracy* (New York, 1973), p. 45.

43. O'Shaughnessy, *The Phenomenon of Political Marketing,* pp. 129–134; Gillian Peele, "Campaign Consultants," *Electoral Studies,* vol. 1, no. 3 (December 1982): 355–362; Mark P. Petracca, "Political Consultants and Democratic Governance," *PS: Political Science & Politics* (March 1989): 13.

44. Pew poll.

45. Larry Sabato, *The Rise of Political Consultants: New Ways of Winning Elections* (New York, 1981), pp. 6, 23.

46. Internet site, quoted on May 1, 1997.

47. In the Pew poll, when consultants were asked why they usually chose their clients, only 16 percent cited candidates' chances of winning as a very important factor; 58 percent cited candidates' beliefs; 55 percent cited money; and 39 percent cited candidates' ability to govern. But the poll did not ask whether consultants select clients whose beliefs they respect, or whose beliefs are *popular.* Eighty-two percent of consultants think that a candidate's "message" is the single most important factor in determining victory. And since most consultants say that they are not motivated by their own political beliefs, they may favor clients whose platforms are likely to be popular. See also Sabato, *The Rise of Political Consultants,* p. 26.

48. Pew poll.

49. Petracca, "Political Consultants and Democratic Governance," p. 13 (comma added).

50. For an ambivalent comment on this issue, see Celinda Lake, "Political Consultants: Opening Up a New System of Political Power," *PS: Political Science & Politics* (March 1989): 28.

51. On the importance of "swing" voters to consultants, see Sidney Blumenthal, *The Permanent Campaign: Inside the World of Elite Political Operatives* (Boston, 1980), p. 6.

52. In the Pew poll, 83 percent said that negative campaigning was more effective than positive campaigning, and 98 percent said that the media paid more attention to it.

53. Quoted in O'Shaughnessy, *The Phenomenon of Political Marketing,* p. 141.

54. World Wide Web site operated by Direct Marketers of Charleston, quoted on May 1, 1997.

55. William Dalbec and Michael Dabadie (of Wirthlin Worldwide), "You Don't Need Every Vote" (Op-Ed), *New York Times,* October 30, 1998, p. A31.

56. Pew poll.

57. Just 42 percent of consultants said that they had a great deal of confidence in the American people on election day (ibid.).

58. Pew poll.

59. Larry Sabato, "Political Influence, the News Media and Campaign Consultants," *PS: Political Science & Politics* (March 1989): 16.

60. Neil A. Lewis, "Clinton Coalition Proves Effective at Raising Money," *New York Times,* March 3, 1992.

61. Alison Mitchell, "A New Form of Lobbying Puts Public Face on Private Interest," *New York Times,* September 30, 1998, pp. A1 and A14. I have described the law firm of Arter & Hadden as a lobbying company because it disclosed sixty-seven lobbying clients in the first six months of 1997. See its federal disclosure at http://www.crp.org/lobby/.

62. David Mathews, *Politics for People: Finding a Responsible Public Voice* (Urbana and Chicago, 1994), pp. 19–20.

63. FEC reports for 1990, analyzed by the author.

64. See Ronald Dworkin, "The Curse of American Politics," *New York Review of Books,* October 17, 1996, pp. 19–24.

65. Trent Lott, quoted by Katharine Q. Seelye, "G.O.P. Blithely Seeks Big Donors," *New York Times,* April 17, 1997, p. A23.

66. Deborah Beck, Paul Taylor, Jeffrey Stanger, and Douglas Rivlin, *Issue Advocacy Advertising during the 1996 Campaign,* Annenberg Public Policy Center, University of Pennsylvania (1997), p. 3.

67. Indeed, Oregon and Washington State have among the highest levels of turnout in the nation. In 1996, turnout as a percentage of voting-age population was 49.08 in the United States, 54.74 in Washington State, and 57.14 in Oregon. But California's turnout (43.9 percent in 1996) has lagged well behind the nation's since 1976, perhaps in part because many voting-age Californians are recent immigrants. Voting guides have not improved matters noticeably in that state. (Source: FEC.)

68. Fishkin has trademarked this term.

69. James Fishkin, *The Voice of the People: Public Opinion & Democracy* (New Haven, Conn., 1995), p. 162.

70. Fishkin, *The Voice of the People,* pp. 179, 189.

71. Almost three-quarters gave it the highest possible rating on a questionnaire (Fishkin, *The Voice of the People,* p. 222). In 1996, the Commission on Presidential Debates held focus groups with over 600 people to help decide what questions to ask the candidates. "An unexpected lesson was that participants lauded the sheer experience of post-debate discussion as much as the debates, bonding like jurists with other panelists and compounding their appetite for politics. 'We didn't intend this; it just happened,' said Diana Carlin, a political scientist who ran the focus groups." See Francis X. Clines, "'Ask Not . . .' 'Military-Industrial Complex . . .' 'but Fear Itself . . .'" *New York Times,* September 23, 1996, p. A12.

72. Federal Communications Act of 1934 (47 USCS §§ 151 et seq).

73. I heard these points made by Alex Castellanos, a prominent political consultant, on March 13, 1997.

74. Woodrow Wilson, *Congressional Government: A Study in American Politics* (Boston, 1896), p. 209.

75. Dan Greenberg, "Slashing Congressional Spending, Part I: Congressional Pay, Pensions, Perks, and Staff," *The Heritage Foundation Backgrounder,* no. 1034 (originally published on May 16, 1995, republished on the Internet at http://www.heritage.org/library/categories/govern/bg1034.html). The average House challenger's "campaign resources" in 1998 amounted to $207,107, according to Common Cause.

76. *New York Times*/CBS poll reported April 8, 1997, p. A14.

5

Journalism in the Public Interest

FREEDOM OF THE PRESS

"The basis of our government being the opinion of the people, the very first object should be to keep that right; and were it left to me to decide whether we should have a government without newspapers or newspapers without a government, I should not hesitate for a moment to prefer the latter." So wrote Thomas Jefferson, in typically provocative style.[1] Thanks in part to him, the Bill of Rights declares: "Congress shall make no law . . . abridging the freedom of speech, or of the press." Justice Potter Stewart once noted that the press is "the only organized private business that is given explicit constitutional protection."[2]

Freedom of the press is important because most of us have little direct contact with politics; what we know comes from reading newspapers and magazines, listening to the radio, or watching television. James Madison argued that American journalists had performed an invaluable service by "canvassing the merits and measures of public men." Politicians' "merits and measures" presumably included their records, platforms, beliefs, and at least their public behavior. Without a free press, voters would not know the "comparative merits and demerits of the candidates for public trust," and consequently their right to govern would be without "value and efficacy."[3]

Madison rightly thought that citizens who have values and preferences should be able to obtain the information necessary to assess and control their leaders. He did not, however, explain how voters can acquire preferences in the first place. Deliberation about ends is another important function of the mass media, and one that requires a somewhat different kind of journalism. When citizens deliberate, the means is often provided by newspapers' letter pages, radio call-in programs, and television talk shows. At their best, newspapers and broadcasts can prevent our local conversations from becoming insular or uninformed. Nothing else can connect our small-scale discussions into one "deliberative national public."[4] Even when we think and talk privately about public affairs, we originally acquire most of our information from journalists. Meanwhile, politicians gather a great deal of their knowledge about *us* from newspapers and television.

Today, the media in the United States are as free, diverse, and bold as they have ever been in human history. I will discuss ways to preserve and enhance First Amendment rights in an age of cable television, media empires, and cyberspace, but I think that the most serious problem lies elsewhere. With rights come responsibilities. We now have a largely free press, one that possesses adequate powers to inform citizens and to cultivate public deliberation. In fact, its powers are enormous and often troubling. We do not have a generally *responsible* press, one that actually serves democracy as well as it could. But there are stirrings of reform within the journalistic profession, and these will play a critical role in the New Progressive Movement.

The original Progressives sought to preserve and enhance the freedom, independence, and effectiveness of the press, so that it could survey government on the public's behalf. First of all, Progressive writers and editors developed a new approach to political journalism, which influenced the leading publications of the day. Traditionally, newspapers and magazines had been partisan outlets, often controlled by politicians or parties. But the Progressives wanted their publications to be independent and nonpartisan. In the popular press, nonpartisanship meant a continuous crusade against powerful people—politicians and industrialists alike—sparing only the publishing magnates themselves. Joseph Pulitzer captured the philosophy of muckraking Progressive journalism in 1907, saying that his newspapers would:

> always fight for progress and reform, never tolerate injustice or corruption, always fight demagogues of all parties, never belong to any party, always oppose privileged classes and public plunderers, never lack sympathy with the poor, always remain devoted to the public welfare, never be satisfied with merely printing news, always be drastically independent, never be afraid to attack wrong, whether by predatory plutocracy or predatory poverty.[5]

The fact that Pulitzer himself could be considered a "predatory plutocrat" did not negate the importance of his creed. His commitment to reform, independence of mind, and the public welfare was classically Progressive, and he turned these ideas into an effective strategy for selling newspapers. Although Pulitzer, Hearst, Scripps, and others of their ilk often protected their friends and harassed their personal enemies, they also competed fiercely for readers who now wanted the press to serve as a public watchdog. In the long run, a newspaper that spared *anyone* lost subscribers. It would be difficult to overstate the importance of investigative journalism in exposing financial scandals, corporate misconduct, and poverty; and many Progressive reforms were the direct result of these muckraking articles. Jacob Riis, Upton Sinclair, Lincoln Steffens, and David Graham Phillips were major figures in the Progressive movement.

Meanwhile, in the more highbrow press, nonpartisanship meant an effort to present a balanced, judicious debate about the public good, unencumbered by partisan loyalties. Progressive reporters were not free of ideology and bias, nor did the sophisticated ones claim to be. Croly and Lippmann of *The New Republic* were men of strong political opinions, as were the non-journalists who frequently contributed to their journal, including Dewey. But they thought that a permanent identification with individuals and parties would undermine their objectivity. The Progressive-Era cult of neutrality, independence, and objectivity has been widely criticized. But there is such a thing as good independent reporting, and journalists like Lippmann set a high standard.[6]

It was also the Progressives who invented modern First-Amendment law. They developed their position, in part, as a reaction to the oppressive sedition acts that Woodrow Wilson signed during the First World War. Wilson's postmaster general, Albert S. Burleson, announced that no one could print and mail any document saying:

> that this government got in the war wrong, that it is in it for the wrong purposes, or anything that will impugn the motives of the Government for going into the war. They can not say that this Government is the tool of Wall Street or the munitions-makers. That kind of thing makes for insubordination in the Army and Navy and breeds a spirit of disloyalty through the country.[7]

Protected by his senatorial immunity, La Follette often said just what Burleson forbade. As a result, the Senate seriously considered impeaching him. La Follette also argued that the war should be financed with higher taxes instead of loans, but an issue of *The Public* that took the same line was suppressed.[8] The experience of being denounced for his political opinions—while others were jailed for expressing the same views—turned La Follette into a militant critic of government censorship. Many Progressives agreed, since public deliberation required a completely free flow of information and ideas. During the war, the Supreme Court upheld the federal sedition acts, but Justices Holmes and Brandeis prepared the ground for a more liberal constitutional doctrine. Just as La Follette made his last run for president, Brandeis summarized the Progressive position on freedom of speech:

> Those who won our independence . . . believed that freedom to think as you will and to speak as you think are means indispensable to the discovery and spread of political truth; that without free speech and assembly discussions would be futile; [and] that with them, discussion affords ordinarily adequate protection against the dissemination of noxious doctrine.[9]

In the 1960s and '70s, the Supreme Court fully articulated a concept that was latent in Madison's and Brandeis's writings: the press as public watchdog. For example, in *New York Times v. United States*, the Court upheld the right of newspapers to publish classified national-security documents that had come into their possession. Where Madison had praised journalists for revealing the "merits and measures" of public officials, Justice Hugo Black now wrote:

> The press was protected so that it could bare the secrets of government and inform the people. Only a free and unrestrained press can effectively expose deception in government. And paramount among the responsibilities of a free press is the duty to prevent any part of government from deceiving the people and sending them off to distant lands to die of foreign fevers and foreign shot and shell. In my view, far from deserving condemnation for their courageous reporting, the *New York Times,* the *Washington Post,* and other newspapers should be commended for serving the purpose that the Founding Fathers saw so clearly.[10]

Although Justice Black was a civil libertarian, his view of press freedom was not strictly a libertarian one. According to civil libertarians, all citizens have perfect rights of thought and speech; journalists are citizens, too, so they can write anything they like. Reporters who exercise their right to free expression need not accept any special responsibilities. By the same token, the libertarian position offers journalists no special *privileges,* such as guaranteed access to government information, automatic admission to courtrooms and legislatures, immunity when called to testify, the right to protect sources and publish classified documents, and so on. Justice Black, by contrast, argued that journalists gain unique rights in return for their service as public watchdogs. The state, as a potential menace, cannot restrain the press with any kind of leash or muzzle. But in return, journalists acquire both the power and the responsibility to bare official secrets, expose corruption, and reveal the policies and characters of public officials.[11] Black's position derived from Madisonian ideas, but especially from Progressive ones: Charles Evans Hughes had argued, for example, that the public required a "vigilant and courageous press" to overcome government "malfeasance and corruption."[12]

This concept of press freedom was an important Progressive contribution, but it is not sufficient today. First of all, journalists do not become free if they are made immune from *government* censorship and prosecution; there is also the important question of private control. Second, journalists do not fulfill their public responsibilities if they simply report acts of government malfeasance. They have a much more constructive role to play in a deliberative democracy.

THE MONEY POWER

The state always poses a threat to free speech because of its power to censor, but so does capital. Newspapers, magazines—and now, broadcast networks—are privately owned, and their owners have economic interests. In 1912, La Follette gave a speech in Philadelphia, in which he charged that "the money power . . .

controls the newspaper press." The public, he said, "is fast coming to understand that wherever news items bear in any way upon the control of government by business, the news is colored; so confidence in the newspaper as a newspaper is being undermined."[13]

La Follette delivered this speech during a hectic presidential campaign and immediately after he had learned that his daughter required a dangerous operation. Speaking before an audience of magazine publishers, he received a hostile welcome and responded by losing his temper and lecturing for two hours. The next morning's press reported that he had suffered a nervous breakdown; editorial writers assailed him for his radical ideas. Although an editor of the *Philadelphia Evening Telegraph* told him that his view of the press was correct, most coverage of his speech was scathing. In fact, it was the ruin of his presidential campaign: prominent Republicans used the news of his "breakdown" or "collapse" as an excuse to back Roosevelt.[14]

But La Follette kept making the same case throughout his career. In 1918, for example, he wrote: "Except for the subserviency of most of the metropolitan newspapers, . . . 65 percent of all the wealth of this country would not now be centralized in the hands of two percent of all the people. And we might today be industrially and commercially a free people, enjoying the blessings of a real democracy."[15] La Follette implied the following argument: the owners of newspapers influenced what was printed; what was printed influenced public opinion; and public opinion influenced policy. Therefore, to some unknown but disproportionate extent, the people who owned the mass media influenced public policy to serve their own interests. As a result, democracy was corrupted.

Let us assume that publishers desire, either consciously or unconsciously, to shape the news in their class interests. They have considerable power to do so, for they can hire and fire editors and reporters at will. Furthermore, their support for elite economic interests may please their advertisers, who provide more than half of their revenue. Newt Gingrich recognized this possibility when he told the Georgia Chamber of Commerce: "the media, which all of you *control* through your advertising, doesn't have a clue what [congressional Republicans] are doing. . . . I would say to all of you, the responsibility for a news media that can't report accurately how the world works rests on those who pay for it, and that's the advertisers."[16]

It would be deeply dangerous if the Chamber of Commerce could pressure media executives to favor the ideology of House Republicans. However, Gingrich's fantasy has not come true, perhaps because the realities of the news business work against it. First of all, facts are stubborn. Although a newspaper can choose what issues to cover, whom to interview, and what adjectives to use, outright falsehood tends to show itself. Second, journalists do not belong to the same class as publishers. The median salary for reporters and correspondents in 1997 was about $22,000, which was only three-fifths of the median family income that year.[17] If what people think and write is influenced by their economic condition, then we would expect publishers to have an elitist slant on the news, but reporters would have working-class values—and newsrooms would be filled with class conflict.

In fact, writers are not at war with publishers over the content of the news. This could mean that management always wins the battle before it starts; perhaps journalists are too weak to think of challenging their employers. But reporters— and even former reporters—rarely complain that their bosses have suppressed their views.[18] Furthermore, if publishers dominated their employees, then we would expect the nonprofit press to be very different from the private media. But there is no discernible difference between the privately owned liberal press (e.g., *The Nation*) and the nonprofit liberal media (e.g., National Public Radio). These facts suggest that publishers and advertisers do not try to control editorial content in their class interests.

The reason, surely, is that their individual, bottom-line interest—selling papers or attracting viewers—conflicts with their abstract and general *class* interests. Since the average newspaper reader is not wealthy, promoting the interests of the rich is a poor way to boost subscriptions. The American public is diverse, and it includes plenty of people with ample disposable income who read conservative journals filled with lavish advertisements. Nevertheless, some rich and conservative publishers make money selling left-liberal publications (such as the *Village Voice*) to niche audiences. The average American, meanwhile, is middle-class and middle-of-the-road politically, and that is where the biggest profits lie.

In general, the drawback of a pure capitalist market is that it assigns votes in proportion to the amount of money that each person can spend. Thus decisions about what should be produced and who should be hired are made in an undemocratic fashion. But a product that costs 25 cents a day is subject to something very much like a democratic vote, in which the most popular item takes the biggest share. If people liked *Socialist Worker* as much as *USA Today,* then its readership would surely grow, although it would start with a small number of distributors. Socialist newspapers in other industrialized democracies have built mass audiences and large corporate advertising accounts. The reason that the American press is largely pro-capitalist is simple: our typical citizen is proudly and authentically bourgeois, and has bourgeois interests.

If the press had an upper-income bias, this would result in a conservative economic slant. However, conservatives complain that the mainstream press has a *liberal* bias. Indeed, polls show that 44 percent of reporters are Democrats; and only 16 percent, Republicans.[19] More specifically, 89 percent of the Washington reporters who were surveyed in one poll stated that they had voted for Bill Clinton in 1992.[20] Meanwhile, the mainstream press either ignores religion or treats it as a fringe movement, when Americans are a deeply pious and church-going people.[21] The left- and right-wing critiques of media bias are mutually compatible, since many elite journalists and editors are secular, upper-income liberals, and thus odious to evangelicals and leftists alike. However, the market for print journalism is an open one, and if the vast majority of American consumers prefer the products of bourgeois liberals to right-wing religious publications or left-wing revolutionary journals, then that choice is probably an honest and genuine one.

Nevertheless, there are grounds for concern. First, publishers cannot pursue elite class interests without losing readers. But this is true only insofar as the market is competitive. In a monopoly situation, both readers and reporters inevitably lose influence vis-à-vis publishers. In fact, the birth of independent, investigative reporting can be traced to an increase in media competition during the Progressive Era. In 1880, there were 971 daily newspapers in America; by 1899, there were 2,226. Even more important was the increase in market penetration. In 1880, there were three times as many American households as there were copies of newspapers printed each day, so most families received no paper. By 1910, however, 120 copies were printed for every 100 families—saturation point.[22] Since some poor people in the South and West still received no newspaper at all, the average urban family must have bought well over one journal a day. Under these circumstances, a publisher could easily lose subscribers to competing newspapers. He therefore catered to his readers, in part by hiring bold, independent, uncontrollable reporters like Sinclair and Steffens.

Compare the current situation, in which 70 newspapers are printed for every 100 households (down from twice that many in 1945), and 98 percent of daily newspapers are local monopolies that get most of their out-of-town news from the Associated Press.[23] Several television networks provide national and international news, but their reporting budgets are so low that they largely rely on the wire services and the *New York Times* for their leads. Meanwhile, the local television news mostly provides live footage of fires, lurid tales of rape and murder, exhaustive sports and weather coverage, silly human interest stories, and mindless chatter. The media do not pursue an obvious class interest, but they do ignore many controversial economic and social issues—which is perhaps a worse outcome. In any large community, there is no shortage of daily horror; but when "the news" consists of graphic violence and disaster, the only lesson we can draw is to fear our fellow citizens and despair for our polity. I doubt that the quality of local news reporting has ever been as bad in the history of America—not excepting the gutter press of the Federalist period or the "yellow" journalism of 1900.

Another reason for concern is the growing influence of a small elite among reporters. The median television journalist may earn $32,000 a year;[24] but ABC pays Diane Sawyer $7 million. She and a few score of her colleagues are media *stars,* recognizable from television appearances even if they are officially newspaper reporters or editorial writers. Their income allows them to act like an elite special interest. For example, Sam Donaldson of ABC, who is paid $2 million a year, has owned sheep and mohair farms that enjoyed federal subsidies of $97,000 during one two-year period.[25] His credibility is suspect when he tries (in Pulitzer's words) to "oppose privileged classes and public plunderers."

In general, media stars have a distorted picture of economic reality. For instance, the Washington press corps responded nonchalantly to reports that Zoe Baird, Clinton's first nominee for attorney general, had hired illegal immigrants as domestic servants. *ABC News* quoted a Bel Air resident who said that this practice was "extremely common." The *Wall Street Journal* described Baird's dilemma as one shared by "thousands of baby-boom parents"—presumably including some of the *Journal*'s employees. On CNN's *Capitol Gang,* Robert Novak said, "I think it is a ridiculous offense. . . . All of [co-panelist Al Hunt's] high-tone social friends have illegals." (Note the verb.) National reporters seemed shocked when talk radio shows and the Capitol switchboard were swamped by angry callers who couldn't forgive a corporate attorney for breaking the law, avoiding social security taxes, and choosing foreign citizens over unemployed Americans.[26]

Similarly, Steven Waldman reports that when President Clinton announced a $10,000-a-year scholarship program, his public audience was wildly enthusiastic, but the White House press corps was unimpressed:

> "Ten thousand dollars?" one reporter said snidely about the annual scholarship. "What's that gonna buy you?"
>
> His buddy agreed. "Yeah, I mean it costs four thousand to send your kid to nursery school."[27]

As Hunt said after the Baird affair, "It may be that we live a life so unlike average citizens that we're not really very attuned to what they're thinking about."[28] To make matters worse, star journalists and pundits now command huge speaking fees from industry groups and other special interests, which raises troubling questions about bias—and even outright corruption. To the extent that elite Washington and New York journalists set the tone for news coverage across the country, there are reasons for concern.

A final reason to worry about the "money power" applies specifically to the broadcast media, which are less open and diverse than print. A newspaper is actually a bundle of separate products: the news stories, the editorials, the advice columns, the comics, and so on. By adding a new feature or viewpoint, the paper stands to pick up extra readers, and it rarely risks losing sales by adding more diversity. Similarly, within its news and editorial pages, the more viewpoints it contains, the more readers it can attract. Those who detest a particular column can simply skip it. Therefore, despite any ideological biases that may be identified in a newspaper like the *New York Times,* its editorial pages are as diverse as the editors know how to make them.[29] Meanwhile, there are always alternative journals for those who find major newspapers unsatisfying, and these journals, too, have been able to attract advertising.

But the electronic media—television and radio—are in some ways more important than print, since 70 percent of Americans cite TV as their major source of news, compared to 20 percent who cite newspapers.[30] However, the electronic media are much less diverse and accessible than books and newspapers. This is primarily because the electromagnetic spectrum has room for only a limited number of channels. Moreover, a television station is not a bundle of separate products, like a newspaper. It can only broadcast one program at a time, and if people don't like it, they will switch channels—perhaps for good. Therefore, broadcasting, more than print, is subject to majority tyranny and a decline to the lowest common denominator.

The government's response to the poor quality of commercial television has been typical of interest-group liberalism. Instead of deliberating about what good TV would look like, Congress has delegated vague powers to the Federal Communication Commission (FCC), which negotiates with broadcasters and the industry lobby. The FCC is supposed to grant free use of the spectrum to whichever applicant would best serve "the public interest, convenience, and necessity." Until deregulation in the 1980s, the FCC translated this general formula into a few significant regulations, notably the Fairness Doctrine, which required broadcasters to cover all issues that were of public importance and to cover them fairly. Thus a local television station could not, in theory, refuse to cover a major strike in its area, nor slant its coverage in favor of one side in the strike. If it did, it would be subject to lawsuits.

It should not be surprising that the FCC has never demanded much under the public interest clause or the now-defunct Fairness Doctrine. Appointed regulators do not have the mandate to debate values, conflicting interests, or public priorities. Besides, they are subject to manipulation by powerful lobbyists who can influence their selection, threaten to erase their rulings through legislation, and hire them after they leave the government. Congress should take the bull by the horns, publicly debate what "the public interest" means in broadcasting, and pass content-neutral requirements for licensees (such as a certain number of minutes devoted to public-affairs programming). Federal courts should then uphold such requirements as enhancements of free speech.

At the same time, Congress should be generous in its subsidies of public television and radio, which present minority views and highly substantive programming. The government could also distribute broadcasting rights in a different way. Since passage of the Communications Act of 1934, the FCC has granted one company total control over each part of the spectrum in each geographical area. Instead, the government could give part of the day to commercial broadcasters and reserve part for nonprofit or public use. Or it could retain control of the spectrum and give out individual broadcast slots to private groups, both commercial and nonprofit. A very modest reform would be to provide free broadcast time for political candidates. The high cost of TV advertising is one cause of politicians' dependence on private money. Along with Sri Lanka, the United States is one of only two countries in the world that do not give politicians free broadcast time.

But whatever changes are made to improve broadcast television, cable TV has become more important, serving three out of five TV-equipped homes.[31] Cable is not subject to content regulation, because it does not use the public's airwaves. Fortunately, it is a relatively open and diverse medium. The copper cables that are most common today can carry more than fifty channels, and fiber-optic lines (made of tiny glass threads) can carry hundreds. Thus the scarcity that has prevailed in broadcasting is no longer necessary on technological grounds. Already, cable companies provide numerous channels serving all kinds of minority interests. They are beginning to resemble newspapers—which sell a large bundle of features instead of a single product—or even newsstands, which offer an even wider variety of information and ideas.

For a few years in the early 1990s, it was thought that the future lay in two-way communications between cable subscribers and media companies. People would use their cable lines to order entertainment and news from firms with huge stocks of movies and information. Traditionally printed material, such as daily newspapers and magazines, would be cheaply transmitted the same way. With this vision in mind, cable, video, news, and entertainment companies rushed to merge. But the conventional wisdom changed in a matter of months. Suddenly, the Internet was the rage, and everyone expected *it* to carry live pictures even more cheaply and conveniently than cable systems. Indeed, the difference between cable television and computer networks may fade over time, as computers begin to carry video programming and televisions gain more complex control systems.

Any prediction about the future of electronic media is liable to look foolish almost before it is made. But we should apply an important legal principle—the "common carrier" idea—whatever the future brings. Today's telephone networks are common carriers, because the utility establishes a price schedule, and then anyone can use its wires to say anything to anyone. Telephone companies own the conduits, but not the content, of communications. This approach turns the telephone network into a free public space, while providing profits to the utilities that own it.

The Internet currently works the same way, because its medium *is* the telephone network. Millions of people and organizations disseminate information in cyberspace, and anyone can communicate with anyone else. Although most of what has appeared on the Internet so far is of low quality, the medium is unfettered. But cable services are different. Since one company provides both the communications conduit and a limited array of programming, it has enormous power to censor and discriminate. If cable lines became the means for distributing newspapers, the problem would only grow more serious. Thus it would be better for the Internet to swallow up cable television, rather than the reverse. At the moment, computer networks seem safely ascendant, and no one talks about a brave new world of cable television. But the telephone lines that transmit the Internet into private homes have limited capacity; they cannot conveniently carry moving pictures. One way to solve this problem is to run fiber-optic wires into everyone's house; another is to use the existing cable lines. In either case, the question arises: Who will own these wires? If TV, radio, electronic mail, telephone, and newspapers are all transmitted into our homes along a single cable, then control over that line will mean control over our lives. It is therefore very important to ensure that networks are managed on a common-carrier basis, with a strict separation between the owners of the conduits and the providers of content. Two cities in the Pacific Northwest, Seattle and Portland, require that local cable lines function as common carriers when they carry Internet data. Experience will show whether this approach works, but it is certainly worth trying.[32]

THE DUTIES OF A FREE PRESS

Concerns about censorship and bias should lead Progressives to defend free expression whenever it is threatened by the government. They should also oppose media monopolies; support public broadcasting and research subsidies; and favor a common-carrier approach to cable-TV and the Internet. All of these measures will help to preserve and enhance the press's role as public watchdog.

In recent years, however, nothing has stopped the press from uncovering scandals and canvassing the merits and measures of powerful people. It has acted as a fierce watchdog, but it has done little to enhance public deliberation. On the contrary, by emphasizing partisan political maneuvering, journalists have sometimes suggested that public talk is irrelevant to the power games that constitute "politics." By concentrating on elections, they have implied that citizens act through the ballot box alone. Their fixation on divisive issues and controversial figures has polarized opinion and made citizens weary of political debate. And their relentless search for scandal and hypocrisy has given all politics an odor of disgrace.

Although I have used survey results in this book, I think that journalists' heavy use of polls is also problematic. Pollsters often ask a random sample of Americans for their individual, unreflective, and uninformed opinion about pre-formulated questions. The aggregated results are then presented as parameters within which politicians and the public *must* operate. We are told, for example, that a given policy is "unrealistic," because 65 percent of the public opposes it. "Public opinion" thus confronts citizens as an alien force, even though it is supposed to be something that they create. Anything worthy of the name should be the result of actual deliberation about ends and values.

During the 1996 presidential campaign, CNN was criticized for broadcasting daily polls that measured fluctuating support for the major candidates. Tom Hannon, the network's political director, replied: "Everyone strives to get a good balance between reporting on polls and reporting on other sorts of campaign news, so that you're not poll-driven. But [a poll] does happen to be the most authoritative way to answer the most basic question about the election, which is who's going to win."[33]

If you have made up your mind about every political issue, and you already know for certain which candidates you will support, then you are ready to cast your vote. In that case, you may indeed think that "Who will win?" is the most basic question about an election. But if this is how you feel, then the whole campaign is not really worth much of your attention, because there is little that you can do to affect the outcome. Like a racing fan, you can only sit back and watch the horses run. Whether this spectacle interests you is a sheer matter of taste. On the other hand, some people have not made up their minds about all the issues and candidates. At least in principle, they are open to evidence and argument. For them, "Who will win?" is *not* the most important question in an election. What they want to know is: "Who *should* win?" To an extraordinary extent, journalists try to answer the first question and ignore the second.

The media's preference for "horse-race" stories over issues has been amply documented with statistics. To take just one example, during the 1996 Republican presidential primary campaign, the candidates conducted a spirited debate about supply-side economics, protectionism, and the role of private charity and the family. But 54 percent of television news reports discussed the "electability" of the various candidates; 17 percent covered their "campaign trail behavior"; and just 15 percent mentioned "their positions on policy issues."[34]

Nor do journalists behave much differently when the next election is still years away and a crucial issue is being decided by the government. For example, in July of 1995, affirmative action became the most prominent domestic policy question. In quick succession, the Supreme Court issued a major decision on the topic; President Clinton took a position in favor of certain kinds of affirmative action; and the regents of the University of California ended all race- and gender-based programs on California state campuses.

Clinton's speech, in which he adopted the slogan "Mend it, don't end it," coincided with the release of a ninety-five-page review of federal affirmative action programs. News coverage uniformly focused on three questions. First, how would Clinton's stance affect the 1996 presidential vote, still eighteen months away? Many reporters noted that his position might prevent a challenge from Reverend Jesse Jackson and mollify angry liberals. But a headline in the *San Diego Union Tribune* stressed the political cost of the president's stance: "What price must Clinton pay? Gleeful GOP thinks he'll lose the support of angry white men."[35]

The *New York Times,* blessed with an advance copy of the review, offered the inside story on the White House's calculations. The *Times* cited anonymous presidential aides who had "concluded not only that [affirmative action] programs worked well, but also that the political risks of tinkering with them now far outweighed any benefit that Mr. Clinton might gain in new support from minority voters." These sources noted that affirmative action "benefitted not just minorities, but also women, whose electoral support the President needs."[36] Nevertheless, many pundits predicted that the issue would help Republicans, especially California Governor Pete Wilson, then a presumed presidential contender. "The interesting thing," said Michele Norris of *ABC News,* "is that both parties will likely use affirmative action as a wedge issue in the '96 elections."[37]

A second "interesting" question, also much discussed, was the following: Did Clinton act from political expediency or rather from principle? In other words, as the *St. Petersburg Times* editorialized: "Once again, a matter of race—this time camouflaged as affirmative action—has become a test of political *character.*"[38] Some thought that Clinton's speech reflected poorly on him. For example, when Howard Fineman of *Newsweek* was asked what he thought of the president's stance, he answered promptly: "Well, what's going on here is presidential politics. . . . Bill Clinton, number one, knows that he's lost the angry white male vote, especially in the South. [To compensate, he] needs those votes of minorities and women in industrial states."[39] Arguing the opposite position, Jeff Greenfield began his syndicated column: "President Clinton did something unusual last week: He took a clear, forceful stand on a controversial issue." Greenfield conceded, "If you are afflicted with terminal 'politicitis,' you can view the speech as an attempt to ward off an independent presidential campaign by Jesse Jackson." But he preferred to see "the president's talk as a sign of what Clinton's critics say he lacks: a sense of a 'core belief,' a conviction deep enough to defend even at the cost of political pain."[40]

In covering Clinton's affirmative action speech, reporters instinctively turned to political strategy and questions of character. As I argued in chapter 3, this kind of coverage has a measurable, negative effect on public trust. Journalists also wanted to know how potential voters had responded to the president's speech. On CNN's *Inside Politics,* Bernard Shaw began his show by saying, "Affirmative action has become the issue of the moment on the presidential campaign trail [remember that the date was *July* 1995], with President Clinton taking the leading defenders' role. If his stance was aimed at bolstering his image with the public, it has apparently worked."[41] Shaw then announced the results of a poll showing that citizens favored the president's position by 46 percent to 38 percent, a marked increase over the previous week.

If some voters changed their minds immediately following Clinton's speech, it was not on the basis of any relevant information. The speech itself was only quoted in tiny snippets; and, as far as I can tell, no newspaper, magazine, or broadcast show addressed the obvious substantive questions: How do federal affirmative-action programs work? When did they begin? Whom do they affect? What can you do if you feel that you have been mistreated? Do some people feel this way? What did the president's review say? Was it accurate? These questions could be dull if they were answered with dry statistics, but a skillful reporter could dramatize them by telling stories about real people whom affirmative action had helped or harmed. There was plenty of time to develop such stories, because the administration's review had been widely anticipated. But I doubt that most reporters read it, let alone analyzed it.

When the actual issue of affirmative action was discussed in the mass media, there was more heat than light. The following exchange from ABC's *This Week with David Brinkley*, broadcast July 23, 1995, was not much worse than the norm:

> SAM DONALDSON: Well, the Reverend Jackson's used the word "corrupt" to describe some of your supporters at that [California Board of Regents] meeting.
>
> Gov. PETE WILSON: Well, that's unfortunate name-calling. It's the kind of childish name-calling that he's guilty of in this morning's *Los Angeles Times,* where he refers to me as the "Susan Smith of national politics," whatever that is supposed to mean.
>
> Rev. JESSE JACKSON: Well, my point is—my point is, in South Carolina—
>
> Gov. WILSON: Well—
>
> Rev. JACKSON: —Susan Smith was desperate. She used an imaginary black man as diversion. When you are desperate because your economy's failing—
>
> Gov. WILSON: Oh that's—that's—
>
> Rev. JACKSON: —you do not have—
>
> Gov. WILSON: —pretty much of a reach.
>
> Rev. JACKSON: —a budget before your legislature—
>
> Gov. WILSON: That is a pathetic—
>
> Rev. JACKSON: —you pull out the race card.
>
> Gov. WILSON: —effort.

It seems unlikely that most viewers and voters admire this kind of discussion. Although substantive policy issues can be dull, nothing is more tedious than a shouting match, unless it's the type of arcane horse-race story that has become common recently. Late in the 1996 presidential campaign, for example, a fairly typical newspaper story might speculate about whether the Dole campaign's decision to buy advertising in California was intended to help Republican House candidates prevail in districts where "soccer Moms" were likely to vote for Clinton—and so on, endlessly. I doubt that these stories sell many papers; indeed, the overall market for political news seems to be shrinking.[42]

If the emphasis on campaign strategy and polls is not driven by public demand, it may come from the supply side: in other words, from journalists. After all, it is *difficult* to write a useful story about affirmative action. First, you may have to read a ninety-five-page report, which even one of its authors called "profoundly boring."[43] Then you ought to talk to a lot of experts and ordinary people, read statutes and law-review articles, and visit agencies. Finally, you have to make arguments and draw conclusions in an area where you lack expertise, credibility, and confidence. How much easier it is to concentrate on the only question that political reporters can discuss with genuine expertise—Who is going to win?

As it turned out, the pundits were mistaken to believe that affirmative action would play an important role in the 1996 race. Meanwhile, they often seem to have no idea what happens in government below the highest, most "political," levels. Nor are they much interested. Howard Kurtz, the *Washington Post*'s media critic, described the scene in the White House pressroom early in 1995, when Newt Gingrich seemed to be governing America from the House of Representatives, and no one was paying any attention to the president:

> Brit Hume is in his closet-size White House cubicle, watching Kato Kaelin testify on CNN. Bill Plante, in the adjoining cubicle, has his feet up and is buried in the *New York Times*. Brian Williams is in the corridor, idling away the time with Jim Miklaszewski.
> An announcement is made for a bill-signing ceremony. Some of America's highest-paid television correspondents begin ambling toward the pressroom door.
> "Are you coming with is?" Williams asks.
> "I guess so," says Hume, looking forlorn.[44]

One would think that a temporary lull in political excitement would provide White House reporters with a precious opportunity. Surely, a slow news day in 1995 was the perfect time to read the government's employment rules in preparation for the coming battle over affirmative action. If such regulations grew unbearably dull, reporters could always cross Pennsylvania Avenue to talk to federal employees about their experience under affirmative action. Or, if they couldn't stand this whole subject, they could read about welfare, Bosnia, the federal budget, monetary policy—anything. Instead, as the White House spokesman, Mike McCurry, observed: "Brit Hume has now got his crossword puzzle capacity down to record time. And some of the reporters have been out on the lecture circuit."[45]

There is one kind of issue that seems to provoke mainstream reporters into action. Whenever there is a scandal in government, we can expect aggressive, independent, investigative reporting: witness the coverage of the Whitewater Affair in the *New York Times,* the *Washington Post,* and the *Wall Street Journal.* Indeed, the *Times* originally revealed the affair, and the press subsequently offered enormous amounts of hard-won information—intricate charts of financial dealings, detailed chronologies, complex legal analysis. As usual, reporters were primarily interested in the question: Who will win? In cases of scandal, however, this question shifts slightly to become: Will the president be indicted? Only congressional committees and the independent counsel can subpoena documents, and only juries can indict and convict, but investigative reporters can try to *foretell* what will happen by gathering information from inside sources. They may also influence the legal outcome by uncovering otherwise unknown facts. "Yet," as Joan Didion wrote in 1996:

> the actual interest of Whitewater lies in what has already been documented: it is "about" the S & L crisis, and therefore offers a detailed and specific look at the kinds of political and financial dealing that resulted in the meltdown of middle-class

confidence. What Whitewater "really means" or offers, then, is an understanding of that meltdown, which is being reported as an inexplicable phenomenon weirdly detached from the periodic "growth" figures produced in Washington.[46]

Didion suggests that we should analyze Whitewater as part of the economic and political history of our times; but this is impossible for reporters who always keep their eyes on the question: Who will win? In fact, journalists generally missed the savings-and-loan story until it became an issue for congressional investigators, because their whole focus was on the inside game of politics.

Fortunately, during the last few years, a new movement, called public or civic journalism, has begun to transform American newspapers, at least beyond the Capital Beltway. This label has been adopted by a loose coalition of reform-minded journalists with diverse ideals and projects. But a common theme unites many of their experiments: the cultivation of public deliberation.

In North Carolina, the *Charlotte Observer* and the local ABC-television affiliate decided to adopt a self-described "public journalism" approach to the 1992 elections. They deliberately ignored political strategy and stopped running wire-service stories that treated the campaign as a competition among professional politicians. Before the campaign began, they polled 1,000 citizens, asking them what issues the candidates should discuss. They then recruited 500 of these people to serve as a "citizens' panel" that would collaborate with journalists to devise questions for candidates to answer. Reporters from the business, health, education, and religion beats covered topics that the panel considered relevant to the election. Members of the panel met directly with some candidates, and some of their deliberations were televised locally.[47]

Rich Oppel, the *Charlotte Observer*'s editor, recalls:

> Voters were intensely interested in the environment. . . . So our reporters went out to senatorial candidates and said here are the voters' questions. Terry Sanford, the incumbent senator, called me up from Washington and said, "Rich, I have these questions from your reporter and I'm not going to answer them because we are not going to talk about the environment until the general election." This was the primary. I said, "Well, the voters want to know about the environment now, Terry." He said, "Well, that's not the way I have my campaign structured." I said, "Fine, I will run the questions and I will leave a space under it for you to answer. If you choose not to, we will just say, 'would not respond' or we will leave it blank." We ended the conversation. In about ten days he sent the answer down.[48]

This example shares several features with many (although not all) other cases of public journalism. First, the *Observer* convened a panel of citizens who influenced the newspaper's decisions about what issues to cover and how. Public journalists argue that reporters should stop taking direction from official press releases and news conferences, and start pursuing the voters' agenda.

Second, the *Observer* assumed an activist stance. Once its readers had expressed concern about environmental policy, the newspaper demanded that the candidates respond. Such activism dismays some opponents of public journalism, who worry that it violates principles of neutrality and detachment. This criticism grew intense as public journalism strengthened its hold on the North Carolina media. During the 1996 campaign, six major daily newspapers and several television stations combined forces to create a consortium known as "Your Voice, Your Vote." Participating newspapers reduced their horse-race coverage and largely stopped following the candidates; instead, they published questionnaires on topics selected by a citizens' poll.

These newspapers thereby gave themselves significant power. For example, they chose to emphasize the issues of "crime and drugs," "taxes and spending," "affordable health care," and "education"; but they passed over several issues that also ranked high in the voters' poll, notably "families and values" and "race relations." The last two issues sharply divided the North Carolina senatorial candidates, who itched for confrontation. The incumbent, Jesse Helms, is a gay-baiting former segregationist; his opponent, Harvey Gannt, is an African American with socially liberal ideas. Both Gannt's campaign manager and at least one House candidate complained bitterly that the newspaper's selection of issues had hurt them politically and affected the outcome of the race. Although Senator Helms won the election, he cannot have been much happier, since he declined to participate in the consortium's questionnaire, and blank spaces were printed under his name.[49]

It is worth noting, however, that "Your Voice, Your Vote" was only part of the *Charlotte Observer's* election coverage; its articles also discussed fund-raising, tactics, personalities, and issues not raised in its poll.[50] Furthermore, North Carolina's public journalists never forced candidates to take any particular position on crime and drugs or the environment. Instead, they compelled politicians to engage in a dialogue with citizens on these issues. Thus public journalists promoted a particular democratic *process* and not a political *outcome.* The underlying idea was that candidates have no automatic right to expect journalists to describe their behavior and statements. Editors—backed by their readers' opinion—may choose to cover issues that candidates would rather avoid. Newspapers and broadcast stations cannot neglect their responsibility as participants and conveners of a democratic dialogue.

The *Wichita Eagle* has dedicated itself, perhaps more than any other paper, to public journalism. Its writers and editors believe that this philosophy influences them even when they are not using citizens' panels or other forms of public deliberation. The *Eagle* claims to be engaged in public journalism whenever it describes constructive public dialogue taking place in the community, and whenever it emphasizes the public's "struggle to find a middle ground." In its news stories, it argues explicitly that the citizens of Wichita should "face up to its problems and come together to solve them."[51]

In short, the *Eagle* intentionally presents a picture of a community in search of consensus, and it editorializes in favor of this process throughout its news pages. In this way, public journalism influences the tone and spirit of the newspaper's daily coverage. The *Eagle* does not shrink from covering strife as well as deliberation, but its editors try to emphasize the community's search for consensus and pragmatic solutions: aspects of public life that mainstream journalists often ignore. For example, the day after a primary election, the *Eagle*'s frontpage, banner headline read: "Folks in the middle seek ways to find common ground." To help them do so, the *Eagle* convened groups of citizens to talk at length about local problems. It then printed summaries of their discussions, along with suggestions from readers and information about relevant organizations.[52]

Of course, all is not perfect in Kansas, and the *Eagle* sometimes openly laments Wichita's failure to solve its problems. In its stories about the city's shortcomings, the newspaper often blames itself. One article was entitled: "1994: Our community is challenged; Wichita had to confront race issue." Discussing a particular racial controversy, the reporter asked, "In our haste to solve the problem, did we miss the opportunity to work our way through it as a community?" And he concluded: "With the best of intentions, we blew the opportunity." The "we" refers to Wichitans in general, but also explicitly to the *Eagle*.

PUBLIC JOURNALISM AND ITS CRITICS

Public journalism has become highly controversial. One common complaint is that reporters who are involved in the movement compromise their obligation to be accurate and objective. For instance, the *Charlotte Observer*'s use of citizens' panels may seem inherently misleading, because it allows the newspaper to cover deliberation when in fact people rarely meet in diverse groups to talk about politics. Similarly, when the *Wichita Eagle* describes "folks in the middle" getting together to hash out their problems, this looks to many hardened political reporters like an obvious falsification of the grim reality. Public journalists, the critics argue, make civil society look better—more civil—than it really is.

In one sense, citizens' panels do distort reality. It would be a mistake to predict aggregate public behavior by observing deliberation. If politicians or journalists want to know how the public at large will vote during the next election, a conventional opinion poll can probably provide the best insights into this behavior. Participants in a roundtable may offer particularly poor insights into the future actions of the whole public, because people who engage in inclusive, informed deliberation will often reach different conclusions from those of their nondeliberating peers.

However, information of great *moral* relevance can be derived from deliberation, since participants share ideas, educate themselves, and defend their values. In deliberation, they do not abandon their right to their own interests and beliefs, but they test them in public discussion. Alexander Hamilton wrote: "The republican principle demands that the deliberate sense of the community should govern the conduct of those to whom they entrust the management of their affairs."[53] Journalists would perform a public service if they helped identify and promote this "deliberate sense."

The decision to emphasize the search for consensus within the larger community raises a different set of issues. For example, the *Wichita Eagle* presented an idiosyncratic picture of the 1994 National Presbyterian Assembly, simply because the *Eagle*'s reporter approached his subject as a public journalist. The national media sent reporters to cover the Presbyterian Assembly, in the expectation that they would find rhetorical fireworks. The *Dallas Morning News* predicted: "The Presbyterian General Assembly that starts Friday . . . is likely to be the most contentious in years." The *Fresno Bee* declared: "It's not life or death for the Presbyterian Church (U.S.A.) as thousands of members gather today in Wichita, Kan. But the church body is flailing and emergency lights are flashing over issues like biblical interpretation, sexuality, and finances." And the Minneapolis *Star Tribune* announced (in a news story): "Fear is stalking American Christendom, slowly, one denomination at a time, corroding the heart and soul of its religious institutions. Fear of change. Fear of heresy. Fear of each other. It has landed, for now, on the 2.8 million-member Presbyterian Church."[54]

The *Wichita Eagle*'s reporter, Thomas B. Koetting, did not ignore the controversy that other newspapers emphasized. But he quoted Presbyterian conferees who deplored division and sought consensus. Public journalists typically go looking for "the folks in the middle," the people in any group who want to reach a constructive agreement. This search may introduce bias into their coverage. But mainstream journalists seek people with polarized opinions, so that they can balance pithy quotes on either extreme of any issue. Even at a church conference, they hope to find "flashing lights" and "flailing bodies." Under these circumstances, public journalists have at least as good a chance of being accurate as mainstream reporters.

Indeed, according to the *Salt Lake Tribune,* the Presbyterian Conference turned out to be "an emotional session that resolved a lot of issues that many thought would divide the faith. . . . Participants left Wichita pleased." Reverend Robert W. Bohl, the new Presbyterian leader, recalled, "It was a laboratory of human grace under pressure. We proved we could deal with our differences and did it. No one went away mad." Although many delegates had arrived "apprehensive"—having "formed opinions on partial information"—one participant remembered that the assembly ended in a scene of "tremendous healing," with delegates hugging and singing "Praise God from Whom All Blessings Flow."[55]

From these quotations, it sounds as if Koetting filed more accurate stories than the rest of the media put together. But not all participants were equally satisfied. One wrote later that "the furor created by a feminist 'Re-Imagining Conference' . . . set the mood, stage and context for decisions made at our General Assembly."[56] So which atmosphere actually predominated at the assembly—"furor" or "tremendous healing"? Someone could have conducted a scientific poll of the delegates, asking them about their impressions of the assembly. But regardless of the results, most journalists would have considered conflict to be the real *news;* and Koetting would have covered the search for consensus.

During the conference itself, the [Louisville, Kentucky] *Courier-Journal* reported that most delegates "milled around, slapping backs, listening to speeches, taking votes," while controversy raged in a small committee room, among a few dozen people."[57] Presumably, Koetting spent his time talking to back-slapping delegates who deplored controversy, while the rest of the press tried to cover the battle inside the committee room. When there is both division and consensus present in a community, either can be covered accurately. Public journalists believe that polarized, unconstructive conflict is far too common in the news, so they seek out examples of successful public discussion.

In short, critics are wrong to say that public journalism cannot be accurate, objective, or truthful. But others complain that public journalists are "activists" who have abandoned the "detachment" that is proper to their profession. According to this argument, reporters should simply describe the world as they find it; they should never attempt to change society in keeping with their values. Max Frankel of the *New York Times* has attacked public journalism by arguing: "Reporters, editors, and publishers have their hands full learning to tell [the news] right. They should leave reforms to reformers." Frankel suggests that a newspaper that identifies itself with a social struggle will be unable to provide "trustworthy observation" of that struggle as it proceeds.[58] Some critics are concerned, too, about the media's power. An activist press, they fear, could alter public life almost at will—and without democratic accountability.

Needless to say, even the news pages of the mainstream press are not free of activism. All news media potentially influence public policy by choosing what stories to cover and how to present them. Many conventional journalists argue that they serve a free society by describing the behavior of politicians, so that citizens may vote wisely. For example, Leonard Downie, executive editor of the *Washington Post* and a critic of public journalism, has said that the duty of the press "is to provide citizens with as much as possible of the information they need to conduct their lives, private and public, and to hold accountable the increasing number of powerful people and institutions that hold sway in our lives."[59] In support of this role, reporters and editors sometimes heroically confront political officials and defend their rights of free speech and access to information. These efforts—just like the convening of citizens' panels—constitute "activism" and turn journalists into "actors on the political stage."[60] At its best, the mainstream press simply promotes a representative democracy instead of a deliberative one.

Representation is an important value. By breaking the Watergate story, Woodward and Bernstein truly helped citizens to judge their elected officials, as did the *New York Times* when it published the Pentagon Papers in order to inform its readers about Vietnam. Justice Black cited its role in enhancing "informed representative government."[61] But, as Cole Campbell, the editor of the *St. Louis Post-Dispatch,* says, "we are coming to realize that deliberative democracy may hold more possibilities than representative democracy, and that covering democracy one way can be just as legitimate as covering it another."[62]

Because the mainstream media are committed to pure representative democracy, they devote vast amounts of space to stories about the tactics and plans of professional politicians, thus suggesting that the inside game is extremely important to the future of the nation. When, in almost every story on policy questions, reporters analyze the "real" (i.e., tactical and selfish) motivations of politicians, they imply that citizens' main political job is to assess the "merits and measures" of their elected officials, so that voters may judge without illusion. Thus the mainstream media advocate representative democracy just as actively and aggressively as the *Wichita Eagle* champions deliberation.

For the same reasons, the mainstream press automatically treats the launching of campaigns, presidential press conferences, and personal attacks as news; but it rarely covers unofficial citizen deliberations. Many mainstream reporters apparently think that there is something "artificial" about convening a group of citizens to discuss politics, but that it is "detached" and "objective" to cover a press conference, even if one candidate calls it to denounce another for cheating or lying. Perhaps mainstream journalists imagine that they belong to an entirely different world from that of candidates, so that reporters are detached observers at news conferences where the candidates are the only actors. But, seen from a more distant perspective, journalists and politicians actually collude in promoting the idea that professionals can take care of politics for us and that we must only judge them after the fact.

Thus, in defense of the *Charlotte Observer* and the *Wichita Eagle,* we can say that their "activism" is similar to that of the mainstream press. In particular, both public journalists and traditional investigative reporters claim to promote democratic *procedures* and not policy outcomes. For example, during Watergate and the Vietnam War, the *Washington Post* and the *New York Times* did not defend their aggressive reporting as beneficial to any policy, party, or politician; rather, they offered information so that the voters might judge national policy for themselves. Similarly, the *Charlotte Observer* and the *Wichita Eagle* do not favor any particular policies in their news pages (at least, no more than any other paper's); rather, they encourage procedures of public deliberation. Their procedural role should assuage their critics' fear that the media is too powerful and unaccountable to play an active role in the political arena.

To encourage deliberation is a procedural goal; to defend the spotted owl would mean promoting particular values and policies. But some issues seem to lie in an intermediate realm. For example, the *Akron Beacon-Journal* won a Pulitzer Prize for its antiracism program, which it described as an example of public journalism. One could argue that racism is a barrier to deliberation, because it undermines the equality and mutual respect that (among other things) distinguish deliberation from less valuable forms of discourse. But one could also argue that opposition to racism is a policy goal—albeit a laudable one—in which case the newspaper may have overstepped its proper bounds.

The *Beacon-Journal* convened biracial discussion groups to discuss racial inequality and provided the participants with data to discuss. This part of its program was typical of public journalism, and so far its goals were narrowly procedural, because citizens could reach any conclusion they chose. But in addition to reporting on the citizen discussions, the newspaper also invited local organizations to devise programs against racism, offering professional support at the newspaper's expense. Finally, it asked readers to take a pledge to fight racism and received 22,000 positive responses. The *Beacon-Journal* estimates that some 10,000 citizens in the Akron area were involved in programs related to race relations by mid-1994. It is difficult to criticize the intentions behind this program, but we should ask whether the *Beacon-Journal*'s role was purely procedural. In my view, no harm would be done if a newspaper actively and openly pursued a political goal (even a more controversial one than racial peace). But that would be a different matter from supporting deliberation, and it would require a separate defense.

Another serious complaint about public journalism is that, by emphasizing the "folks in the middle," it may cause newspapers to exclude or denigrate people at the political and cultural margins. These people may be too outnumbered and disrespected, or their views may be too radical to be discussed calmly in a citizens' panel. Public journalists respond that the mainstream press devotes too much space to reporting the inflammatory remarks of implacable political enemies. But if public journalism became the dominant philosophy, people who *actually were* implacable enemies might find themselves ignored, in favor of citizens who happened to be politically moderate enough that they could deliberate together.

For example, people who think that abortion is cold-blooded murder have good reasons not to deliberate with "pro-choice" activists about pragmatic solutions to their common problems. The same is true of people who believe that "pro-life" activists are misogynists who want to punish women for exercising their sexual autonomy. Some public journalists have argued that both sides in this dispute can—and should—work together toward common ends: for example, promoting adoption in order to reduce the number of abortions.[63] But any such compromise would undermine the respective goals of the two movements, if (among other things) they want to expose pervasive evil by employing dramatic symbols, provoking stark conflicts, and demonizing their opponents.

Some political movements thrive by deliberately clashing with uncompromising enemies. Public journalists do not want to aid this variety of activism, however, for it divides civil society, polarizes public opinion, and prevents deliberation.[64] Yet these tactics have an honorable history. One master of the art of polarization was Martin Luther King, Jr. In 1962, King's Southern Christian Leadership Conference nearly foundered in Albany, Georgia, when the segregationist authorities, led by Police Chief Laurie Pritchett, played the role of moderates, avoiding confrontation and even joining the Civil Rights leaders in prayer. As a result of this disaster, the SCLC deliberately chose Birmingham, Alabama, as the site of its next campaign: "Project C" (for "Confrontation"). While Chief Pritchett had managed to look like one of the "folks in the middle," Birmingham's Bull Connor was bound to use violence against peaceful demonstrators.

Before the SCLC arrived in Birmingham, Connor was unseated by a white moderate candidate. But King did not wait to see whether the new commissioner might dismantle segregation voluntarily; instead, he rushed to confront Connor. By sending schoolchildren on peaceful marches, the SCLC was able to provoke Connor into using firehoses and dogs, thus driving a nail into the coffin of Jim Crow. When police first used violence against marchers in Birmingham, the SCLC leaders "were jumping up and down, elated. . . . They said over and over again, 'We've got a movement. We've got a movement. We had some police brutality. They brought out the dogs. We've got a movement.'"[65]

Meanwhile, a group of white clergymen published an advertisement in which they accused Dr. King of coming into their community from the outside, stirring up tension, and interfering with a process of local, peaceful change that would have led to justice. Many in the African-American business community also opposed King's protests, claiming that they could work with Birmingham's white moderates toward orderly change. If public journalists had existed in those days, they might have written stories headed, "Folks in Birmingham seek common ground." On the other hand, they might have ignored King, who was no ordinary Birmingham citizen but rather a political leader with a national constituency, bent on creating tension, confrontation, and crisis.

Indeed, King wrote in his "Letter from a Birmingham Jail" that "the creation of tension [is] a part of the work of the nonviolent resister. This may sound shocking. But I must confess that I am not afraid of the word *tension*." And he acknowledged that the "purpose of the direct action is to create a situation so crisis-packed that it will inevitably open the door to negotiation." By "negotiation," King meant a discussion about the proper *way* to desegregate Birmingham; but he considered desegregation itself to be nonnegotiable. Thus he never genuinely wanted to deliberate with Bull Connor about common values. Instead, he hoped to force a capitulation by the city government on the issue that divided racists from believers in civil rights. Told that the forthcoming administration might end segregation of its own accord, King replied: "My friends, I must say to you that we have not made a single gain in civil rights without determined legal and nonviolent pressure." Asked to wait for change, King declared: "This 'Wait' has almost always meant 'Never.'" Finally, called an "extremist," he embraced the label—for "Was not Jesus an extremist in love? . . . Was not Amos an extremist for justice?"[66]

It should give us pause to realize that King's methods were inconsistent with some of public journalism's values. The Civil Rights Movement gave a new birth to democracy in America, and some writers in the mainstream press helped its progress. But public journalists might not have been friendly to King's tactics, so perhaps we should distrust public journalism.

On the other hand, it could be that the example of the Civil Rights Movement, while glorious, has been overapplied. Confrontation was a necessary tactic to achieve basic democratic rights when these were denied to people on the basis of their race, but it is not a good way to solve the contemporary problems of a divided civil society. In that case, journalists should stop looking for the next Dr. King, stop paying attention to spurious imitators on the right and left, and start quoting the folks in the middle. Public journalism, on this theory, is a necessary successor to the adversarial press of the 1960s.

A third interpretation suggests that confrontation is always necessary when basic political fairness is threatened: for example, when a class of people is denied the vote, constitutional rights, or equal access to government. Democracy must be deliberative, but it also must be fair: and without basic fairness, deliberation is a pointless exercise. In that case, the press always ought to cover confrontational movements that allege injustice in the basic rules of political engagement, even when their claims are suspect, because such allegations deserve a hearing. But reporters should use other tactics—notably those of public journalism—to cover policy disputes that do not involve issues of basic political or constitutional fairness.

Finally, we might say that the essence of public journalism is a commitment to democracy. In that case, a thoughtful version of the movement might have been far more helpful in 1955 than the approach of the mainstream press was at that time. After all, the national media was severely remiss in not describing racism, discrimination, and disenfranchisement when black leaders merely pointed them out; it took violent confrontation to attract reporters to the South. As Pat Watters and Reese Cleghorn, themselves journalists who followed the Civil Rights Movement, observe: "Violence makes news; a folk outpouring of faith and belief in the best achievements of man's moral and political thought—which was the heart of the movement—does not." Even at the height of the movement, they argue, the wire services showed an "amoral tendency to view a profound moral crisis in the South in cliché perspective, so that it came to seem like a baseball game, complete with box scores of broken heads." Furthermore, the press was particularly interested in conflicts among the Civil Rights organizations: the national media came to Albany in 1962 because "it was supposed to be the place for a showdown clash between SCLC, SNCC, and the NAACP."[67] Thus we could conclude that a genuine form of public journalism, appropriate to the age of Jim Crow, might have made the turmoil of the Civil Rights Movement unnecessary.

King and his allies would not have had to dramatize racism by provoking violence, if the press had covered African Americans' complaints without such prompting.

I have emphasized public journalism's potential for marginalizing political radicals and insurgents. A different problem may arise when public journalists champion civic responsibility to the exclusion of personal expression. They claim that the press as an institution "belongs to" the public, despite the fact that media corporations are privately owned. At a time when private property is worshiped as an idol, it is pleasant to encounter a movement that stresses the public responsibility of the private sector.[68] However, there is a risk if we demand exclusively public benefits from reporters and other writers. For newspapers are not only money-making corporations and public institutions; they are also stages for autobiography, eccentric opinion, and personal style. Aesthetic freedom and diversity may suffer if writers are exclusively called to serve public ends.

Public journalism's theorists owe a strong, acknowledged debt to Dewey, who argued that the sole criterion of value was a capacity to make the social world a better place.[69] "Unless subjective intents and thoughts are to terminate in picturesque utopias or dogmas irrelevant to constructive action," he wrote, "they [must be] subject to objective requirements and tests." By "objective tests," he meant the criterion of public acceptance. Thus he condemned "capricious pragmatism based on exaltation of personal desire; consolatory estheticism based on capacity for wringing contemplative enjoyment from even the tragedies of the outward spectacle; refugee idealism based on rendering thought omnipotent in the degree to which it is ineffective in public affairs."[70] Each of these failings is manifest in today's press.

But there is also a tradition in American thought that celebrates the vision of eccentric individuals, people who do not always care very much about the public—or who even hold it in contempt. Henry David Thoreau, for example, was a classic "refugee idealist," who wrote:

> It is not a man's duty, as a matter of course, to devote himself to the eradication of any, even the most enormous, wrong; he may still properly have other concerns to engage him; but it is his duty, at least, to wash his hands of it, and, if he gives it no thought longer, not to give it practically his support. . . . As for adopting the ways which the State has provided for remedying the evil, I know not of such ways. They take too much time, and a man's life will be gone. I have other affairs to attend to. I came into this world, not chiefly to make this a good place to live in, but to live in it, be it good or bad.[71]

If this statement expresses Thoreau's contempt for politics and the state, he felt much the same way about civil society. "The community has no bribe," he wrote, "that will tempt the wise man."[72] Thoreau abandoned both the state and his human community for Walden, where he wrote about his private life, pro-

claiming that his duty was to give his readers "a full dose of himself."[73] Here he
spoke for an entire American tradition (including also Ralph Waldo Emerson and
George Santayana) that has consistently championed privacy over an invasive
public domain.

Perhaps most daily journalists lack opportunities for unfettered self-expres-
sion, in which case they would lose nothing if they had to serve civil society. But
the last time that an idealistic movement influenced the press, it was New Journalism, which called for more freedom, more individuality, and more self-expres-
sion. The New Journalism made space for Joan Didion, Norman Mailer, Janet
Malcolm, John McPhee, Hunter S. Thompson, Gary Wills, and Tom Wolfe, at
least some of whose work is autobiographical and subjective, and not particularly
dedicated to social improvement. Perhaps the New Journalism made few inroads
at daily newspapers, but it transformed magazines and free weekly papers.

As long as New Journalists do not harm deliberation, they can coexist comfortably with public journalists. But the two movements will clash if a writer emerges
who has a strong, interesting, eloquent voice, but who denigrates the public or
engenders conflict. For example, the *New York Times* presumably gave Maureen
Dowd license to write in her distinctive style because her strong personality
would entertain readers and enliven the newspaper.[74] In that case, the *Times*'s
values were consistent with the ideals of New Journalism. But Dowd's relentless
cynicism and consuming interest in the powerful must be anathema to public
journalists. Dowd is perhaps not a very good example of any journalistic values.
Nevertheless, we are entitled to ask whether editors should reject contributions
that are eloquent, witty, arresting, and idiosyncratic, just because they harm
rather than enhance public deliberation. If so, we may in the end trade aesthetic
values for pragmatic ones, to the detriment of journalism as an art.

PUBLIC JOURNALISM AND WATCHDOG JOURNALISM

Public journalism should, I think, be combined with free, personal expression—
and also with a measure of traditional, watchdog-style reporting. Public journalists boast that their coverage begins with the public and ends with government,
instead of vice versa. For example, they convene citizens' panels and ask the participants to set the agenda for their coverage, instead of taking direction from
politicians and official interest groups. But let us imagine that a citizens' panel
was convened in a Rust Belt city that suffered from high unemployment because
of local plant closings. The citizens might initially place jobs at the top of their
agenda, asking the newspaper to cover employment issues extensively. After re-
questing and receiving information from reporters, the deliberating citizens
might decide that the cause of the local plant closing was a leveraged buy-out on
Wall Street. After even more informed deliberation and collaboration with reporters, they might conclude that the buy-out had occurred because of a change in

financial regulations. Further investigation might reveal that this regulatory change had occurred because Wall Street interests had financed congressional campaigns. At the end of the process, the public deliberators might call for campaign-finance reform.

But by then, ten years of rampant corruption could have occurred unobserved; and the basic problem might not even be campaign finance anymore. At any point during those ten years, experts and insiders could have told reporters that election laws required reform. In fact, they would have faxed numerous press releases to the newspaper about that very subject. But their effort to set the agenda would have been ignored in favor of the citizens' panel.

Thus it seems to me that public journalism should coexist with, and not replace, issue-based political and financial reporting.[75] This has already begun to happen. For instance, the *Asbury Park* (New Jersey) *Press* stumbled across a major story about real-estate fraud while working on a public-journalism project in its community. The *Press* "diverted" two reporters from its civic journalism team to work on the investigation and also hired forensics experts and real-estate appraisers. Ultimately, federal racketeering charges were filed against the developers whose misdeeds the *Press* had discovered. Meanwhile, its civic journalists were convening forums to talk about the more general problem of urban blight.[76] Thus, up to a point, there are plenty of resources available for both investigative and public journalism; and even more space and talent would become available if newspapers reduced their coverage of politicians' personalities, private behavior, and tactics. However, at some point the growth of public journalism would have to come at the cost of substantive political coverage—and this would involve a genuine loss for democracy. With this reservation, we should embrace public journalism as an important element of democratic renewal.

NOTES

1. Quoted by the Commission on the Freedom of the Press, *A Free and Responsible Press* (Chicago, 1947), which is excerpted in *Freedom of the Press from Hamilton to the Warren Court*, ed. Harold L. Nelson (Indianapolis, 1967), p. 397.

2. Potter Stewart, "Or of the Press," *Hastings Law Journal* 26 (1975): 631, 633.

3. James Madison, report on the resolutions of the Virginia General Assembly in opposition to the Alien and Sedition Acts, in Jonathan Eliot's *Debates in the Several State Conventions on the Adoption of the Federal Constitution,* vol. 4 (Philadelphia, 1937), pp. 570, 575.

4. Benjamin I. Page, *Who Deliberates? Mass Media in Modern Democracy* (Chicago, 1996), p. 14, note 12.

5. Pulitzer, cable of April 10, 1907, in *Freedom of the Press,* ed. Nelson, p. 409.

6. We should remember, however, that openly partisan newspapers are often more effective than independent journals at mobilizing the mass electorate. Like party "machines," partisan journals tend to increase political participation, but they also empower

their own leaders, simplify issues, and exacerbate political differences. Neither their advantages nor their disadvantages should be overlooked.

7. Nelson, *Freedom of the Press,* pp. xxxiii–xxxiv.

8. This according to William Hard, "Mr. Burleson, Espionagent," *The New Republic* (May 10, 1919): 43.

9. Brandeis, concurring opinion (joined by Holmes), in *Whitney v. California,* 274 U.S. 371, at 375.

10. *New York Times Co. v. United States,* 403 U.S. 717.

11. See Timothy Gleason, *The Watchdog Concept: The Press and the Courts in Nineteenth-Century America* (Ames, Iowa, 1989), p. 16

12. *Near v. Minnesota,* 283 U.S. 697 (1931), at 722.

13. Robert M. La Follette, speech at the Annual Banquet of the Periodical Publishers' Association, February 2, 1912, in *The Political Philosophy of Robert M. La Follette, as Revealed in His Speeches and Writings,* ed. Ellen Torelle (Madison, Wis., 1920), p. 349.

14. David P. Thelen, *Robert M. La Follette and the Insurgent Spirit* (Madison, Wis., 1985), pp. 90–92.

15. *La Follette's Magazine* (April 1918) in *The Political Philosophy of Robert M. La Follette,* ed. Torelle, p. 349.

16. Kevin Sack, "Gingrich Attacks Press as Out of Touch," *New York Times,* April 23, 1997, p. A22; italics added.

17. Department of Labor, 1997 National Occupational Employment and Wage Estimates; 1997 *Statistical Almanac of the United States.*

18. See Page, *Who Deliberates?* pp. 72–74 (cf. pp. 38–39, note 10). Page notes, however, that writers' and editors' belief in their own autonomy could be mistaken, because the mechanisms of control employed by owners could be subtle and even unintentional.

19. William Glaberson, "Increasingly, Reporters Say They're Democrats," *New York Times,* November 18, 1992, p. A20.

20. Howard Kurtz, "Dole Attack Rings True with Some in Press," *Washington Post,* October 27, 1996, p. A22.

21. See Garry Wills, *Under God: Religion and American Politics* (New York, 1990), pp. 15–25.

22. Bruce M. Owen, *Economics and Freedom of Expression: Media Structure and the First Amendment* (Cambridge, Mass., 1975), tables 2A–1 and 2A–5, pp. 64 and 69.

23. Michael Delli Carpini and Scott Keeter, *What Americans Know about Politics and Why It Matters* (New Haven, Conn., 1996), p. 113; Ben Bagdikian, "The 50, 26, 20 . . . Corporations That Own Our Media," at http://www.wco.com~dragon22/bofairmedia.html.

24. Figure for 1996, from the Bureau of Labor Statistics, *1998–1999 Occupational Outlook Handbook.*

25. James Fallows, *Breaking the News: How the Media Undermine American Democracy* (New York, 1996), pp. 78, 37.

26. All this is described in Page, *Who Deliberates?* pp. 77–105. I have quoted from pp. 82, 83, and 87.

27. Steven Waldman, *The Bill: How the Adventures of Clinton's National Service Bill Reveal What Is Corrupt, Comic, Cynical—and Noble—About Washington* (New York, 1995), p. 70, quoted in Fallows, p. 80.

28. Quoted in *Who Deliberates?* by Page, p. 98.

29. However, Benjamin Page argues that in one important case (the Gulf War), the opinion pieces and letters that appeared on the *Times*'s Op-Ed page were neatly balanced to the hawkish and dovish side of the *Times*'s own position, thereby suggesting that the editors were moderate and reasonable. Certain points of view (e.g., Iraq's complaints about Kuwait's prewar behavior) were overlooked. See Page, *Who Deliberates?* pp. 17–42.

30. This is a 1988 statistic. See CRS Report to Congress, "Negative Campaigning in National Politics," September 18, 1991, p. 10.

31. Source: National Cable TV Association, March 1992.

32. Sam Howe Verhovek, "AT & T Fights for Control of Its Cable Lines in Struggle over Internet Access," *New York Times,* February 15, 1999, p. A12.

33. James Bennet, "Polling Provoking Debate in News Media on Its Use," *New York Times,* October 4, 1996, p. A24.

34. Center for Media and Public Affairs, press release, April 15, 1996.

35. Amy Bayer, "What Price Must Clinton pay? Gleeful GOP Thinks He'll Lose the Support of Angry White Men," *San Diego Union Tribune,* July 20, 1995, p. A21.

36. Todd S. Purdum, "President Shows Fervent Support for Goals of Affirmative Action," *New York Times,* July 19, 1995, p. A1.

37. ABC, "This Week with David Brinkley," July 23, 1995.

38. "Good for America," unsigned editorial, *St. Petersburg Times,* July 21, 1995, p. 12A—italics added.

39. CNN, "Capital Gang," July 23, 1995.

40. Jeff Greenfield, "On Affirmative Action, Clinton Takes a Stand," *Chicago Sun-Times,* July 23, 1995, p. 30.

41. CNN, "Inside Politics," July 24, 1995.

42. The percentage of Americans who said that they had read the previous day's newspaper declined from 71 in 1965, to 58 in 1994, and then to 45 in 1995. Source: Times Mirror Center for the People and the Press, April 6, 1995, pp. 9, 29, cited in *Getting the Connections Right: Public Journalism and the Troubles in the Press*, by Jay Rosen (New York, 1996), p. 19. See also Felicity Barranger, "In Washington Is There News after Scandal?" *New York Times,* February 15, 1999, p. C1, reporting a net loss of two million viewers for national news broadcasts in 1998 and 1999.

43. Christopher Edley, Jr., "The Road to Clinton's Big Speech: An Insider's Account of the Affirmative Action Battle," *Washington Post,* July 23, 1995, p. C1.

44. Howard Kurtz, "The Snooze at 11: White House Correspondents Wait while Nothing Happens," *Washington Post,* March 24, 1995, quoted in *Breaking the News,* by Fallows, p. 33.

45. Kurtz, "The Snooze at 11," p. 33.

46. Joan Didion, "The Deferential Spirit," *New York Review of Books,* September 19, 1996, p. 18.

47. Lisa Austin, "Public Life and the Press: A Progress Report," Project on Public Life and the Press, funded by the Knight Foundation, housed at New York University, 1994.

48. Jay Rosen, "Where Is Public Journalism? The Search for a New Routine," remarks to Project on Public Life and the Press Spring Seminar, American Press Institute, Reston, Virginia, March 24–25, 1995.

49. See William E. Jackson, Jr., "The Press Cops Out," *New York Times,* October 7, 1996; and Michael Kelly, "Media Club," *The New Yorker,* November 4, 1996, pp. 45–49.

50. Jennie Buckner, "Assault on 'Public Journalism,'" *Washington Post,* October 31, 1996, p. A21.

51. *Wichita Eagle,* quotes circulated at the American Press Institute (April 1995).

52. See Rosen, *Getting the Connections Right,* pp. 40–41.

53. The 71st Federalist, in *The Federalist Papers* (New York, 1961), pp. 432.

54. Jennifer Nagorka, "Presbyterians' Gathering Likely to Be Divisive," *Dallas Morning News,* June 10, 1994, p. 35A; John G. Taylor, "Presbyterians Will Face Tough Issues at Assembly," *Fresno Bee,* June 10, 1994, p. B3; Martha Sawyer Allen, "A Schism on Women: 'Re-Imagining' Meeting Splits Presbyterians," *Minneapolis Star-Tribune,* p. 1B. See also "Presbyterians Lose Link to the Media," *Chicago Tribune,* June 17, 1994, p. 10, describing a church "wracked" [sic] with "internal dissent."

55. Peter Scarlet, "Presbyterian Head Preaches Reconciliation," *Salt Lake Tribune,* July 9, 1994, p. B1.

56. William G. Nottage-Tracey, "Assembly Took Traditional Stands" (editorial), *Omaha World-Herald,* August 11, 1994, p. 23.

57. Todd Murphy, "Presbyterian Panel Trying to Deal with Feminism Uproar," *Courier-Journal,* June 15, 1994, p. 7C.

58. Max Frankel, "Fix-It Journalism," *New York Times Magazine,* May 21, 1995, p. 28.

59. Tony Case, "Public Journalism Denounced," *Editor and Publisher* (November 12, 1996): 14.

60. This is Downie's critical assessment of public journalists. See Case, "Public Journalism Denounced," p. 15.

61. *New York Times v. United States,* 403 U.S. 73 (1971). Justice Stewart (joined by Justice White) invokes the value of "an enlightened citizenry—an informed and critical public opinion which alone can here protect the values of democratic government." The majority is correct, but their notion of informing and enlightening the public involves a transfer of information *from* reporters *to* individual readers. On this view, deliberation is evidently not part of a newspaper's core responsibility.

62. Cole Campbell, remarks to the James K. Batten Symposium of Civic Journalism, September 13, 1995, quoted in *Getting the Connections Right,* by Rosen, p. 17.

63. Davis Merritt, Jr. (editor of the *Wichita Eagle*), "Public Journalism: What It Means, How It Works," in *Public Journalism: Theory and Practice*, by Jay Rosen and Davis Merritt, Jr. (Dayton, Ohio: Kettering Foundation, 1994), p. 24.

64. See, e.g., Merritt, "Public Journalism: A Movement toward a Basic Cultural Change." Paper circulated at the American Press Institute, Reston, Virginia, March 24–26, 1995, p. 2 (adapted from a column printed in The *Wichita Eagle* on October 30, 1994). Merritt writes: "[Information] arrives at our eyes and ears packaged in hopeless insolubility. It is framed by both politicians and journalists as a contest between black-and-white [sic], presented through the words of experts and absolutists. Each of the framers has a stake in continuing the argument; none has a stake in resolving it. Those who do have a stake in resolution—average citizens—are frustrated by the . . . polarized presentation of issues."

65. James Forman, quoted by David J. Garrow, *Bearing the Cross: Martin Luther*

King, Jr., and the Southern Christian Leadership Conference (New York, 1986), pp. 239–240.

66. "Letter from a Birmingham Jail," in *I Have a Dream: Writings and Speeches That Changed the World,* by Martin Luther King, Jr., ed. James M. Washington (New York, 1992), pp. 86–87, 88, 94, punctuation altered.

67. Pat Watters and Reese Cleghorn, *Climbing Jacob's Ladder: The Arrival of Negroes in Southern Politics* (New York, 1967), pp. 55, 73, n. 10; 277, n. 14.

68. Contrast Michael Kinsley's view: "elected officials are public servants. They are employees of the taxpayers, and whatever gives them value as public speakers—whether it is merely their fame, or their inside-Washington insights, or their actual power over the course of the nation—rightly belongs to the public and not to them. Journalists are not public servants." Kinsley, "Confessions of a Buckraker," *The New Republic* (May 1, 1995): 18.

69. See, e.g., Jay Rosen, "Making Things More Public: On the Political Responsibility of the Media Intellectual," *Critical Studies in Mass Communication* 11 (1994): 368–369, 377.

70. John Dewey, *Experience and Nature* (La Salle, Ill., 1958), pp. 181, 198.

71. Henry David Thoreau, "Civil Disobedience" (1849), in *Civil Disobedience and Other Essays* (New York, 1993), pp. 6, 8

72. "Life without Principle," in ibid., p. 78.

73. Quoted by Leonard J. Waks, "Experimentalism and the Flow of Experience" Unpublished paper. p. 51.

74. Susan Stamberg interviewed Edwin Diamond, a media critic, about Maureen Dowd's writing and other changes at the *Times*: see "The Road to Making the *New York Times* Reader-Friendly," National Public Radio, Weekend Edition, February 19, 1994.

75. Jay Rosen agrees. "It is true," he writes, "that the watchdog role is fundamental to journalism and should never be compromised." Remarks to the Associated Press Managing Editors National Convention, Philadelphia, Pennsylvania, October 12, 1994, p. 2.

76. The *Asbury Park Press* Civic Journalism Team, "House of Cards Tumbles out of Asbury Park Civic Journalism Project," *Civic Catalyst,* published by the Pew Center for Civic Journalism (Fall 1997): 1, 2, 6.

6

Legislation and Regulation

DELIBERATION IN LEGISLATURES

As a young professor, Woodrow Wilson outlined a position that he would maintain until he retired from the White House thirty-three years later. He argued that "government by discussion" was "the only tolerable sort of government for a people which tries to do its own governing." He pushed this axiom to a fairly radical conclusion, holding that "instruction and guidance in public affairs" were *more* important legislative functions than the making of laws.

The future governor and president held legislatures to high standards:

> For the instruction and elevation of public opinion in regard to national affairs there is needed . . . public discussion of a peculiar sort: a discussion in which every feature of each mooted point of policy shall be distinctly brought out, and every argument of significance pushed to its farthest point of insistence, by recognized leaders in that body; and, above all, a discussion upon which something . . . evidently depends. It is only a discussion of this sort that the public will heed; no other sort will impress it.[1]

In Wilson's classically Progressive rhetoric, we can detect several important ideas: that principled arguments ought to have actual power over legislation; that the government's work should be publicly visible ("suffused in a broad daylight of discussion"); and that "sober, purposeful, business-like talk upon public questions" is "of great value."[2] We can clarify Wilson's position by specifying what he *opposed:* secrecy, mendacity, triviality, force, and mere bargaining.

Any proponent of democracy will worry about the first four problems, perhaps hoping that they can be remedied by campaign-finance reform, open-meeting laws, skillful journalism, and the election of honorable politicians in fair elections. But not everyone decries bargaining, which often seems both necessary and praiseworthy in a peaceful society. In a recent book, however, Joseph Bessette analyzes several varieties of bargaining that often seem to *replace* deliberation: namely, "the logroll, the compromise (or splitting the difference), and the use of side-payments."[3] In the first case, I support your bill—even though I don't necessarily believe in its merits—because you have agreed to vote for mine. In the second case, we split the difference between our respective positions, even though neither of us believes that the compromise is in the public's best interest. And in the third case, I persuade you to support my position by giving you something of value. Gifts of money are illegal, but politicians can offer political assistance, committee assignments, and campaign support in return for votes.

Progressive reformers denounced these techniques as the very opposite of government by discussion. But the reformers had intellectual opponents in their own time. For instance, Arthur Bentley wrote in 1908:

> Log-rolling is a term of opprobrium. This is because it is used mainly with reference to its grosser forms. . . . Log-rolling is, however, in fact, the most characteristic legislative process. When one condemns it "in principle," it is only by contrasting it with some assumed pure public spirit which is supposed to guide legislators, or which ought to guide them, and which enables them to pass judgment in Jovian calm on that which is best "for the whole people." Since there is nothing which is best literally for the whole people, group arrays being what they are, the test is useless, even if one could actually find legislative judgments which are not reducible to interest-group activities.[4]

Bentley conceded that "along with all this log-rolling in all its forms goes a great activity of reasoning, theorizing, and argument, and at times the argument seems to be the cause of all that is happening." But public or legislative debate was always merely "a technical agency for the [underlying] transaction" among interest-groups—a way of signaling bids, specifying demands, or demonstrating the size of one's coalition. "Argument under certain conditions is a greater labor-saver than blows, and in it the group interests more fully unfold themselves. But beneath all the argument lies strength. The argument can get no farther than the strength goes."[5]

Bentley was one of the founders of the tradition in political science that interprets "all phenomena of government" as "phenomena of groups pressing one another, forming one another, and pushing out new groups and group representatives (the organs or agencies of government) to mediate the adjustments."[6] This tradition helps to legitimize interest-group liberalism—a regime in which public officials *openly* perform "specified governing functions for the underlying groups of the population."[7] If Bentley was right about the character of all politics, then Wilson's criteria of legislative deliberation were naive. Bentley argued on the basis of anecdotes and theoretical assumptions, but a great wealth of statistical analysis has since accumulated, which interprets legislation as the interplay between interest-group pressures and politicians' desire to maximize their odds of reelection. Although few analysts claim that bargaining and self-interest are the *sole* forces in government, these factors seem to predict political outcomes to an impressive degree.

Nevertheless, Bessette offers several reasons to distrust any strictly statistical analysis that purports to unmask the true character of lawmaking. First of all, simply by looking at numbers, we cannot tell whether a given compromise is a mechanical splitting-of-the-difference or rather a deliberative achievement that occurs when erstwhile opponents come to share each other's point-of-view. Second, it may happen that 90 percent of legislators reach their positions on a particular bill by talking and applying informed and sincere judgments. If, however, the legislature remains closely divided, then a few politicians may be able to decide the outcome under the influence of side payments and logrolling arrangements. If such cases are common, then statistics will show a correlation between interest-group pressure and legislative outcomes, even though most legislators are not influenced by power or money to any degree. Third, a committee may openly engage in mechanical difference-splitting, as for instance when House and Senate negotiators combine bills from their respective chambers. Nevertheless, deliberation and public reason could determine the heart of the legislation and ensure its passage.[8]

Thus we usually need a detailed historical or journalistic study of any legislation to reveal the balance of reason, principle, self-interest, and force that guided each person who helped to write, shape, and pass it. In many cases, the results are heartening. Bessette writes, "Given the theoretical formulations that seemingly deny any real importance to reasoning about the public good in Congress, it is striking how many case studies describe the lawmaking process in the House and Senate as largely a rational effort to do good."[9] He then offers several impressive stories about lawmakers—and whole committees or houses of Congress—who have struggled to legislate in the public interest.

But these stories have a disturbingly recurrent feature, illustrated in the case of Senator John Culver (D-IA). Culver is described plausibly as a "serious-minded legislator who doggedly pursued his view of the public interest in a few specific fields, using principally the weapons of facts and arguments." So far, so good— but Culver denounces many of his *colleagues* for making reelection their "be-all and end-all," even at the price of "core principles or beliefs."[10] Similarly, several politicians describe their Pauline conversions from full-time campaigners to responsible lawmakers. These conversions, while praiseworthy, typically occur after years of congressional service.[11]

It seems safe to conclude, then, that some legislators seek the public good, regardless of interest-group pressures, and that others do not. Likewise, there may be times when a whole legislature acts as a truly deliberative body, allowing arguments to shape its decisions—but on other occasions, the same legislature may engage in logrolling and back-scratching. If both conditions are possible, then we need a clear picture of good lawmaking and a plan for encouraging it to happen.

Like Bessette, I think that we should begin with cases. Early in 1991, Congress debated whether to authorize a war against Iraq. Polls showed the nation divided on this grave issue, and many Americans disagreed with the final decision. Nevertheless, the congressional debate was widely seen as exemplary—as an instance of deliberative representative government. If Congress typically behaved with such dignity, then public confidence would rise, and all forms of political participation would become more attractive.

Newsday's Paul Vitello wrote: "They say this was the longest debate in the history of Congress, and in fact the members spoke for three days and two nights, one after the other, with no pauses between, as if they were citizens at a town meeting waiting in line to be heard, which is sort of what they are. This is the closest thing to a national town meeting that we get."[12] And in the *Atlanta Constitution,* Mike Christensen wrote, "On the floors of the House and Senate, and in the Capitol corridors, the mood was somber, the debate earnest rather than spirited. Lawmakers discussed the issue rather than arguing it, and they shook hands with serious faces. Those who won the votes expressed no joy in their victory."[13]

Representatives discussed such sophisticated issues as the potential for long-term health problems if Iraq used poison gas, and the effect of a Middle Eastern war on Lithuania (which was about to be occupied by Soviet troops). Vitello wrote, "Some speeches in the debate on war and peace were clumsy, but most were much better than that and a few were eloquent. . . . The voice of Congress was beautiful and strange. Watching from the gallery was like watching a soliloquy by one soul at war with itself: angry, cajoling, soothing, mimicking, prideful, ashamed, cocky, practical, impractical, fearful, brave, dishonest with itself, honest with itself, in succession, in hour after hour of self-excoriation."[14]

In an ideal deliberative democracy, the reasons and values that arose in public conversations would actually determine government policies, with the best reasons overcoming the others. The congressional debate on Desert Storm probably did not decide the outcome, because many members had made up their minds before the formal speeches began. Still, we can call the debate "deliberative," because it reflected a serious process of thinking, talking, and listening that had taken place *off* the floor of Congress.

Representative John Dingell (D-MI) explained that he found voting difficult because there were "valid arguments on both sides of the issue." "I have listened, read, thought, agonized and prayed for wisdom and guidance over the hard choices before us," he said, and "I pray our judgment is wise and good."[15] Even if speeches by Dingell and others did not determine the final vote, they were evidently worth listening to. Representative Joan Kelly Horn (D-MO), for example, spent "more than six hours in the House Chamber, seldom moving," as members filed to the well to make their statements. She opposed the use of force but praised the debate.[16]

If the decision to authorize Operation Desert Storm was unusually deliberative, this was partly because of the solemnity of the issue, which drew the best from legislators. We cannot expect such a distinguished performance before every vote; but deliberation usually seems absent even when Congress considers other weighty matters. For instance, the 1993 House vote on the North American Free Trade Agreement (NAFTA) was decided not because of arguments on either side, but because the Clinton administration promised wavering representatives new federal funding for their districts and small-scale tariff agreements that could cost hundreds of millions of dollars in the aggregate. These favors were available to House members who were willing to bargain but not to anyone who had articulated a principled position on either side. Meanwhile, labor and environmental issues were relegated to vague "side agreements," thus giving the appearance that "any pretense to legislative deliberation had been abandoned."[17]

Even in this case, perhaps most members of Congress voted on the basis of principle, and bargaining determined the passage of NAFTA only because Congress was closely divided. Then it would be unfair to accuse legislators (as a group) of being unprincipled. One can also argue that bargaining is *appropriate* in a specific range of cases that includes the NAFTA debate: namely, those in which the parties disagree about uncertain empirical facts but not about principles. Gutmann and Thompson argue that bargaining is the *only* way to resolve such disputes. But I think they are partially wrong about the NAFTA debate, which did not reflect "consensus on the moral values" and "conflict about whether NAFTA would serve them."[18] On the contrary, there was a crucial moral disagreement between those who favored aggregate economic growth and those who were most concerned about vulnerable minorities in the American work force. Partly because interest-group bargaining was prominent, this moral conflict was not publicly aired.

Why, then, was the debate over Desert Storm unusually deliberative? First, although some American corporations had interests in the Gulf, I doubt that campaign money affected the outcome. The vote was unambiguous, a simple yea or nay on a matter that might cost many lives. Incumbents knew that they would be required to defend, not only their votes, but also their public statements and reasons before an attentive electorate.[19] No sensible politician would risk infuriating voters in order to please a contributor who had given a few thousand dollars.

Perhaps more important, the Gulf War vote followed months of press coverage, which varied in quality but was far more substantive and extensive than usual. Most journalists analyzed the pros and cons of intervention, without dwelling on American politics.[20] It is true that major news organs took a common editorial line (sanctions first, then war), and their news coverage was neither comprehensive nor completely fair. For instance, they contemptuously passed over the idea of a grand deal that would resolve both the Palestinian and the Kuwaiti questions.[21] The *Seattle Times*'s "Reader Advocate," Colleen Patrick, accused her colleagues of treating the Gulf crisis as a "John Wayne" confrontation between George Bush and Saddam Hussein. Too many stories described military press conferences, she thought, and not enough provided independent views of the oil industry or arms sales to Iraq. There were too many "personal accounts" of American soldiers and not enough "scrutiny of the institutions and individuals who can so easily put thousands of American lives at risk."[22] Despite all the coverage, the public was left with some important misunderstandings. For instance, most people thought that the United States had warned Iraq that we would protect Kuwait by force, whereas our government had actually given Saddam Hussein ambiguous signals.[23] Still, newspapers and broadcasts were full of information and unorthodox opinions. Citizens could hear George Bush calling Saddam "worse than Hitler," but they could also watch the Iraqi foreign minister explaining his country's position. Pacifist arguments were widely covered.

Partly because news and ideas were available, the public deliberated *before* Congress began its formal debate. At kitchen tables, in veterans' halls, in classrooms and supermarket aisles, people discussed the prospect of war. From their own experience, they knew what a serious discussion would sound like. Presumably, some legislators participated in these unofficial conversations as parents, spouses, and neighbors, and then they did their best to meet the voters' expectations by acting deliberatively and civilly in Congress.

The Gulf War debate was free, then, of the major problems that are discussed in other chapters: financial corruption, journalistic abuses, and an inattentive public. But these are not the only factors that can frustrate official deliberation—structures and procedures of government also matter. The debate to authorize Desert Storm was public; the rules were simple and transparent; and every member's vote counted equally. The same is not true when complex legislation winds its way through committees or when regulatory agencies settle disputes among interest groups. With the Gulf War example in mind, we should ask: How can our government be reformed so that its vital decisions are *routinely* guided by sober, rational, public, and fair debate?

LEGISLATIVE PROCEDURES AND LOBBYING

The first place to look is to legislative rules and procedures, which are traditional targets of reform. The Progressives argued that a powerful speaker, a seniority system, and important caucuses and conference committees made Congress unrepresentative and unaccountable, and allowed members to cut private deals instead of deliberating publicly.[24] A half-century later, Ralph Nader and John Gardner revived these arguments. Nader started from the premise that parliamentary procedures had a strong influence on legislative outcomes. "In the intense inner world of Congress," he wrote, "strategic use of *rules, precedents, customs, and courtesies* spells power—who has it, who keeps it, who uses it and to what substantive ends."[25] He and his allies therefore sought to change the rules in the interests of fairness, opening meetings, requiring public votes, subjecting committee chairs to secret-ballot elections, and weakening their powers. In the interests of efficiency, legislators may choose to elect powerful leaders, but citizens ought to retain equal weight no matter how junior their own representatives may be. This is possible if legislative leaders are elected by the rank-and-file in fair elections and if the legislature's work is done in public.

But it seems to me that little can be accomplished through parliamentary reforms. The underlying structure of Congress is established by the Constitution, which describes a bicameral legislature whose members decide their own rules by majority vote. This structure ensures that congressional procedures will normally satisfy a majority of members, who represent the majority of Americans. Party leaders can sometimes amass excessive power, but they cannot do this by erecting unfair rules, which are easily overturned. Rather, they sometimes control *elections* by managing primaries, making personal appearances, and determining the flow of private money. When they are able to influence elections, they can create an oligarchy within Congress.

In short, parliamentary procedures normally reflect the underlying campaign-finance regime, not vice versa. For instance, it wasn't the parliamentary reforms of the 1970s that decentralized power in the House; it was the Federal Election Campaign Act (FECA), which made parties virtually irrelevant and individual candidates masters of their own finances. Immediately after FECA was enacted, twenty-nine new committees and subcommittees were created to satisfy incumbents who had become independent enough to demand private baronies, and who knew that chairmanships would help them to raise funds. By the end of the 1970s, fully half of all Democratic representatives and all but one Democratic senator chaired a committee or a subcommittee.[26]

Twenty years later, Newt Gingrich managed to return considerable power to the speaker's office, but he would have failed if he hadn't first invented novel ways to pump money into House elections: $60 million in 1998–99 alone.[27] Rank-and-file Republicans owed him their jobs, which partly explains why they allowed him to amass parliamentary power. When they decided to replace him, they turned to Representative Bob Livingston (R-LA), who had raised $800,000 for his House colleagues in the previous year. Although he couldn't survive adultery charges, Livingston initially defeated the other contenders for the speakership because (among other things) he had distributed so much campaign money.[28] His replacement, J. Dennis Hastert (R-IL), was no slouch at fundraising himself, having collected over $1 million for his own campaign in 1998. Upon assuming the speakership, Hastert immediately set a "frenetic pace" on the national fundraising circuit, raising $350,000 for House Republicans in two months.[29]

Since it is nearly impossible to reallocate power by changing congressional rules, we should direct our energies toward reforming campaign finances so as to promote equality and transparency within Congress. There are, however, times when parliamentary procedures are worth reforming—not to change the distribution of power within a legislature, but to force the whole body to act deliberatively and accountably. For instance, Senate rules are supposed to encourage deliberation by requiring sixty votes to cut off debate and force a vote. But this rule is abused so badly that Progressive principles require its abolition. Senators know that they can threaten to filibuster any bill that lacks sixty supporters. As soon as one senator issues such a threat, the bill is typically removed from consideration, because Congress has many other items to consider. Thus, far from encouraging debate, filibusters allow senators to avoid dealing with bills unless they have the support of a super-majority. Even the House relies on filibusters in the Senate to block bills that have public support, such as campaign-finance legislation. There is nothing sacrosanct about the principle of majority rule, a principle from which the Constitution departs by creating a bicameral legislature and by giving the president a veto. But to add to those checks a sixty-vote threshold in the Senate is to bias the whole system in favor of the status quo.

Just as filibusters permit the Senate to avoid unpleasant votes, so secrecy serves the interests of incumbent politicians as a class; thus it should not be tolerated except when it is absolutely necessary. It allows representatives to make deals that would embarrass them if they had to work before an attentive public. What Brandeis wrote of banks is also true of legislatures: "Sunlight is said to be the best of disinfectants; electric light the most efficient policeman."[30] Besides, Progressives want the public to assess the quality of congressional deliberations, not just the laws that Congress ultimately enacts. In other words, they want the public to judge procedures as well as outcomes, and this is impossible if a legislature conducts some of its business in secret.[31]

The legislative process at all levels of government has been made much more public by the adoption of "sunshine" laws, mostly passed in the early 1970s, which prevent committees from meeting in secret. These provisions are important, but they can only work successfully if they are part of a comprehensive approach to government reform. If lobbyists who control access to huge campaign contributions can also carefully observe committee deliberations, then the public might be better off with closed meetings. Senator William Packwood (R-OR) once said:

> Common Cause simply has everything upside down when they advocate "sunshine" laws. When we're in the sunshine, as soon as we vote, every trade association in the country gets out their mailgrams and their phone calls in twelve hours, and complains about the members' votes. But when we're in the back room, the senators can vote their conscience. They vote for what they think is the good of the country. Then they can go out to the lobbyists and say: "God, I fought for you. I did everything I could. But Packwood just wouldn't give in, you know. It's so damn horrible."[32]

If it is true that elected representatives cannot act responsibly except in private, then our democracy is deeply corrupt. We would then have to choose between publicity, which would allow voters to assess their representatives' behavior, and secrecy, which would permit representatives to deliberate.[33] Indeed, the existing campaign-finance regime gives legislators reason to fear and favor special interests. In a fair democratic system, however, openness would help to keep elected officials accountable to the public and not to special-interest contributors. Therefore, once campaign finances are reformed, virtually all deliberative bodies should be required to face public scrutiny. The only two exceptions should be narrowly construed: they involve confidential personnel issues and matters of national security.

The ideal of publicity also requires disclosure of lobbyists' behavior. Today, federal courts would presumably void La Follette's policy, which was to forbid all private contacts between lobbyists and Wisconsin legislators and to require their written communications to be disclosed.[34] The courts are appropriately concerned about rules that would deter citizens from exercising their constitutional right to petition government for the redress of grievances. Members of unpopular minorities might be afraid to contact elected leaders if the details of their requests were subject to disclosure. However, the public has a right to know who is conducting large, sophisticated lobbying campaigns and how much money is being spent. We should be able to gauge the degree to which legislators are influenced by particular lobbies and lobbyists. This would be a relevant factor to consider at election time. For their part, representatives have an interest in knowing how much money is being spent to influence them.

Since 1995, federal lobbyists have been required to disclose expensive efforts, but not all states have passed equivalent legislation. Besides, the federal statute omits so-called grassroots lobbying, or efforts to drum up letters, calls, and e-mails to Congress. This is now a billion-dollar phenomenon,[35] and those responsible generally want to conceal their own role. A common tactic is to set up front groups that conduct lobbying without disclosing the source of their funds even to their own members. For example, Small Businesses for Advertising Choice (SBAC) was actually a project of the seven Regional Bell Operating Companies—hardly small businesses. They paid a professional creator of grassroots organizations, ABRH Consulting Group of Washington, D.C., to create SBAC as a tool for fighting telephone regulation.[36] Informed Citizens for the Environment (ICE), a.k.a. the Information Council on the Environment, has run ads disputing global warming theories and is funded by power companies.[37] The American Council for Health Care Reform (sponsors unknown) sent mass mailings that alleged that the "goal of the Clinton health care plan is the total elimination of Medicare." These letters warned of "jail time if you buy extra care" under the Clinton proposal.[38]

Every level of government should require disclosure of efforts to influence officials—whether direct or indirect—that consume significant amounts of money. But even if disclosure makes the political system more transparent and deliberative, it cannot make it fair. At least $1.2 billion (and possibly as much as $8.4 billion) is spent to influence the federal government each year, and 80,000 people are said to be employed for this purpose.[39] Some lobbying is directed at the executive branch. But if we assume (conservatively) that lobbyists spend half of their time and money influencing Congress, then more than $7 million may be spent—and more than 60 people employed—to influence *each* member of Congress. At the state level, roughly 30,000 organizations are registered to lobby; in New York State alone they disclosed almost $50 million of expenses in 1995.[40] The effect of all this cash is sure to distort the democratic process in favor of those with deep pockets.

We can divide expensive lobbying activities into four categories, each of which requires a different response. First, lobbyists underwrite political campaigns by making donations of hard or soft money, by acting as fundraisers, and by contributing to legislators' PACs so that officials can pass money on to other politicians. The powerful lobbying firm of Patton, Boggs & Blow even has a computer that will advise clients about the members of Congress to whom they should contribute money, depending upon their legislative interests.[41] These practices would become impossible if large political donations were replaced with public funds.

Second, lobbyists give goods and services directly to lawmakers or their staffs. For instance, they provide travel to retreats and conventions; they give free meals and tickets to legislators to use or distribute to others; they host parties at conventions; they contribute to foundations or charities controlled by legislators; they set up scholarships or charities in the lawmakers' names in their districts; they underwrite legislators' legal defense funds; and they provide jobs for their spouses and dependents. Since these practices give wealthy interests access—and may sometimes actually buy influence—they should be banned. To grasp the value of access, we need only consider the fact that companies were willing to pay $30,000 for the explicit right to lobby members of the National Foundation for Women Legislators, which is hardly the nation's most powerful group of lawmakers.[42]

Opponents of tough ethics rules often cite trivial gifts, such as cups of coffee, which need not be prohibited. But in the aggregate, gifts constitute a serious threat to integrity. In Connecticut, for instance, one state legislator accepted $1,450 in food and drink in 1995, as well as $145 in gifts. Among other specific favors, he received a cruise (accompanied by a lobbyist) and a $110 meal at a business conference in Wisconsin.[43] The New Jersey Chamber of Commerce traditionally rents an Amtrak train to carry lobbyists, politicians, and businesspeople to Washington for what is known familiarly as the "pub-crawl on wheels" or the "pork-barrel express."[44] In states like New York, where the disclosure requirement can be evaded easily, abuses may be even more serious.

Limits on the value of individual gifts are generally ineffective, since lobbyists give repeatedly, give to numerous members and their staffs, and "bundle" gifts with others who share their goals. At the federal level, all gifts and services of monetary value have been banned since 1995—a Progressive victory.[45] Unfortunately, travel was exempted, and wealthy lobbies have therefore taken to offering free trips to luxury hotels and resorts around the world.[46] Wisconsin and some localities have passed better rules, but they should be made universal, and constant vigilance should be exercised to prevent lobbyists from circumventing the law.

Third, some lobbyists use their contacts and experience as former government officials to win influence for their clients. According to the *New York Times,* "To a breathtaking extent, Government service has become required training for almost every aspiring lobbyist—and lobbying, far from being scorned, has become a routine second career." The *Times* reported in 1998 that "at least 128 former members of Congress are now working as lobbyists."[47] The starting salary for an ex-representative in the lobbying business was as much as $500,000 in 1993.[48] One powerful Senate aide actually postponed his starting date at J. P. Morgan & Company to finish drafting securities legislation sought by the banking industry.[49]

The "revolving door" between legislatures and lobbying firms is troubling for three reasons. It raises the prospect that incumbent lawmakers and staff may curry favor with companies that might later employ them as lobbyists. It suggests that former insiders who have friends in the legislature, and who may be owed favors, can exercise disproportionate influence on legislation—regardless of the merits of their views. Finally, the revolving door offers wealthy interests yet another way to turn money into power: by employing former lawmakers. Legislators and staff members should not be able to seek employment at firms they have overseen, and they should be forbidden to lobby their former institutions until several years have elapsed. Some former representatives manage lobbying efforts or work on grassroots lobbying campaigns without directly contacting their former colleagues, and such activities should count as "lobbying" for the purposes of a revolving-door law.[50] Opponents claim that worthy citizens will not enter government service if they are forbidden to lobby afterward. In fact, revolving-door regulations are an excellent way to screen out people with such mercenary motivations.

Finally, lobbyists sell skills, knowledge, and contacts that they have acquired in legitimate ways: by studying issues, working for other lobbyists, reading the legislative record, or just hanging around the statehouse. The availability of such expertise means that wealthy interests can buy political advantage. Nevertheless, we cannot prevent American citizens from petitioning the government, no matter how skillfully. It is also impossible to prevent organizations from commissioning *research,* even though this is a major source of influence. Nor can we stop them from asking their own members, employees, and customers to contact Congress—also a common and effective practice. The proper response is not to ban, or even to regulate, these activities, but to change the way that Congress makes laws so that the public interest is paramount. If we succeed, then private lobbying will lose some of its allure.

TAX REFORM

Representative Dick Armey (R-TX) recently wrote that "the tax code is the largest playground for Washington's vast and growing lobbying industry."[51] Armey noted that no other issue is mentioned as often on lobby disclosure reports. Presumably, some special interests *want* Congress to complicate the tax system, because they believe that they can purchase competitive advantages by lobbying. Other firms then feel obliged to hire lobbyists so that their interests are not overlooked in the scramble for privilege. This partly explains why the tax code has swollen to 555 million words.[52] Armey concluded: "while there will always be lobbyists in Washington, there would be far fewer if Congress used the tax code to raise revenue efficiently for the federal government and . . . treated every American the same. [A] simple, neutral law . . . would have a chilling effect on the lobbying industry and transform the entire political culture in Washington."[53]

Although Armey correctly cited tax law as the leading target of lobbying in 1996, only a quarter of the registered groups that hired lobbyists that year disclosed an interest in taxes. Lobbyists work on so many types of legislation that even a major change in the tax system would not affect most of them. Still, there are reasons to suspect that tax lobbying is especially harmful to the public interest. Consider this example: baking companies may treat some drivers as contractors instead of employees, thereby avoiding taxes; but other companies may not. Why? Because bakers "have a better lobbyist," according to a staff member for the Ways and Means Committee.[54] We cannot force the American Bakers Association to hire less skillful lobbyists, nor can we deny companies their First Amendment right to petition Congress, but we can require all tax laws to be simple and general. As Armey writes, "Because our tax system lacks any coherent principle . . . tax policy has evolved into a free-for-all for special interests."[55] The solution is to make the tax code so uncomplicated that it is pointless to lobby on behalf of any narrow interest.

The current system gives a strategic advantage to organized interests over people who seek diffuse and general goals, such as efficiency, economy, or fairness. Special interests can be motivated to defend each loophole and deduction in the tax code, and it is difficult to mobilize widespread opposition to narrow deductions if they are taken one at a time: people do not care enough about each provision. For instance, in order to promote alternatives to imported oil, the federal government gives companies an "alternative fuel production credit" that will cost the Treasury about $5.9 billion between 1996 and 2002.[56] In theory, Congress could abandon this credit and instead appropriate money every year to subsidize selected firms—especially Archer-Daniels-Midland, which controls about half of the domestic ethanol market and has already gained about $6 billion from the ethanol tax credit.[57] An annual subsidy would have exactly the same effect as the current tax break, but Congress wouldn't dare to pass an appropriation for

A.D.M., even though the company has given $4 million to parties and campaigns since the 1970s.[58] Instead, Congress gives the aid covertly by means of a tax provision that mentions no names and conceals the final cost.

With its hundreds of pages of fine print, the federal budget is complicated enough, but at least taxpayers can see how much money is being appropriated for each program. Tax breaks may cost just as much as appropriations, but their price is impossible to predict with any certainty. Justice Robert Jackson of the Supreme Court remarked that the tax code of his day was "beset with invisible boomerangs."[59] For government and business alike, this means that planning is unnecessarily difficult. Because it is opaque and unpredictable, tax policy is not subject to rational assessment, and Congress cannot be held properly accountable for its economic decisions. In particular, it is difficult for anyone to understand the government's priorities, since tax breaks of unknown size cannot be measured against spending programs. The same is true when new taxes are enacted in such a complex legal environment. As a congressional commission concluded, "Because of political pressures against tax increases, Congress and the President often raise taxes by enacting cumbersome and impossibly complex rules, making it difficult for taxpayers to understand whose taxes are being increased, and by how much."[60]

In addition to being unfair and opaque, a complex tax system is highly inefficient. Just before Congress enacted a mountain of new tax provisions in the 1998 budget, its own Joint Economic Committee found: "By artificially distorting relative prices, targeted tax cuts alter taxpayers' choices and disrupt the efficient operation of markets. Their inefficiency prevents policy makers from lowering the tax rate to the greatest extent possible, so that tax credits have little, if any, impact on working, saving, and investment."[61] If, however, the government abolished shelters and deductions, this would generate new revenue without arbitrarily influencing people's private behavior. It would also reduce the cost of tax preparation and compliance, which has been estimated as $75 billion per annum.[62]

Recent revelations about inefficiency and malfeasance within the Internal Revenue Service offer a final reason to simplify taxes. A limited number of people who are paid standard government salaries cannot be expected to police a system of amazing complexity and subtlety. Most people who really understand the tax code work in the private sector, advising clients how to outwit the IRS. Millions of Americans could be charged with violating the law, either because they have encountered fundamentally ambiguous provisions, they have misunderstood the rules, or they have deliberately cheated, knowing that the law is too complicated to be enforced. Given all this noncompliance, the IRS must use arbitrary criteria to select people for audits. (If its criteria were predictable, then unscrupulous people would know how to avoid being investigated.) Thus we should not be shocked when IRS agents harass taxpayers who cannot afford lawyers, when they provide contradictory advice, or when their enforcement decisions are arbitrary. Meanwhile, in the absence of reliable deterrence, dishonest citizens tend to benefit at the expense of ordinary people, and the unscrupulous rich are the luckiest of all. Under these circumstances, many people do not act with civic virtue, nor do they trust their fellow citizens. It is hard to act honestly when you believe that others will cheat; yet trust and integrity are important habits to develop in a democratic society.[63]

Vast majorities of the population favor across-the-board income tax simplification, as the comprehensive reform of 1986 showed. But the 1986 bill simply traded off some overall tax simplification for reductions in upper-income rates, without changing the process by which tax bills are written. Immediately after passage of the bill, new deductions and loopholes began to proliferate. By 1996, about 5,400 changes had been made.[64] As long as the House Ways and Means Committee and the Senate Finance Committee are able to write detailed tax bills, distortions are bound to be included in the code. Instead, Congress should pass a simple tax bill and then alter its own rules to make new deductions impossible to pass. A true simple tax would have a standard deduction for dependents, a smooth progressive curve, and no other wrinkles.

The argument for tax simplification applies to loopholes that benefit the poor as well as those that help the rich. In a 1993 editorial, the *Washington Post* conceded that a new tax credit for corporations that build low-rent housing could well be a "costly way to generate housing for the poor," and that vouchers might be more efficient. Nevertheless, the *Post* applauded passage of this credit on the ground that (unlike a spending program) it would be immune to budget-cutting by conservatives.[65] Since tax credits are practically invisible and are defended by the construction industry, they survive through all economic and ideological climates. But a program that is immune to being cut under any circumstances is an example of bad government, even if we happen to like its goals. Democracy means subjecting public choices to public debate; yet the *Post* favored the tax credit for low-income rental units precisely because debate would be avoided.

The deduction for charitable contributions raises a serious problem for Progressives. On the one hand, it is inequitable, because only a small number of people have enough income to justify itemizing their federal tax deductions. As a result, working people must devote a substantial portion of their incomes to supporting unglamorous government functions like repaying the national debt, while rich people are able to reduce their tax burdens if they donate to their favorite charities. "What is more," writes the philanthropy expert Lester Salamon, "much of private giving flows not to those in greatest need but to functions with a significant 'amenity' value to the givers."[66] For instance, instead of paying taxes, a millionaire can endow the local concert hall that he and his friends attend, thereby purchasing considerable prestige at a state-subsidized price.

On the other hand, Progressives believe that civil society is an essential ingredient of democracy and that it must consist of diverse, independent, and adequately funded private institutions. If the charitable tax deduction were repealed, then contributions to the nonprofit sector would probably fall by about 10 percent.[67] This is especially troubling since nonprofits face serious financial difficulties at present. It is unlikely that the federal government would replace the shortfall with new grants, and even if it did, Congress would never fund private programs that were unpopular. But organizations that represent minority interests and values must flourish, or else civil society will not serve its function as a check on majority rule.

The solution is to repeal the charitable deduction and divide the money saved by the number of people in America, producing a sum of about $85 per capita.[68] Each citizen should be able to designate a nonprofit organization to receive this amount direct from the Federal Treasury. Congress could enlarge the per capita allocation if it decided that civil society needed further subsidy. As a result, most federal funds would flow to popular organizations and programs, but some money would go to unpopular ones. Every citizen would have an equal say in the allocation of public money, and both pluralism and fairness would be served.

REGULATORY REFORM

A national commission recently found that the tax code is so baffling that IRS regulations actually make matters clearer, removing ambiguities that Congress has created.[69] This is evidence of extremely poor legislation. But usually the reverse is true: as complicated and obscure as statutes may be, administrative rules are worse. About twenty-five rules are issued for each law that Congress enacts, filling roughly 70,000 pages of the *Federal Register* every year.[70] These rules are collected in the *Code of Federal Regulations,* which is now so complex and arcane that hardly anyone can benefit from it without the services of legal specialists, string-pulling politicians, and well-financed lobbyists. The general interest is rarely served, and public confidence is undermined.

Progressives were largely responsible for the origins of administrative regulation at both the state and the federal levels. They hoped that efficient, professional regulatory bodies would act on the public's behalf. But to ensure that these bodies really would carry out "the well formulated judgment and the will of the people," they placed them under the control of elected legislatures.[71] "In dealing with complex economic subjects," Thomas McCarthy wrote, "the legislature lays down general principles—determines the general policy and turns over to appointive commissioners the responsibility for the administration of these principles."[72]

This is the theory. However, since the last years of the Progressive Era, reformers have worried that special interests may intervene to ensure that regulations *do not* reflect the will of the public or the legislature. Narrow groups can focus their resources and attention to influence regulatory bodies on specific issues, whereas ordinary citizens have only a limited stake in most government decisions. Concentrated pressure often defeats diffuse public opinion, even when the public's interest is quite clear. This is a problem for government in general, but it is most serious in regulation. Congress cannot easily pass a law that benefits a tiny minority at general expense, because each member's vote might become a campaign issue. Administrative agencies, however, are much less accountable.

Congress often passes unobjectionable statutes, like the one that requires the secretary of agriculture to manage produce markets so as to maintain farmers' incomes, ensure reasonable prices for consumers, and serve the public interest. Under the authority of this law, the Department of Agriculture has enacted quotas for fruit, milk, and other foods that cost average families as much as $500 each year and benefit only large agricultural firms. But whenever the department considers abolishing quotas, powerful members of Congress intervene behind the scenes to preserve them. Their actions are virtually impossible to detect, because the only votes they have cast are vacuous declarations of the public interest. When administrative agencies produce less than ideal results, members of Congress can score points by "investigating" them. Meanwhile, they can utter platitudes on the campaign trail, until voters reasonably come to believe that elections don't matter.[73]

Even when statutes are not fatally vague or contradictory, agencies usually have too little money and staff to prosecute all violators. Instead, they must negotiate compliance agreements with lawyers who represent regulated companies. They also issue general rules and advisory opinions to put flesh on the skeleton of the law. But as soon as a rule is issued, it is appealed; and as soon as one agency devises a regulation, another produces contradictory standards. This is a comfortable setting for organized interests, who expect to renegotiate the same economic issues perpetually. Soon their official representatives become routine participants in bureaucratic administration.

Indeed, Washington has turned into what William Greider calls "The Grand Bazaar," staffed by at least 100,000 "lawyers, lobbyists, trade-association and public-relations specialists, consultants, and corporate reps."[74] Similar "regulatory communities" exist in most state capitals. A common phenomenon is the "iron triangle," in which legislative aides turn to friendly bureaucrats for information and assistance with constituent services; administrators rely on legislative staff to maintain their appropriations and perquisites; and lobbyists work comfortably with both groups. Since all of these people typically hold their jobs for long periods, they come to know one another well and learn to protect their collective interests, regardless of their bosses' changing agendas.

Like tax deductions, laws that delegate regulatory powers to bureaucrats have hidden costs. If the federal government decides to clean up an environmental problem, the expense will be borne by all taxpayers, and it will be recorded in the federal budget so that voters can decide whether the government's priorities are appropriate. If, on the other hand, Congress empowers the Environmental Protection Agency to regulate factory emissions, then consumers and workers will bear some of the cost. But the size of the burden (both to each individual and to the overall economy) will be virtually impossible to estimate. Members of Congress who want to address problems *without* having to find new federal revenues often prefer to delegate authority to bureaucrats rather than make hard choices themselves.

Legislation is difficult to change, but administrative rules are always open to appeal, amendment, reinterpretation, and exception. Madison argued that "mutable policy . . . poisons the blessings of liberty itself." Government by the people can hardly be said to exist, he wrote, "if the laws be so voluminous that they cannot be read, or so incoherent that they cannot be understood; if they be repealed or revised before they are promulgated, or undergo such incessant changes that no man, who knows what the law is today, can guess what it will be tomorrow."[75] In a state managed by administrators, decisions about how to interpret vague statutes and when to enforce regulations often become more important than the underlying laws. But whereas the public can grasp deliberations about broad public policy, they cannot possibly follow endless negotiations about details. Hence, there is an almost inevitable tendency for special interests to prevail over general ones.

Even if regulators intend to serve the public good and manage to avoid becoming entangled with narrow interests, the mere fact that they are powerful specialists can undermine democratic values. The technical discourse of experts can eclipse public deliberation about ends. Consider, for example, the idea of a gross national product. GNP can be measured, and its growth or decline is affected by macroeconomic policies that are (at least roughly) understood by experts. The greater the GNP, the wealthier we are, and the more revenue can be collected with an income tax. Therefore, both parties now assume that growth in GNP is one basic measure of government policy. Administrative agencies are instructed to estimate the costs of proposed regulations on "the economy" (measured by GNP); and the Federal Reserve—an extremely powerful regulatory body—is supposed to manage capital markets with the overriding purpose of maximizing gross production of goods and services. Voters usually reject administrations that preside over recessions and reelect politicians who promote growth. In this way, technical experts have set the terms of the national debate.

But GNP is a value-neutral measurement: a pornographic video adds just as much as a book of poetry, and it is immaterial whether Bill Gates earns his fifteen billionth dollar or a homeless man makes his first. If I stay home with my child, I contribute nothing to GNP, but if I leave her watching television commercials while I go out drinking, I add twofold. Layoffs and the exploitation of natural resources can increase GNP; a peaceful walk in the woods contributes nothing. In short, more GNP is not necessarily better. Why, then, do we focus on it so obsessively? An important reason is that GNP can be understood technically; it treats all economic transactions as commensurable, measurable units. If, on the other hand, we choose to discuss the value of leisure versus income, environmental protection versus material production, art versus entertainment, or housework versus wage labor, then no expert advice can settle the issue. We have to deliberate about these questions in a legislature or in civil society. A clear danger of the regulatory state is that it blocks such deliberation by turning social policy over to value-neutral experts, who appear to have wisdom that they actually lack. It also gives Congress, whose chief responsibility is to deliberate, the chance to duck its duty.

The Progressives viewed citizens as the chief deliberators, legislatures as policy-making bodies, and administrative bureaus as mere "arms" of the legislature. However, one recent textbook on administrative law flatly states, "Although there may be academic squabbles over the degree of power that bureaucracies have acquired, there is virtually no disagreement over the fact that the old dichotomy between policy making and administration is gone and that administrative agencies now perform both functions, fused into one institution." For example, Congress has delegated the right to "determine just and reasonable rates" to the Federal Power Commission; the task of defining "the public interest, convenience, and necessity" in broadcasting to the Federal Communications Commission; and the authority to "prevent an unfair or inequitable distribution of voting power among security holders" to the Securities and Exchange Commission.[76] Congress has not even attempted to define "just rates," the "public interest," or "unfair voting power." Locke proposed that "the legislative cannot transfer the power of making laws to any other hands. For it being but a delegated power from the people, they, who have it, cannot pass it over to others."[77] This precept was made explicit in the Constitution, which assigns "all legislative powers" to Congress.[78] Basic democratic theory tells us that bureaucracies should not legislate; but they do, and often their decisions are made by mid-level career officials who owe their jobs neither to the voters nor to elected officials, but to other career bureaucrats.

During the Progressive Era—and again during the reform revival of the 1970s—modest steps were proposed that might prevent gross regulatory abuses if they were implemented consistently. Campaign-finance reform and lobby regulation would curb the power of special interests in both Congress and the executive branch. Revolving-door provisions would prevent regulators from being quickly hired by the industries that they have regulated. Officials could also be prevented from overseeing businesses that had previously employed them.

The Open Meeting Act of 1976 ensures that reporters and members of the public can observe federal rulemaking sessions.[79] However, most people cannot afford to appear at rulemaking sessions, and nonexperts cannot produce effective written comments. The Constitution gives every citizen the right to a legal defense, but this right was meaningless for poor people until indigent defendants were guaranteed free legal counsel. Along similar lines, the constitutional right to petition government (including administrative agencies) could become more than a paper provision if lobbying were made affordable. Financial support could be provided for needy organizations and individuals who wanted to provide information in support of their views. Conservative and pro-business groups would be just as eligible for the money as liberal or radical organizations, but any applicant would have to show some kind of public-interest rationale as well as financial need. The federal grants would be distributed by an independent board.[80]

The reformers of the 1970s also favored "sunset" provisions that would cause rules (and even whole agencies) to expire automatically unless they received explicit legislative reauthorization every five years. This reform would guarantee public debate and accountability and put vested interests on the defensive. There is little chance that Congress would limit the duration of its own statutes one by one, but liberals and conservatives might reach the following grand accord. Although each conservative politician supports some federal programs, most would gladly approve a law that automatically terminated *all* regulations and agencies after five years, because they dislike more programs than they support. Some liberals might be persuaded to join them, realizing that liberalism is doomed unless the government has a public mandate. With a sunset rule in place, Congress could still act dramatically: raising taxes, spending money, and banning harmful behavior. But every intervention would come soon after a public vote. Programs would not remain in place simply because of inertia, once public support had waned.

Conservatives often endorse a more Draconian solution to the evils of the administrative state. Deregulation, they argue, is the only way to stop corruption, smash iron triangles, end the rule of value-neutral specialists, and save us from regulations that are unfair, inflexible, or both. But deregulation means ceding public authority to the market; it narrows the public's authority. Although people often say that they want less regulation, a broad majority of Americans consistently favors state action to protect health, safety, consumer interests, workplace fairness, and other core values that are not well served by the market. No democratic society in the world refrains from government intervention, because people understandably want to control their environment. The solution, then, is an improved means of control, not laissez-faire.

Thirty years ago, Theodore Lowi proposed a simple alternative that has not yet been tried. He argued that the Supreme Court should enforce its doctrine that Congress may not delegate legislative functions to the executive branch. This would mean reviving the *Schechter* decision of 1934, which has been largely forgotten although never repealed.[81] Congress had passed the National Industrial Recovery Act as a keystone of the New Deal. One provision allowed the president to approve regulatory codes drawn up by industrial associations that met certain criteria. The live poultry dealers of New York City devised a code that mandated minimum pay and maximum hours for their workers, banned child labor, and set health standards. President Roosevelt signed the code, thus making it enforceable as a federal law. This was an example of a liberal policy: a state intervention to protect workers and reduce unemployment. It was also an example of *interest-group* liberalism, because the regulations were devised by a private association and approved and enforced by the executive branch without deliberation in Congress. The president's only statutory instructions from Congress were to further the "public interest" and to ensure "fair competition."

Writing for a unanimous court, Chief Justice Charles Evans Hughes (an old Progressive) ruled the National Industrial Recovery Act unconstitutional, partly because it left concepts like "fair competition" entirely to the discretion of trade associations and the president. Hughes wrote, "Congress is not permitted to abdicate or to transfer to others the essential legislative powers with which it is . . . vested."[82] Perhaps La Follette would have agreed, for he had argued that Congress should legislate conservation policies that Theodore Roosevelt had preferred "to leave to the discretion of the Secretary of the Interior."[83] Certainly La Follette's friend Brandeis joined the unanimous court with enthusiasm.

The *Schechter* decision was part of the assault on the New Deal from which the Court retreated in 1937. It did not become an important precedent, because it "fell under a cloud" when liberals associated it with the "discredited constitutional doctrines" of the anti-Roosevelt Supreme Court.[84] Although *Schechter* was never repealed, many subsequent laws have clearly failed its test.[85] Nevertheless, the Supreme Court could revive it tomorrow, declaring most of the federal regulatory apparatus unconstitutional. (As it has in other cases, the judiciary should give legislatures time to review each area of regulation before it actually abolishes any agency.[86]) Conservatives would be delighted to see bulwarks of the New Deal and the Great Society tumble. But liberals should be almost equally relieved. For reasons that I described earlier, administrative rule-making has failed to deliver its promised benefits to the poor and disadvantaged. Regulations are burdensome and omnipresent, but rarely effective or equitable. Their main effect is to diminish confidence in government. And if government lacks public support, then it will not be given adequate resources to assist those who need its help.

The *Schechter* doctrine would prevent Congress from delegating its legislative responsibilities, but it would not preclude state intervention in the economy. Consider an issue that has not yet received adequate attention from the federal government: day care. Many parents are either unwilling or unable to stay home with their children. The quality of baby-sitting and education for young children is often abysmal, and there is no reason to believe that the market can provide acceptable services for everyone. The government is involved, but not consistently. At present, most states do not license child-care providers who work in their own homes, nor do most states annually inspect licensed centers. In forty-one states, no training is required to become a child-care provider.[87]

The interest-group liberal response would be to increase regulation, using federal agencies to promulgate and enforce national rules intended to bring even the most backward states up adequate standards. So perhaps the Children's Bureau in the Department of Health and Human Services would be directed to close any child-care facility that it found "unsafe" or "inadequate." This office would work with the day-care industry to set standards, which it would try to enforce by inspecting a limited number of the nation's child-care centers. But it would lack the personnel necessary to visit most facilities, and any decision to close one would be subject to appeal. Large organizations would use federal regulations to keep small firms out of the business; small firms would seek exemptions from Congress. The total number of providers might shrink, and the cost per child might rise from its already unmanageable average of more than $4,000 per year. Meanwhile, the government *might* provide funding to eligible centers or grants to selected families—but there is little money in the budget and much aversion to new taxes.

If *Schechter* were revived, then Congress could not allow bureaucrats to define "safe and adequate" day care. Either Congress or state legislatures would have write their own definitions, or else parents would be left to assess the quality of child-care facilities for themselves. But *Schechter* would not prevent federal inspectors from shutting down facilities that violated clear laws—including new bills that Congress passed and the president signed. Nor would *Schechter* stop Congress from giving generous grants to low-income families with children. Once these families had market-power, they could buy the services that they wanted. Voters would be much more likely to support such new entitlement programs if Americans did not associate the federal government with burdensome and arbitrary regulations.

In general, once regulatory agencies were denied discretion, the perennial public demand for state action would begin to press in new directions. I suspect that people would ultimately favor simple, efficient, transparent, but *ambitious* federal initiatives such as vouchers, cash transfers, and a guaranteed minimum income. But, of course, it would be up to us as a public to decide what we wanted.

PARTNERSHIPS WITH LOCAL BODIES

Another solution to the dilemmas of federal regulation is for Congress to form partnerships with deliberative bodies at the state or local level. In *Schechter,* Chief Justice Hughes noted that social problems often arise from "complex conditions involving a host of details with which the national Legislature cannot deal directly." Legislation must be "adapted" to these realities, or else it will be ineffective or burdensome—or both.[88] Recognizing this problem, the New Deal Congress delegated its legislative powers to the executive branch. While condemning this approach as unconstitutional, the Supreme Court noted that *states* could be left to manage intrastate markets. Brandeis, following the Democratic Party line of his youth, was particularly enthusiastic about states as laboratories of democracy.[89]

But the truth is that their legislatures are no better equipped than Congress to handle the "host of details" involved in any complex regulatory matter. They have the advantage of physical closeness but would be ill-equipped to regulate markets (such as the New York poultry trade) that cross state lines. And since many of us move frequently and do business in many locations simultaneously, we don't want to live under fifty different regulatory regimes. Furthermore, when Congress requires state or local governments to manage selected issues, it generates unfunded mandates. It is not healthy for federal politicians to claim credit for solving social problems, while passing the costs to local authorities.

Thus federalism is no way to improve regulation, and conservatives rightly see it as a tactic to limit government and to enlarge the scope of the market. Nevertheless, there may be ways for local bodies to assist with federal administration, thereby addressing the problem that general laws don't usually fit specific circumstances. In earlier chapters I described a long tradition of Progressive experimentation at the local level, from Wilbur Phillips's Social Unit Plan of 1919 to the Community Action programs of the 1960s. These experiments differed from the New Deal's self-regulatory trade associations in one crucial respect: they established *democratic* bodies, open to all members of the communities they served. The Live Poultry Industry of the City of New York did not include any consumers or workers. By contrast, the Social Unit Plan was a democratically organized voluntary association. As such, it was a great success and worthy of emulation—but it was no substitute for government regulation, because its only power was to raise and spend philanthropic money. However, the Social Unit Plan was a model for the Community Action Associations of the War on Poverty, which were democratic bodies, chartered by the federal government, that issued rules and managed some public resources within their areas.

As I noted in chapter 2, the Community Action program became embroiled in sometimes violent disputes about representation—about who should sit on each community board. The new bodies were supposed to reflect their neighborhoods better than traditional elected governments had. But if board members were chosen by voters, then Community Action agencies began to look much like traditional city councils, except that turnout was unusually low in their elections. The alternative was to choose members in a nontraditional way, finding the kind of "authentic" community representatives who might not win formal elections. In some cases, this meant choosing established leaders (ministers, association presidents, and the like) to serve ex officio. But often, as Tom Wolfe noted, militancy was treated as evidence of authenticity. "If you were outrageous enough, if you could shake up the bureaucrats so bad that their eyes froze into iceballs and their mouths twisted into smiles of sheer physical panic . . . then they knew you were the real goods. They knew you were the right studs to give the poverty grants and community organizing jobs to. Otherwise they wouldn't know."[90] This was no way to improve accountability or efficiency or to encourage widespread participation. To make matters worse, Community Action boards competed with existing elected bodies that should have been forums for democratic self-government.

Fruitless disputes about representation arose because Community Action boards were granted powers (albeit limited ones) to make formal decisions. It therefore seemed very important to decide who could vote. Most people assumed that the backgrounds of board members would determine their opinions. For instance, a board with even a narrow majority of African-American militants would produce different results from one dominated by machine appointees. When people risked being outvoted, they often turned to undemocratic methods, such as patronage and even civil unrest.

This is not an attractive model. But in the New Progressive Era, local agencies could be reconceived as *deliberative* bodies. In deliberation, the exact balance of membership is not important, because people are expected to change their values in response to arguments. Deliberation is unlikely when the primary purpose of a body is to make decisions by majority vote. But rules can be written to discourage majority voting and to encourage consensus-building and mutual persuasion. In that case, no one will bother to fight divisive battles over membership. In fact, nobody has to be excluded from a deliberative body, except perhaps for bad conduct. And these bodies need not compete with established local legislatures, because their function is different. They may even make the job of traditional politicians easier.

Consider the recent example of "watershed partnerships." Water has long been the subject of bitter disputes in most places west of the Mississippi. Economic conflicts are exacerbated by differences in ideology and culture among such groups as miners, ranchers, urban consumers, environmentalists, hunters, and Native American nations. To make matters worse, watersheds are sensitive systems that cross state lines; water-use or pollution in one place affects everywhere else. Thus each watershed is vulnerable to the behavior of all who own, use, or regulate any part of it, including federal, state, and local governments, tribes, and private landowners of all types. From the outside, battles over land-use in Western watersheds often look so contentious that no resolution can be reached until the federal government acts forcefully, perhaps using armed agents to administer its unpopular regulations.

But actually, all the interests involved are harmed by conflict and would benefit from consensus, if one could be reached. With this in mind, at least seventy-six local groups across the West have convened completely voluntary meetings of interested parties.[91] Since the resulting "partnerships" have no power to issue regulations, there are few conflicts over membership. Anyone who wants to participate is invited; anyone who disagrees with the group may opt out without fear of becoming subject to its decisions. On other hand, some of the participants have power, so they can work out significant mutual agreements. Landowners and corporations can promise to curb unpopular behavior; environmental groups can waive their rights to sue; and government agencies can manage public lands and resources according to the desires of the group.[92]

Some watershed partnerships merely serve as neutral forums for public discussion and education—inviting speakers, sponsoring town meetings, and so on.

These groups "build better community relations as participants learn to understand and respect each other."[93] In Robert Putnam's terminology, they create social capital: habits of trust and cooperation. But the achievements of some partnerships go well beyond the intangible. For instance, the Topanga-Las Virgenes Resource Conservation District (near Los Angeles) organized about 160 entities that jointly developed a "Coordinated Resource Management Plan" for their watershed. A similar plan for the Upper Carson River in Nevada and California was signed by "government agencies, the Washoe Tribe, state assembly members, local community leaders, ranchers, conservation groups and homeowners associations."[94] Since important players find these plans at least tolerable and prefer them to constant strife, they voluntarily assent to their provisions. The resulting peace benefits everyone.

As we should expect, there have been failures. The Bitterroot Water Forum in Montana fell apart due to friction among members. The Clear Creek Watershed Forum in Colorado was actually started by the EPA; it failed because of hostility to the agency, and then reconstituted itself as a local discussion group that has lasted but lacks the capacity to invent constructive plans. The San Pedro Coordinated Resource Management Group in Arizona originally required consensus, but newcomers kept showing up and voting "no," leading to general frustration. For similar reasons, the Upper Rogue Watershed Council in Oregon now requires an 80 percent super-majority for any decisions. People who are outvoted in this council may ignore its decisions; they may even subvert the whole process.[95]

Notwithstanding these inevitable failures, the watershed partnerships represent a model that could be adopted in other areas of domestic policy, including transportation, poverty programs, and economic development. If Congress stopped delegating its legislative responsibilities to regulatory agencies, then it would need an alternative way to manage complex issues that require federal action. One idea is to ask local voluntary groups to try to reach consensus. Once they had developed generally acceptable and detailed plans, Congress could order federal agencies to enforce them. Instead of asking administrators to pursue ill-defined values, laws would mandate compliance with specific agreements, like the Upper Carson River Water Management Plan. Federal officials would participate in developing these plans and would articulate the national interest in local debates, but ultimately Congress would decide the law. As a beneficial by-product, we might see growth in civic participation, for local self-government teaches (in John Adams's words) "the habit of discussing, of deliberating, and of judging public affairs."[96]

When local groups *failed* to reach consensus, legislatures (from county councils to Congress) would have to rule, because nothing represents the public's will more authentically than an elected body. But nothing makes a legislature's job easier than a locally generated consensus.

A strikingly successful instance of this model has already occurred. Second to watersheds, national forests are perhaps the most bitterly contested resources in the West. Specifically, forests in the Sierra Nevada range provide habitats for endangered spotted owls and chinook salmon, jobs for loggers, and water that flows to millions of Californians, producing hydroelectricity on its way toward the Pacific.[97] These conflicting uses have stimulated lawsuits, lobbying battles, and violence. But in 1993, local environmentalists and government officials began open discussions in the Quincy, California, public library. These talks ultimately produced an agreement that was acceptable to forty-one signatories, including "sport fishing groups, conservation clubs, wild river clubs, timber companies, county commissioners, land and trails trusts, women in timber chapters, the local Audubon Society, and even one person . . . who describes herself as a 'Quincy resident and independent thinker.'"[98] All these parties feared that a huge federal forest would burn to the ground if the Forest Service continued to manage it with existing techniques; but efforts to change the status quo had always led to political and legal deadlocks. The Quincy Library plan called for timber companies to log the forest in such a way as to preserve wildlife and prevent devastating fires; in return, environmental groups would stay out of court. The plan also called for action by the National Forest Service, which was reluctant to comply. But by a 429–1 vote, the House of Representatives passed legislation to *force* compliance, inspired by what an opponent in Washington called "the popular appeal of 'community consensus.'"[99] The Senate ultimately concurred and the plan became law.

Its main opponents were federal employees and large environmental organizations, including the national office of the Audubon Society, which parted company with its own chapter in Quincy. The fact that national groups rejected the local "community consensus" does not automatically prove that they were wrong. Congress should always hold hearings before it approves locally generated plans, inviting national experts to testify about scientific and legal issues and the national interest. The only consensus that is evidence of truth is a global one, and the Quincy group—for all its unanimity—could have erred.

A coalition of 140 groups, including the National Resources Defense Council, the National Audubon Society, and the Wilderness Society, raised scientific arguments against the Quincy Plan (to which the local group's academic advisers responded).[100] But some of their arguments concerned the *process* of deliberation. For example, Steven Evans of Friends of the River objected that the Quincy Library Group would be "elevated above the rest of the general public," because the Forest Service would be forced to consult with them.[101] Louis Blumberg of the Wilderness Society denounced the Quincy process as "only one special interest group."[102] And Mike Leahy of the National Audubon Society worried that "a relatively small group of citizens [could] dictate public forest management, rather than agency officials receiving input from the public at large. . . . Thus, opportunities for true public participation are eliminated."[103]

The question, for course, is whether "true public participation" ever occurs under traditional procedures. Since the Progressive Era, organizations with national lobbying offices have influenced administrative agencies such as the Forest Service, but the "public at large" has rarely had any discernible impact.[104] Environmental groups in Washington lobby for their conception of the national interest (an honorable role even when they are wrong), but they are frequently stalemated by lobbyists for corporations. This is the flawed system that they rose to defend when Congress considered the Quincy Library bill. Local deliberation has its own dangers, but it is far more promising than bureaucratic rulemaking.

Even if the regulatory state is dismantled, executive-branch agencies will always have to administer federal assets, from national forests to military bases. Proponents of watershed partnerships have articulated an important principle to guide these efforts: "Government should *participate as a member of the community.*"[105] It can do so by convening and funding local deliberative bodies, by providing technical support and advice, but also by more modest (and less intrusive) steps, such as sending its own workers to meetings. At the same time, it can relax the law that governs advisory bodies. Watershed partnerships arguably fall under the Federal Advisory Committee Act (FACA), which covers all boards "established or utilized by one or more agencies" of the federal government.[106] FACA was passed and amended during the 1970s, and it reflects the good-government ideas of the time: open-meeting rules, a sunset clause, full disclosure of documents, and a mandate that any board's membership be "fairly balanced."[107] There are also provisions to ensure federal *control:* for instance, an employee of the government must chair or attend all meetings and may adjourn them unilaterally.[108] FACA is "a major impediment for some watershed partnerships for both procedural and substantive reasons."[109] The balance requirement would mandate changes in the composition of some partnerships; the conflict-of-interest rules would block many interests from participating at all; and the government-control clause would scare some groups away.

In fact, this law would have blocked the Quincy Library process, but for the intervention of the agriculture secretary, Dan Glickman. The former chief of the Forest Service argued that it was "patently illegal" for an executive named Red Emmerson, "who owns Sierra Pacific," to be "involved in the Quincy Library Group." He said:

> They're a nonprofit charter, and they're violating, not following, the forest plan. But the Secretary of Agriculture just turns around and says, "OK, you guys can manage these two and a half national forests." They're not properly chartered, and they're sitting there cutting deals back and forth. . . . I like co-operation, but I don't like Emmerson; who the hell turned over my national forests to him?[110]

The pronoun "my" may reflect the perspective of a citizen who commendably views the national forests as *public* property; but it is hard not to suspect a proprietary attitude on the part of this retired federal official. This kind of thinking will have to change before local deliberation is allowed to work. Unfortunately, the ideas of the Progressive-Era conservationists die hard. As Samuel Hays writes, "Their entire program emphasized a flow of authority from top down and minimized the political importance of institutions which reflected the organized sentiment of local communities."[111]

It should be noted, however, that elements within the Forest Service have long been friendly to grassroots deliberation. Indeed, some of the agency's experiments paved the way for the Quincy Library Group. Carmen Sirianni and Lewis Friedland write, "The U.S. Forest Service invited widespread participation in the 1970's, but when this proved ineffective in altering the adversarial paradigm, it moved to other measures. These included extensive use of dispute resolution, open planning, trust-building, and public-leadership development to engage varied constituencies."[112] The Watershed Partnership Movement can be traced to this shift within the Forest Service. As for the national environmental movement, it played an essential and positive role in the Quincy Library process—even though it objected to the endgame. Logging companies would not have come to the library to talk if their activities hadn't been virtually halted by the Endangered Species Act. Under laissez-faire conditions, they could have cut old-growth trees without pausing to deliberate. But federal environmental laws forced them to negotiate, and these laws would never have passed without effective lobbying by national organizations. The possibility of deliberation is always affected by background legal conditions, and we should be grateful to public-interest lobbies for improving the law. The environmental groups only erred, I think, by denouncing the deliberation that they had made possible.

The Forest Service is not alone in wanting to encourage public deliberation as an alternative to other forms of "citizen participation." Reforms passed in the 1970s often required regulatory bodies (or regulated companies) to hold public meetings before they could act. For the most part, this approach has turned out badly. Representatives of special interests inevitably attend public meetings, where they make speeches that duplicate the content of their letters and advertisements. Miscellaneous citizens also attend—and what they say is sometimes cogent—but often their angry comments simply cancel one another out. As a result, such sessions are unpleasant, uninformative, and sparsely attended.

Power companies in Texas are one group of regulated businesses that must "consult the public" regularly. Their executives are justifiably dissatisfied with public meetings as a method of consultation. Several major Texas utilities have therefore asked James Fishkin to conduct Deliberative Polls for them. In 1996, for example, the Central and South West Corporation of Houston brought a representative sample of 250 customers together for a weekend to read background materials, hear presentations by assorted experts, and deliberate. The fourteen visiting experts ran the gamut from environmental activists to commercial customers and city development officials. A similar group had previously approved the background papers, which presented several options for increasing wattage. After absorbing information and sharing views, customers showed a willingness to shift their positions dramatically. For example, most participants increased their support for efficiency programs and lost faith in renewable energy sources such as solar power and wind—although their highest priority was a balanced mix of energy supplies. They were also willing to endorse appropriate *costs* for benefits like cleaner air. Deliberating customers of the West Texas Utilities Company, for instance, said that they would pay $7.83 a month to "ensure that renewable energy plants were part of the resource mix."[113]

Citizens who participated expressed enthusiasm about the process, with more than 70 percent giving it a "10" on a ten-point scale.[114] Utility companies were equally happy, because they gained useful information about public attitudes and political cover for the difficult decisions that they would have to make. Citing the opinion of various outside interests, Fishkin writes that the utilities "scrupulously followed" the outcomes of the deliberative poll.[115] But no one was happier than the national environmental groups, which interpreted the citizens' endorsement of energy efficiency as a vindication of their own position.[116] The Texas Public Utility Commission also embraced the results as a valid expression of public opinion; indeed, the Commission now *requires* utilities to use Deliberative Polls or similar mechanisms.[117] This idea has very wide potential in all areas of government regulation—from neighborhood zoning to national tobacco policy.

Before closing this section, I will mention a final alternative to regulation. Unions and employers can negotiate contracts that manage contentious issues in the workplace. Unlike national regulations, collective-bargaining agreements can fit local realities and be understood by everyone whom they affect. As Richard Rothstein (formally of the Amalgamated Clothing and Textile Workers union) has written:

> Regulation, with its paper work, legal fees, and administrative time, is . . . burdensome because it can't account for meaningful differences between firms. Health and safety regulators, for example, make rules applying evenly to all workplaces. This may lead to detailed procedures covering equipment that in one workplace may be no danger, while other more serious hazards are ignored.
>
> A collective bargaining advantage is that workers and management together may agree on practical solutions to problems that resist regulation. Private dispute resolution procedures are more efficient and more nuanced than lawsuits. Lengthy, legalistic, and expensive labor-management arbitration procedures are still briefer, more informal, and cheaper than court cases. Employers, as well as unions, would rather face arbitrators than judges.[118]

It is true that unions and companies sometimes share goals that conflict with community interests, so collective bargaining is not a panacea. Compared to federal regulation, however, it could be a superior way to manage wages, job security, safety, and work rules. This approach will not succeed until we have democratic unions in which corruption plays no significant role. We will also need *reinvigorated* unions with enough members to challenge corporations directly. (For more on labor reform, see chapter 7.)

THE NATIONAL SECURITY APPARATUS

The problems of expertise, centralization, and bureaucratic discretion are nowhere more serious than in the federal agencies whose function is to protect our "national security." These agencies share a penchant for secrecy that would be unimaginable in the EPA or the Education Department. As Senator Daniel Patrick Moynihan (D-NY) recently wrote: "*secrecy is a mode of regulation.* In truth, it is the ultimate mode, for the citizen does not even know that he or she is being regulated. Normal regulation concerns how citizens must behave, and so regulations are widely promulgated. Secrecy, by contrast, concerns what citizens may know; and the citizen is not told what may not be known."[119]

Except in the field of nuclear energy, the government classifies information by administrative fiat, not by statutory law. "Thus, what commonly is referred to as 'government secrecy' more properly could be termed 'administrative secrecy' or 'secrecy by regulation.'"[120] Under the authority of various executive orders, about three million people—federal officials, military officers, and private contractors—are able to decide what public information will be classified. Even after the Cold War, these people still classify documents about 3.6 million times each year, thereby enlarging a confidential hoard of data that is already billions of pages long and decades old.[121]

Classified documents (including the millions that are destroyed before they are ever disclosed) tell the story of our government's actions at home and abroad—actions funded by American citizens, conducted under our authority, and executed in our name. Members of the "intelligence community" strenuously defend the use of secrecy, arguing that full publicity would allow foreign powers to steal our assets; to identify, capture, and torture our spies and informants; and to gain information that might threaten our physical safety. Even giving away information that is inherently valueless to our enemies is said to be dangerous, because it may reveal the sources and methods that were used to gather it.

But if secrecy has benefits, it has clear costs as well. In the most literal sense, the price of classification approaches $6 billion per year.[122] What's more, vast amounts of public money are spent, momentous decisions are made, and sometimes lives are lost as a result of secret government activities, yet those responsible often escape accountability because their decisions are invisible to the public. Describing his experience investigating allegations that American prisoners of war remained alive in Southeast Asia, Senator John Kerry (D-MA) said, "I do not think that more than . . . a couple of hundred pages of the thousands of [secret] documents we looked at had any current classification importance, and more often than not they were documents that remained classified or were classified to hide negative political information, not secrets."[123] Such experiences suggest that rampant classification is a threat to democratic self-government.

In the interests of accountability, procedures for classifying federal documents should not be left to the discretion of the executive branch. Congress should pass a statute granting the authority to classify documents to a limited set of officials, for limited purposes. One of these officials would be required to take personal and formal responsibility for any decision to classify a document. Within the document itself, the precise reasons for its classification would be stated. There would be a presumption in favor of disclosing all documents after a limited period, but a different official from the one who originally classified any record would be able to reclassify it for specific and necessary reasons. Law-enforcement officials would audit some secret documents to determine that the reasons for their classification were permissible under the law. Any federal official who classified a document in order to conceal information about someone's misbehavior would be subject to prosecution.

Along with classification, covert action poses one of the most serious threats to democracy in the national-security field. Covert action describes any government activity that is not publicly acknowledged—from a hostage-rescue mission to an undeclared war. The degree of secrecy involved differs widely. For example, U.S. involvement in Nicaragua and Afghanistan during the 1980s was technically covert, although widely recognized. Many argue that some covert actions are justifiable and even necessary; few would quarrel with a secret effort to free hostages, for example. But some CIA projects, from the Bay of Pigs to the anti-Saddam efforts in Iraq, have failed miserably. Clark Clifford, an author of the 1947 National Security Act, which gave authority for covert actions, testified forty years later:

> Covert activities have become numerous and widespread, practically constituting a routine component of our foreign policy. And with these activities have come repeated instances of embarrassing failure—where the goals of the operation themselves were not fulfilled and unforeseen setbacks occurred instead. I believe that on balance covert activities have harmed this country more than they have helped us.[124]

Even the two covert actions that are most often cited as "unblemished triumphs"—the CIA-sponsored coups in Iran in 1953 and Guatemala in 1954—both ended in long-term disaster for American interests. And we have no idea what unnecessary costs and losses were incurred during these actions, nor what moral principles were violated, because the CIA destroyed all of the relevant documents. As Theodore Draper has written, "The CIA has much to hide and decided to do it in the most effective way—by destroying the official record. This auto-da-fé of paperwork is a self-accusation."[125] Senator Moynihan adds that major failures are inevitable in a system dominated by secrecy. In the Cold War era, he writes, "error became a distinctive feature of the [national security] system. This is easy enough to explain. As everything became secret, it became ever more difficult to correct mistakes. Why? Because most of the people who might spot the mistakes were kept from knowing about them because the mistakes were classified."[126]

Under the Intelligence Oversight Act of 1980, the executive branch must keep the Intelligence Committees of the House and Senate "fully and currently informed" of intelligence activities. Agencies must give Congress prior notification of "significant anticipated intelligence activities" and furnish any information requested by the Intelligence Committees.[127] However, executive-branch officials are often reluctant to tell Congress everything it might want to know; and, for its part, Congress has sometimes been accused of carrying out its oversight responsibilities with insufficient zeal. Under the National Security Act, members of the Intelligence Committees must "protect from unauthorized disclosure all classified information relating to intelligence sources and methods." This responsibility prevents them from taking unilateral action beyond the committee chamber when they object to intelligence activities. Whatever oversight they do conduct is therefore secret; and it is not clear to what degree they have investigated "illegal intelligence activity and significant intelligence failure," as required by the National Security Act. But to judge by the public record, their first response has often come years after the alleged abuses.

Following the advice of a Twentieth-Century Fund task force, I think that at least the following moderate steps should taken to reform covert action. The president should be required to notify congressional oversight committees *in advance* whenever a covert action is undertaken, except in emergencies, when the White House would be given two days in which to report the action. The oversight committees should be able to block the covert operation by a super-majority vote. Several cabinet members (the director of central intelligence, the attorney general, and the secretaries of state and defense) should have to express their departments' views of the operation in writing. As a matter of policy, covert action should be undertaken only to serve a publicly articulated policy when other options are impossible.[128]

Roughly one-fifth of Americans believe that their government is involved in at least one large-scale conspiracy.[129] Paranoia is hardly a civic virtue. Citizens ought to make critical and informed judgments, and on this ground we can criticize people who believe (for instance) that the federal government is plotting with the United Nations and space aliens to control the world. On the other hand, some degree of distrust is understandable, given the long record of deceit, error, and lawlessness in the secret parts of the government. Nor is fair to ask people to exercise discriminating judgment when they are denied information about precisely who is responsible for federal policies. Since we cannot hold individuals accountable, the natural tendency is to blame abstractions—"the government," "the elite"—for sins that are actually committed by specific agencies and administrations. Especially after the demise of the Soviet Union, it is time to consider another severe threat to American institutions: public distrust. This problem can be solved in time, but only if the government genuinely embraces openness and accountability.

NOTES

1. Woodrow Wilson, *Congressional Government: A Study in American Politics* (Boston, 1896), pp. 302, 297, 85.

2. Wilson, *Congressional Government,* pp. 297, 82.

3. Joseph M. Bessette, *The Mild Voice of Reason: Deliberative Democracy and American National Government* (Chicago, 1994), p. 58.

4. Arthur F. Bentley, *The Process of Government* (1908; reprint, Evanston, 1935), pp. 370–371.

5. Bentley, *The Process of Government*, pp. 372, 360–361.

6. Bentley, *The Process of Government*, p. 269.

7. Bentley, *The Process of Government*, p. 261.

8. Bessette, *The Mild Voice of Reason*, pp. 61, 71, 72. In *Federalist,* no. 50 (*The Federalist Papers*, ed. Clinton Rossiter [New York, 1961] p. 319), Madison describes an interesting case in which empirical evidence shows that a legislature was too partisan to deliberate. But see also Hamilton's remark that "differences of opinion, and the jarring of parties in [the legislature], though they may sometimes obstruct salutary plans, yet often promote deliberation and circumspection, and serve to check excesses in the majority." (Federalist, no. 70, p. 427.)

9. Bessette, *The Mild Voice of Reason.* p. 100.

10. Bessette, *The Mild Voice of Reason.* pp. 129, 131, quoting Elizabeth Drew, *Senator* (New York, 1978), p. 90.

11. Bessette, *The Mild Voice of Reason.* pp. 133, 145, 146. Jane Mansbridge also cites studies that show evidence of congressional deliberation on particular issues. See her "Self-Interest and Political Transformation," in *Reconsidering the Democratic Public*, ed. George E. Marcus and Russell L. Hanson (University Park, Penn., 1993), p. 94. These studies prove that deliberation *sometimes* counts, but again it is hard to tell how often.

12. Paul Vitello, "Congress at Its Best—and Worst," *Newsday,* Nassau and Suffolk edition, January 13, 1991, p. 5.

13. Mike Christensen, "Congress Gives Nod to War: Votes Show Deep Rift on Hill," *The Atlanta Constitution,* January 31, 1991, p. A1.

14. Vitello, "Congress, Best and Worst," p. 5.

15. William J. Eaton, "Members Delve within Selves to Cast Their Votes," *Los Angeles Times,* January 13, 1991, p. A1. The first quoted sentence is Eaton's paraphrase, not Dingell's words.

16. Charlotte Grimes, "Somber: Hectic Day of Grappling with Call for War," *St. Louis Post-Dispatch,* January 13, 1991, p. B6.

17. Joseph M. Bessette, "Deliberation in American Lawmaking," *Report from the Institute for Philosophy and Public Policy,* vol. 14, no. 1/2 (Winter/Spring 1994): 23.

18. Amy Gutmann and Dennis Thompson, *Democracy and Disagreement,* (Cambridge, Mass., 1996), p. 72.

19. During the debate, there was a marked increase in the audience for C-SPAN and public television, which carried it live. See David Gonzalez, "Confrontation in the Gulf: TV Companies Finding Interest in Gulf Debates," *New York Times,* January 13, 1991, section 1, part 1, page 12. According to a poll conducted on January 11–13, only 33 percent of the public knew that Congress had authorized war. But the congressional vote was held on January 12, and awareness presumably increased thereafter. (CBS News/*New York Times* poll, reported in the Roper Center's "Public Opinion Online.")

20. Even an article on the political risks for Republicans and Democrats had to concede that "partisan politics was starkly absent from Congress' momentous votes." Paul Houston, "News Analysis: Both Parties Have Big Stake in Vote," *Los Angeles Times,* January 13, 1991, p. A10.

21. See Benjamin I. Page, *Who Deliberates? Mass Media in Modern Democracy* (Chicago, 1996), pp. 17–42.

22. Colleen Patrick, "Truth Can Be a Casualty before a Shot's Been Fired," *Seattle Times,* January 13, 1991, p. A17.

23. Michael Delli Carpini and Scott Keeter, *What Americans Know about Politics and Why It Matters* (New Haven, Conn., 1996), p. 100, citing Justin Lewis and Michael Morgan, *Images/Issues/Impact: The Media and Campaign '92* (Amherst: Publisher, 1992).

24. For two representative examples, see Walter Weyl, *The New Democracy* (New York, 1914), pp. 116–117, 315 n. 2; and Robert M. La Follette, "The Iniquity of the 'Conference' System," remarks in the U.S. Senate, July 26, 1916, in *The Political Philosophy of Robert M. La Follette, as Revealed in His Speeches and Writings,* ed. Ellen Torelle (Madison, Wis., 1920), p. 19.

25. Nader's introduction to The Ralph Nader Congress Project, Ted Siff and Alan Weil, directors, *Ruling Congress: A Study of How the House and Senate Rules Govern the Legislative Process* (New York, 1975), p. xi.

26. David Vogel, *Fluctuating Fortunes: The Political Power of Business in America* (New York, 1989), p. 203.

27. Juliet Eilperin, "Hastert Drawing Crowds—of Lobbyists," *Washington Post,* March 10, 1999, p. A11.

28. Peter Overby reporting on "All Things Considered," National Public Radio, November 11, 1998.

29. Eilperin, "Hastert Drawing Crowds," p. A11.

30. Louis Brandeis, *Other People's Money* (New York, 1932), p. 92.

31. Gutmann and Thompson cite anecdotal evidence to suggest that publicity "is quite consistent with ordinary log-rolling." For them, "the main contribution of publicity is not to make politics public-spirited but simply to make it public so that citizens can decide together what kind of politics they want" (*Democracy and Disagreement,* p. 127).

32. Jeffrey H. Birnbaum and Alan S. Murray, *Showdown at Gucci Gulch: Lawmakers, Lobbyists, and the Unlikely Triumph of Tax Reform* (New York, 1987), p. 260. Between 1924 and 1993, the names of representatives who had signed "discharge petitions" (to move legislation to the House floor without committee consideration) were kept secret, on the ground that otherwise lobbyists could pressure members to sign.

33. See Gutmann and Thompson, *Democracy and Disagreement,* pp. 364–365, n. 7; and Bessette, *The Mild Voice of Reason,* pp. 221–228.

34. Robert M. La Follette, *Autobiography* (Madison, Wis., 1960), p. 128.

35. This is my estimate, based largely on a survey by *Campaigns & Elections* that showed $800 million being spent on grassroots lobbying in 1993, and again in 1994. Spending must have increased by at least 20 percent since then, because the tobacco companies' efforts in 1998 alone consumed about $40 million. See Alison Mitchell, "A New Form of Lobbying Puts Public Face on Private Interest," *New York Times,* September 30, 1998, p. A14.

36. Cindy Skrzycki, "Companies Adopt Grass-Roots Lobbying Tactics to Push Programs," *The Washington Post,* February 3, 1992, p. A6.

37. Matthew L. Wald, "Pro-Coal Ad Campaign Disputes Warming Idea," *The New York Times*, July 8, 1991, p. D2.

38. Robert Pear, "'Liars' Try to Frighten Elderly on Health Care, Groups Say," *New York Times,* May 27, 1994, p. A18. See also Jane Fritsch, "Sometimes, Lobbyists Strive to Keep Public in the Dark," *New York Times,* March 19, 1996, p. A1.

39. See chapter 2, note 85, for data and methodology.

40. Clifford J. Levy, "Huge Rise in Spending on State Lobbying," *New York Times,* March 14, 1996, p. B1.

41. *New York Times,* March 3, 1992.

42. Michael Wines, "From a Lawmakers' Group, an Old Fund-Raising Lesson," *New York Times,* December 5, 1996.

43. Jonathan Rabinowitz, "State Legislatures Tighten the Rules on Lobbyists' Gifts," *New York Times,* May 3, 1996, p. A1.

44. Carl J. Meyer, "The Importance of Being Anyone at All," Op-Ed essay, *New York Times,* August 26, 1995, section 1, p. 19.

45. See a memorandum to all members, officers, and employees of the House of Representatives, from the Committee on Standards of Official Conduct (Nancy L. Johnson, Chairman; Jim McDermott, Ranking Democratic Member), December 7, 1995 (available on the World Wide Web at http://www.house.gov/ethics/giftrule.html).

46. Ruth Marcus, "Private Interests Ensure That Lavish Trips for Congress Endure," *Washington Post,* November 7, 1997, p. A1.

47. Jill Abramson, "The Business of Persuasion Thrives in Nation's Capital," *New York Times,* September 29, 1998, p. A22.

48. Saundra Torry, "As the Revolving Door Turns—Now You See Them, Now You Don't," *Washington Post,* March 22, 1993, p. F5.

49. Jane Fritsch, "Securities-Bill Staff Has Ties to the Industry," *New York Times,* May 5, 1995, p. A1.

50. Abramson, "The Business of Persuasion," p. A22.

51. "Washington's Lobbying Industry: A Case for Tax Reform" (at http://flattax.-house.gov/wsj0696.htm).

52. Richard W. Stevenson, "House Votes to Dump Tax Code by 2003," *New York Times,* June 18, 1998, p. A32.

53. Dick Armey, "How Taxes Corrupt," reprinted from the *Wall Street Journal,* June 19, 1996 (at http://flattax.house.gov/wsj0696.htm).

54. David E. Rosenbaum, "Tax Bill's Complexities Often Aid the Wealthy," *New York Times,* June 16, 1997, p. B10.

55. Armey, "How Taxes Corrupt."

56. Source: Citizens for Tax Justice, "Tax Expenditures, Fiscal 1996–2002, A Detailed List" at http://www.ctj.org/html/download.html.

57. Douglas Frantz, "Dole and Ethanol Industry Count on Each Other," *New York Times,* April 16, 1996, p. A16.

58. Tim Weiner, "It's Dwayne's World: Archer-Daniels's Influence Is Wide as Well as Deep," *New York Times,* January 16, 1997, p. D1.

59. *Arrowsmith et al. v. Commissioner of Internal Review,* 73 S. Ct. 74 (dissenting opinion).

60. Senator Bob Kerrey and Representative Rob Portman, co-chairs, *A Vision for a New IRS: Report of the Commission on Restructuring the Internal Review Service* (Washington, D.C.: 1997), p. 43.

61. Joint Economic Committee, "The Inefficiency of Targeted Tax Policies," April 1997, quoted by Donald C. Alexander, "This Is Not How You Spell Relief," Op-Ed, *Washington Post,* August 29, 1997, p. A19.

62. Joel Slemrod's estimate, cited in *A Vision for a New IRS,* Kerray and Portman, p. 41. W. Kurt Hanson puts the cost at 10 percent of the gross domestic product: "Try the Flat Tax" (Op-Ed), *Wall Street Journal,* May 14, 1993.

63. *A Vision for a New IRS,* Kerrey and Portman, p. 41.

64. Armey, "How Taxes Corrupt."

65. "Some Increased Aid for Housing" (editorial), *The Washington Post,* August 12, 1993, p. A26.

66. Lester M. Salamon, *Holding the Center: America's Nonprofit Sector at a Crossroads,* a Report for the Nathan Cummings Foundation (1997), p. 24.

67. Salamon, *Holding the Center,* p. 25, citing Charles T. Clotfelter and Richard Schmalbeck, "The Impact of Fundamental Tax Reform on Nonprofit Organizations," in *Economic Effects of Fundamental Tax Reform* by Henry J. Aaron and William G. Gale (Washington, D.C., 1996), pp. 211–243.

68. The total cost of individual and corporate charitable tax deductions in 1997 was forecast at $21.2 billion (of which $2.2 billion was accounted for by corporations). See Citizens for Tax Justice, "Tax Expenditures, Fiscal 1996–2002, a Detailed List."

69. *A Vision for a New IRS,* Kerrey and Portman, p. 41.

70. Steven J. Cann, *Administrative Law* (New York, 1995), p. 20.

71. La Follette's address at the Republican Platform Convention, 1910, in *The Political Philosophy of Robert M. La Follette,* ed. Torelle, p. 182.

72. Charles McCarthy, *The Wisconsin Idea,* (New York, 1912), pp. 45–46.

73. David Schoenbrod, *Power without Responsibility: How Congress Abuses the People through Delegation* (New Haven, Conn., 1993), pp. 4–9, 19–20.

74. William Greider, *Who Will Tell the People? The Betrayal of American Democracy* (New York, 1992), p. 107.

75. *The Federalist,* no. 62, p. 381.

76. Cann, *Administrative Law,* pp. 9, 76.

77. John Locke, *The Second Treatise of Civil Government,* chapter 11, section 141.

78. Article I, section 1.

79. This is part of the Administrative Procedures Act, 5 U.S.C. 552b.

80. See Joan B. Aron, "Citizens' Participation at Government Expense," in *Comparative Policy and Citizen Participation,* ed. Charles R. Foster (New York, 1980), pp. 54–69. "Intervenor funding" was a live issue in the Carter years, but it fell prey to the wholesale assault on government that Reagan initiated.

81. *A. L. A. Schechter Poultry Corporation v. United States,* 295 U.S. 495. I am not recommending that the Supreme Court revive the part of *Schechter* that cited the interstate commerce clause to prevent Congress from regulating hours and wages (*Schechter,* at 550). Contrary to Justices Hughes and Cardozo, work rules in one state *may* affect interstate trade. And restrictions on federal power limit the capacity of the American people to control their environment. See also Rehnquist's concurring opinion in the *American Petroleum Institute* case, 448 U.S. 607, at 674–675, 686.

82. *Schechter,* at 529–530.

83. Samuel P. Hays, *Conservation and the Gospel of Efficiency: The Progressive Conservation Movement 1890–1920* (Cambridge, Mass., 1959), pp. 85–6; cf. David P. Thelen, *Robert M. La Follette and the Insurgent Spirit,* (Madison, Wis., 1985), p. 60.

84. Rehnquist in the *American Petroleum Institute* case, at 675, 687.

85. To mention just one example, section 655 (a) of the Occupational Safety and Health Act gives the Secretary of Labor the power to turn industry-generated standards into enforceable federal regulations. It is thus almost identical to the procedure that was voided in *Schechter.* (I am indebted to my colleague Mark Sagoff for this reference.) See also *In the Matter of the Contested Election of Loretta Sanchez to the House of Representatives to the United States Congress,* United States District Court for the Central District of California, 1997 U.S. Dist. LEXIS 14607: "The only two cases in which the Supreme Court has declared a delegation of legislative power unconstitutional are often described as aberrations and are easily distinguishable. . . . In fact, extremely broad delegations of legislative power have been upheld as constitutional by the Supreme Court. See, e.g., *Mistretta v. United States,* 488 U.S. 361, 102 L. Ed. 2d 714, 109 S. Ct. 647 (1989) (upholding Congress's statutory delegation of broad power to issue binding sentencing guidelines to Sentencing Commission); *Skinner v. Mid-America Pipeline Co.,* 490 U.S. 212, 104 L. Ed. 2d 250, 109 S. Ct. 1726 (1989) (concluding the broad delegation of taxing power to an executive agency was constitutional). But see also the very recent *American Trucking* decision (175 F. 3rd. 1027).

86. Schoenbrod, *Power without Responsibility,* pp. 175–177.

87. Children's Defense Fund, "Inadequate Child Care Strains America's Working Families," (November 4, 1997) at http://www.childrensdefense.org//ccfact.html.

88. *Schechter,* at 529–530.

89. Schoenbrod, *Power without Responsibility,* p. 39, citing Arthur Schlesinger, *The Politics of Upheaval* (Boston, 1960), p. 280.

90. Wolfe, "Mau-Mauing the Flak Catchers" in *Radical Chic & Mau-Mauing the Flak Catchers* (New York, 1970), p. 98.

91. University of Colorado Natural Resources Law Center, *The Watershed Source Book: Watershed-Based Solutions to Natural Resource Problems* (1995), pp. 2–3 through 2–5.

92. Jo Clark, for the Western Governors' Association, *Watershed Partnerships: A Strategic Guide for Local Conservation Efforts in the West* (February 1997), p. 50.

93. Clark, *Watershed Partnerships,* p. 3.

94. *The Watershed Source Book,* pp. 1–10 through 1–11, 1–12, 1–20.

95. Ibid., 1–33, 1–48.

96. Quoted by Joseph Bessette, *The Mild Voice of Reason,* p. 41.

97. "Quincy Library Group Background," at http://www.qlg.org/publichtml/contents/overview.htm.

98. Statement of Chairman Don Young (R-AK) during the Committee on Resources mark-up of the Quincy Library Group Community Stability Act (May 21, 1997), available at http:/www.qlg.org/publichtml/bill/dyoung.htm.

99. "Dear Senator" letter by Mike Leahy of the National Audubon Society (September 17, 1997), available at http://www.igc.apc.org/igc/econet/hl/9709221595/hl7.html.

100. See Ed Marston, "The Timber Wars Evolve into a Divisive Attempt at Peace," *High Country News,* vol. 28, no. 18 (September 29, 1997); Leahy, "Dear Senator"; a memorandum to "interested parties" from David Edelson and Sami Yassa of the NRDC (September 20, 1996); a letter from Louis Blumberg of the Wilderness Society (February 13, 1997); and other documents, all accessible via http://www/qlg.org.

101. Steve Evans, letter to Chairman Don Young, May 20, 1997, at ibid.

102. Marston, "The Timber Wars Evolve into a Divisive Attempt at Peace."

103. Evans, letter to Chairman Young.

104. This fact was acknowledged by Michael McCloskey of the Sierra Club, according to Jon Margolis, "How a Foe Saved the Quincy Library Group's Bacon," *High Country News,* vol. 29, no. 18 (September 29, 1997). On the rise of private organizations as a response to the new power of the Interior Department during the Progressive Era, see Hays, *Conservation and the Gospel of Efficiency,* p. 274.

105. Clark, *Watershed Partnerships,* p. 43

106. 5 U.S. Code Appendix §3 (2) c. Indeed, partnerships have been treated as if they were covered by FACA, although perhaps section §4 (c) could excuse them: "Nothing in this Act shall be construed to apply to any local civic group whose primary function is that of rendering a public service with respect to a Federal program."

107. §5 (b) 2.

108. §10 (e).

109. Clark, *Watershed Partnerships,* p. 62.

110. Marston, "The Timber Wars Evolve into a Divisive Attempt at Peace."

111. *Conservation and the Gospel of Efficiency,* p. 272.

112. Carmen Sirianni and Lewis Friedland, "Civic Innovation and American Democracy," on the Civic Practices Network home page (http://www.cpn.org/sections/newcitizenship/change.html), reprinted from *Change,* vol. 29, no. 1 (January–February 1997).

113. Larry Jones, "Educated Opinions," *Electric Perspectives* (January/February 1997), pp. 10–17.

114. Jones, "Educated Opinions," p. 17.

115. James Fishkin, *The Voice of the People: Public Opinion & Democracy* (New Haven, Conn., 1995), p. 201.

116. See the following press releases: "We Want Clean Energy!—El Paso Electric Customers Send Clear Message" (by Karl Rábago, Environmental Defense Fund, August 25, 1997), "Deliberative Poll Shows Ark-La-Tex Residents Want Clean Energy (Rábago, February 27, 1997) and "South Texans Speak Loudly and Clearly for a Clean Electric Energy Future" (EDF, undated).

117. Fishkin, *The Voice of the People,* p. 201.

118. Richard Rothstein, "New Bargain or No Bargain," *The American Prospect,* no. 14 (Summer 1993) at http://epn.org./prospect/14/14roth.html.

119. *Report of the Commission on Protecting and Reducing Government Secrecy* (1997), Senate Document 105–2, 103d Congress: Chairman's Foreword, p. xxxvi. Cf. Gutmann and Thompson, *Democracy and Disagreement,* pp. 121–126, on "deep secrets."

120. *Report of the Commission on . . . Secrecy,* main text, p. 5.

121. *Report of the Commission on . . . Secrecy.,* pp. xxii, xxvii, xxiv.

122. *Report of the Commission on . . . Secrecy.,* p. 10.

123. Remarks at a markup session of the Senate Committee on Foreign Relations, quoted in *Report of the Commission on . . . Secrecy.,* p. xxxii.

124. Statement of Clark M. Clifford before the Senate Select Committee on Intelligence, December 10, 1987, p. 3.

125. Draper, "Is the CIA Necessary?" *New York Review of Books,* August 14, 1997, p. 19.

126. Danice Patrick Moynihan, "The Peace Dividend," *New York Review of Books,* vol. 37, no. 11 (June 28, 1990), p. 3.

127. 50 U.S.C. 413, (a) (1–3).

128. See Twentieth Century Fund, Task Force on Covert Action and American Democracy, *The Need to Know: The Report of the Twentieth Century Fund Task Force on Covert Action and American Democracy* with a background paper by Allan E. Goodman and Bruce D. Berkowitz (New York, 1992).

129. James Davison Hunter and Carl Bowman, *The State of Disunion: 1996 Survey of American Political Culture*, with fieldwork conducted by the Gallup Organization, Inc., for the University of Virginia's Post-Modernity Project (Charlottesville, Va., 1996).

7

Civil Society

When we advocate deliberative democracy and a healthy interaction between the state and civil society, we must be careful not to fall into utopian clichés. Rousseau thought that he would recognize a "well-ordered city" because there "every man flies to the assemblies." In his view, civic participation should be fulfilling—not a necessary evil, a defensive tactic, or a chore. But Rousseau realized that most people would not love politics unless they lived in small, self-governing communities of social and economic equals. Only then could all questions be decided consensually, because everyone's interests would be identical. "Among the happiest people in the world, bands of peasants are seen regulating affairs of state under an oak, and always acting wisely. . . . The first man to propose [a law] merely says what all have felt, and there is no question of factions or intrigues or eloquence."[1] Instead of Rousseau's peasants, other enthusiasts have envisioned toga-clad sages deliberating in a marble amphitheater, and hardy Anglo-Saxons at the hustings. Norman Rockwell tried to show us what the earnest American workingman would look like when he rose to speak at a PTA meeting.

It is important *not* to define the New Progressive Movement as an effort to make these clichés come true. People have various and conflicting interests, so the "latent causes of faction are . . . sown in the nature of man."[2] And since we are always divided into factions, political interactions are never reliably pleasant. They are struggles for power and goods, in which deceit, intimidation, collusion, and secrecy are never entirely absent. Given these costs, the potential benefits of participation are not sufficient to entice everyone into politics. It is rational and inevitable that some people will opt out. There are other things to do in life.

Nevertheless, it would be good if a higher percentage of Americans voted, read newspapers, talked about public affairs, joined associations, and chose organizations that were public-spirited and diverse. Citizens who participated in these ways would make the government's job easier. They could resolve some issues by reaching consensus and applying their own voluntary labor, leaving formal institutions to concentrate on matters that are inherently contentious or that require coercion. While participating civically, people would acquire information and broaden their perspectives, so their political demands would grow more rational and coherent. Honorable politicians would find helpful partners in an engaged public. As for corrupt officials, they would be threatened by citizens who read newspapers and joined civic associations.

It is not utopian to imagine a 25- or even 50-percent increase in the Index of Deliberation presented in chapter 3. That much improvement in levels of public engagement would, I think, encourage better government. In turn, better government would increase trust and confidence and make people more likely to participate civically. We have certainly seen the opposite: a vicious cycle of official misconduct and public withdrawal, each reinforcing the other. The start of a modest upward spiral should be the chief goal of the New Progressive Movement.

The first thing that the government can do to improve civil society is to get its own house in order, restoring its reputation for accountability and integrity. In addition, the state could transform its most tangible connection to organized civil society—the tax code. In discussing tax reform generally, I have proposed that we should replace the federal deduction for charitable contributions with vouchers that each person could donate to any registered nonprofit organization. This would surely cause a major redistribution of philanthropic money from prestigious national and cultural institutions (traditionally patronized by the wealthy) toward local groups that build social capital and serve less privileged clienteles.[3] All things being equal, it would be a shame if Harvard University and the Metropolitan Museum of Art lost revenue as a result of a tax reform—but all things are *not* equal. Given limited amounts of state-subsidized philanthropic money, the lion's share should go to nonelite institutions. Moreover, a voucher system would encourage organizations of all types to recruit volunteers, because people who worked for a particular group might also give it their vouchers. A voucher system would thus alter the market for civic participation by raising the value of—hence the demand for—people without special wealth or ability. As James Fishkin writes, "Vouchers would give organizations incentives to take seriously the interests of those who are now left out of the dialogue." Vouchers would also reshape the market by encouraging "the continual, competitive creation of new organizations," especially ones that could attract people who are currently unorganized.[4]

Furthermore, the government could use grassroots deliberative forums to advise legislatures; and public money could be given to political parties to support deliberation and participation. If these two reforms were implemented, then habits of discussion and cooperation might spread through civil society. Meanwhile, the news media could play a more civic role if journalists saw themselves not just as watchdogs and purveyors of information but also as participants in public deliberation.

All these ideas are promising, but government agencies, political parties, and reporters are not the only agents of civic renewal. There are also crucial roles to be played by nongovernmental organizations, schools, and citizens. The rest of this chapter presents recommendations to them.

But the nature of these recommendations depends on our response to a theoretical problem. Some people argue that civil society is the foundation of democratic government and that it is composed of *all* nonprofit organizations. If this is true, then philanthropies and membership organizations deserve official tolerance, favorable tax treatment, and voluntary support—almost without exception. Perhaps not every group is equally laudable, but the value of civil society lies in its vast *diversity* of institutional forms and purposes. Other people hold, however, that the point of civil society is to cultivate habits of cooperation, trust, civility, participation, community autonomy, and/or mutual respect. Just as corrupt and unresponsive state agencies deserve criticism, so nonprofits that are exclusive, hierarchical, paranoid, uncivil, or bureaucratic should be reformed or disbanded—if necessary, by judicial fiat.[5]

John Dewey held that democratic ideals should be incorporated "into *all* the relations of life." A "humanist view of democracy," he wrote, should have an impact "upon education, science and art, morals and religion, as well as industry and politics."[6] We can call this the "congruence" thesis: the belief that private groups should always mimic democracies. I think that Dewey was wrong, because people should be able to join the Catholic Church (the original "Hierarchy") and other organizations that choose *not* to use democratic deliberation to make all of their decisions. It is true that American Catholicism has been strongly influenced by democratic and participatory values, as have other denominations. But the only people who can decide internal matters are a religion's own members, who may understandably refuse to put democratic values ahead of theological beliefs when the two conflict. The departing president of the National Conference of Catholic Bishops recently observed that "endless debate . . . may actually be a healthy thing in the secular culture. But it can be out of place in the church."[7] His position can be assailed, but only on theological grounds; it is not self-evident that a church should be democratic. Similarly, a democratic state requires the equal participation of men and women. But civil society would be weaker and less diverse if it lost its exclusively female organizations.

The loss would be less lamentable if citizen's militias, or NIMBY (not-in-my-back-yard) associations, vanished from civil society. Nevertheless, as Nancy Rosenblum argues, we "cannot shepherd adults into presumptively benign groups, and if we *could* compel association, there is no assurance that model arrangements would effectively influence dispositions in intended ways." She rejects the thesis that egalitarian and civil organizations necessarily promote these values in the larger society, nor does she believe that exclusive and authoritarian groups always turn their members into bad citizens. Even if "we are subject to (or inflict) prejudice, arbitrariness, or deference in one domain, we may be able to exhibit an iota of tolerance, say, in public arenas or fairness in hiring. Which is why fear for the effects of association on members' overall disposition and conduct (liberal fear of traditionalist groups and vice versa) may be exaggerated."[8]

In short, pluralism and autonomy are civil society's chief virtues, and they should restrain us from interfering with voluntary associations or officially discriminating among them. Still, it would be a mistake to declare that every private organization is immune from criticism. Groups that spread hate or paranoia certainly need to be confronted, at least with moral arguments. Progressives should also try to reform those organizations that claim to be democratic, open, and public-spirited but that do not live up to these ideals. When they work well, such organizations help to keep the government accountable. They are also arenas in which their members can participate politically. Dewey held that democratic participation was the single most valuable human activity; we can meet him halfway and declare it one admirable endeavor among others. On these grounds, we ought to challenge some nonprofit associations to become more democratic, for to leave them alone would be a missed opportunity.

PHILANTHROPIES AND CIVIL INVESTING

If civil society is defined as the realm in which individuals deliberate and cooperate on equal terms to solve common problems, then foundations stand somewhat apart from it. On one hand, they may cultivate democracy by sponsoring useful institutions or processes. For example, Community Development Corporations (CDCs) have an impressive record of building and renovating property in devastated areas. They also allow residents to participate effectively—and they wouldn't exist without an initial grant from the Ford Foundation.[9] It is helpful, too, when philanthropies take it upon themselves to *solve* problems that merely require money and expertise, thereby freeing democratic organizations to concentrate on more contentious issues. If, for instance, a foundation agrees to pay for inoculations that are beyond the means of a local government, then the local authorities and citizens can worry about other matters. It would be even better if government agencies in poor areas had enough public money to perform such functions themselves; but if their budgets remain inadequate, then philanthropies can help.

These cases illustrate healthy relationships between foundations and citizens. However, philanthropies may instead hurt deliberative democracy by acting in the same harmful ways that we sometimes expect from the government. In 1995, a group of grassroots leaders told interviewers that "foundations too often set themselves up as experts who know what is best for communities that they actually know very little about." This attitude can harm local institutions that rely on philanthropic money. One leader recalled, "[our] whole grass roots identity got lost because [a foundation] came in with all these experts and pretty much told everybody how you do things." Local organizations that happen to employ well-trained and educated grant-writers can negotiate foundations' red tape, but other groups are often shut out. Grant-makers can also force local associations to follow arbitrary schedules and procedures, or to address fashionable issues that don't seem important at the community level.

Since the grant-seeking process is competitive, local groups must strive to look both unusual and superior to their neighbors—rather than work together. Furthermore, donors sometimes look for excessively concrete results when they demand reports and assess their grantees. Thus local groups cannot spend too much time on matters that evaluators tend to overlook, such as the quality of local relationships or the breadth of civic involvement.[10]

Finally, foundations manage tax-exempt (that is, quasi-public) funds without democratic accountability. Many charities receive government money, which obliges them to follow state regulations and priorities; but this is not true of grant-making foundations—"perhaps the only institutions in society that do not depend in any significant way on outside resources."[11] Since they are lightly regulated and self-governing, their autonomy is extraordinary. There are unmistakable advantages to this approach. Philanthropies exhibit (potential) pluralism and flexibility that are impossible in formal government, and they are insulated from the harmful aspects of politics, such as patronage and majority tyranny. But the disadvantages are equally clear. The expected pluralism, for one thing, has failed to materialize. Peter Frumkin writes, "Most of the large foundations have evolved into highly professional bureaucracies that look strikingly similar to one another in their organizational structures and grantmaking practices. . . . Not surprisingly, when one peruses the annual reports of foundations working in the same geographical area, the names of a small group of non-profit organizations begin to appear over and over again in the grant lists of foundations."[12]

To make matters worse, nonprofit organizations can spend their money in self-serving ways, building luxurious headquarters, paying their officers high salaries, holding conventions in exotic settings, or buying positive publicity for their donors. The Ford Foundation's home in a Manhattan skyscraper has a twelve-story atrium and "terraced indoor gardens, a dense green jungle four stories high, suggesting a dream dreamt by Nebuchadnessar of Babylon and executed by Mies van der Rohe."[13] Many local leaders believe "that foundations are very comfortable places to work precisely because they allow themselves very high administrative costs. At the same time, [local] organizations say that their own requests for modest operating funds are turned down repeatedly."[14] The frustration that community activists express about their donors is shared by many average citizens. In 1992, just 27.2 percent of Americans expressed at least "quite a lot" of trust in private and community foundations. Four percent more said that they trusted federated appeals like the United Way, whose financial scandals had yet to be publicized. Thus foundations enjoyed less trust than the military or public schools, and they were exactly on a par with the (generally despised) media.[15]

If philanthropies are distrusted and have an ambiguous relationship to deliberative democracy, then they are in the same condition as government, and they need a dose of Progressive reform. To avoid the dangers of centralized power, it would be best if this reform were voluntary and self-generated. Fortunately, there is something to build on: the nascent Civil Investing movement. This movement is in some ways the latest version of the drive that began in the 1950s to organize poor communities, to increase citizen participation, to train local leaders, and to create democratic or insurgent groups. (See chapter 2.) But a new episode began in the mid-1990s, when a group of about forty foundation executives resolved to "strengthen social capital and/or to promote deliberative democratic participation."[16] They decided to help build communities in which people belonged to many organizations and informal groups, ideally with overlapping memberships. They also wanted citizens to trust one another and to believe in their own ability (and responsibility) to solve problems by working across boundaries such as race and class.[17]

One theorist of Civil Investing, Mark Gerzon, writes:

> In the past, foundations have operated as extensions of their benefactors' social visions. . . . While the donor-driven grant-making role of philanthropy can . . . have significant, positive impact on certain social problems in specific geographic areas, it does not necessarily enhance the self-governing capacities of communities. At worst, grants from outside the community can become just another external influence seeking to shape the community's future. . . . We need a philanthropy in which the community *decides,* for itself, what it needs.

Thirty years ago, any advocate of community organizing (including foundation executives) would have agreed. But the community-action programs of that era tried to influence who had the *power* to make political decisions, whereas Civil Investors are more worried about the quality of communities' talk. Gerzon continues, "When citizens engage in a deliberative process and choose to use available resources for specific purposes . . . , they are building community" and gaining "experience, however modest, in self-governance."[18]

Gutmann and Thompson offer good reasons to focus on deliberation rather than power. They concede that certain economic, political, and perhaps cultural conditions are necessary to permit perfectly fair deliberation.

> We do not presume that these background circumstances are easily created or maintained. But citizens and officials should not use the injustice of inequalities in liberty and opportunity as an excuse for neglecting to deliberate or failing to develop a more deliberative form of democracy. On the contrary, because deliberative democracy relies on reciprocity, publicity, and accountability, it stands a better chance of identifying and meliorating social and economic injustices than a politics that relies only on power, which is more likely to reproduce or exacerbate existing inequalities.[19]

In other words, even under the worst conditions, deliberation can reveal what is wrong; it can also help to create strong new coalitions. It is a mistake to give people power without first asking them to deliberate, for only deliberation can tell us who should be empowered and how. Talk without power is empty; power without talk is blind.

In practical terms, Civil Investing means that foundations either make grants that are specifically designed to promote discussion and mutual trust, or else assess the impact of their regular grants on social capital (i.e., trust and habits of cooperation). Some try to aid the kinds of informal groups that cannot apply for grants. Thus a foundation might build a laundry room in a public housing project partly in order to encourage the residents to talk. Or it might provide space and food for a deliberative body like the Quincy Library group. Meanwhile, as Marvin Cohen of the Chicago Community Trust explains, grant-makers have begun to ask of any proposal: "Are we presented with an opportunity to build bridges among the citizenry, to promote dialogue and mutual understanding, to open up new possibilities for pursuing the public good?"[20]

Although I think that the Civil Investing movement is promising, it must move beyond two distracting issues. First, much of the discussion among interested foundation executives has concerned the negative effects of professionalism (or expertise) on their relationships with grantees.[21] Citizens cannot address their own problems—the argument goes—if foundation executives claim to have scientific answers. Furthermore, the prevailing criteria for making and assessing grants are said to be distorted by professional prejudices, such as a demand for quantifiable results, a bias in favor of applicants who have formal credentials, and a division of social problems into rigid disciplinary fields (economics, public health, education, and so on). Finally, donors and grantees apparently behave like professionals and clients, respectively—not like partners who can deliberate together about ends and means.

This critique echoes the writings of Jane Addams and Mary Simkhovitch, Settlement House leaders during the Progressive Era, who resisted pretensions to expertise. Addams blamed the "scientific methods" of Chicago's Bureau of Organized Charity for the death of a poor father whom she had tried to help. Haunted by the memory of this case, she wrote, "I learned that life cannot be administered by definite rules and regulations; that wisdom to deal with a man's difficulties comes only through some knowledge of his life and habits as a whole."[22] Addams initially fought municipal corruption and disliked the Chicago Democratic machine, but she learned to hold elitist reformers in equally low regard. Of local politicians, she wrote: "They are corrupt and often do their work badly; but at least they avoid the mistake of a certain type of business men who are frightened by democracy, and have lost their faith in the people."[23]

Since Addams's time, democracy has often been troubled by professionals who apply their disciplines in inappropriate ways. However, despite the rise of degree programs in philanthropy, the truth is that most foundation executives are *not* professionals or experts. Their methods of evaluation are often haphazard and lax, especially when they assess community-based groups.[24] They may tell local organizations how to operate, thereby acquiring undue influence—but not because of their educational credentials or their specialized methods. Indeed, no one would listen to them at all if it weren't for their money. So what distorts the relationship between donors and grantees is not expertise but financial dependence. If their conversations fail to exhibit the candid, egalitarian, critical, and open-ended qualities that we prize in deliberation, that's because those who need money must strive to please those who have it.

Civil Investors like to discuss public deliberation, consensus, and trust, when their predecessors in the community-organizing movement used to analyze money and power. This shift is in some ways constructive, for citizens can improve their communities even while power remains unequally distributed. But it is not healthy for people to overlook questions of money and power *when they have it.* Local leaders will act as subservient clients of foundation officers as long as the latter manage huge funds. Therefore, Progressive foundations ought to cede some degree of financial control.

This can be done in relatively modest ways. For instance, foundations should make grants to support the basic operating costs of community-based, deliberative organizations. The money should be guaranteed for (say) five years at a time, subject only to basic accounting standards. Then the recipients would be able to decide for themselves how to allocate their resources, without worrying that funds will quickly disappear if they displease foundation executives.

Any group that seems likely to promote deliberation and social capital should be eligible for such long-term, unrestricted grants. In some inner-city, rural, and immigrant communities, the most obvious candidates are *churches* and other religious congregations. Historically, foundations have been reluctant to support religious bodies, sometimes out of secular bias or sheer snobbery, but sometimes because the purpose of a congregation (to praise the Lord and save souls) is not mentioned in the typical philanthropic charter. But while congregations carry out their religious duties, they also provide civic and political benefits that can be useful to their whole communities. Church members vote, volunteer, and trust others more than nonmembers do. So secular foundations should not ignore religious bodies as recipients of long-term grants.

A second distracting issue concerns assessment. Proponents of Civil Investing argue that certain forms of evaluation burden local groups with unnecessary red tape, overlook social capital, or involve foundation executives in micro-management. Indeed, no philanthropy should retract its money from a democratic organization just because of a premature assessment. Members of grassroots groups should be consulted about the criteria of success that they will have to meet. They should then participate in their own evaluation, and they shouldn't be compelled to satisfy outside experts before they've had a chance to operate independently for some time. However, Civil Investors sometimes overstate the case against expert evaluators (the "Chi-Square Crowd") by arguing that *any* assessment is inappropriate, especially if it uses numerical data. It seems to me that foundations have a duty to weigh the success and efficiency of Civil Investment grants compared to more traditional forms of philanthropy, using whatever data they can find.

To be sure, there are sometimes better things to do with scarce resources than to collect precise statistics when a rough assessment would suffice. Nevertheless, such instruments as polls, interviews, focus groups, and records of attendance or membership would help to show whether Civil Investing worked. If, for instance, a project built trust, then it would affect answers to survey questions about attitudes toward others. If it improved the relationship between citizens and their local government, then randomly selected residents would recognize the improvement. If it increased participation, then attendance at local events would rise measurably. Evaluators could also look for more concrete outcomes, assigning due credit when deliberative bodies managed to design consensus plans, or when churches lowered the crime rate in their vicinity.[25] Of course, even the best programs can fail to produce tangible results because of bad luck or because external factors have caused matters to grow worse. But this is equally true for conventional philanthropy, so it is wrong to argue (as some Civil Investing advocates have) that traditional charity and welfare programs have failed. Perhaps service-delivery programs are highly efficient, and a shift to Civil Investing would cause net harm. This is the threshold question that foundations must ask—and a measure of professionalism wouldn't hurt.

MEMBERSHIP ORGANIZATIONS

A second type of nonprofit organization also requires reform: public-interest membership groups or citizens' lobbies. For the most part, members of these organizations simply send money to buy the services of professional lobbyists. Pure mailing-list groups do not build strong connections from citizen to citizen, nor do they allow their members to set their national agendas. It is true that many public-interest lobbies are organized democratically, with elected boards, state affiliates, and even referenda—but most of their members have so little commitment and knowledge that the professional staff dominate. To take just one example, the "Center for Science in the Public Interest receives 75 percent of its revenues from over 80,000 members, yet these contributors play no role in directing the affairs of the organization or in determining its goals."[26]

This is not a sufficient reason to condemn mailing-list organizations, for perhaps they allow ordinary people to influence public policy (albeit indirectly) and to gain political information at a reasonable cost. However, their effectiveness has declined, as groups on the Right have played those on the Left to a stalemate, and all nonprofit organizations have lost influence to corporate lobbyists, public-relations experts, and the mass media. In 1971, the economist Mancur Olson theorized that large voluntary groups that sought "social goods" (such as political reform, public morality, or justice) could not attract members without also offering specific incentives such as subsidized insurance. Even people who didn't join or give money to these groups would benefit from their activities. Since choosing to be a "free rider" was rational (in economists' terms), the vast majority of people would do so. Soon after Olson published *The Logic of Collective Action,* his theory seemed threatened by the rise of public-interest organizations.[27] Common Cause recruited 230,000 members in its first year; Public Citizen had 175,000 contributors by the mid-seventies.[28] But collectively these groups managed to recruit much less than 1 percent of the American people—mostly wealthy individuals for whom a $20 membership fee was a negligible expense. Meanwhile (as Olson's theory might have predicted), commercial organizations were able to overcome the free-rider problem by spending money. Companies could stir up "grassroots" pressure, and media figures could boost their ratings by disseminating political messages.

The handwriting was on the wall by 1994, when a coalition including Common Cause, Public Citizen, the U.S. Catholic Conference, and Ross Perot's United We Stand America supported a bill to require disclosure of lobbying expenses. Following their customary procedures, these groups tried to alert their members, some of whom obediently called Congress to support the legislation. It passed in both houses and seemed to face only the formality of a final-passage vote. But then the radio talk-show host Rush Limbaugh took to the air, charging that the bill would require all church members to register if their denominations lobbied. As a matter of fact, only paid lobbyists were covered, and religious organizations were explicitly exempted. Nevertheless, angry callers besieged the Capitol and the legislation died.[29]

At that moment, it was clear that the model pioneered by Robert La Follette's Citizens' Legislative Service (and resurrected by John Gardner's Common Cause) required a thorough overhaul. Pure mailing-list groups, facing irrelevance, should now consider implementing a *chapter* structure, borrowing the best models from Amnesty International, the League of Women Voters, the American Civil Liberties Union, the Audubon Society, the National Rifle Association, and the Christian Coalition. To varying degrees, these groups ask their local bodies to discuss issues and to initiate action. Since the chapter structure requires myriad presidents, secretaries, and treasurers, it teaches leadership skills. It also brings people together to act cooperatively, thereby building social capital. Because chapters of different organizations can meet and share resources, they may increase the overall capacity of their communities to solve problems. Finally, chapters acquire power and information, so they can sometimes hold their own national organizations accountable.

There is certainly a practical drawback to the chapter structure. Since mass mailings raise a lot of money, they allow consumer and environmental groups to operate in Washington. For instance, the Southern Policy Law Center earned twice what it spent on its direct-mail campaign during the 1980s, which targeted the resurgent Ku Klux Klan. After Ronald Reagan was shot, Handgun Control quickly recruited 450,000 members by sending an appeal.[30] Another option is door-to-door canvassing, which has worked financially for groups like ACORN and the Clean Water Action Project—but it is little more participatory or deliberative than mass mailings are. Compared to these methods, chapters are better for civil society, but the funds that they generate may not repay the cost of establishing them. Most of the successful chapter-based associations are old, their local affiliates having formed slowly over the decades. The main exception is the Christian Coalition, but even it is an alliance of pre-existing churches. Thus it is not clear that groups like Handgun Control could afford to transform themselves into coalitions of local chapters. Nor would citizens have enough to do as chapter members of single-issue lobbies, so some groups might have to broaden their agendas—and thereby lose legislative focus.

Nevertheless, mailing-list organizations should experiment with the chapter model, at least on a small scale. There are three major reasons for them to do so. First, their traditional methods are losing clout, and they would draw strength from a chapter structure. Politicians are no longer impressed by telephone calls from a few voters, because corporate lobbyists can generate these calls almost at will; but elected officials might respect chapters that were active in their districts. Second, local bodies offer social benefits (such as friendship and entertainment) that attract some people to join and to stay active. For instance, many people probably belong to the Sierra Club because of its nature walks, and to the National Rifle Association because of its firearms classes. Finally, there is a public-interest rationale for establishing a chapter structure. Common Cause, Public Citizen, and similar groups are committed to democracy, which requires broad deliberation. But by raising money through the mail, they do not promote civil society; they may even divert resources away from more participatory groups. Therefore, national membership associations should devolve some responsibility to local bodies in an effort to create social capital. The nation's largest mailing-list organization, the American Association of Retired Persons, has already taken this lesson to heart and is trying to increase the civic responsibilities and capacities of its volunteers and chapters.[31]

UNIONS

Like philanthropies and citizen's lobbies, labor unions require reform to live up to their democratic promise. Once labor has reformed itself, modern Progressives should embrace it with greater enthusiasm than their predecessors (including Robert La Follette) mustered. Indeed, Progressives should do more than wait for union reform—they should actively seek it. For unions are not just special interests or lobbies; they are necessary components of a modern democracy, whose strength and internal culture are matters of deep public concern.

During the original Progressive Era, the basic political issue for unions was toleration. They had been legal since a court decision of 1842, but the judicial system often treated their behavior as conspiratorial under common law, using injunctions to block strikes and federal troops to enforce injunctions. Under these circumstances, Samuel Gompers said that labor "asks no favors from the State. It wants to be left alone and to be allowed to exercise its rights."[32] Progressives agreed that it was unfair to allow capitalists to combine into state-chartered corporations, while treating combinations of workers as conspiracies.[33] Two surviving Progressives, George Norris and Fiorello LaGuardia, were responsible for the legislation that finally gave employees collective-bargaining rights—"to exercise *actual* liberty of contract and freedom . . . of labor."[34]

La Follette's friend John Commons, who often advised him on labor matters, considered unions to be organized economic factions that deserved as many rights and as much respect as companies, but no more. "In the final analysis," he wrote, "the legality or illegality of a labor union turns on the opinion of the judge or the [government] executive or the public as to the public purpose of the union. If it exists only for a private purpose, then even its persuasive efforts are illegal. If it performs a public purpose, then its effort to strengthen its bargaining power by persuasion is lawful. . . . Does it, or does it not, serve a public purpose? Each person must decide for himself."[35] Commons personally favored unions, holding that they served a useful function as counterweights to business, but he did not view them as part of the Progressive Movement. They were a faction to be treated fairly, but firmly—to be held at arm's length, lest their narrow interests corrupt public officials.

During the battle over railroad regulation in 1907, La Follette argued (according to David Thelen) that "the need of the travelling public for safety was more important than the greed of either railway officials or [unionized] workers." When the president of the Seamen's Union asked La Follette to reform working conditions at sea, the senator introduced landmark legislation but on the condition that it contained safety provisions to prevent a repeat of the *Titanic* disaster.[36] Since La Follette always claimed that his bills transcended partial interests in the name of the public good, perhaps he, too, viewed unions as nothing better than factions. Even if labor and management worked out mutually acceptable deals on an equal footing, their bilateral negotiations would only serve the national interest by chance—if at all. Ultimately, then, rules regarding minimum wages and work conditions should be set by the government, after legislators had deliberated about the conflicting demands of workers, consumers, and capitalists.[37] La Follette never said any of this publicly, but his tactful silence could be attributed to the fact that he needed to keep the ambivalent AFL within his coalition. Many unions did back him in 1924, but Gompers grudgingly remarked: "It looks as if we are forced to turn to La Follette."[38] Perhaps the feeling was mutual.

If we defined "democracy" as majority rule, then unions would actually be undemocratic, for they represent narrow groups of workers who can hold the community hostage if they control strategic interests. But democracy does not mean majority rule; it means a fair search for consensus. And this is most likely when each faction can block extremely unfavorable outcomes—not by exercising a simple veto, but by taking arduous defensive actions, such as a strike. American workers never strike lightly, for the costs and risks are high. Still, because of their power to withhold labor, unions may be able to force the nation to discuss work conditions, job security, and wages. If the ratio of profit to salary and the nature of work are negotiated in bargaining sessions and in legislatures, then reason and persuasion may temper pure force. But frank and constructive negotiations are unlikely to occur unless workers are organized.

Furthermore, unions can be seen as parts of civil society and not simply as market institutions. Like other voluntary associations, they cultivate trust, disseminate information, and encourage both cooperation and discussion among their members.[39] Their decline is the most salient fact about American civil society since 1950, and their renewal must be part of a successful Progressive movement. This is especially important because unions have certain unique functions that cannot be handled by other associations.

Collective bargaining can resolve issues in the workplace without the dilemmas that beset regulatory agencies. When unions and managers sit across the bargaining table, they can devise agreements that are understood and approved by the rank-and-file, and that fit local realities. This makes unions useful institutions—but hardly unique, because collective bargaining resembles other forms of negotiation. But unions *are* unique in that they allow workers to discuss the economic conditions of their own lives, to debate tactics for bettering their situations, and then to take collective and binding action in their mutual interest. Other associations offer these opportunities separately: we can talk about economics in a reading group and take action by changing our own jobs; we can think about tactics at the office or on a sports team and act in common in a soup kitchen. But no other organization links these components into one (potentially) seamless whole. Unions are not primarily places in which some people get together to help others, nor where each helps herself, but where every member can assist everyone else by implementing democratic decisions.

On the other hand, unions resemble small states, so they can fail in all the ways that governments can. Corruption has been a consistently serious problem in the American labor movement, virtually ruining what should be a pillar of Progressive democracy. Thus union members, reporters, and law-enforcement officials should relentlessly pursue dishonest labor leaders. But even without actual corruption, union executives can develop interests that conflict with those of ordinary workers. In a union, discussion, decision-making, and action should all be linked—but these links can easily be broken, with the rank-and-file bearing all the risks and distant leaders making the important decisions.

Once again, part of the blame lies with interest-group liberalism, whose quintessence is the National Labor Relations Board (NLRB). In the board's first years, under Franklin Roosevelt, it basically let labor and industry fight their own battles, and unions organized on a vast scale. But the 1947 Taft-Hartley Act, passed by conservatives over President Truman's veto, brought labor firmly under the control of bureaucrats and courts. Congress empowered the NLRB to define "good-faith negotiation" and "collective bargaining" and then to enforce its definitions nationwide, interfering in almost every aspect of unions' internal organization and bargaining practices.[40] The NLRB treats organizations (unions) as surrogates for an entire interest (labor), and it views a few union officials as representatives of the whole rank-and-file. Sixty years of regulation have produced what the board acknowledges is a "highly specialized area of the law"; as a result, labor attorneys are often the "chief negotiators" for both sides in any labor dispute.[41] To address the concerns of people who are outside the system, the law provides a formal—but very difficult—method for organizing workers into recognized "bargaining units," which can then elect leaders and hire lawyers. In all these respects, the NLRB is an epitome of interest-group liberalism.

Delegation is a common way to avoid difficult moral conflicts that should be resolved by elected officials or by civil society. In this case, we might expect Congress, state legislatures, unions (and other private groups), or the NLRB to deliberate about such matters as the prevailing wage for each occupation, the acceptable level of risk, and the extent of job security. But state legislatures are discouraged from addressing labor concerns by the broad scope of federal law. They may set minimum standards, but they rarely intervene in particular disputes between workers and companies. Unions, for their part, are hierarchical and dominated by experts, so they don't promote deliberation among ordinary Americans. Congress avoids its deliberative responsibilities by delegating authority to the NLRB. One senator who helped to create it explained: "When employees have chosen their organization, when they have selected their representatives, all [we propose] to do is to escort them to the door of the employer and say, 'Here they are, the legal representatives of your employees.' What happens behind those doors is not inquired into."[42] Finally, the NLRB, like all regulatory agencies, is ill-equipped to deliberate about values and ends. It has established bargaining rules, but it has no mandate to seek just or wise decisions.

Procedural fairness is a purported goal, but the NLRB's dominant purpose is *peace.* The idea is to create a stable equilibrium between labor and capital so that the national economy does not suffer from strikes or unnecessary layoffs. To this end, federal law demands negotiation before confrontation, long-term contracts instead of short-term ones, and centralized union power as a substitute for the unpredictable behavior of autonomous locals. Since each International is now legally responsible for its own members' behavior once a contract is signed, it becomes in effect an arm of the state.

Given the weakness of unions in the marketplace, the importance of labor regulations, and the political power of organized special interests, American unions have naturally shifted their attention from strikes and collective bargaining toward campaign contributions and lobbying. Instead of confronting corporations directly, they often apply pressure to Democratic politicians in the hope that they can win favorable legislation. It is not too much of an exaggeration to say that the AFL-CIO is now a federation of PACs and not a coalition of unions.

By the 1960s, the whole regime of interest-group liberalism was ripe for a Progressive critique. The authors of the Port Huron Statement (who met at a labor retreat) criticized American political institutions as bureaucratic, unaccountable, inequitable, and amoral. Most people, they argued, had no meaningful opportunities for political participation, and there was little discussion of the public good. Around the same time, students of the union movement leveled exactly the same complaints against the AFL-CIO. For instance, Stanley Aronowitz wrote:

> Trade unions have fallen victim to the same disease as the broader electoral and legislative system. Just as the major power over the state has shifted from the legislative to the executive branch of government, power over union affairs has shifted from the rank and file to the corporate leaders, the trade union officials, and the government. Trade unions are regulated by the state both in their relations with employers and in their internal operations. Moreover, the problems of union leadership have been transformed from political and social issues to the routines of contract administration and internal bureaucratic procedures, such as finances. The union leader is a business executive. His accountability is not limited to the membership—it is extended to government agencies, arbitrators, courts of law, and other institutions which play a large role in regulating the union's operations.[43]

All this remains true twenty-five years later. Today we may be seeing the first glimmers of a labor revival, but it is not clear that unions have yet restored internal democracy—not even to the degree that the government has.

One reason for the lack of participation within unions is (as Aronowitz notes) the "alleged technical nature of collective bargaining in the modern era." Negotiations inevitably involve some technical matters, but often collective bargaining becomes more complex than necessary because the federal bureaucracy turns conflicts of values and interests into legal puzzles. "Not only leaders and representatives of the local membership sit at the union's side of the bargaining table, but lawyers, insurance and pension experts, and sometimes even management consultants as well; the rank-and-file committees tend to be relegated to advisory or window-dressing functions or simply play the role of bystander."[44]

This problem is familiar from other fields—and not easy to solve. But labor's other dilemmas are even less tractable. Above all, the structure of contemporary industry makes local self-government difficult within unions. During the Great Depression, CIO unions relied heavily on shop stewards: industrial workers who provided free, elected leadership for groups of twenty-five to thirty peers. When a dispute arose on the floor, the shop steward would leave his or her post to settle the matter with the company's foreman, sometimes threatening an immediate "job action." After the Second World War, however, companies centralized their organizations, taking discretion away from their own foremen, and thereby made shop stewards almost irrelevant.[45] This was the trend in large manufacturing companies that employed skilled labor, but that whole sector shrank as new jobs were created in highly decentralized industries composed of small firms, contractors, and contingent workers. Such industries have so far proved almost impossible to unionize. Therefore, the number of firms in which a shop-steward system would still work is vanishingly small.

The regulatory system that governs unions was attacked in the sixties for making the relationship between labor and management excessively bureaucratic and constrained. But today it seems more passé than harmful, for it only applies to "skilled workers—principally professionals and technicians but also some skilled craftspersons—[who] perform core functions for firms to which they are attached on a more-or-less permanent basis."[46] For the rest of the population, labor law is largely irrelevant—but so are unions.

The membership of American unions must be expanded, and labor organizations must be reformed internally. In the struggle for raw numbers, the AFL-CIO has recently taken the lead by putting money and energy into recruitment.[47] Workers also have a role to play: they should vote "yes" to unionization whenever they have the opportunity to do so. And public law should be reformed to give labor organizers a better chance of success. Under current rules, once 30 percent of the workers in a given unit sign cards indicating a preference to unionize, a secret-ballot election must be held to decide whether a union shall be recognized. Before the vote, employers can hold anti-union meetings, isolate labor activists from the rest of the workers, and litigate every detail of the campaign, including the definition of the "bargaining unit," the date and time of the election, and the list of eligible voters. The NLRB is supposed to guarantee that employers do not fire union proponents or threaten to close plants if they are unionized. But the AFL-CIO charges that about 10,000 workers are dismissed annually for advocating unions, and that even the token penalties for violating federal regulations are rarely assessed until elections are long over.[48] Thomas Geoghegan, a labor lawyer, writes that "if you put on a union button at work . . . it can be shown to a reasonable certainty that you will be fired." He calls the NLRB at its worst "a bloodless, bureaucratic death squad."[49]

If the NLRB is indeed ineffective, this would be typical of interest-group liberalism, for the government hardly ever employs enough officials to enforce its complicated regulations equitably. It would be better for Congress to pass a very simple rule accompanied by effective sanctions. Some experts argue that the original postcard petition should suffice to certify a union—as in Canada, and as in the United States before the Taft-Hartley Act of 1947. Geoghegan may be right to say, "I can think of nothing, no law, no civil rights act, that would radicalize this country more, democratize it more . . . than to make this one tiny change in the law: to let people join unions if they like, freely and without coercion, without threat of being fired, just as people are permitted to do in Europe and in Canada."[50]

Geoghegan advocates this "tiny" change with due irony, because repeal of Taft-Hartley would require a very hard fight. Equally difficult would be to repeal state "right-to-work" laws, which forbid the establishment of union shops. Unless a union represents everyone, employers can discriminate against its members, even to the point of firing them. Opponents of the union shop argue that it violates individuals' right to negotiate privately in the labor market. But when we enter a social contract, we give some of our private property rights to the state in return for the power to vote. We do this because we recognize that private property without a state is insecure; democracy is a better bargain than anarchy. Likewise, workers should be able to trade their private bargaining rights for membership in a democratic union—and they shouldn't have to agree unanimously to unionize. If, after all, the United States Constitution had required unanimous popular consent for its ratification, then we would never have become a nation.

A smaller percentage of American workers are represented by unions today than before the creation of the NLRB.[51] Labor's condition is so grave that some people have suggested voluntarily returning to the pre-New Deal arrangement. In those days, unions were never recognized by the national government. If enough workers wanted to form a union, they struck and picketed the plant to keep replacements ("scabs") from entering it. If they used physical coercion, they were subject to arrest—and often they were arrested even when their behavior was legal. They were almost inevitably fired en masse. But they sometimes forced employers to recognize them as a union, especially when the surrounding community and local government backed them. Today, authorities should refrain from intervening on the employer's side of an extra-legal strike when the issue is unionization. One major wildcat action could have a salutary effect on American labor relations.

Whether or not the new efforts at recruitment prove to be successful, labor must reform its own procedures and culture to become more democratic. Unions can start by allowing members to elect both bargaining teams and International presidents directly. They should also grant the equivalent of Home Rule to locals, whenever this is possible. As a side benefit, devolution of power may increase membership, because participatory organizations are attractive to join. Dorothy Sue Cobble, a labor historian, believes that the AFL's "willingness to grant autonomy to its affiliates" helped it to grow between 1886 and 1955. She recommends that the AFL-CIO revive an old procedure that allowed any seven workers of "good character" who supported the labor movement to petition the national AFL for a union charter. They did not have to be part of an existing union, nor did their occupation have to be unionized to any degree. But these "federal locals"—of which there were as many as 20,000—were little cells that built unions from the bottom up. Cobble argues that this model has become relevant again "with the increase of a mobile, contingent workforce."[52]

Unfortunately, there is little hope for such reforms (nor would they be adequate) until the labor movement develops an internal civil society. As in politics, so in unions: voluntary associations are necessary checks against the power of the central administration. Effective campaigns for reform can only be organized by voluntary groups, which will continue to serve as forums for deliberation and dissent even in completely democratic unions.

So far, there is only one significant example of a voluntary reform organization within the labor movement: Teamsters for a Democratic Union (TDU). This is a group of about 10,000 members—Teamsters, retirees, and spouses—who each pay between $20 and $30 in membership dues and elect their own leaders. When the Teamsters were controlled by the Mafia, and dissidents could be beaten even for speaking at meetings, TDU was formed to advocate free speech, nondiscrimination, and direct democracy. When it supported Ron Carey for Teamsters president, TDU acted much like a political party—a useful role in any electoral system. But it wasn't implicated in the fundraising scandals that ended Carey's career, nor have its activities been limited to electioneering. Above all, it advocates an ideology: the "social union" instead of the "business union." While the latter provides professional services to its members, the former seeks to organize all workers and involve them in common efforts. Ken Paff, TDU's national organizer, has said, "We have to build an organizing-model union that shows the rest of labor that democracy works—it makes our union stronger and puts money in the members' pockets. . . . TDU needs to lead the way."[53] Although most other unions are already more democratic that the Teamsters, they all need the equivalent of TDU. In fact, each should have *several* competing voluntary associations within its own ranks.

SCHOOLS AND CIVIC EDUCATION

Public schools, which educate the vast majority of Americans, are not formally part of civil society, for they are state institutions. But we ask them to teach skills and values—such as deliberation, disciplined thought, political participation, association, leadership, and reciprocity—that are essential to what Tocqueville called *"la vie civile."* They are not the only institutions that teach these habits, but they must provide at least a minimum level of civic instruction for students whose families and neighborhood or religious associations are inadequate. What's more, schools host extracurricular organizations that are as significant as anything in adult civil society. Indeed, they are *especially* important, because their young members may learn habits of association that last for a lifetime.

The story of American civic (or democratic, or political) education in the twentieth century is the story of repeated Progressive critiques that never seem to have much impact. Before 1900, classes were often taught with the aid of catechisms modeled on those used in religious instruction. The opening chapter of the Reverend Dr. Joseph Alden's *Young Citizen's Manual* (1869), entitled "Origin of Civil Society and Government," typified this approach:

1. *Why do men live together in society?*
   Because God has made men to live together in society.
2. *How does that appear?*
   God has given to men a social nature, which renders society necessary to their happiness and improvement.[54]

Most early manuals also reprinted the entire texts of the Constitution and the Declaration of Independence. Students were either asked catechistic questions about these documents or else required to learn them entirely by heart. Accounts of civic education in the nineteenth-century classroom conjure up a vivid scene: a teacher stands in front of a class, instructing students about the structure and functions of their government and drilling them on the political rights and responsibilities they will possess as adults.

Progressives had more advanced pedagogical ideas, emphasizing student participation and practical experience. They also opposed the traditional focus on the official structures of government, because they wanted to prepare students for life in civil society. Thus they advocated "a consideration of such topics as family, church, and public opinion in the new courses in civics for the elementary and secondary schools."[55] A movement called "community civics" became influential after 1910, receiving the official sanction of the U.S. Bureau of Education in 1915.[56] The second chapter of a 1924 civics textbooks discussed what we would call "civil society," including "lodges, clubs and societies whose primary propose is to develop good fellowship within their membership, but in so doing . . . serve as a means of training their members to be of greater assistance in the affairs of the entire community."[57]

If the purpose of civic education is to prepare students for life in civil society, then extracurricular activities can obviously play a crucial role. Writing in 1930, Charles Clinton Peters (a follower of Dewey) explained:

Participation in . . . clubs may give pupils valuable experience in the techniques of group leadership, group cooperation, and of group discussion, ability to convince others, the necessary confidence for speaking to a group, practice in evaluating group leaders, and appreciation of persons outside of one's own social class by reason of democratic intermingling and cooperation with them. Almost inevitably these clubs will give some training of value for citizenship.[58]

Community service programs seemed especially promising to Deweyan reformers, and they have been attempted periodically ever since. Reformers have also claimed that students learn democratic skills and ideals by experiencing democracy at work in their schools. As Peters wrote: "Very great gains for civic education are claimed from 'pupil self-government.' It is pointed out that such organization is really a miniature of the state, and hence training and experience in it are of a piece with training in the actual functioning of political government."[59] By 1930, student governments and school newspapers were standard in American high schools, in large part because Progressives had advocated them as tools for civic education.[60]

This was a lasting accomplishment, but most of the other Progressive ideas have been repeatedly proposed, sporadically implemented, and then allowed to languish. To be sure, Progressive approaches can be found here and there in American classrooms. Even the rather unimaginative civics text used in Georgia schools in the 1980s suggested that an elementary school class should discuss jobs that needed to be done in the classroom, and then elect students to perform them.[61] More radical experiments are currently taking place in Florida, where "micro-society elementary schools . . . try to prepare students for life. They have their own court systems, student police departments, banks, malls, legislatures, etc. The students apply for jobs and are selected based on a number of qualifications. Micro is integrated into all subject areas in a variety of ways."[62] Nevertheless, civics classes remain largely devoted to the study of government, and the "accepted wisdom in the political science profession is that [such] classes have little or no effect on the vast majority of students."[63] Adults who have passed through them do not know appreciably more about politics than other people do, nor are they more likely to vote.

One way to test the impact of conventional civics classes is look at trends over time. Since educational opportunities have generally broadened, and 87 percent of students still report that they have studied civics for at least one semester, we should expect adults' knowledge of politics and government to have improved.[64] However, Michael Delli Carpini and Scott Keeter calculate that the proportion of the public who could correctly answer a question about civics climbed by 6 percent between 1959 and 1964—and then steadily *declined* by 8 percent until 1991. The temporary increase in civic knowledge around 1964 was a result of significantly better answers to questions concerning civil rights, and the credit obviously belongs to the Civil Rights Movement. This evidence suggests that schooling has not improved civic knowledge.[65] As Samuel Popkin writes, "the hoped-for *deepening* of the electorate has not occurred, because an increase in education is not synonymous with an increase in civics knowledge."[66]

Although the conventional wisdom holds that civics classes are irrelevant, this view has been complicated by recent information. In 1988, the National Assessment of Educational Progress (NAEP) found some positive relationships between civics education and students' knowledge. Putting it together with previous studies, I think that we can reach the following tentative conclusions. First, students do gain information by attending civics classes, although we don't know for how long they retain it. Second, classes are most helpful at improving those forms of knowledge that are *not* immediately useful for political action. Successful participation is competitive; to get results from voting, lobbying, or donating money, you must possess at least as much information as other people have. Information acquired in school might help people with low social status or wealth to overcome barriers to participation, but only under the following three conditions: they must gain ground on their most privileged competitors, they must retain what they learn in the classroom, and they must update it as the political situation evolves.

Although civics classes matter, they don't come close to overcoming the effects of ability, motivation, and social status. The civic knowledge of high school seniors improves if they have taken a sustained and/or recent civics course, but a much more significant variable is their plan for life after graduation.[67] Those who intend to go to college are the best students and the future bourgeoisie; they are also the best informed about civics, regardless of the courses that they have taken. For all we know, civics instruction may actually exacerbate the differences in participation between elite adults and poor ones.[68]

Still, classes seem to improve people's general understanding of our political system, albeit modestly; and graduates seem to retain this understanding in adulthood, even though they may not learn concrete political information like the names of their elected officials. Likewise, regression analysis suggests that education improves knowledge of the Constitution, although it doesn't increase people's awareness of current events.[69] Even if general knowledge is not closely connected to political participation, it is presumably worth having. For one thing, it may help people to become more *rational* agents. Michael Delli Carpini and Scott Keeter have found that political knowledge changes people's political preferences in a regular and explicable fashion. For instance, Americans with very little political knowledge answer questions about domestic policy more or less randomly, and they choose between Democrats and Republicans irrespective of their own policy preferences. Those with substantial knowledge, however, choose according to rational self-interest. The wealthy ones express conservative views and vote Republican; the poor prefer liberal policies and Democratic candidates.[70] While self-interest is not the highest form of civic virtue, it meets a minimal test of rationality.

Finally, the data show that *methods* of teaching matter. The NAEP asked students how they had been taught civics, and many described a scene from a nineteenth-century schoolhouse, complete with textbooks, frequent quizzes, and short-answer exercises. Less than half of the students said that they wrote reports even once a month. The more frequently they had to memorize facts from the textbook, the *worse* they performed on the NAEP. Quizzes also seemed to lower their performance on this national standardized test. On the other hand, participation in mock trials and elections seemed to be effective. Covering a variety of topics also helped, as did discussion of current events.[71]

Given the history of repeated reform efforts, it seems almost futile to propose once more that students should be prepared, through a combination of experience and formal study, to govern themselves in both civil society and politics. Most of the barriers to this ideal are not conceptual; they are the familiar ones that plague *all* educational reform efforts—large classes, inadequate budgets, inattentive parents, ill-prepared teachers, and low expectations. Furthermore, if additional money or energy becomes available for education, it should not necessarily be devoted to civics, because basic literacy serves democracy as much as civic knowledge does.

But we can take some modest steps without undue cost and thereby advance the Progressive agenda even if education does not generally improve. First, we should pay attention to the state of extracurricular activities, recognizing that the best groups are seedbeds of civic virtue. In the past quarter-century, sports teams and student governments have lost one-fifth of their members; participation in newspapers and yearbooks has shrunk by almost 30 percent; but honorary societies have grown by similar margins.[72] Perhaps teenagers have mimicked their elders, many of whom have left participatory local groups for professional associations. The reason is probably not economic, for teenagers who hold paid jobs are *more* likely than their peers to volunteer in the community.[73] And although the decline of athletics and journalism could be attributed to school budget cuts, student governments do not require much money. I suspect that high school politicians (never social idols) have met ridicule during this period of widespread hostility to politics and government. But they report strikingly high levels of community service, which indicates that some of them, at least, are trying to serve democracy and civil society.[74] If schools lack the necessary resources or will to revive student governments, newspapers, and sports teams, then adult groups ought to help. After all, their future members will be drawn from today's scholastic clubs and organizations.

Second, we should carefully examine the service-learning movement, which tries to combine volunteering with academic work, and social action with reflection. This movement has received explicit support from the federal government as one of the National Education Goals for the year 2000. The Corporation for National Service defines "service-learning" as any service activity that is integrated into the curriculum with structured discussion and writing opportunities. Several studies have found that service programs with "high intellectual content" have positive effects on classroom performance.[75] However, no clear correlation has yet emerged between voluntary service and political efficacy or knowledge.[76]

The rhetoric—if not the reality—of service-learning has become very common. The vast majority of schools now arrange volunteer activities, and 16 percent of students report that community service is required. More than half of student volunteers say that they are given opportunities either to talk about their service in class, to write about it, or to get academic credit for it.[77] Furthermore, it is possible that service-learning has increased the number of students who volunteer regularly. Although the absolute number of teenaged volunteers remains small, the growth since 1991 has been on the order of 25 percent.[78] Service-learning is certainly within the mainstream of Progressive educational thought, and it deserves support when it works. But we should not hesitate to criticize particular programs—or even the entire movement—if the quality of instruction is low.

Philosophically, Progressives could find merit in the idea of *mandatory* social service. "Required volunteering" is an oxymoron, but there is nothing wrong with forcing students to do things that may make them into better citizens. If we can require the study of a foreign language (or attendance in gym class), then we can compel social service in order to teach civic skills. In Maryland, every high school student must now perform community service to graduate. A poll has found that two-thirds of American students would support such a program nation-wide.[79] But the Maryland requirement is too new to be evaluated, and it should be imitated with caution. According to a federal survey, the *lowest* levels of regular community service occur in schools that require—but do not organize—service activities. The highest levels occur in the opposite kinds of schools, ones that arrange volunteer efforts without requiring them.[80] Thus considerable damage could be done if millions of students were forced to volunteer before constructive opportunities had been created for them. A valuable volunteer experience can turn a young person into an active, able, responsible citizen for life, but an ill-conceived idea may only build cynicism, water down the curriculum, reduce the graduation rate, and waste everyone's time. It would be wise to impose service requirements cautiously, one institution at a time, and only after large and successful voluntary programs had been established.

A third idea would be easier to implement. Roughly 700 newspapers ("the schoolmasters of the common people") provide free copies for use in schools. In the third grade, students can read selected articles, learn about headlines and by-lines, discuss the meaning of pictures, and meet reporters. In a high school civics class, students can complete daily assignments using the newspaper, interview reporters about their methods, and visit the newsroom. Independent studies show that such programs improve students' knowledge of politics; they also help with reading, writing, and math skills from kindergarten to twelfth grade.[81] If students were taught how to derive useful information from newspapers, they would overcome one significant barrier to civic participation. Statistics show that regular readers are politically and civically engaged. Meanwhile, publishers would gain financially from an increase in readership, so perhaps more of them could be persuaded to provide free copies and other assistance. The American Newspaper Publishers Association advises its members to start such programs in order to ensure that the "young people of today [become] newspaper readers to-morrow."[82]

A final idea has applications well beyond the classroom, for it can appeal to highly educated adults as well as to young schoolchildren. Two organizations, the National Issues Forums (NIF) and the Study Circles Resource Center, promote deliberation by training moderators for discussion groups; they also provide background materials that can be used in these sessions. According to the NIF,

"More than 5,000 civic and education organizations—high schools and colleges, libraries, service organizations, religious groups, and other types of groups— convene Forums and study circles in their communities as part of the National Issues Forums. Each participating organization assumes ownership of the program, adapting the NIF approach and materials to its own mission and to the needs of the local community."[83] Every year, the Public Agenda Foundation publishes three NIF "issue books"—each on a different topic of national importance—that offer information and several contrasting points of view to help structure discussions. They resemble the brochures that Wisconsin's Department of Debating and Public Discussion used to publish during La Follette's administration. Meanwhile, the Study Circles Resource Center provides "Busy Citizen's Discussion Guides" on topics like "violence in our communities." The idea is to guide discussions that can lead to constructive local action.

An ideal study circle looks like this: "A dozen people are comfortably seated around a living room or meeting room, one speaking, several others looking like they would like to make a point, one skimming an article as if searching for a particular item, another scanning the group, and the others listening attentively."[84] Although this scene takes place in a home (or perhaps in a church basement), National Issues Forums and study circles can also be used in classrooms. In fact, the NIF issue books are perfect for guiding discussions in civics class. There are Spanish translations and special versions for adults who are still learning to read. Several teachers who have used the books agree that "deliberation allows students to view their place in politics differently, to see the possibility of change, and to keep asking themselves, 'What can I do?'" Students, meanwhile, report that they have transferred aspects of the Forum process to family and social situations. One said, "I use my deliberation skills when working with my friends. I tend to have a hot temper and argue my point and don't listen to anybody else, but have honestly tried to listen to other sides and work to find common ground."[85]

On a larger scale, schools can host deliberative meetings for their whole communities—including their students. To mention just one example, study circles in South Portland, Maine, have considered drug and alcohol abuse and ways to restructure the town's middle schools. More than 1,000 people have attended, and high school students have presided as moderators.[86] Students have also been trained to moderate study circles on racial issues in schools that are racially divided.[87] Clubs as well as teachers and administrators could make use of these models.

CITIZENS

Most of this book has been devoted to analyzing the institutions that either encourage civic participation or block it. I have not exhorted citizens to exercise their individual responsibilities. The most serious problem is not a lack of personal initiative, I believe, but rather frustration caused by malfunctioning institutions, including Congress, the news media, unions, and schools. Even if some citizens are remiss, readers of this book do not need exhortation—and I lack the moral standing to give it.

Still, we can all exhort *ourselves* with roughly the following argument. Citizenship is a public office, not completely different from the presidency in that it also has powers and responsibilities. Exercising these responsibilities need not be a chore; it can be one of the best parts of life. For Aristotle, politics was the second noblest activity (after philosophical contemplation), and we can rate it at least among the best five or six human endeavors—certainly well above watching TV. But even if politics is not my personal avocation, I cannot ask other people to bear all of its burdens for me. Perhaps the advantage that I gain from voting does not repay me for the labor of going to the polls, but I want *someone* to vote, and I cannot morally exempt myself from demands that I would place on others. The same is true of volunteering and petitioning the government: these are universal duties.

Some hold the exaggerated view that American government is thoroughly corrupt and that all participation is fruitless or ignoble. If this were true, then we should declare a crisis and zealously strive to reform public life; apathy would be a crime. But actually, citizens ought to make informed and discriminating judgments, not wholesale denunciations. Assuming, then, that American politics has both good and bad aspects, we have no excuse for opting out. After all, we have plenty of choice, for if electoral politics seems repellent, there are also private associations to join (or vice versa).

To inform ourselves, we should read newspapers and magazines and engage in face-to-face discussions with diverse people. The best discussions tend to occur within certain kinds of organizations: religious congregations that span racial and economic boundaries, civic groups, public schools, some electronic "chat rooms," certain fraternal and sororal groups, and associations whose main purpose is to promote deliberation. Their activities are not to everyone's taste, but everyone should give deliberation a try.

We should not act without first talking, but neither should we be satisfied with talk alone. After we have discussed political issues, we should vote, lobby, and (if necessary) protest. We should also donate our voluntary labor to communities and associations, especially those that are organized democratically and that promote some version of the public good. Finally, we should recognize that most groups (whether political or nonpartisan, public or private) need *leadership,* and that becoming a leader can be an obligation as well as an opportunity.

When the delegates to the Constitutional Convention emerged from their final meeting in 1787, a crowd of citizens awaited them. The most recognizable delegate was probably Benjamin Franklin, who had spent most of his long life in service to Philadelphia. One onlooker, Mrs. Samuel Powel, shouted, "Well, Doctor, what have we got, a Republic or a Monarchy?" "A Republic," Franklin replied, "if you can keep it."[88] Franklin's answer would have satisfied Robert M. La Follette, who believed that all Americans must struggle to preserve their institutions of self-government, even in times of peace and prosperity. La Follette and the other Progressives kept Franklin's Republic alive so that we would face the same challenge in our time. We still have a representative government, capable of deliberating fairly about the common good—but only if *we* can keep it.

NOTES

1. Jean-Jacques Rousseau, *The Social Contract,* trans. G. D. H. Cole (London: 1913, new ed. 1993), book 3, chapter 15 (p. 266); book 4, chapter 1 (p. 274).

2. James Madison, *Federalist,* no. 10, in *The Federalist Papers,* ed. Clinton Rossiter (New York, 1961), p. 79.

3. Lester M. Salaman, *Holding the Center: America's Nonprofit Sector at a Crossroads,* a report for the Nathan Cummings Foundation (1997), p. 27.

4. James Fishkin, *The Dialogue of Justice: Toward a Self-Reflective Society* (New Haven, Conn., 1992), pp. 198–199.

5. See Jean L. Cohen, "American Civil Society Talk," in *Civil Society, Democracy, and Civic Renewal,* ed. Robert K. Fullinwider (Lanham, Md., 1999), pp. 55–85; and Nancy L. Rosenblum, "The Moral Uses of Pluralism," in *Civil Society, Democracy, and Civic Renewal,* ed. Fullinwider, pp. 255–271.

6. John Dewey, *Freedom and Culture* (1939; reprint, New York, 1963), pp. 124–125 (Dewey's emphasis).

7. Associated Press, "Bishop Urges More Respect for Authority," *New York Times,* November 17, 1998, p. A17.

8. Rosenblum, "The Moral Uses of Pluralism," pp. 261, 266.

9. Testimony of Paul Grogan, president of the Local Initiatives Support Corporation, before the National Commission on Civic Renewal, May 19, 1997.

10. Patrick L. Scully and Richard C. Harwood, *Strategies for Civil Investing,* a Harwood Group study (1995), pp. 10–13.

11. Peter Frumkin, "Strangled Freedom," *The American Scholar,* vol. 64, no. 4 (Autumn 1995): 590.

12. Frumkin, "Strangled Freedom," pp. 590, 595.

13. David Samuels, "Philanthropical Correctness," *The New Republic* (September 18 and 25, 1995): 28.

14. Scully and Harwood, *Strategies for Civil Investing,* p. 9.

15. Independent Sector (Virginia A. Hodgkinson, Murray S. Weitzman, et al.), *Giving and Volunteering in the United States: Findings from a National Survey* (Washington, D.C., 1992), table 5.1.

16. Kathryn E. Merchant, "Foundations Develop Social Capital," *Civic Partners: A Report from the Pew Partnership for Civic Change* (1997), p. 27.

17. See, e.g., the *1995 Annual Report* of the Mary Reynolds Babcock Foundation, entitled *Building Bridges.*

18. Mark Gerzon, "Reinventing Philanthropy: Foundations and the Renewal of Civil Society," *The National Civic Review* (Summer–Fall 1995): 190–192.

19. Amy Gutmann and Dennis Thompson, *Democracy and Disagreement* (Cambridge, Mass., 1996), p. 349.

20. Marvin R. Cohen, "An Exercise in Civility," The Chicago Community Trust: A Project Eighty Report (June 1995): draft, pp. 37–38.

21. Source: author's minutes from Civil Investing seminars held on April 24–25, 1996 (Atlanta), and November 7–8, 1996 (New York City). See also Mary Ann Zehr, "Getting Involved in Civic Life," *Foundation News & Commentary* (May/June 1996): 26.

22. Jane Addams, *Twenty Years at Hull-House* (New York, 1960), p. 123.

23. Jane Addams, *Democracy and Social Ethics,* (1902; reprint, New York, 1911), pp. 224–225.

24. Samuels, "Philanthropical Correctness," pp. 29, 32. For evidence of the rise of professionalism within philanthropy, see Frumkin, "Strangled Freedom," pp. 595–597.

25. Many of these ideas are contained in a draft "Social Capital Impact Statement" that is being written by the Saguaro Seminar. This seminar is co-chaired by Robert Putnam of Harvard and Lewis Feldstein of the New Hampshire Charitable Foundation.

26. John M. Holcomb, introduction to the Foundation for Public Affairs' *Public Interest Profiles, 1988–1989,* p. 5.

27. For a mixed verdict, see Andrew S. McFarland, *Common Cause: Lobbying in the Public Interest* (Chatham, N.J., 1984), pp. 57–58.

28. David Vogel, *Fluctuating Fortunes: The Political Power of Business in America* (New York, 1989), pp. 104, 102.

29. See David S. Cloud, "Leaders Turn to Arm-Twisting to Pass Gift Ban in House," *Congressional Quarterly Weekly Reports,* October 1, 1994, p. 2756; Cloud, "GOP and Interest Groups Dig in to Dump Gift Ban in Senate," *Congressional Quarterly Weekly Reports,* October 8, 1994, p. 2854; Eliza Newlin Carney, "In the Enemy Camp on Lobby Reform," *National Journal* (October 8, 1994): 2354; and personal reports.

30. Holcomb, introduction, pp. 6, 22.

31. Source: personal communication with Dr. Gretchen Straw of the AARP.

32. Quoted by John B. Howe, "The Role of Industrial Relations in Achieving Social Equity: A Comparison of Labor Laws in Australia and the United States," *Labor Law Journal,* vol. 48, no. 6 (June 1997): 346.

33. John R. Commons, *Industrial Goodwill* (New York, 1919), p. 47.

34. Norris-LaGuardia Act of 1932, 47 Stat. 70 (1932), 29 U.S. Code §102 (1998), emphasis added.

35. See Commons, *Industrial Goodwill,* p. 46.

36. David P. Thelen, *Robert M. LaFollette and the Insurgent Spirit* (Madison, Wis., 1985), pp. 59, 111–12.

37. Cf. Sidney and Beatrice Webb, *Industrial Democracy* (New York, 1897), in *Theories of the Labor Movement,* by Simeon Larson and Bruce Nissen (Detroit, 1987), p. 202.

38. C. Wright Mills with Helen Schneider, *The New Men of Power: America's Labor Leaders* (New York, 1948), p. 206.

39. For statistics, see chapter 3.

40. Archibald Cox and John T. Dunlop, "Regulation of Collective Bargaining by the National Labor Relations Board," *Harvard Law Review* 63 (1950): 390.

41. *Patrick Cudahy, Inc.,* 1987–88 CCH NLRB at 33, 535.

42. Cox and Dunlop, "Regulation of Collective Bargaining," quoting Senator Walsh from the *Congressional Record,* vol. 79 (1935), p. 7660.

43. Stanley Aronowitz, *False Promises: The Shaping of American Working Class Consciousness* (Durham, N.C., 1992; 1st ed., 1973), p. 220. This passage is anticipated by Mills, *The New Men of Power,* p. 105.

44. Aronowitz, *False Promises,* p. 220.

45. Ibid., p. 253.

46. Jonathan P. Hiatt, General Counsel, AFL-CIO, "Union Survival Strategies for the Twenty-First Century" (1996), at http://135.145.28/139/publ/press96/pr03203.html.

47. John J. Sweeney, with David Kusnet, *America Needs a Raise* (Boston, 1996), pp. 125–126 and passim.

48. Sweeney, *America Needs a Raise,* p. 82; Richard Rothstein, "New Bargain or No Bargain" at http://135.145.28/139/publ/press96/pr03203.html.

49. Thomas Geoghegan, *Which Side Are You on? Trying to Be for Labor When It's Flat on Its Back* (New York, 1992), pp. 253, 257.

50. Geoghegan, *Which Side Are You On?* p. 276.

51. Rothstein, "New Bargain or No Bargain."

52. Dorothy Sue Cobble, "The New Unionism: Structural Innovations for a Revitalized Labor Movement," *Labor Law Journal,* vol. 48, no. 8 (August 1997): 440–442

53. Martha Gruelle, "Labor vs. Capital: A Referendum on Union Democracy; Teamsters Vote to Stay the Democratic Course," *Multinational Monitor,* vol. 18, no. 3 (March 1997), at http://prince.essential.org/monitor/hyper/mm0397.06.html.

54. Quoted in *The Improvement of Civics Instruction in Junior and Senior High Schools* by Arnold W. Brown (Ypsilanti, Mich., 1929), p. 11.

55. Brown, *The Improvement of Civics Instruction,* p. 28.

56. Brown, *The Improvement of Civics Instruction,* p. 32: quoting U.S. Bureau of Education Bulletin, 1915, no. 23.

57. Clyde B. Moore, *Civic Education: Its Objectives and Methods for a Specific Case Group: A Study in Educational Sociology* (New York, 1924), p. 2.

58. Charles Clinton Peters, *Objectives and Procedures in Civic Education* (New York, 1930), p. 125.

59. Peters, *Objectives and Procedures in Civic Education,* p. 129.

60. See Brown, *The Improvement of Civics Instruction,* p. 37, quoting the *Report of the North Central Association* (1920), p. 35A: "most schools seem to place great faith in the civic training afforded by the school papers, debating clubs, mock elections, and other types of student co-operating organizations."

61. Mary A. Hepburn and Edwin L. Jackson, *Citizenship Education for Elementary Grades: Lessons for K–6* (Athens, Ga., 1985), pp. 19–20.

62. Source: Annette Boyd Pitts, executive director of the Florida Law Related Education Association. Personal communication, July 25, 1995.

63. Richard G. Niemi and Jane Junn, *Civic Education: What Makes Students Learn,* p. 16 (citing a large literature). Nie et al. are sure that formal civics instruction has no impact on concrete political knowledge (see *Education and Democratic Citizenship in America* [Chicago, 1996] p. 72). See also Michael Delli Carpini and Scott Keeter, *What Americans Know about Politics and Why It Matters* (New Haven, Conn., 1996), p. 183.

64. The statistic comes from Niemi and Junn, *Civic Education,* table 4–1.

65. Delli Carpini and Keeter, *What Americans Know about Politics,* pp. 122, 117. According to Benjamin I. Page and Robert Y. Shapiro, *The Rational Public: Fifty Years of Trends in Americans' Policy Preferences* (Chicago, 1992), pp. 10–11, Gallup polls showed a significant increase in public knowledge of the Bill of Rights between 1954 and 1989—but these were two "snapshot" surveys, with no intervening information. Again, I suspect that the Civil Rights Movement and the Warren Court did more than schools and universities to increase awareness of the Bill of Rights.

66. Samuel Popkin, *The Reasoning Voter: Communication and Persuasion in Presidential Campaigns* (Chicago, 1991), p. 36.

67. Niemi and Junn, *Civic Education,* table 6–1.

68. Although the NAEP shows mild positive effects from coursework, its questions concern government structure and civil rights—just the subjects that are stressed in civics classes. If students were asked about current events or whether they planned to vote, I suspect that the correlation with social and economic status would be even stronger, and the effects of classes would be correspondingly weaker.

An assessment of the Agency for International Development's adult civic education programs in Poland and the Dominican Republic found that "civic education may not have as broad an impact on the democratic characteristics of individuals as is often expected." The effect of school programs was weak and transitory; what really encouraged participation was the opportunity to participate and the existence of group networks. See A.I.D. (Christopher A. Sabatini, Gwendolyn G. Bevis, and Steven E. Finkel), *The Impact of Civic Education Programs on Political Participation and Democratic Attitudes,* January 27, 1998, pp. 54, 25.

69. Delli Carpini and Keeter, *What Americans Know about Politics,* pp. 191, 197–198. Nie et al. present a graph (*Education and Democratic Citizenship in America,* p. 34) that shows a 20-percent jump in knowledge of "democratic principles" between those with nine years of education and those with ten. The tenth year of school (i.e., ninth grade) was the traditional time for civics classes, so this graph suggests that civics instruction may raise awareness of fundamental democratic values. The authors do not mention this jump—they merely describe the increase as monotonic—so I cannot tell whether their sample is large enough to permit comparisons between people who differ by just one year of schooling.

70. Delli Carpini and Keeter, *What Americans Know about Politics,* pp. 243, 253.

71. Niemi and Junn, *Civic Education,* tables 4–10, 4–11, p. 97, table 6–1.

72. U.S. Department of Education, National Center for Education Statistics (NCES), using National Longitudinal Studies of 1972, 1980, and 1988 ("High School and Beyond").

73. See NCES (Mary Jo Nolan, Bradford Chancy, and Chris Chapman), *Student Participation in Community Service Activity,* NCES 97–331, (Washington, D.C., 1997), table 3. There are, however, correlations between volunteering and three background variables: family income, number of guardians in the household, and parents' educational status. See ibid., table 4.

74. Nolan et. al., *Student Participation,* table 3.

75. See Nolan et. al., *Student Participation,* p. 2.

76. Richard Niemi, "Family Socialization for Civic Responsibility" Unpublished manuscript. pp. 12–16.

77. Nolan et al., *Student Participation,* table 12; p. 16.

78. The percentage of students who report daily or weekly volunteering has increased from 8.7 to 10.8 since 1991. Comparing 1980 and 1994, the change is smaller (just 9 percent) because there was a decline during the 1980s. Source: NCES, citing the University of Michigan's *Monitoring the Future* study, 1994.

79. "Poll Finds Students Back Volunteer Rules," *The Chronicle of Philanthropy,* vol. 7, no. 23 (September 21, 1995): 11.

80. Nolan et al., *Student Participation,* table 7.

81. American Newspaper Publishers Association Foundation, *A Brief Introduction to the Newspaper in Education Concept* (Washington, D.C., 1990), pp. 1, 16 (quoting Henry Ward Beecher), 24 (citing several studies). Niemi and Junn cite an additional study from Argentina: *Civic Education,* p. 18.

82. American Newspaper Publishers Association Foundation, *Newspaper in Education: A Guide for Weekly Newspapers* (Washington, D.C., 1991), p. 3

83. Official literature posted at http://www.vote-smart.org/issues/Immigration/nif.-html.

84. Study Circles Resource Center, *The Study Circles Handbook* (Pomfret, Conn., 1993), p. 3.

85. Kristin Cruset, "Can Deliberation Be Taught in the Classroom?" *Kettering Foundation Connections,* vol. 8, no. 2 (December 1997): 21.

86. "Bringing Youth Voices into Democracy's Conversation," *Focus on Study Circles, The Newsletter of the Study Circles Resource Center,* vol. 7, no. 4 (Fall 1996): 1.

87. David Ruenzel, "Crucial Conversations: Study Circles Help Students Talk Constructively about Race," *Teaching Tolerance* (Spring 1997): 19.

88. I am grateful to Harry Boyte for using this anecdote in my hearing. I have found it (minus punctuation) in *The Records of the Federal Convention of 1789* ed. Max Ferrand (New Haven, Conn., 1934), vol. 3, p. 85. For background, see William G. Carr, *The Oldest Delegate: Franklin in the Constitutional Convention* (Newark, Del., 1990), p. 122. The original source is James McHenry, a delegate from Maryland.

A Summary of Principles and Proposals

Americans will always disagree about important issues. Since we differ in our interests and values, any law will anger some of us, just as it pleases others. Yet if the state fails to act because it lacks public consensus, then people—especially poor and weak ones—will have no effective protection against the coercive behavior of their fellow citizens, private corporations, and foreign interests. Under these circumstances, unanimous consent is a fantasy, perfect freedom is unattainable, and politics is a permanent contest with winners and losers at every stage.

Nevertheless, we can all agree that the rules of this contest should be fair and that results should emerge only after thoughtful discussion. These two abstract principles—fairness and deliberation—enjoy near-unanimous support. Making them more concrete, we can agree that:

1. In the political arena, everyone should count equally and the best argument should prevail. If politicians need large amounts of private money to win elections, then the political system cannot be fair. Therefore, fundamental campaign-finance reform is essential, and it will require at least partial public funding of campaigns. Whenever possible, this money should support campaign activities that promote deliberation, such as televised debates, voter guides, and Deliberative Polls. We also need tough ethics laws and lobby disclosure to reduce the power of money after election day.
2. There is a real difference between special-interest laws and public-interest legislation. Only the latter has a rationale that can be put in general terms and publicly defended. Certain methods of legislation—especially targeted tax breaks and bills that delegate power to regulatory agencies—are prone to special-interest pressure. Therefore, democracy would benefit from fundamental tax reform and a ban on legislative delegation.
3. No institution is sacrosanct. The public, as long as it acts fairly and deliberatively, can interfere with the market, the media, and nonprofit institutions. However, if public discussion is to remain fair and deliberative, then no

argument or perspective may be suppressed. Thus citizens have rights of association and expression that cannot be overruled by the majority.

4. People mainly talk about social and economic issues within organizations: unions, religious congregations, political parties, neighborhood associations, social clubs, and the like. These institutions must be strengthened and their internal affairs made more deliberative. One way to increase membership is to replace the tax deduction for charitable contributions with a voucher system. Meanwhile, membership organizations should create local chapters; labor unions should become more democratic and develop internal civil societies; and philanthropies should form partnerships with deliberative groups.

5. Lawmakers should consult deliberative bodies of citizens as often as possible—creating them, if necessary. These bodies would seek consensus solutions that could be written into law, but they would not purport to "represent" their communities, for representation is best achieved by elected legislatures.

6. Journalists can serve democracy by assisting the public in its deliberations. This means providing relevant information and disseminating ideas, but also convening public meetings and consulting groups in civil society. Since freedom of discussion is threatened by private media ownership, we need strong antitrust regulation, a common-carrier approach to cable-TV and the Internet, and statutes that mandate substantive news coverage.

7. Leaders who try to serve the public interest have nothing to fear from publicity, but special interests thrive in secrecy. Therefore, official deliberations and negotiations should take place in public. If covert action is incompatible with democratic principles, then the United States must refrain from covert action.

8. Deliberative democracy has its own canon of virtues: public-spiritedness, trust, respect for other people's opinions, cooperativeness, intellectual honesty, social concern, and a desire to achieve consensus where possible. An unfair political system discourages these virtues by making them seem pointless. But political reform is not enough; people must learn to act as citizens in a deliberative community. Civic education is an important function of public schools and voluntary groups, and it can be done better.

Index

About the Author

Peter Levine has previously published *Nietzsche and the Modern Crisis of the Humanities* (1995); *Something to Hide,* a novel about politics (1996); and *Living without Philosophy: On Narrative, Rhetoric, and Morality* (1998). He graduated from Yale in 1989 with a B.A. in philosophy. He then studied at Oxford on a Rhodes Scholarship, receiving his doctorate in 1992. For the next two years, Levine was a research associate at Common Cause, helping that organization to lobby for campaign-finance reform and government ethics. In 1993, he became a research scholar at the Institute for Philosophy and Public Policy at the University of Maryland. Since 1987, he has worked part-time for the Charles Kettering Foundation, of which he is now an associate. He is also deputy director of the National Commission on Civic Renewal, chaired by Senator Sam Nunn and William Bennett. He lives in Washington, D.C., with his wife and two children.